The Guptas Ate My HOMEWORK!

By Stephen Francis & Rico

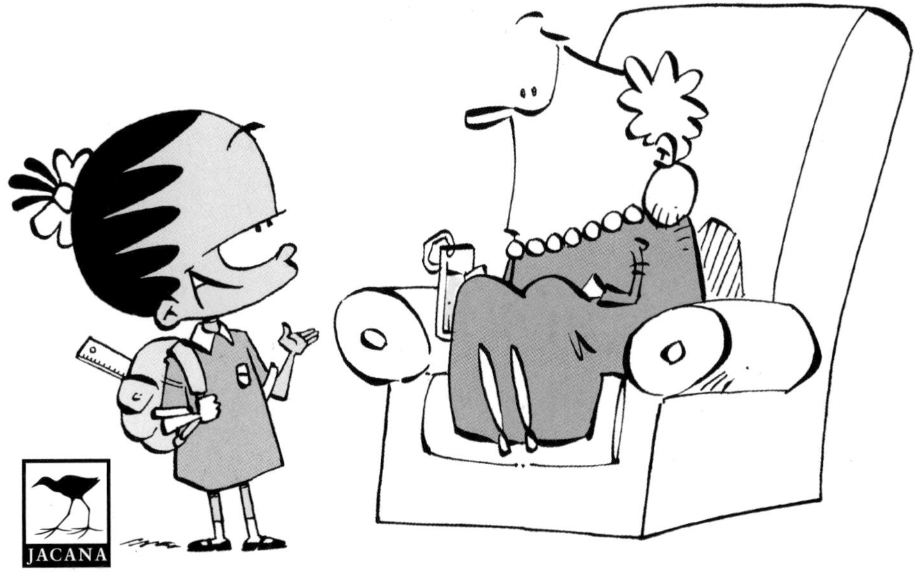

JACANA

To our loving wives ... who often give us the headlines, the deadlines ... and sometimes even the punchlines

Published in 2018 in South Africa by
Jacana Media
10 Orange Street, Auckland Park, 2092
PO Box 291784, Melville, 2109
www.jacana.co.za

ISBN 978-1-4314-2732-1
Job number 003397

Printed by **novus print**, a Novus Holdings company

OTHER MADAM & EVE BOOKS

Madam & Eve Collection (Rapid Phase, 1993, reprint 1999)
Free At Last (Penguin Books, 1994)
All Aboard for the Gravy Train (Penguin Books, 1995)
Somewhere over the Rainbow Nation (Penguin Books, 1996)
Madam & Eve's Greatest Hits (Penguin Books, 1997)
Madams are from Mars, Maids are from Venus (Penguin Books, 1997)
It's a Jungle Out There (David Philip, 1998)
International Maid of Mystery (David Philip, 1999)
Has anyone seen my Vibrating Cellphone? (interactive.Africa, 2000)
The Madams are Restless (Rapid Phase, 2000)
Crouching Madam, Hidden Maid (Rapid Phase, 2001)
Madam & Eve, 10 Wonderful Years (Rapid Phase, 2002)
The Maidtrix (Rapid Phase, 2003)
Gin & Tonic for the Soul (Rapid Phase, 2004)
Desperate Housemaids (Rapid Phase, 2005)
Madams of the Caribbean (Rapid Phase, 2006)
Bring me my (new) Washing Machine (Rapid Phase, 2007)
Madam & Eve Unplugged (Rapid Phase, 2008)
Strike While The Iron Is Hot (Jacana, 2009)
Twilight of the Vuvuzelas (Jacana, 2010)

Mother Anderson's Secret Book of Wit & Wisdom (Jacana, 2011)
The Pothole at the End of the Rainbow (Jacana, 2011)
Twenty (Jacana, 2012)
Keep Calm and Take Another Tea Break (Jacana, 2013)
Send in the Clowns (Jacana, 2014)
Shed Happens (Jacana, 2015)
Take Me to Your Leader (Jacana, 2016)
Hadeda La Land (Jacana, 2017)
Jamen sort kaffe er pa mode nu, Madam! (Gyldendal, Denmark, 1995)
Jeg gyver Mandela Skylden for det her! (Gyldendal, Denmark, 1995)
Alt under kontrol I Sydafrika! (Bogfabrikken, Denmark, 1997)
Men alla dricker kaffet svart nufortiden, Madam! (Bokfabrikken, Sweden, 1998)
Madame & Eve, Enfin Libres! (Vents D'Ouest, France, 1997)
Votez Madame & Eve (Vents D'Ouest, France, 1997)
La coupe est pleine (Vents D'Ouest, France, 1998)
Rennue-Ménage à deux (Vents D'Ouest, France, 1999)
En voient de toutes les couleurs (Vents D'Ouest, France, 2000)
Madame vient de Mars, Eve de Venus (Vents D'Ouest, France, 2000)
Madam & Eve (LIKE, Finland, 2005)

MADAM & EVE APPEARS REGULARLY IN:
*Mail & Guardian, The Star, Saturday Star, Herald, Mercury, Witness, Daily Dispatch, Cape Times, Pretoria News,
Diamond Fields Advertiser, Die Volksblad, EC Today, Kokstad Advertiser, The Botswana Advertiser, The Namibian.*

TO CONTACT MADAM & EVE:
PO Box 413667, Craighall 2024, Johannesburg, South Africa
ricos@rico.co.za
www.madamandeve.co.za
Follow Madam & Eve on Facebook: www.facebook.com/madamandevecartoon
Follow Madam & Eve on Twitter @madamevecartoon

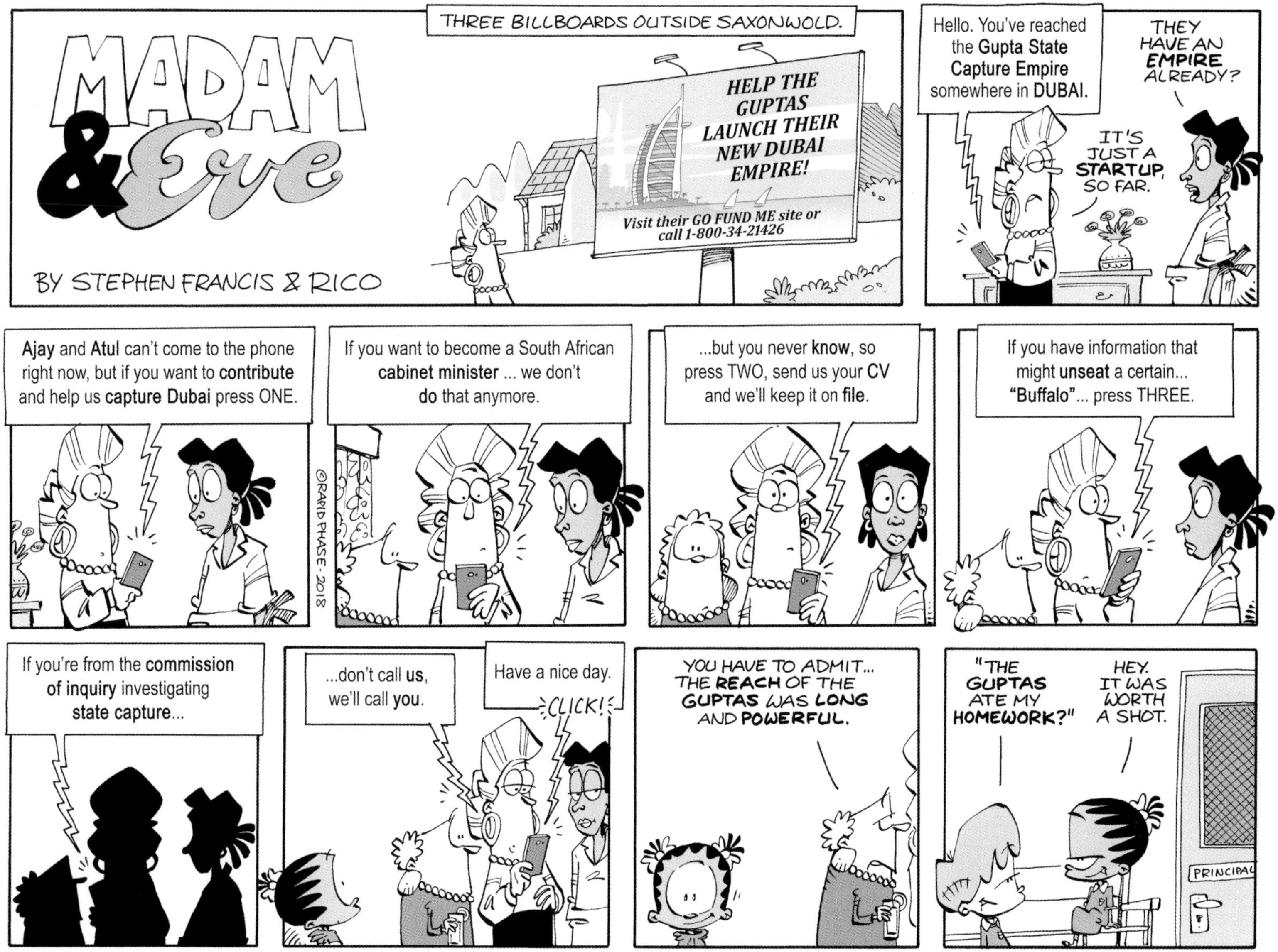
THREE BILLBOARDS OUTSIDE SAXONWOLD.
MADAM & Eve
BY STEPHEN FRANCIS & RICO
HELP THE GUPTAS LAUNCH THEIR NEW DUBAI EMPIRE!
Visit their GO FUND ME site or call 1-800-34-21426
Hello. You've reached the Gupta State Capture Empire somewhere in DUBAI.
THEY HAVE AN EMPIRE ALREADY?
IT'S JUST A STARTUP, SO FAR.
Ajay and Atul can't come to the phone right now, but if you want to contribute and help us capture Dubai press ONE.
©RAPID PHASE · 2018
If you want to become a South African cabinet minister ... we don't do that anymore.
...but you never know, so press TWO, send us your CV and we'll keep it on file.
If you have information that might unseat a certain... "Buffalo"... press THREE.
If you're from the commission of inquiry investigating state capture...
...don't call us, we'll call you.
Have a nice day.
CLICK!
YOU HAVE TO ADMIT... THE REACH OF THE GUPTAS WAS LONG AND POWERFUL.
"THE GUPTAS ATE MY HOMEWORK?"
HEY. IT WAS WORTH A SHOT.
PRINCIPAL

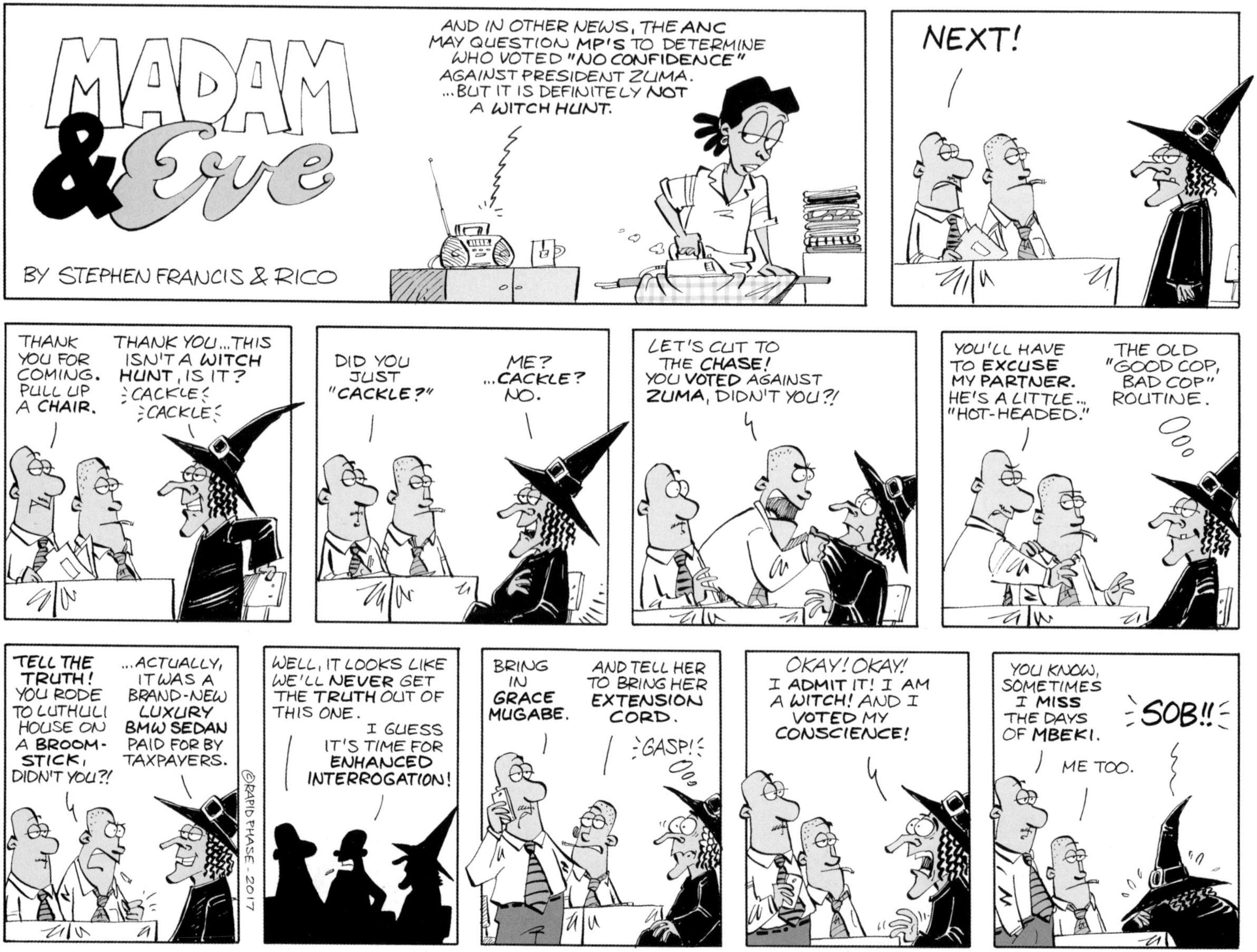
MADAM & Eve
BY STEPHEN FRANCIS & RICO
AND IN OTHER NEWS, THE ANC MAY QUESTION MP'S TO DETERMINE WHO VOTED "NO CONFIDENCE" AGAINST PRESIDENT ZUMA. ...BUT IT IS DEFINITELY NOT A WITCH HUNT.
NEXT!
THANK YOU FOR COMING. PULL UP A CHAIR.
THANK YOU... THIS ISN'T A WITCH HUNT, IS IT? CACKLE CACKLE
DID YOU JUST "CACKLE?"
ME? ...CACKLE? NO.
LET'S CUT TO THE CHASE! YOU VOTED AGAINST ZUMA, DIDN'T YOU?!
YOU'LL HAVE TO EXCUSE MY PARTNER. HE'S A LITTLE... "HOT-HEADED."
THE OLD "GOOD COP, BAD COP" ROUTINE.
TELL THE TRUTH! YOU RODE TO LUTHULI HOUSE ON A BROOM-STICK, DIDN'T YOU?!
...ACTUALLY, IT WAS A BRAND-NEW LUXURY BMW SEDAN PAID FOR BY TAXPAYERS.
©RAPID PHASE - 2017
WELL, IT LOOKS LIKE WE'LL NEVER GET THE TRUTH OUT OF THIS ONE.
I GUESS IT'S TIME FOR ENHANCED INTERROGATION!
BRING IN GRACE MUGABE.
AND TELL HER TO BRING HER EXTENSION CORD.
GASP!
OKAY! OKAY! I ADMIT IT! I AM A WITCH! AND I VOTED MY CONSCIENCE!
YOU KNOW, SOMETIMES I MISS THE DAYS OF MBEKI.
SOB!!
ME TOO.

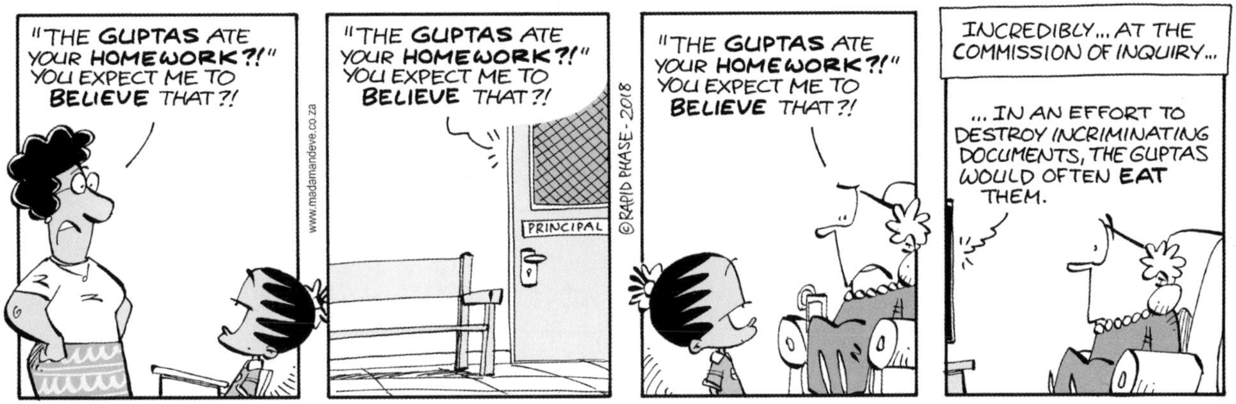
"THE GUPTAS ATE YOUR HOMEWORK?!" YOU EXPECT ME TO BELIEVE THAT?!
www.madamandeve.co.za
"THE GUPTAS ATE YOUR HOMEWORK?!" YOU EXPECT ME TO BELIEVE THAT?!
PRINCIPAL
©RAPID PHASE-2018
"THE GUPTAS ATE YOUR HOMEWORK?!" YOU EXPECT ME TO BELIEVE THAT?!
INCREDIBLY... AT THE COMMISSION OF INQUIRY...
... IN AN EFFORT TO DESTROY INCRIMINATING DOCUMENTS, THE GUPTAS WOULD OFTEN EAT THEM.

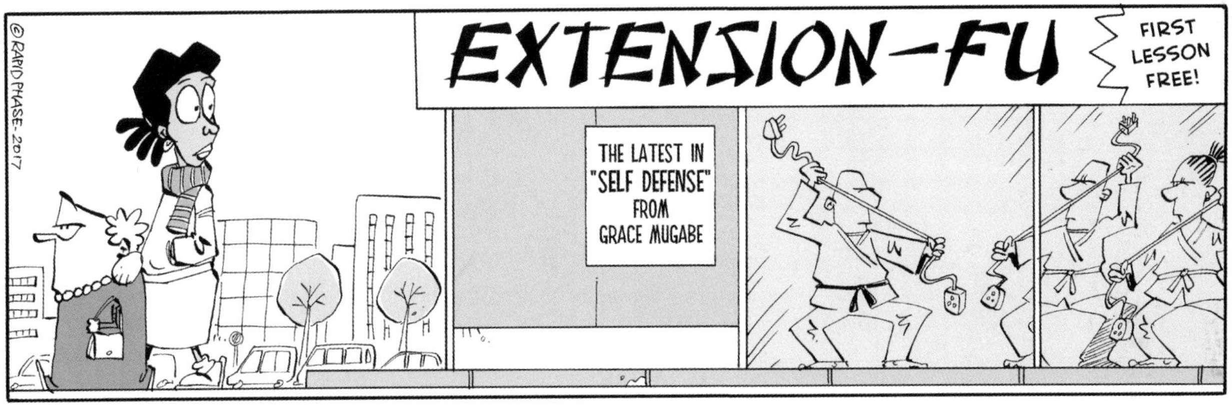
© RAPID PHASE-2017
EXTENSION-FU
FIRST LESSON FREE!
THE LATEST IN "SELF DEFENSE" FROM GRACE MUGABE

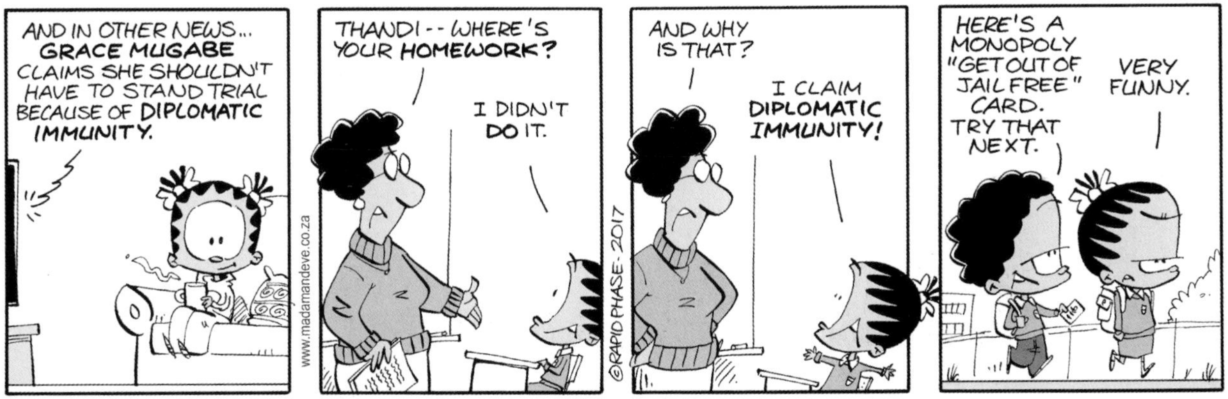
AND IN OTHER NEWS... GRACE MUGABE CLAIMS SHE SHOULDN'T HAVE TO STAND TRIAL BECAUSE OF DIPLOMATIC IMMUNITY.
www.madamandeve.co.za
THANDI -- WHERE'S YOUR HOMEWORK?
I DIDN'T DO IT.
©RAPID PHASE-2017
AND WHY IS THAT?
I CLAIM DIPLOMATIC IMMUNITY!
HERE'S A MONOPOLY "GET OUT OF JAIL FREE" CARD. TRY THAT NEXT.
VERY FUNNY.

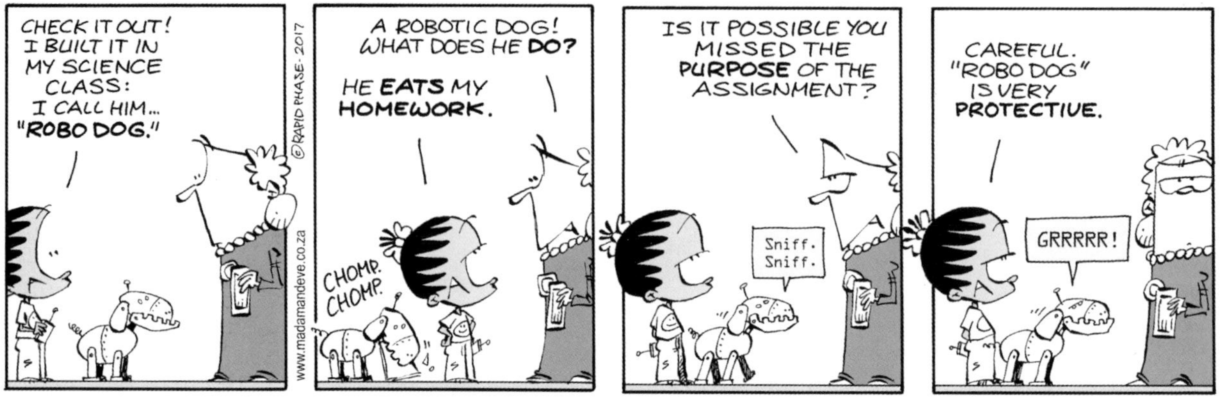
CHECK IT OUT! I BUILT IT IN MY SCIENCE CLASS: I CALL HIM... "ROBO DOG."
©RAPID PHASE-2017
www.madamandeve.co.za
A ROBOTIC DOG! WHAT DOES HE DO?
HE EATS MY HOMEWORK.
CHOMP. CHOMP.
IS IT POSSIBLE YOU MISSED THE PURPOSE OF THE ASSIGNMENT?
Sniff. Sniff.
CAREFUL. "ROBO DOG" IS VERY PROTECTIVE.
GRRRRR!

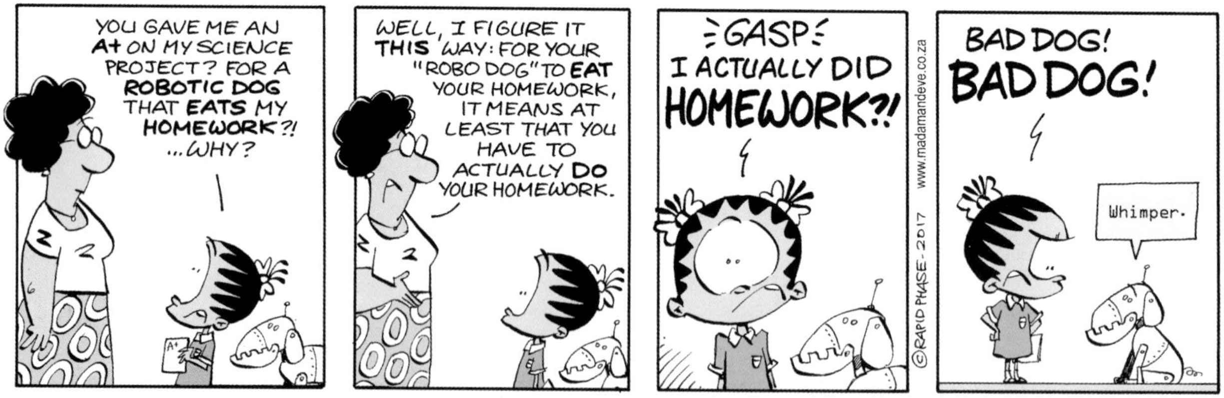
YOU GAVE ME AN A+ ON MY SCIENCE PROJECT? FOR A ROBOTIC DOG THAT EATS MY HOMEWORK?! ...WHY?
WELL, I FIGURE IT THIS WAY: FOR YOUR "ROBO DOG" TO EAT YOUR HOMEWORK, IT MEANS AT LEAST THAT YOU HAVE TO ACTUALLY DO YOUR HOMEWORK.
GASP
I ACTUALLY DID HOMEWORK?!
www.madamandeve.co.za
©RAPID PHASE-2017
BAD DOG!
BAD DOG!
Whimper.

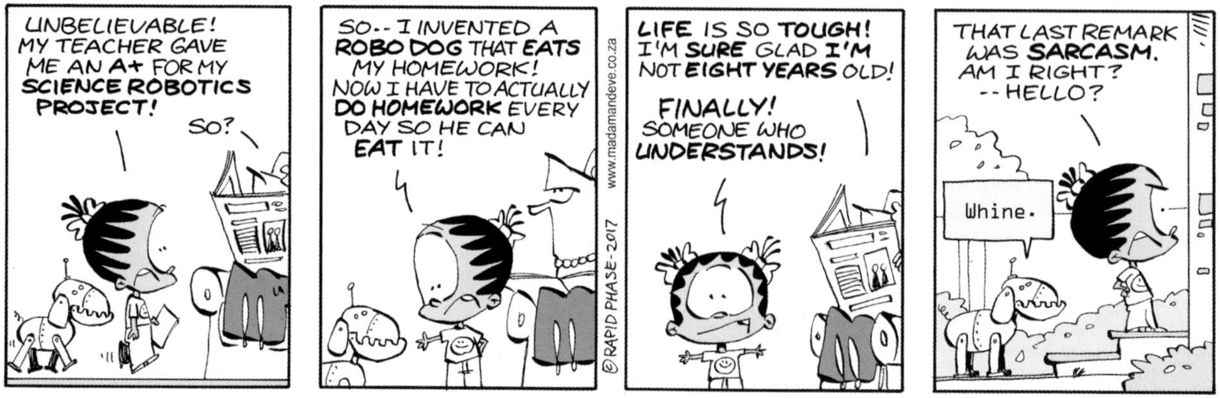
UNBELIEVABLE! MY TEACHER GAVE ME AN A+ FOR MY SCIENCE ROBOTICS PROJECT!
SO?
SO-- I INVENTED A ROBO DOG THAT EATS MY HOMEWORK! NOW I HAVE TO ACTUALLY DO HOMEWORK EVERY DAY SO HE CAN EAT IT!
www.madamandeve.co.za
©RAPID PHASE-2017
LIFE IS SO TOUGH! I'M SURE GLAD I'M NOT EIGHT YEARS OLD!
FINALLY! SOMEONE WHO UNDERSTANDS!
THAT LAST REMARK WAS SARCASM. AM I RIGHT? --HELLO?
Whine.

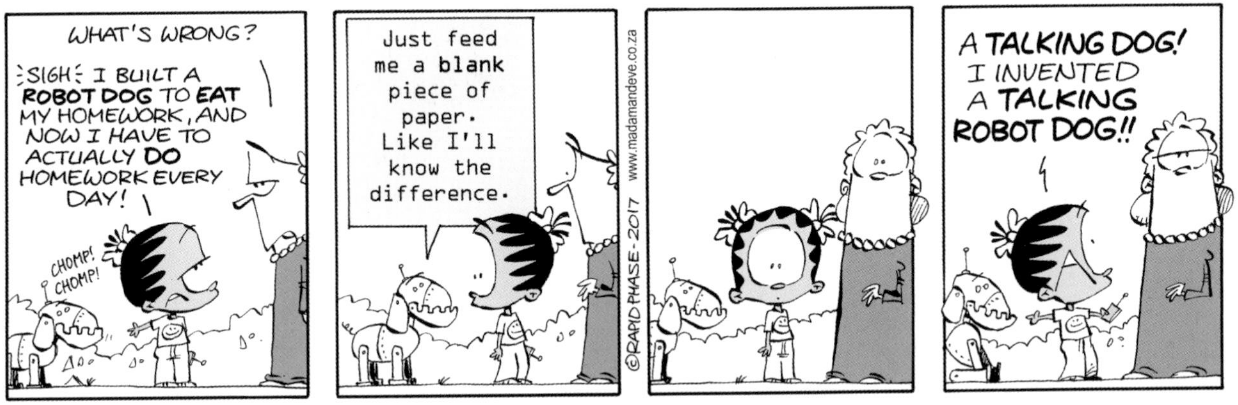
WHAT'S WRONG?
:SIGH: I BUILT A **ROBOT DOG** TO **EAT** MY HOMEWORK, AND NOW I HAVE TO ACTUALLY **DO** HOMEWORK EVERY DAY!
CHOMP! CHOMP!
Just feed me a **blank** piece of paper. Like I'll know the difference.
©RAPID PHASE - 2017 www.madamandeve.co.za
A **TALKING DOG!** I INVENTED A **TALKING ROBOT DOG!!**

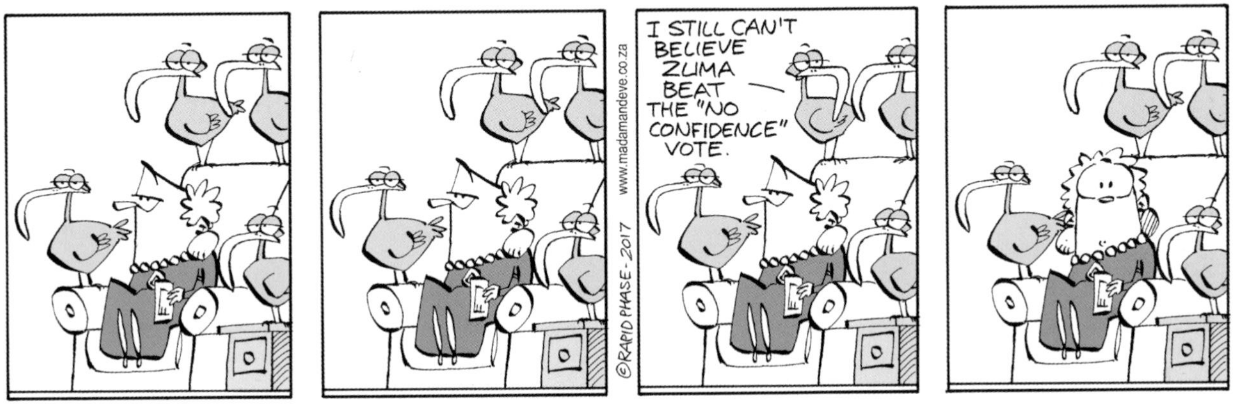
©RAPID PHASE - 2017 www.madamandeve.co.za
I STILL CAN'T BELIEVE ZUMA BEAT THE "NO CONFIDENCE" VOTE.

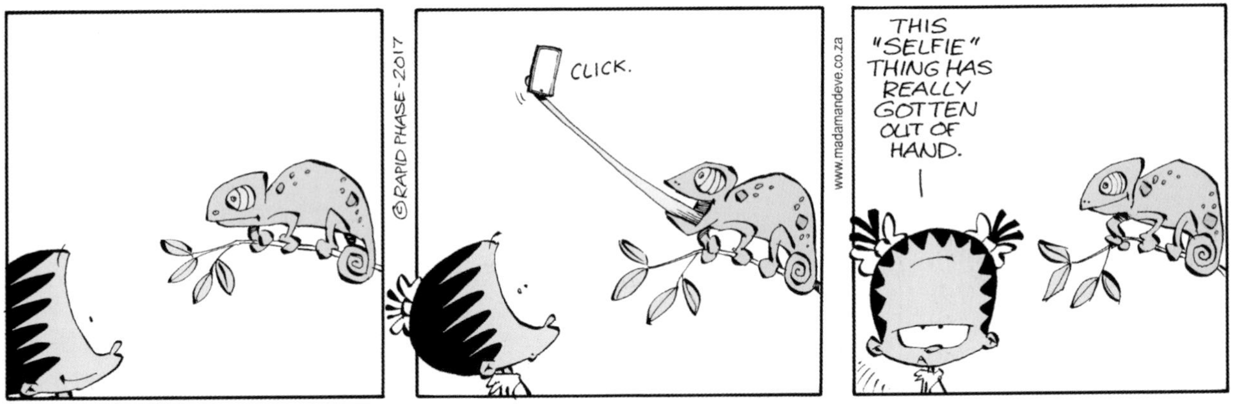
©RAPID PHASE - 2017
CLICK.
www.madamandeve.co.za
THIS "SELFIE" THING HAS REALLY GOTTEN OUT OF HAND.

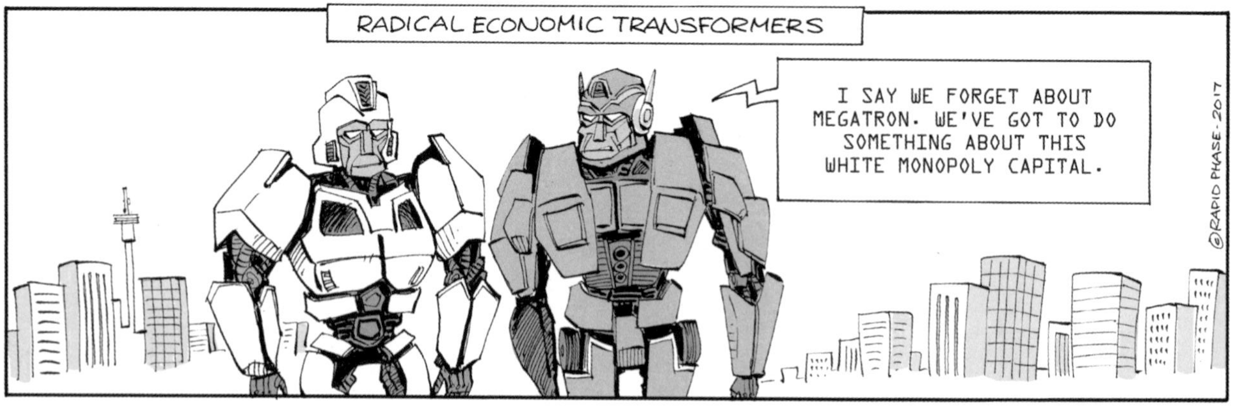
RADICAL ECONOMIC TRANSFORMERS
I SAY WE FORGET ABOUT MEGATRON. WE'VE GOT TO DO SOMETHING ABOUT THIS WHITE MONOPOLY CAPITAL.
©RAPID PHASE · 2017

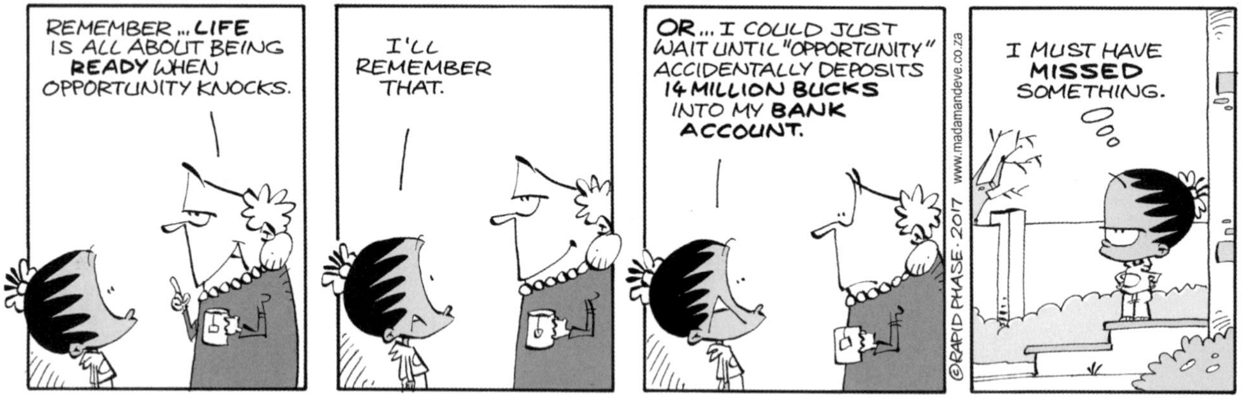
REMEMBER... LIFE IS ALL ABOUT BEING READY WHEN OPPORTUNITY KNOCKS.
I'LL REMEMBER THAT.
OR... I COULD JUST WAIT UNTIL "OPPORTUNITY" ACCIDENTALLY DEPOSITS 14 MILLION BUCKS INTO MY BANK ACCOUNT.
©RAPID PHASE · 2017 www.madamandeve.co.za
I MUST HAVE MISSED SOMETHING.

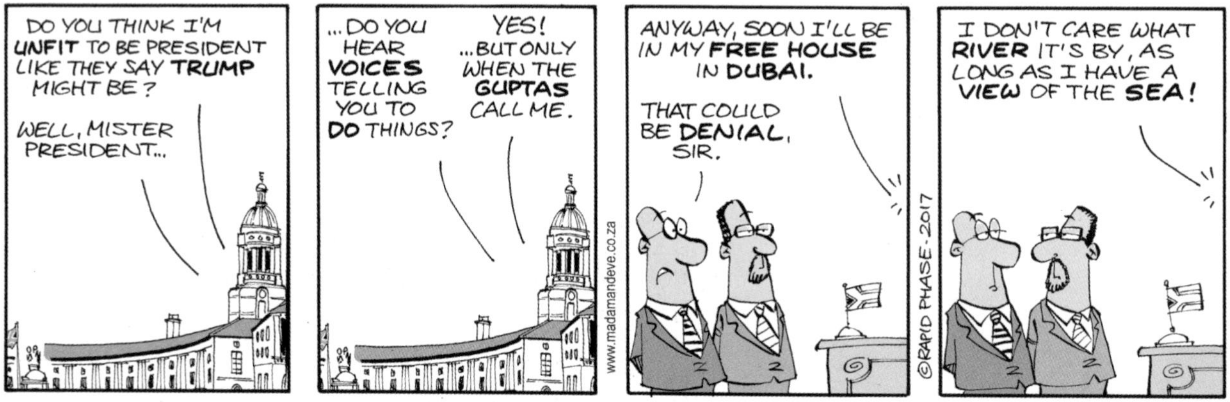
DO YOU THINK I'M UNFIT TO BE PRESIDENT LIKE THEY SAY TRUMP MIGHT BE?
WELL, MISTER PRESIDENT...
...DO YOU HEAR VOICES TELLING YOU TO DO THINGS?
YES! ...BUT ONLY WHEN THE GUPTAS CALL ME.
www.madamandeve.co.za
ANYWAY, SOON I'LL BE IN MY FREE HOUSE IN DUBAI.
THAT COULD BE DENIAL, SIR.
©RAPID PHASE · 2017
I DON'T CARE WHAT RIVER IT'S BY, AS LONG AS I HAVE A VIEW OF THE SEA!

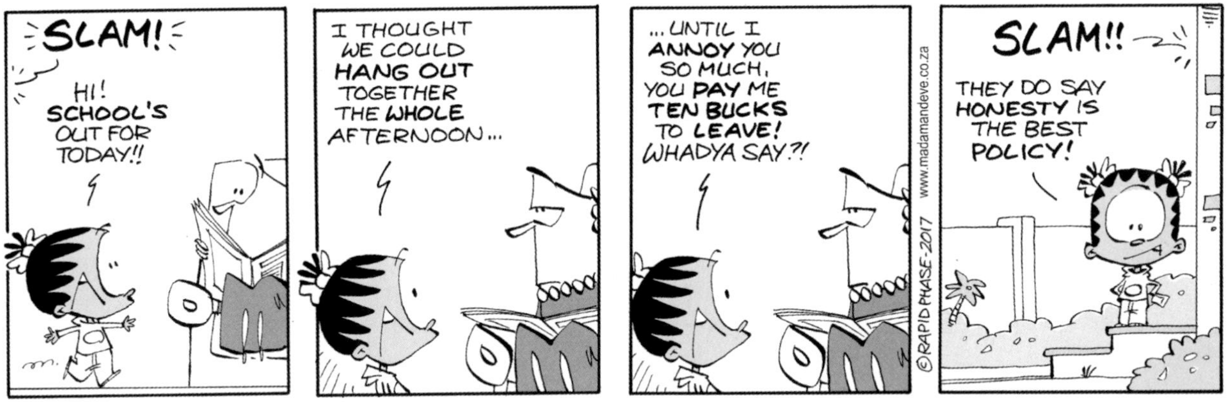
SLAM!
HI! SCHOOL'S OUT FOR TODAY!!
I THOUGHT WE COULD HANG OUT TOGETHER THE WHOLE AFTERNOON...
...UNTIL I ANNOY YOU SO MUCH, YOU PAY ME TEN BUCKS TO LEAVE! WHADYA SAY?!
©RAPID PHASE-2017 www.madamandeve.co.za
SLAM!!
THEY DO SAY HONESTY IS THE BEST POLICY!

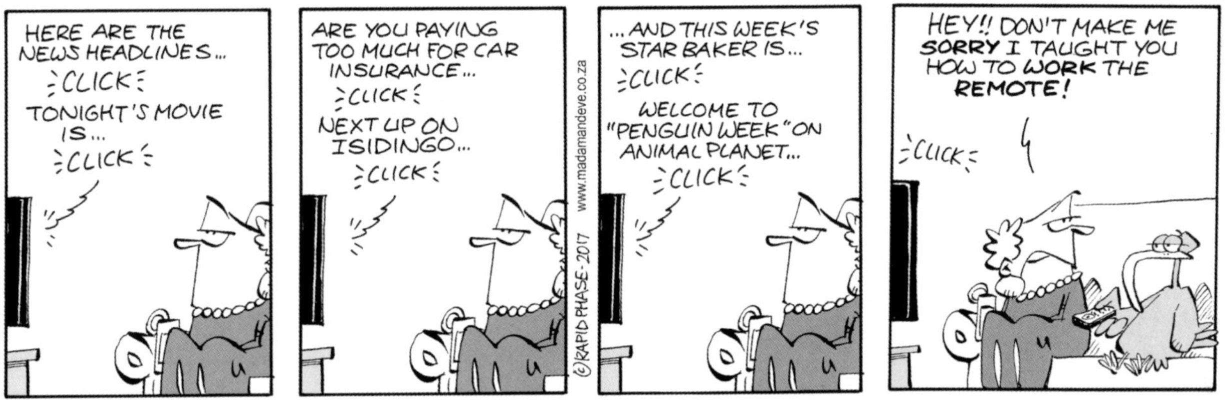
HERE ARE THE NEWS HEADLINES...
CLICK
TONIGHT'S MOVIE IS...
CLICK
ARE YOU PAYING TOO MUCH FOR CAR INSURANCE...
CLICK
NEXT UP ON ISIDINGO...
CLICK
©RAPID PHASE-2017 www.madamandeve.co.za
...AND THIS WEEK'S STAR BAKER IS...
CLICK
WELCOME TO "PENGUIN WEEK" ON ANIMAL PLANET...
CLICK
HEY!! DON'T MAKE ME SORRY I TAUGHT YOU HOW TO WORK THE REMOTE!
CLICK

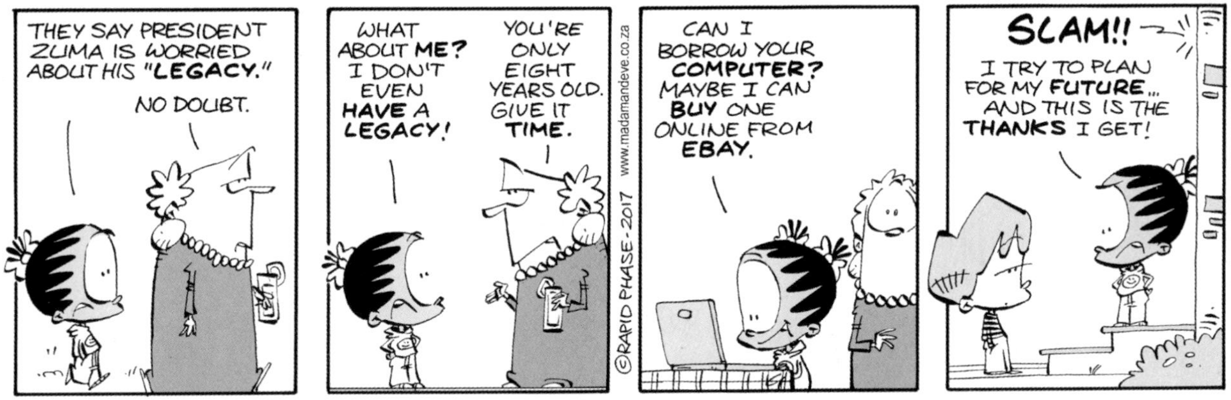
THEY SAY PRESIDENT ZUMA IS WORRIED ABOUT HIS "LEGACY."
NO DOUBT.
WHAT ABOUT ME? I DON'T EVEN HAVE A LEGACY!
YOU'RE ONLY EIGHT YEARS OLD. GIVE IT TIME.
©RAPID PHASE-2017 www.madamandeve.co.za
CAN I BORROW YOUR COMPUTER? MAYBE I CAN BUY ONE ONLINE FROM EBAY.
SLAM!!
I TRY TO PLAN FOR MY FUTURE... AND THIS IS THE THANKS I GET!

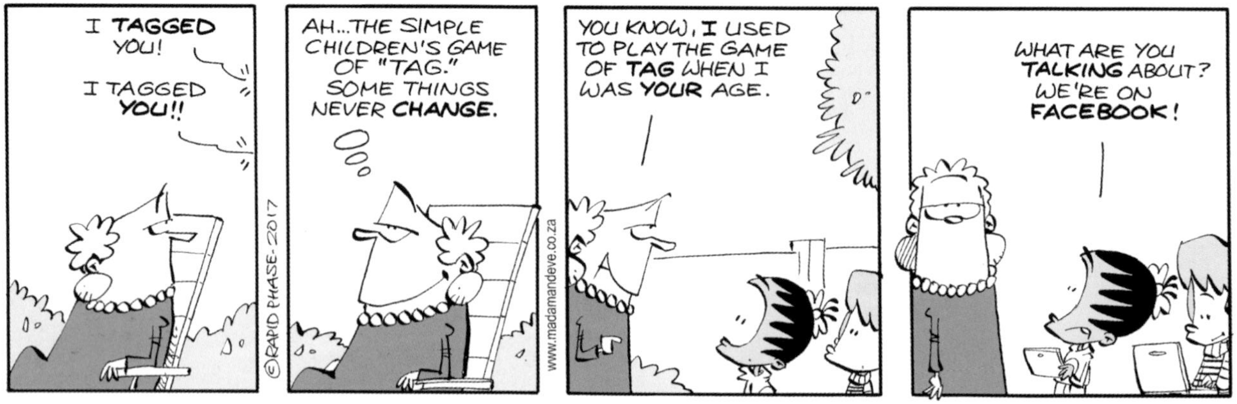
I TAGGED YOU!
I TAGGED YOU!!
AH... THE SIMPLE CHILDREN'S GAME OF "TAG." SOME THINGS NEVER CHANGE.
©RAPID PHASE-2017
www.madamandeve.co.za
YOU KNOW, I USED TO PLAY THE GAME OF TAG WHEN I WAS YOUR AGE.
WHAT ARE YOU TALKING ABOUT? WE'RE ON FACEBOOK!

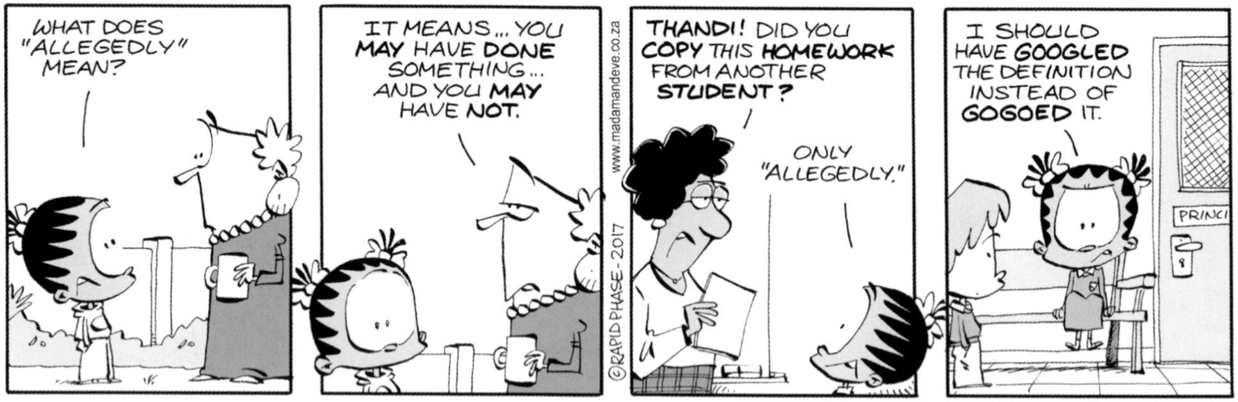
WHAT DOES "ALLEGEDLY" MEAN?
IT MEANS... YOU MAY HAVE DONE SOMETHING... AND YOU MAY HAVE NOT.
©RAPID PHASE-2017
www.madamandeve.co.za
THANDI! DID YOU COPY THIS HOMEWORK FROM ANOTHER STUDENT?
ONLY "ALLEGEDLY."
I SHOULD HAVE GOOGLED THE DEFINITION INSTEAD OF GOGOED IT.
PRINCI

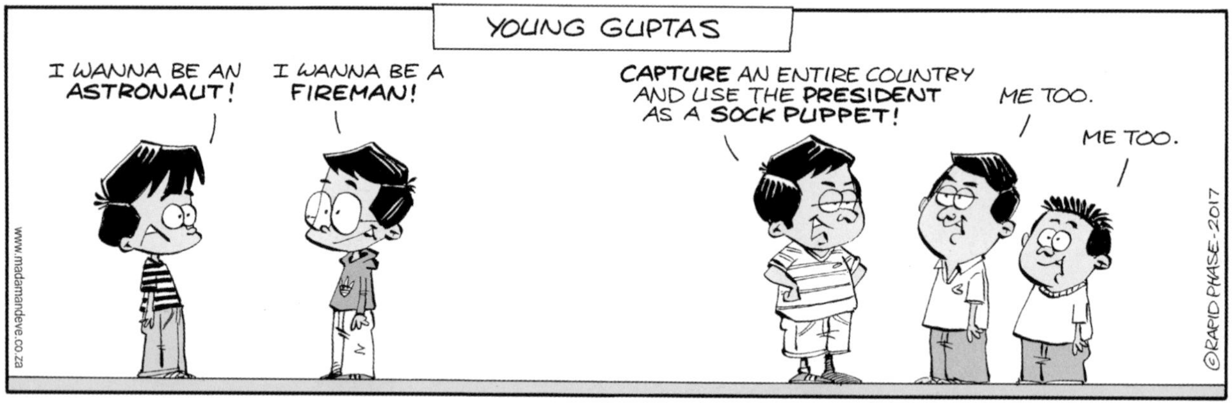
YOUNG GUPTAS
www.madamandeve.co.za
I WANNA BE AN ASTRONAUT!
I WANNA BE A FIREMAN!
CAPTURE AN ENTIRE COUNTRY AND USE THE PRESIDENT AS A SOCK PUPPET!
ME TOO.
ME TOO.
©RAPID PHASE-2017

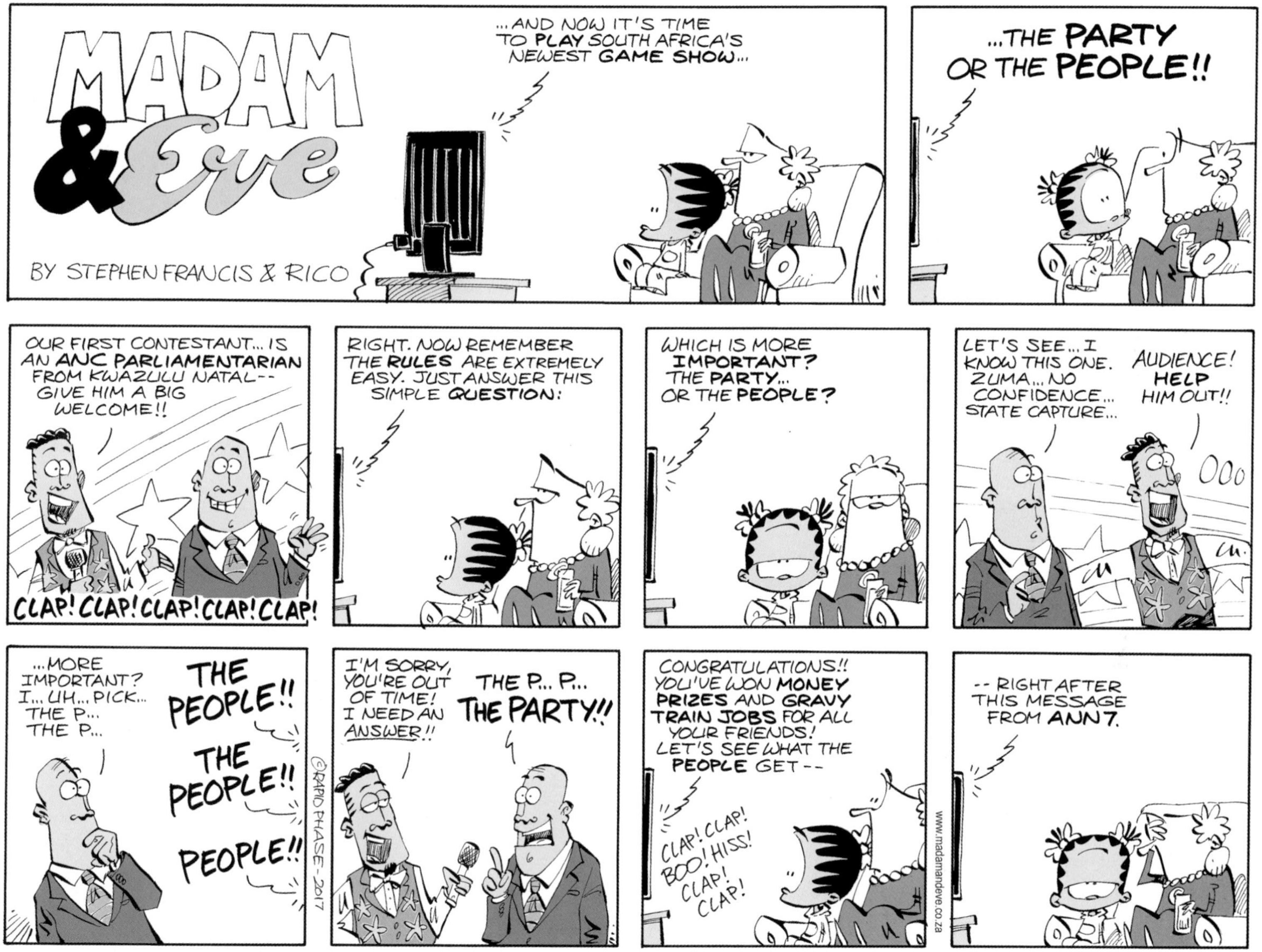
MADAM & Eve
BY STEPHEN FRANCIS & RICO
...AND NOW IT'S TIME TO PLAY SOUTH AFRICA'S NEWEST GAME SHOW...
...THE PARTY OR THE PEOPLE!!
OUR FIRST CONTESTANT... IS AN ANC PARLIAMENTARIAN FROM KWAZULU NATAL-- GIVE HIM A BIG WELCOME!!
CLAP! CLAP! CLAP! CLAP! CLAP!
RIGHT. NOW REMEMBER THE RULES ARE EXTREMELY EASY. JUST ANSWER THIS SIMPLE QUESTION:
WHICH IS MORE IMPORTANT? THE PARTY... OR THE PEOPLE?
LET'S SEE... I KNOW THIS ONE. ZUMA... NO CONFIDENCE... STATE CAPTURE...
AUDIENCE! HELP HIM OUT!!
OOO
...MORE IMPORTANT? I... UH... PICK... THE P... THE P...
THE PEOPLE!!
THE PEOPLE!!
PEOPLE!!
©RAPID PHASE-2017
I'M SORRY, YOU'RE OUT OF TIME! I NEED AN ANSWER!!
THE P... P... THE PARTY!!
CONGRATULATIONS!! YOU'VE WON MONEY PRIZES AND GRAVY TRAIN JOBS FOR ALL YOUR FRIENDS! LET'S SEE WHAT THE PEOPLE GET --
CLAP! CLAP! BOO! HISS! CLAP! CLAP!
www.madamandeve.co.za
-- RIGHT AFTER THIS MESSAGE FROM ANN7.

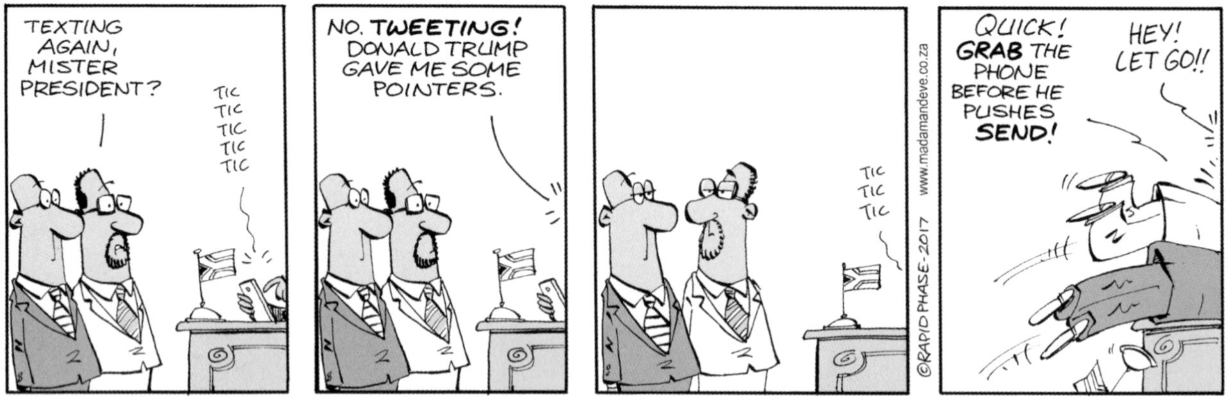
TEXTING AGAIN, MISTER PRESIDENT?
TIC TIC TIC TIC TIC
NO. **TWEETING!** DONALD TRUMP GAVE ME SOME POINTERS.
TIC TIC TIC
©RAPID PHASE · 2017 www.madamandeve.co.za
QUICK! **GRAB** THE PHONE BEFORE HE PUSHES **SEND!**
HEY! LET GO!!

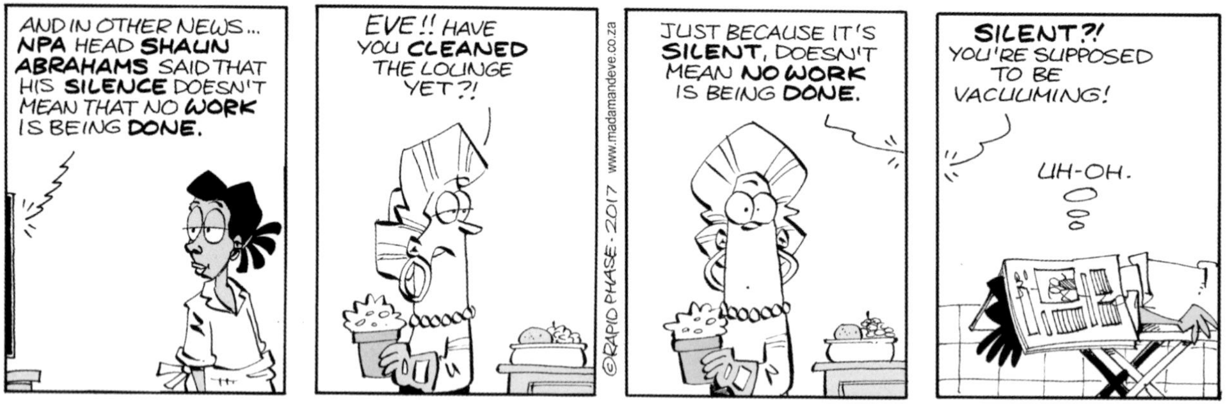
AND IN OTHER NEWS... **NPA** HEAD **SHAUN ABRAHAMS** SAID THAT HIS **SILENCE** DOESN'T MEAN THAT NO **WORK** IS BEING **DONE.**
EVE!! HAVE YOU **CLEANED** THE LOUNGE YET?!
©RAPID PHASE · 2017 www.madamandeve.co.za
JUST BECAUSE IT'S **SILENT**, DOESN'T MEAN **NO WORK** IS BEING **DONE.**
SILENT?! YOU'RE SUPPOSED TO BE VACUUMING!
UH-OH.

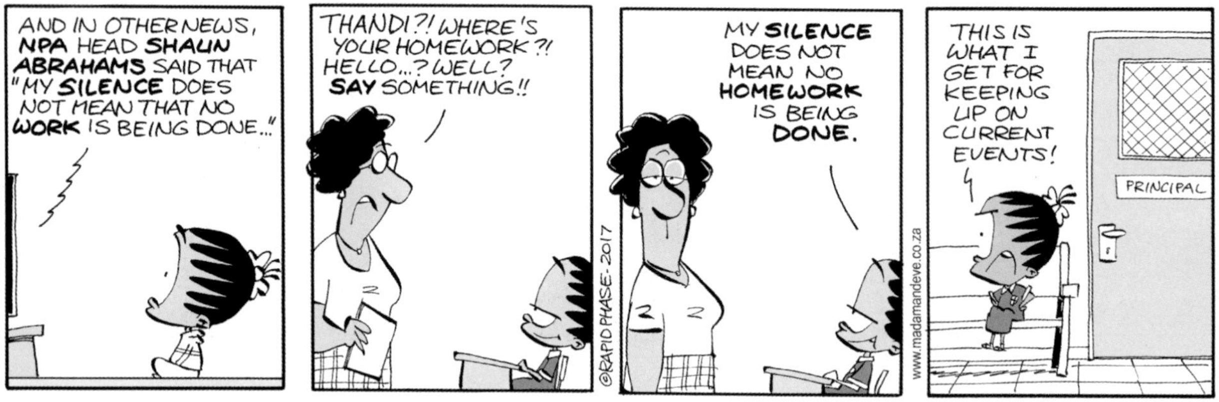
AND IN OTHER NEWS, **NPA** HEAD **SHAUN ABRAHAMS** SAID THAT "MY **SILENCE** DOES NOT MEAN THAT NO **WORK** IS BEING DONE..."
THANDI?! WHERE'S YOUR HOMEWORK?! HELLO...? WELL? **SAY** SOMETHING!!
©RAPID PHASE · 2017
MY **SILENCE** DOES NOT MEAN NO **HOMEWORK** IS BEING **DONE.**
www.madamandeve.co.za
THIS IS WHAT I GET FOR KEEPING UP ON CURRENT EVENTS!
PRINCIPAL

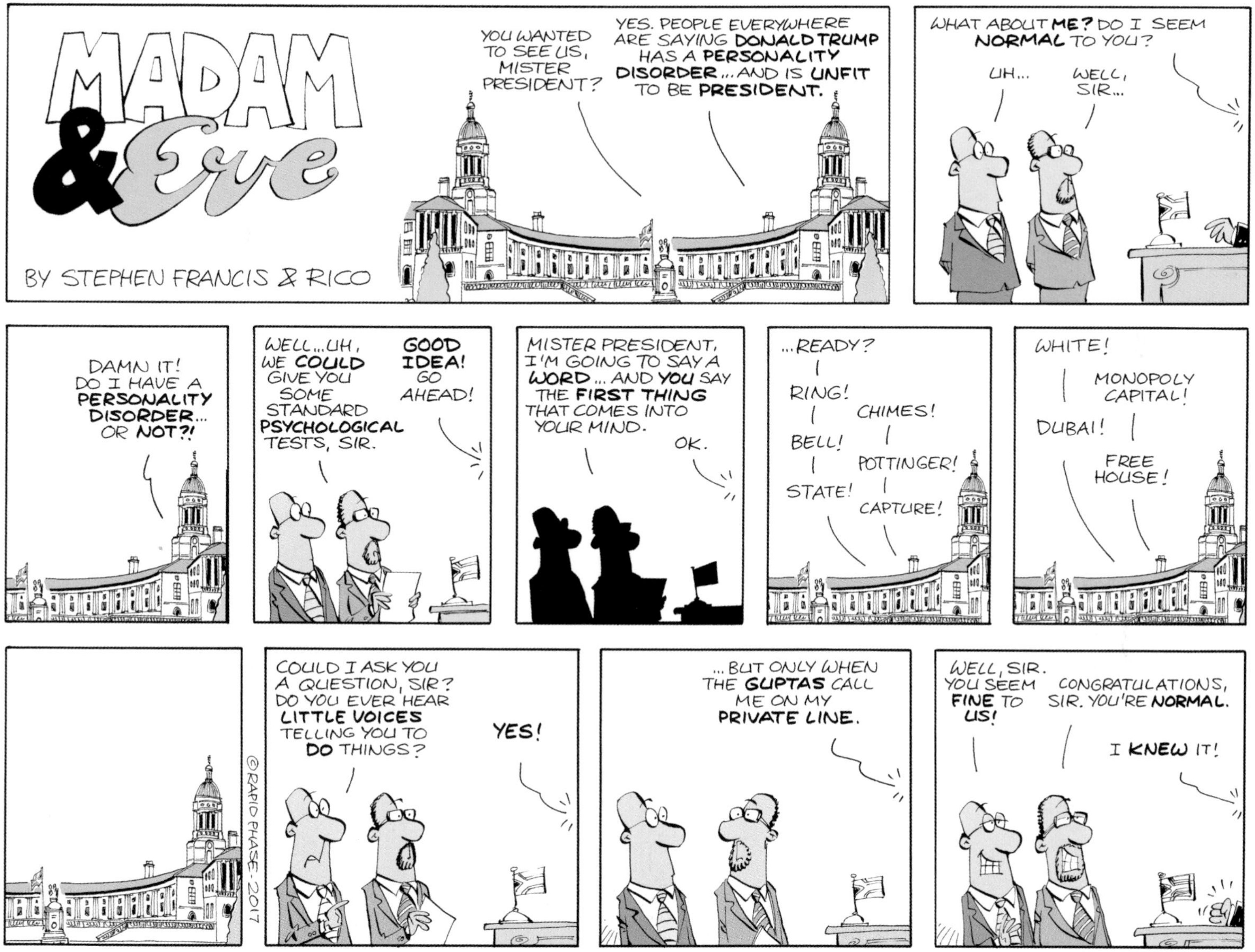
MADAM & Eve
BY STEPHEN FRANCIS & RICO
YOU WANTED TO SEE US, MISTER PRESIDENT?
YES. PEOPLE EVERYWHERE ARE SAYING DONALD TRUMP HAS A PERSONALITY DISORDER... AND IS UNFIT TO BE PRESIDENT.
WHAT ABOUT ME? DO I SEEM NORMAL TO YOU?
UH...
WELL, SIR...
DAMN IT! DO I HAVE A PERSONALITY DISORDER... OR NOT?!
WELL...UH, WE COULD GIVE YOU SOME STANDARD PSYCHOLOGICAL TESTS, SIR.
GOOD IDEA! GO AHEAD!
MISTER PRESIDENT, I'M GOING TO SAY A WORD... AND YOU SAY THE FIRST THING THAT COMES INTO YOUR MIND.
OK.
...READY?
RING!
CHIMES!
BELL!
POTTINGER!
STATE!
CAPTURE!
WHITE!
MONOPOLY CAPITAL!
DUBAI!
FREE HOUSE!
© RAPID PHASE · 2017
COULD I ASK YOU A QUESTION, SIR? DO YOU EVER HEAR LITTLE VOICES TELLING YOU TO DO THINGS?
YES!
...BUT ONLY WHEN THE GUPTAS CALL ME ON MY PRIVATE LINE.
WELL, SIR. YOU SEEM FINE TO US!
CONGRATULATIONS, SIR. YOU'RE NORMAL.
I KNEW IT!

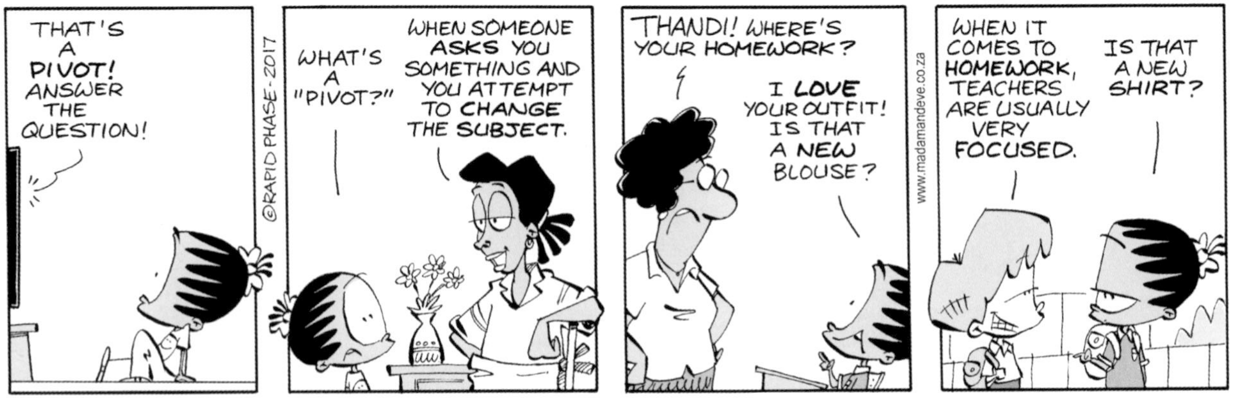
THAT'S A PIVOT! ANSWER THE QUESTION!
©RAPID PHASE · 2017
WHAT'S A "PIVOT?"
WHEN SOMEONE ASKS YOU SOMETHING AND YOU ATTEMPT TO CHANGE THE SUBJECT.
THANDI! WHERE'S YOUR HOMEWORK?
I LOVE YOUR OUTFIT! IS THAT A NEW BLOUSE?
www.madamandeve.co.za
WHEN IT COMES TO HOMEWORK, TEACHERS ARE USUALLY VERY FOCUSED.
IS THAT A NEW SHIRT?

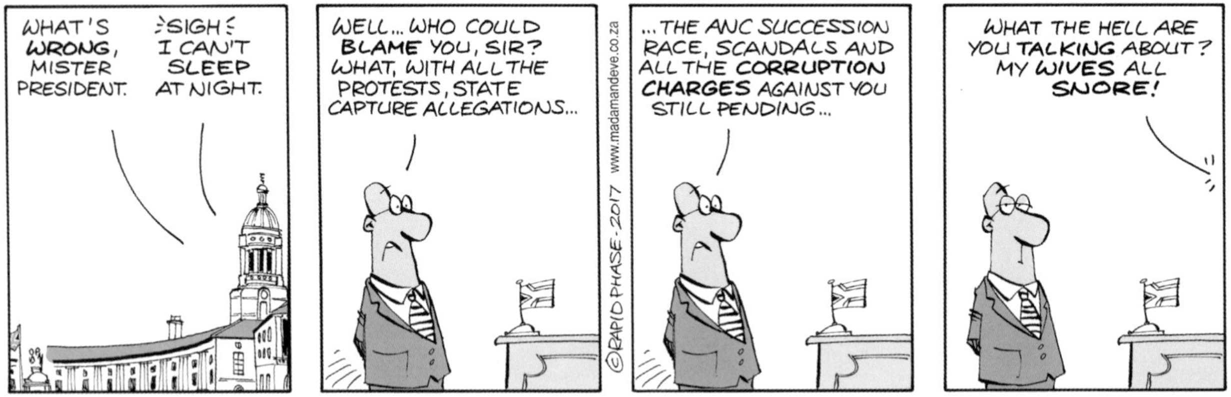
WHAT'S WRONG, MISTER PRESIDENT.
SIGH I CAN'T SLEEP AT NIGHT.
WELL... WHO COULD BLAME YOU, SIR? WHAT, WITH ALL THE PROTESTS, STATE CAPTURE ALLEGATIONS...
©RAPID PHASE · 2017 www.madamandeve.co.za
...THE ANC SUCCESSION RACE, SCANDALS AND ALL THE CORRUPTION CHARGES AGAINST YOU STILL PENDING...
WHAT THE HELL ARE YOU TALKING ABOUT? MY WIVES ALL SNORE!

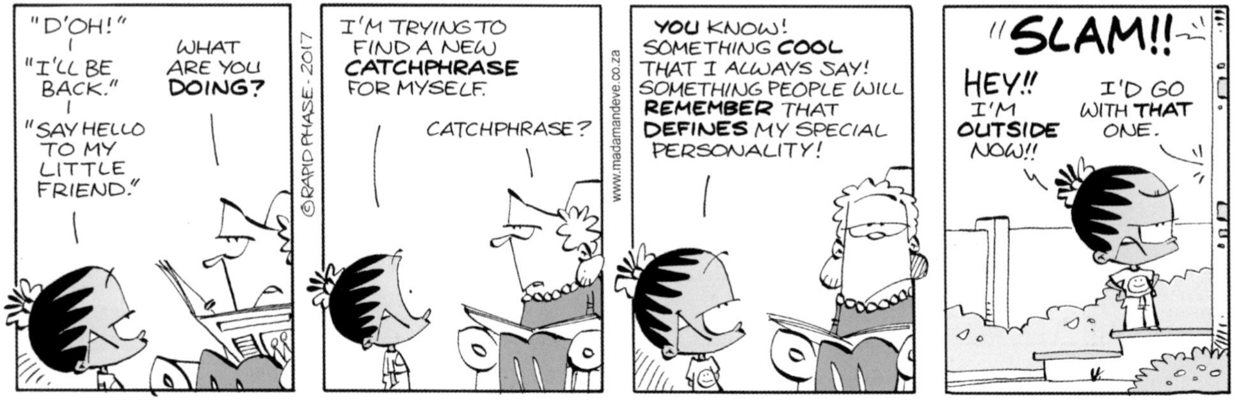
"D'OH!"
"I'LL BE BACK."
"SAY HELLO TO MY LITTLE FRIEND."
WHAT ARE YOU DOING?
©RAPID PHASE · 2017
I'M TRYING TO FIND A NEW CATCHPHRASE FOR MYSELF.
CATCHPHRASE?
www.madamandeve.co.za
YOU KNOW! SOMETHING COOL THAT I ALWAYS SAY! SOMETHING PEOPLE WILL REMEMBER THAT DEFINES MY SPECIAL PERSONALITY!
SLAM!!
HEY!! I'M OUTSIDE NOW!!
I'D GO WITH THAT ONE.

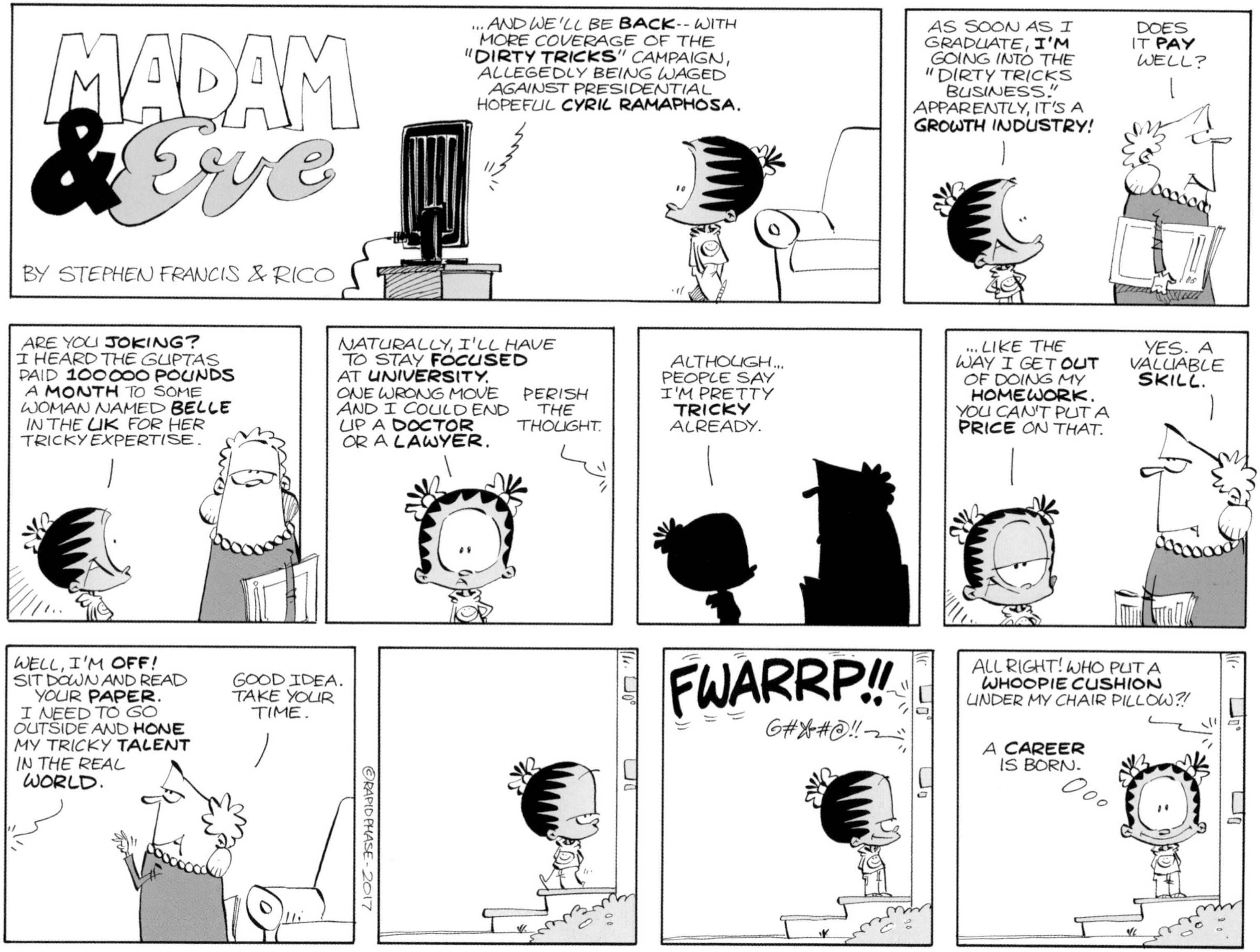
MADAM & Eve
BY STEPHEN FRANCIS & RICO
...AND WE'LL BE **BACK**-- WITH MORE COVERAGE OF THE "**DIRTY TRICKS**" CAMPAIGN, ALLEGEDLY BEING WAGED AGAINST PRESIDENTIAL HOPEFUL **CYRIL RAMAPHOSA.**
AS SOON AS I GRADUATE, **I'M** GOING INTO THE "DIRTY TRICKS BUSINESS." APPARENTLY, IT'S A **GROWTH INDUSTRY!**
DOES IT **PAY** WELL?
ARE YOU **JOKING?** I HEARD THE GUPTAS PAID **100 000 POUNDS** A **MONTH** TO SOME WOMAN NAMED **BELLE** IN THE **UK** FOR HER TRICKY EXPERTISE.
NATURALLY, I'LL HAVE TO STAY **FOCUSED** AT **UNIVERSITY.** ONE WRONG MOVE AND I COULD END UP A **DOCTOR** OR A **LAWYER.**
PERISH THE THOUGHT.
ALTHOUGH... PEOPLE SAY I'M PRETTY **TRICKY** ALREADY.
...LIKE THE WAY I GET **OUT** OF DOING MY **HOMEWORK.** YOU CAN'T PUT A **PRICE** ON THAT.
YES. A VALUABLE **SKILL.**
WELL, I'M **OFF!** SIT DOWN AND READ YOUR **PAPER.** I NEED TO GO OUTSIDE AND **HONE** MY TRICKY **TALENT** IN THE REAL **WORLD.**
GOOD IDEA. TAKE YOUR TIME.
©RAPID PHASE-2017
FWARRP!!
G#*#@!!
ALL RIGHT! WHO PUT A **WHOOPIE CUSHION** UNDER MY CHAIR PILLOW?!
A **CAREER** IS BORN.

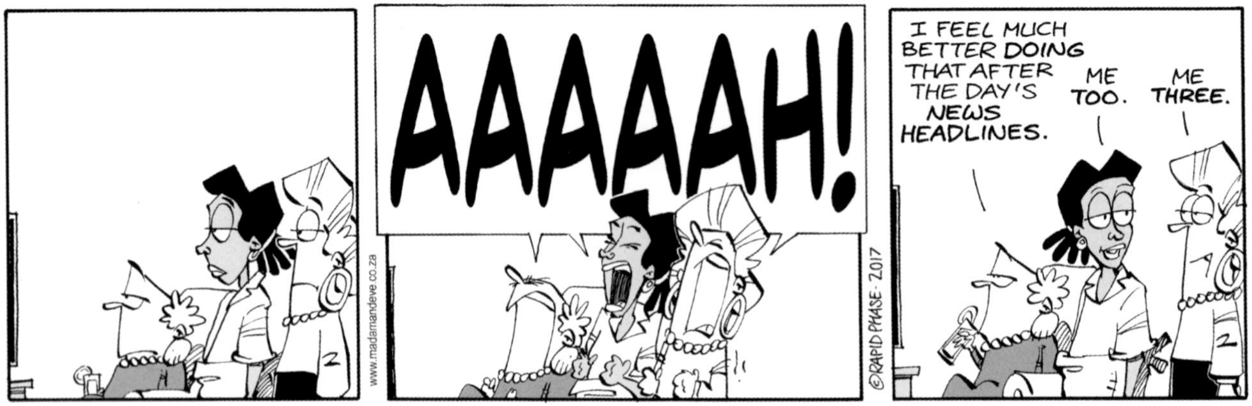
AAAAAH!
www.madamandeve.co.za
I FEEL MUCH BETTER DOING THAT AFTER THE DAY'S NEWS HEADLINES.
ME TOO.
ME THREE.
©RAPID PHASE · 2017

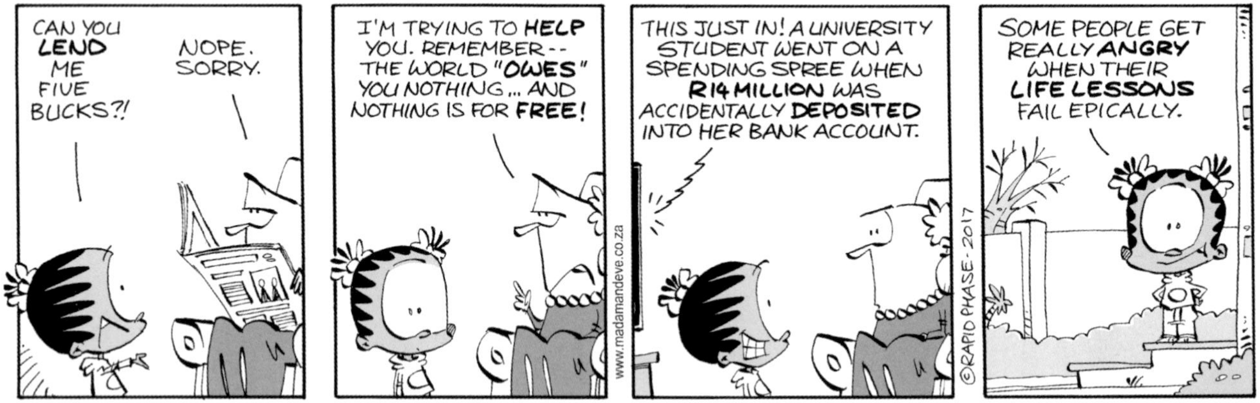
CAN YOU LEND ME FIVE BUCKS?!
NOPE. SORRY.
I'M TRYING TO HELP YOU. REMEMBER -- THE WORLD "OWES" YOU NOTHING... AND NOTHING IS FOR FREE!
www.madamandeve.co.za
THIS JUST IN! A UNIVERSITY STUDENT WENT ON A SPENDING SPREE WHEN R14 MILLION WAS ACCIDENTALLY DEPOSITED INTO HER BANK ACCOUNT.
©RAPID PHASE · 2017
SOME PEOPLE GET REALLY ANGRY WHEN THEIR LIFE LESSONS FAIL EPICALLY.

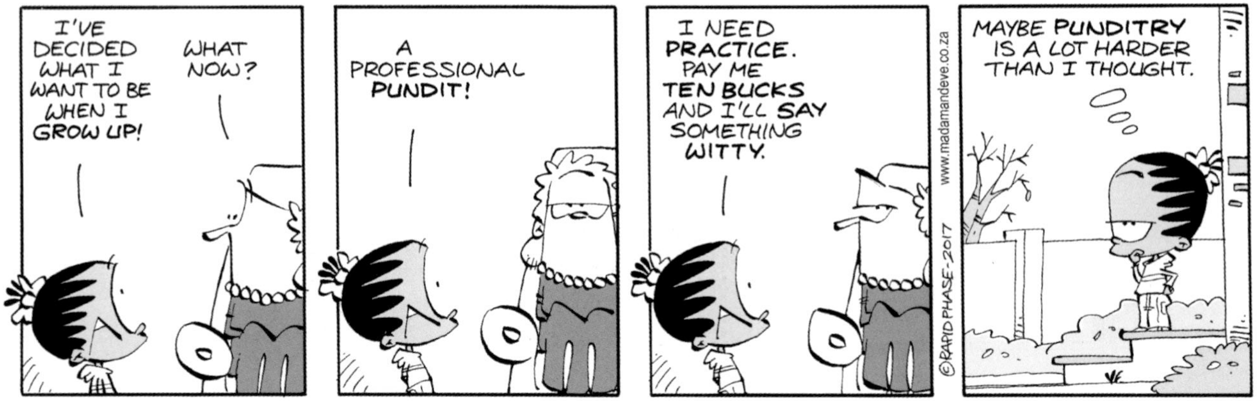
I'VE DECIDED WHAT I WANT TO BE WHEN I GROW UP!
WHAT NOW?
A PROFESSIONAL PUNDIT!
I NEED PRACTICE. PAY ME TEN BUCKS AND I'LL SAY SOMETHING WITTY.
www.madamandeve.co.za
©RAPID PHASE · 2017
MAYBE PUNDITRY IS A LOT HARDER THAN I THOUGHT.

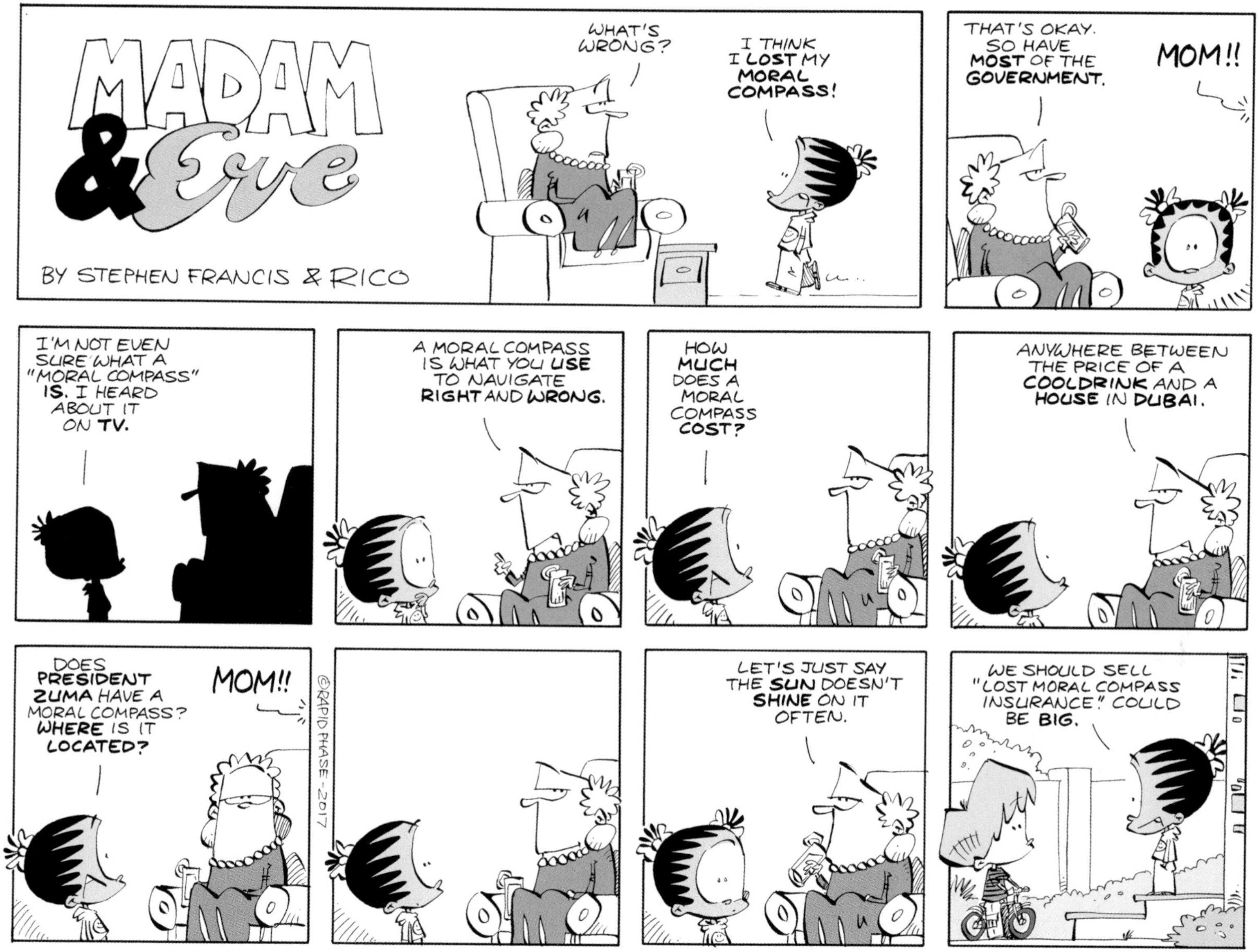
MADAM & Eve
BY STEPHEN FRANCIS & RICO
WHAT'S WRONG?
I THINK I LOST MY MORAL COMPASS!
THAT'S OKAY. SO HAVE MOST OF THE GOVERNMENT.
MOM!!
I'M NOT EVEN SURE WHAT A "MORAL COMPASS" IS. I HEARD ABOUT IT ON TV.
A MORAL COMPASS IS WHAT YOU USE TO NAVIGATE RIGHT AND WRONG.
HOW MUCH DOES A MORAL COMPASS COST?
ANYWHERE BETWEEN THE PRICE OF A COOLDRINK AND A HOUSE IN DUBAI.
DOES PRESIDENT ZUMA HAVE A MORAL COMPASS? WHERE IS IT LOCATED?
MOM!!
©RAPID PHASE-2017
LET'S JUST SAY THE SUN DOESN'T SHINE ON IT OFTEN.
WE SHOULD SELL "LOST MORAL COMPASS INSURANCE." COULD BE BIG.

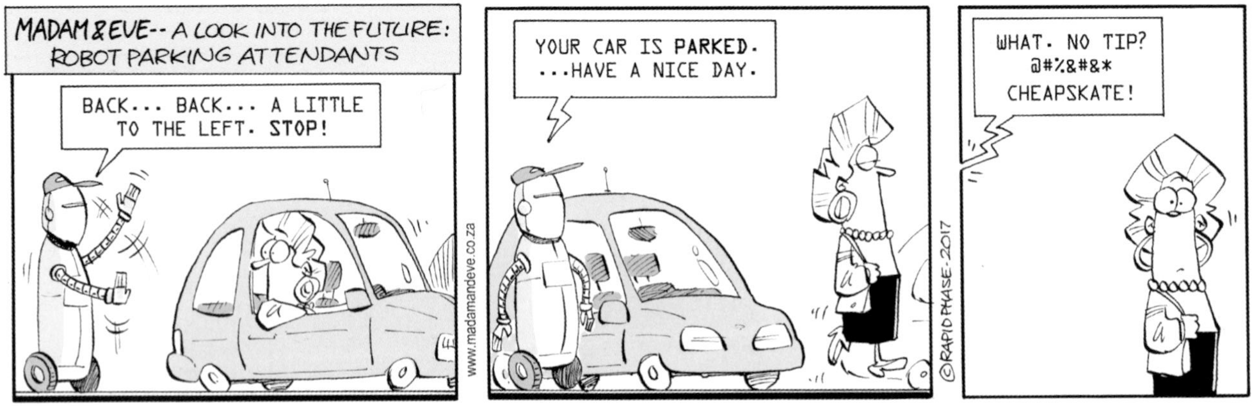
MADAM & EVE-- A LOOK INTO THE FUTURE: ROBOT PARKING ATTENDANTS
BACK... BACK... A LITTLE TO THE LEFT. STOP!
www.madamandeve.co.za
YOUR CAR IS PARKED. ...HAVE A NICE DAY.
©RAPID PHASE-2017
WHAT. NO TIP? @#%&#&* CHEAPSKATE!

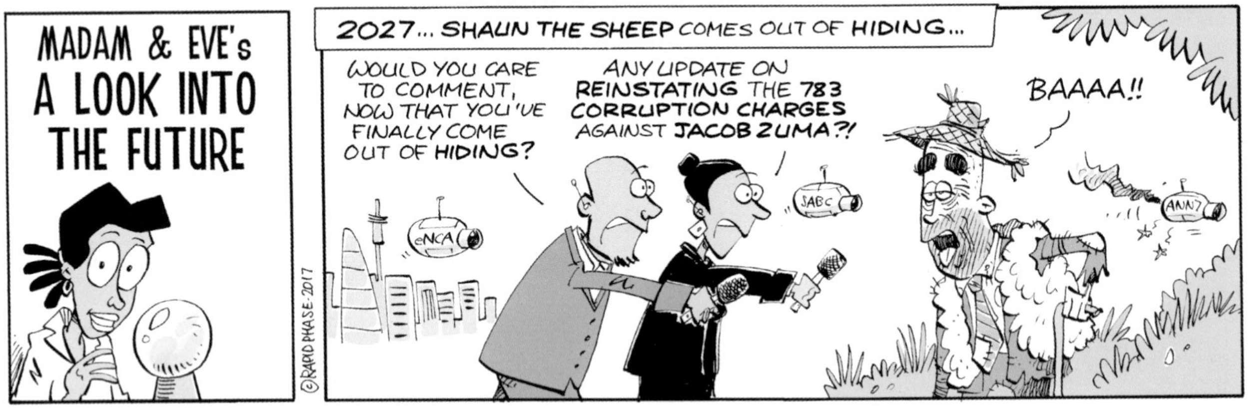
MADAM & EVE's A LOOK INTO THE FUTURE
©RAPID PHASE-2017
2027... SHAUN THE SHEEP COMES OUT OF HIDING...
WOULD YOU CARE TO COMMENT, NOW THAT YOU'VE FINALLY COME OUT OF HIDING?
ANY UPDATE ON REINSTATING THE 783 CORRUPTION CHARGES AGAINST JACOB ZUMA?!
BAAAA!!
eNCA
SABC
ANN7

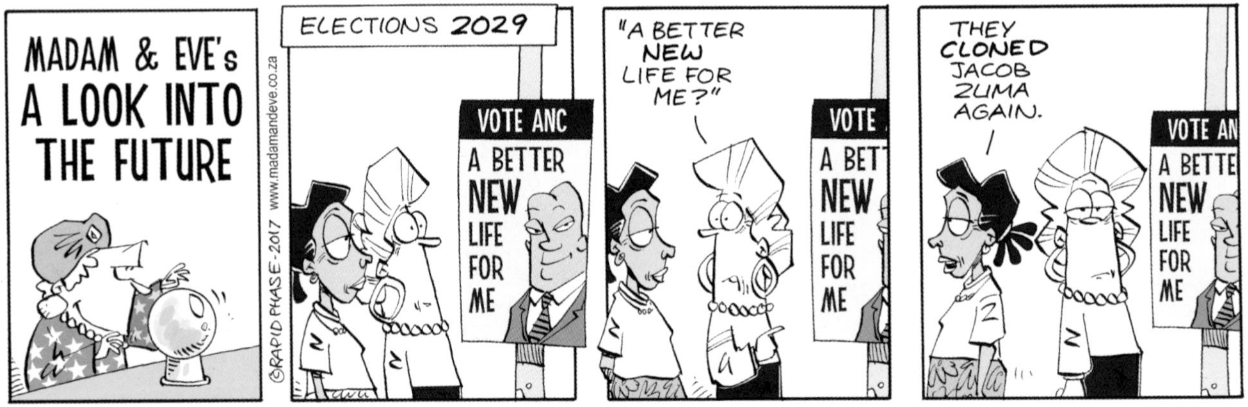
MADAM & EVE's A LOOK INTO THE FUTURE
©RAPID PHASE-2017 www.madamandeve.co.za
ELECTIONS 2029
VOTE ANC
A BETTER NEW LIFE FOR ME
"A BETTER NEW LIFE FOR ME?"
THEY CLONED JACOB ZUMA AGAIN.

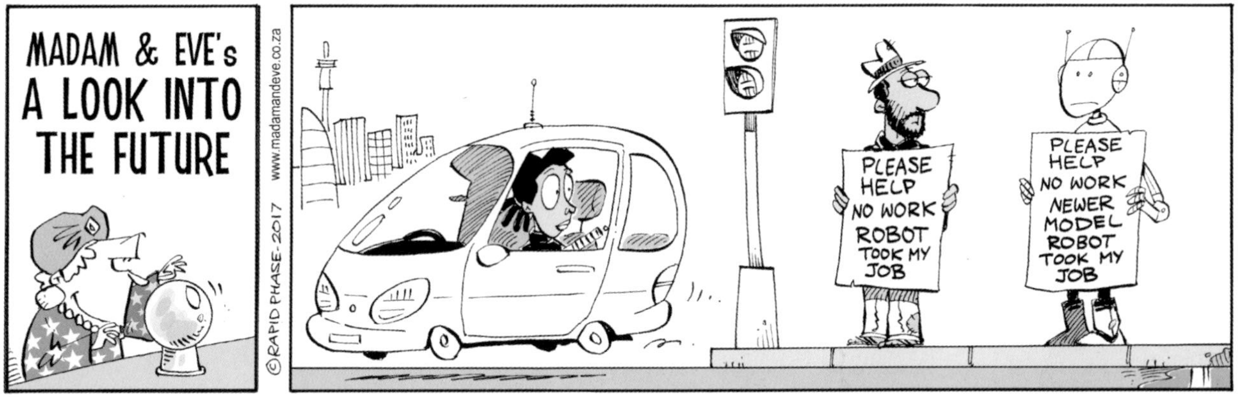
MADAM & EVE's A LOOK INTO THE FUTURE
©RAPID PHASE-2017 www.madamandeve.co.za
PLEASE HELP NO WORK ROBOT TOOK MY JOB
PLEASE HELP NO WORK NEWER MODEL ROBOT TOOK MY JOB

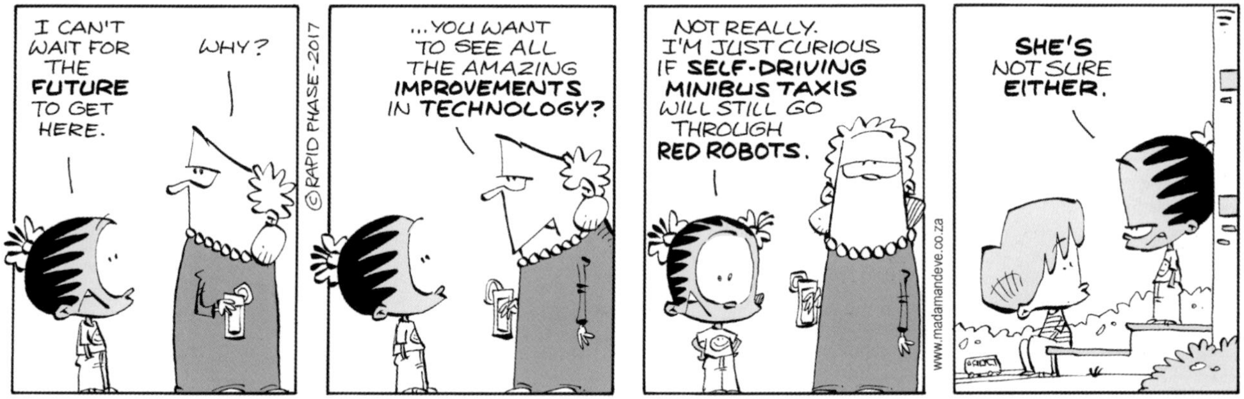
I CAN'T WAIT FOR THE **FUTURE** TO GET HERE.
WHY?
©RAPID PHASE-2017
...YOU WANT TO SEE ALL THE AMAZING **IMPROVEMENTS** IN **TECHNOLOGY?**
NOT REALLY. I'M JUST CURIOUS IF **SELF-DRIVING MINIBUS TAXIS** WILL STILL GO THROUGH **RED ROBOTS**.
www.madamandeve.co.za
SHE'S NOT SURE **EITHER**.

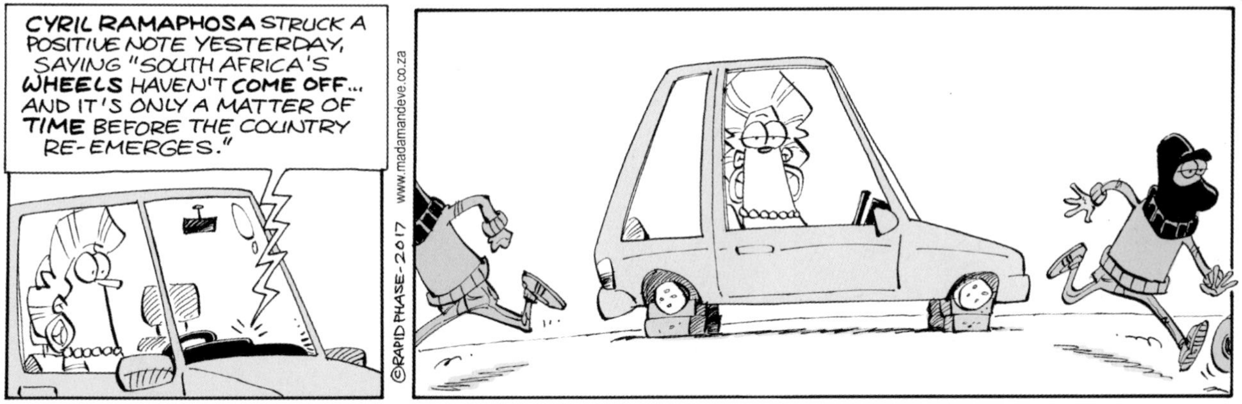
CYRIL RAMAPHOSA STRUCK A POSITIVE NOTE YESTERDAY, SAYING "SOUTH AFRICA'S **WHEELS** HAVEN'T **COME OFF**... AND IT'S ONLY A MATTER OF **TIME** BEFORE THE COUNTRY RE-EMERGES."
©RAPID PHASE-2017 www.madamandeve.co.za

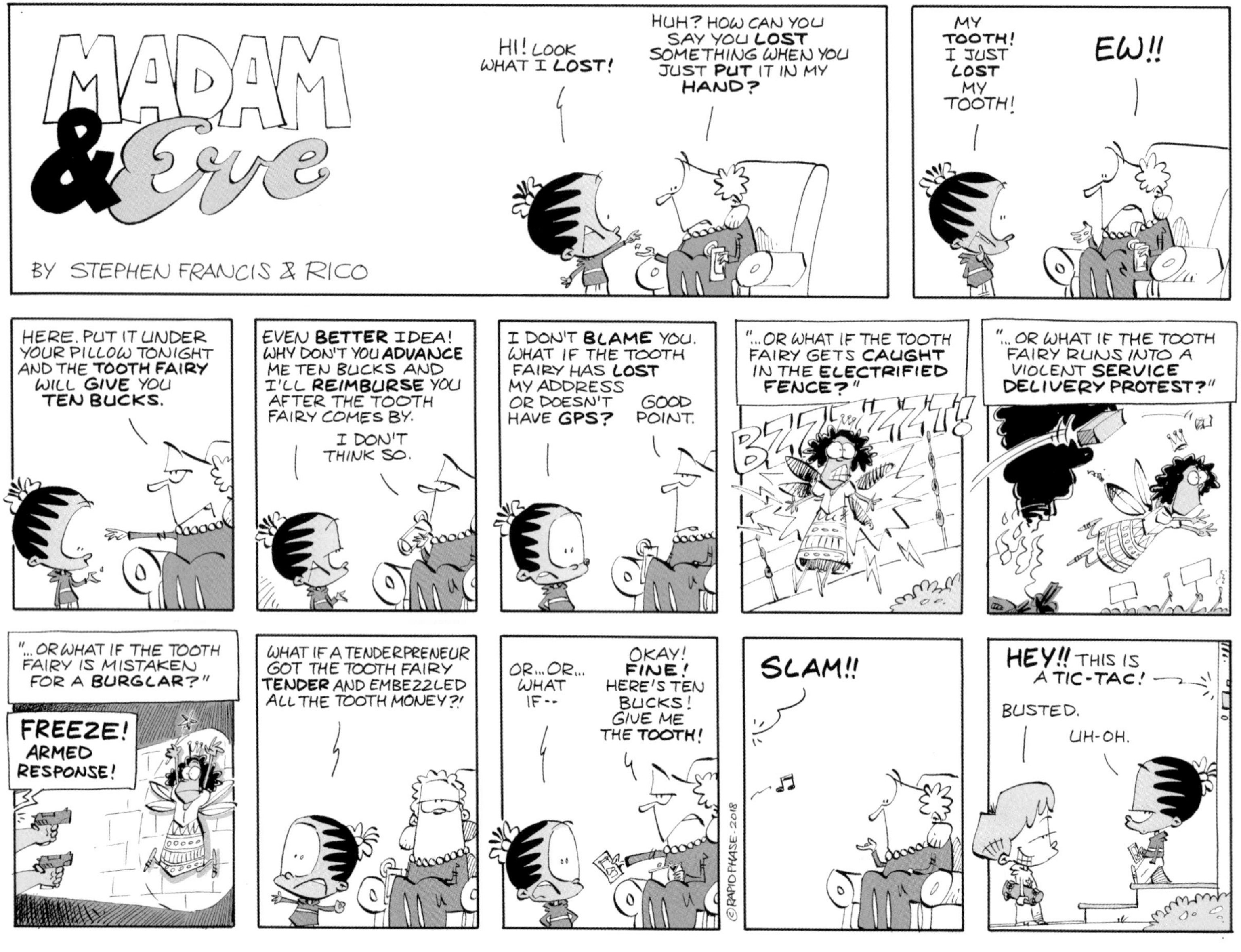
MADAM & Eve
BY STEPHEN FRANCIS & RICO
HI! LOOK WHAT I **LOST**!
HUH? HOW CAN YOU SAY YOU **LOST** SOMETHING WHEN YOU JUST **PUT** IT IN MY **HAND?**
MY **TOOTH!** I JUST **LOST** MY TOOTH!
EW!!
HERE. PUT IT UNDER YOUR PILLOW TONIGHT AND THE **TOOTH FAIRY** WILL **GIVE** YOU **TEN BUCKS.**
EVEN **BETTER** IDEA! WHY DON'T YOU **ADVANCE** ME TEN BUCKS AND I'LL **REIMBURSE** YOU AFTER THE TOOTH FAIRY COMES BY.
I DON'T THINK SO.
I DON'T **BLAME** YOU. WHAT IF THE TOOTH FAIRY HAS **LOST** MY ADDRESS OR DOESN'T HAVE **GPS?**
GOOD POINT.
"...OR WHAT IF THE TOOTH FAIRY GETS **CAUGHT** IN THE **ELECTRIFIED FENCE?**"
BZZZZZZZT!
"...OR WHAT IF THE TOOTH FAIRY RUNS INTO A VIOLENT **SERVICE DELIVERY PROTEST?**"
"...OR WHAT IF THE TOOTH FAIRY IS MISTAKEN FOR A **BURGLAR?**"
FREEZE! ARMED RESPONSE!
WHAT IF A TENDERPRENEUR GOT THE TOOTH FAIRY **TENDER** AND EMBEZZLED ALL THE TOOTH MONEY?!
OR...OR... WHAT IF--
OKAY! **FINE!** HERE'S TEN BUCKS! GIVE ME THE **TOOTH!**
©RAPID PHASE·2018
SLAM!!
HEY!! THIS IS A TIC-TAC!
BUSTED.
UH-OH.

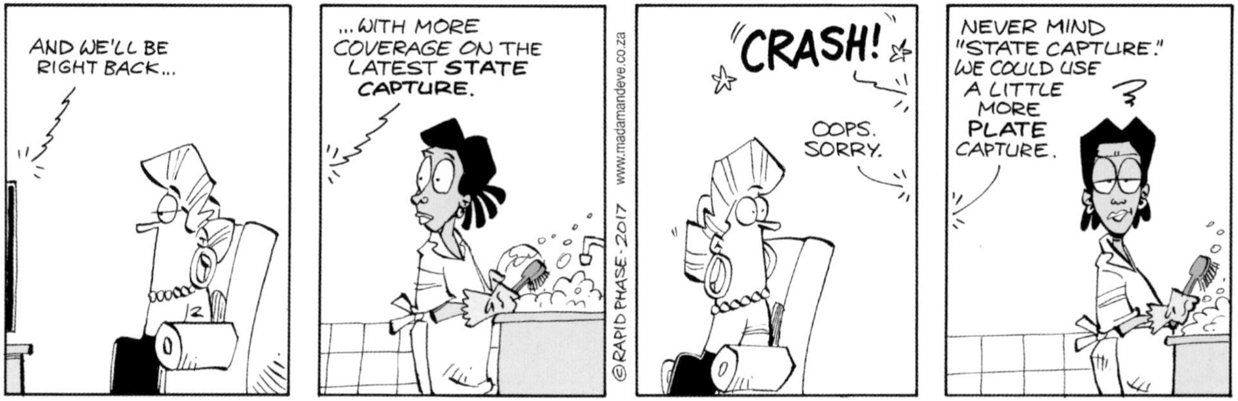
AND WE'LL BE RIGHT BACK...
...WITH MORE COVERAGE ON THE LATEST STATE CAPTURE.
©RAPID PHASE-2017
www.madamandeve.co.za
CRASH!
OOPS. SORRY.
NEVER MIND "STATE CAPTURE." WE COULD USE A LITTLE MORE PLATE CAPTURE.

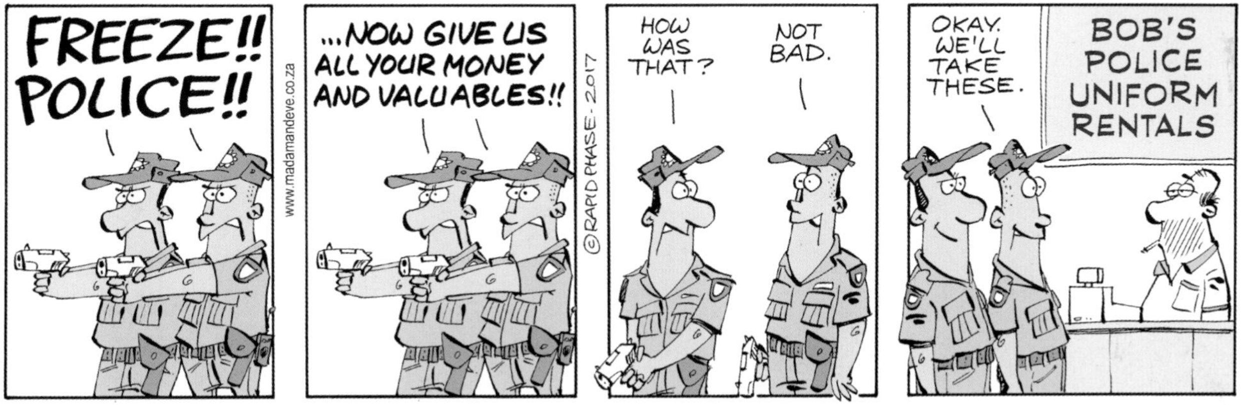
FREEZE!! POLICE!!
www.madamandeve.co.za
...NOW GIVE US ALL YOUR MONEY AND VALUABLES!!
©RAPID PHASE-2017
HOW WAS THAT?
NOT BAD.
OKAY. WE'LL TAKE THESE.
BOB'S POLICE UNIFORM RENTALS

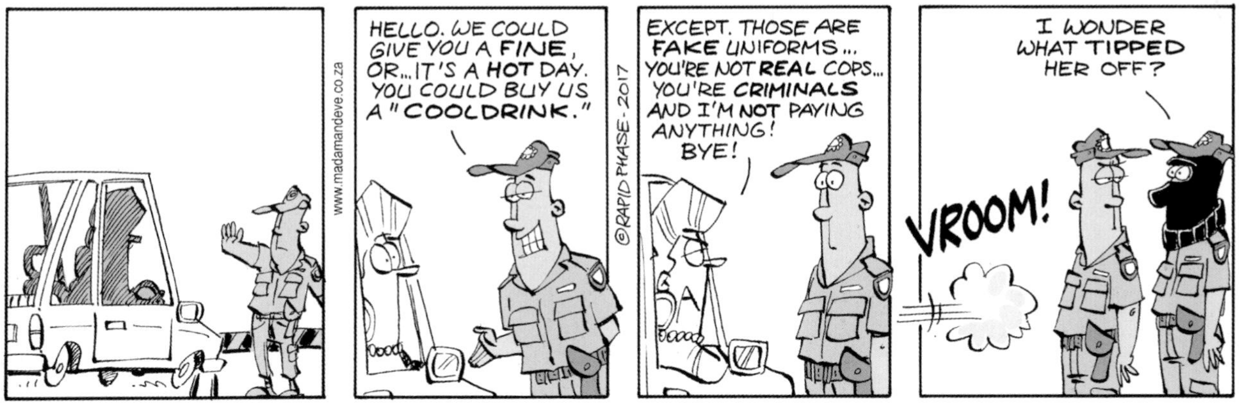
www.madamandeve.co.za
HELLO. WE COULD GIVE YOU A FINE, OR...IT'S A HOT DAY. YOU COULD BUY US A "COOLDRINK."
©RAPID PHASE-2017
EXCEPT. THOSE ARE FAKE UNIFORMS... YOU'RE NOT REAL COPS... YOU'RE CRIMINALS AND I'M NOT PAYING ANYTHING! BYE!
VROOM!
I WONDER WHAT TIPPED HER OFF?

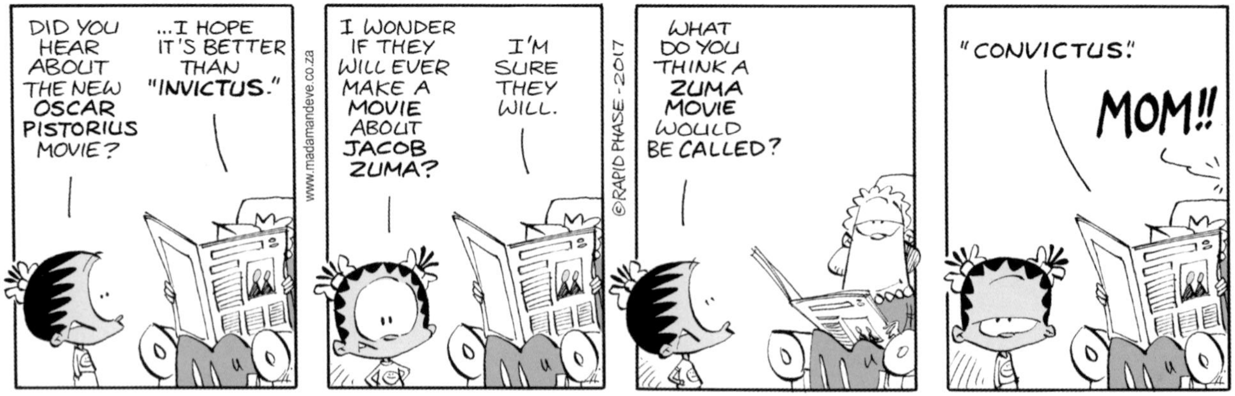
DID YOU HEAR ABOUT THE NEW OSCAR PISTORIUS MOVIE?
...I HOPE IT'S BETTER THAN "INVICTUS."
www.madamandeve.co.za
I WONDER IF THEY WILL EVER MAKE A MOVIE ABOUT JACOB ZUMA?
I'M SURE THEY WILL.
©RAPID PHASE-2017
WHAT DO YOU THINK A ZUMA MOVIE WOULD BE CALLED?
"CONVICTUS."
MOM!!

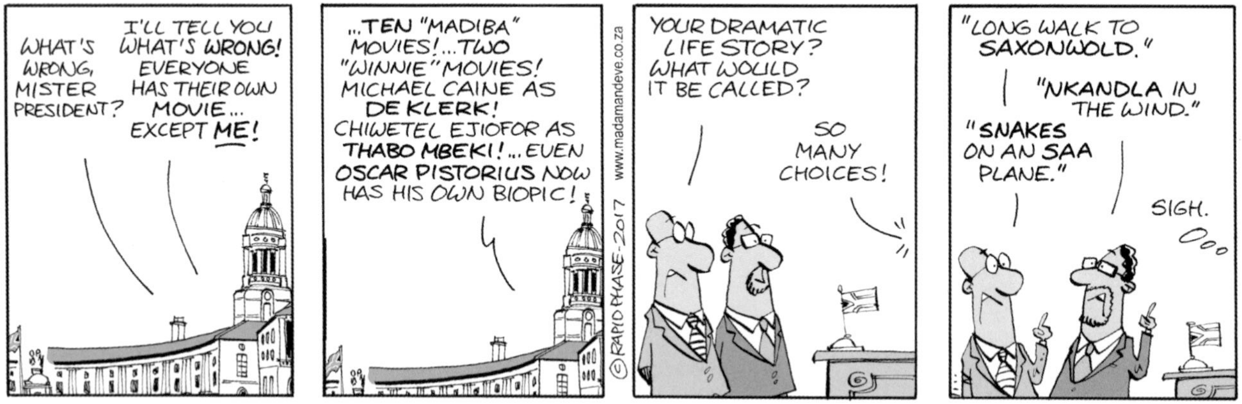
WHAT'S WRONG, MISTER PRESIDENT?
I'LL TELL YOU WHAT'S WRONG! EVERYONE HAS THEIR OWN MOVIE... EXCEPT ME!
...TEN "MADIBA" MOVIES!...TWO "WINNIE" MOVIES! MICHAEL CAINE AS DE KLERK! CHIWETEL EJIOFOR AS THABO MBEKI!...EVEN OSCAR PISTORIUS NOW HAS HIS OWN BIOPIC!
©RAPID PHASE-2017
www.madamandeve.co.za
YOUR DRAMATIC LIFE STORY? WHAT WOULD IT BE CALLED?
SO MANY CHOICES!
"LONG WALK TO SAXONWOLD."
"NKANDLA IN THE WIND."
"SNAKES ON AN SAA PLANE."
SIGH.

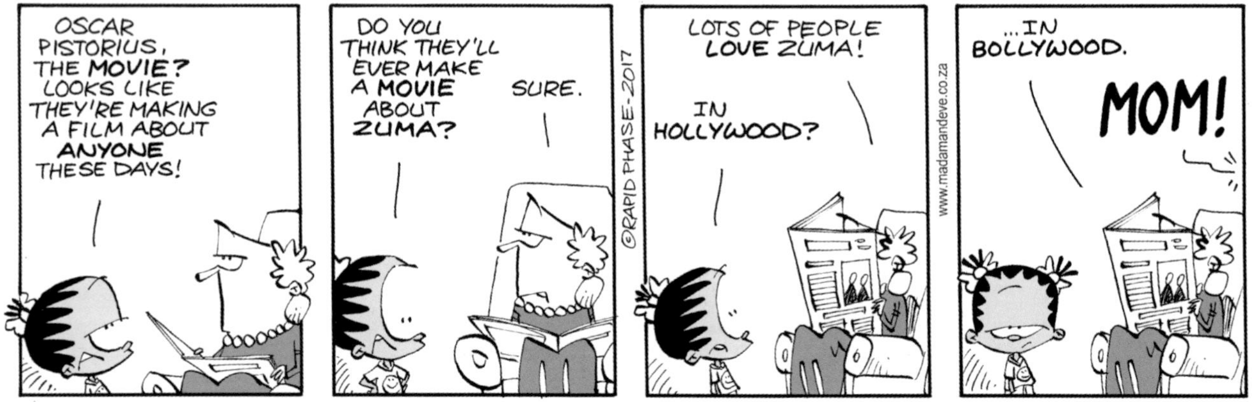
OSCAR PISTORIUS, THE MOVIE? LOOKS LIKE THEY'RE MAKING A FILM ABOUT ANYONE THESE DAYS!
DO YOU THINK THEY'LL EVER MAKE A MOVIE ABOUT ZUMA?
SURE.
©RAPID PHASE-2017
LOTS OF PEOPLE LOVE ZUMA!
IN HOLLYWOOD?
www.madamandeve.co.za
...IN BOLLYWOOD.
MOM!

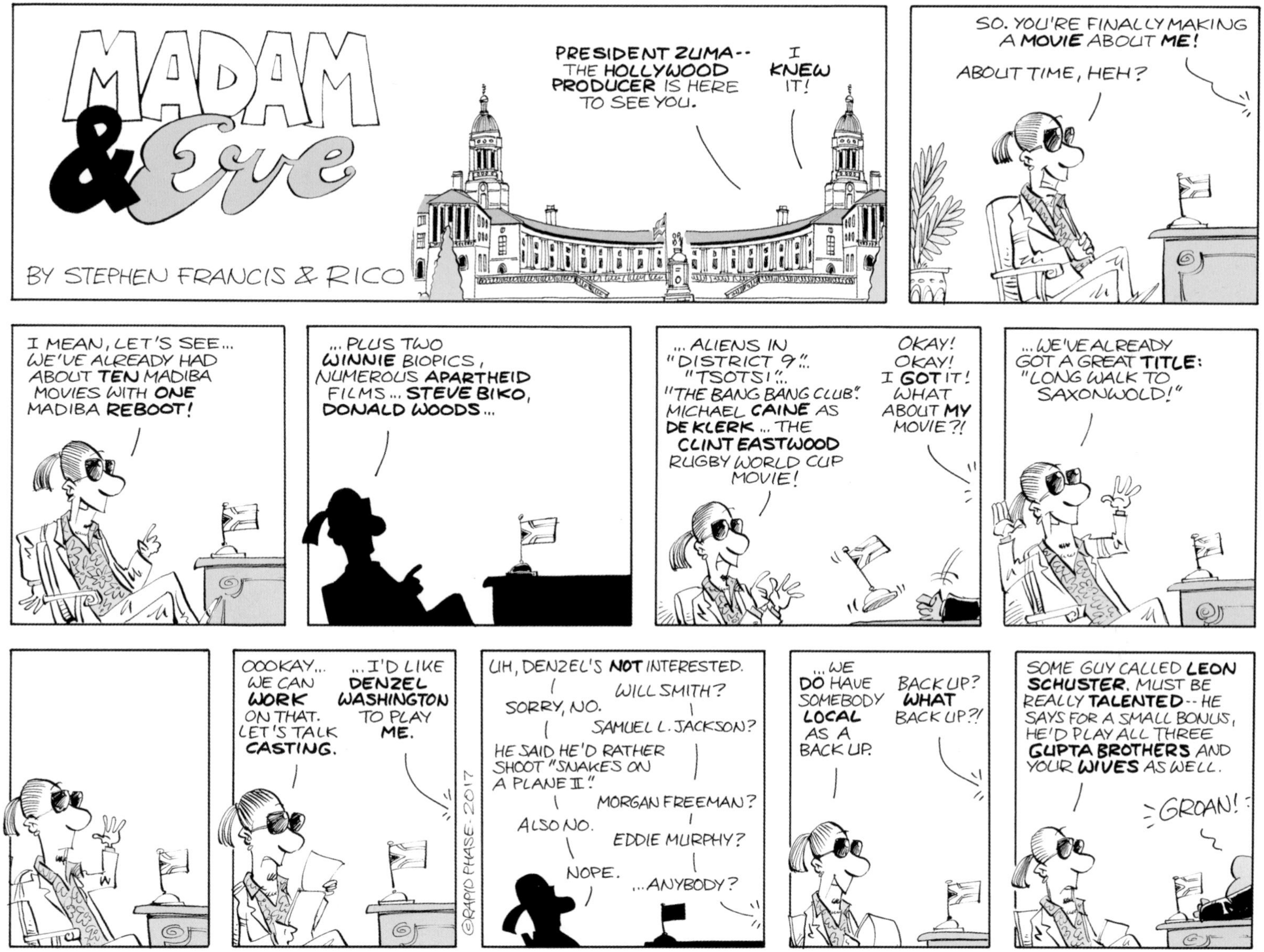
MADAM & Eve
BY STEPHEN FRANCIS & RICO
PRESIDENT ZUMA-- THE HOLLYWOOD PRODUCER IS HERE TO SEE YOU.
I KNEW IT!
SO. YOU'RE FINALLY MAKING A MOVIE ABOUT ME!
ABOUT TIME, HEH?
I MEAN, LET'S SEE... WE'VE ALREADY HAD ABOUT TEN MADIBA MOVIES WITH ONE MADIBA REBOOT!
...PLUS TWO WINNIE BIOPICS, NUMEROUS APARTHEID FILMS... STEVE BIKO, DONALD WOODS...
...ALIENS IN "DISTRICT 9"... "TSOTSI"... "THE BANG BANG CLUB". MICHAEL CAINE AS DE KLERK... THE CLINT EASTWOOD RUGBY WORLD CUP MOVIE!
OKAY! OKAY! I GOT IT! WHAT ABOUT MY MOVIE?!
...WE'VE ALREADY GOT A GREAT TITLE: "LONG WALK TO SAXONWOLD!"
OOOKAY... WE CAN WORK ON THAT. LET'S TALK CASTING.
...I'D LIKE DENZEL WASHINGTON TO PLAY ME.
©RAPID PHASE · 2017
UH, DENZEL'S NOT INTERESTED.
WILL SMITH?
SORRY, NO.
SAMUEL L. JACKSON?
HE SAID HE'D RATHER SHOOT "SNAKES ON A PLANE II"
MORGAN FREEMAN?
ALSO NO.
EDDIE MURPHY?
NOPE.
...ANYBODY?
...WE DO HAVE SOMEBODY LOCAL AS A BACK UP.
BACK UP? WHAT BACK UP?!
SOME GUY CALLED LEON SCHUSTER. MUST BE REALLY TALENTED-- HE SAYS FOR A SMALL BONUS, HE'D PLAY ALL THREE GUPTA BROTHERS AND YOUR WIVES AS WELL.
GROAN!

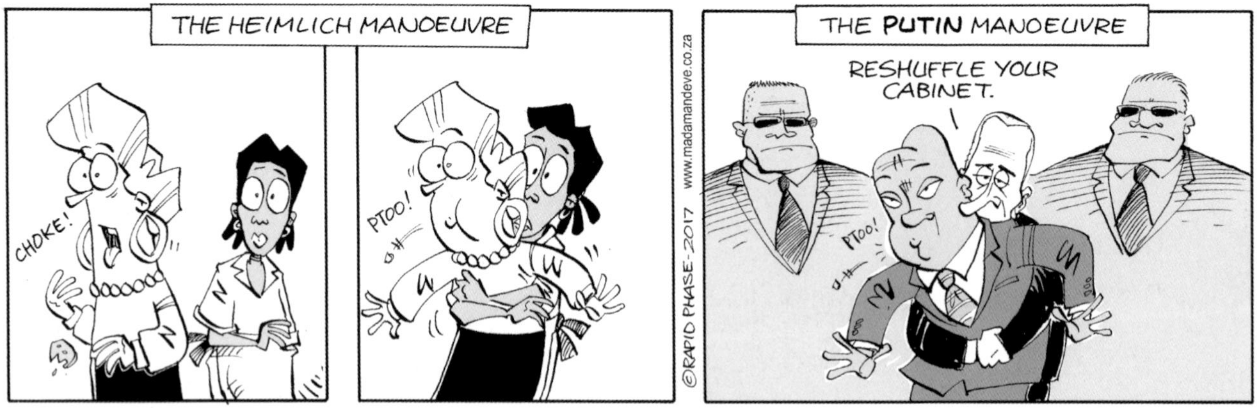
THE HEIMLICH MANOEUVRE
CHOKE!
PTOO!
THE PUTIN MANOEUVRE
RESHUFFLE YOUR CABINET.
PTOO!
©RAPID PHASE-2017 www.madamandeve.co.za

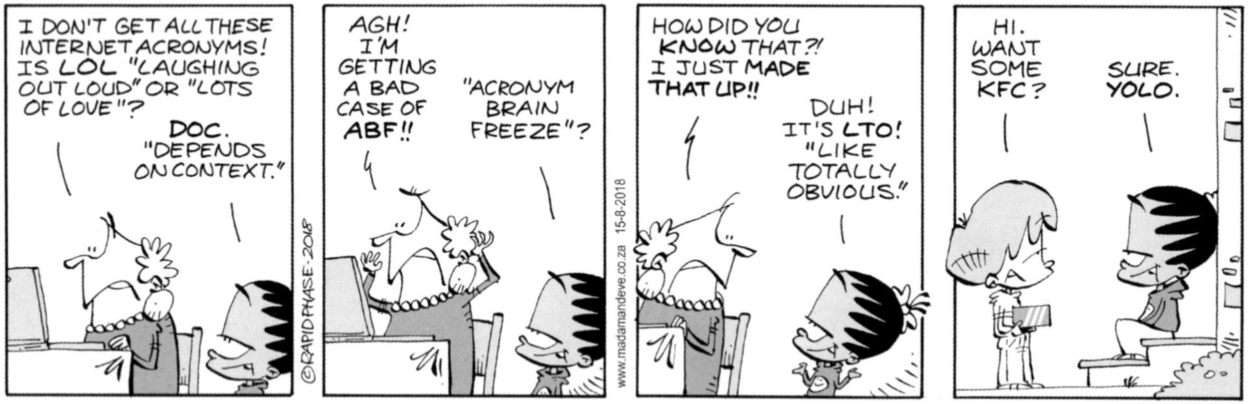
I DON'T GET ALL THESE INTERNET ACRONYMS! IS LOL "LAUGHING OUT LOUD" OR "LOTS OF LOVE"?
DOC. "DEPENDS ON CONTEXT."
©RAPID PHASE-2018
AGH! I'M GETTING A BAD CASE OF ABF!!
"ACRONYM BRAIN FREEZE"?
www.madamandeve.co.za 15-8-2018
HOW DID YOU KNOW THAT?! I JUST MADE THAT UP!!
DUH! IT'S LTO! "LIKE TOTALLY OBVIOUS."
HI. WANT SOME KFC?
SURE. YOLO.

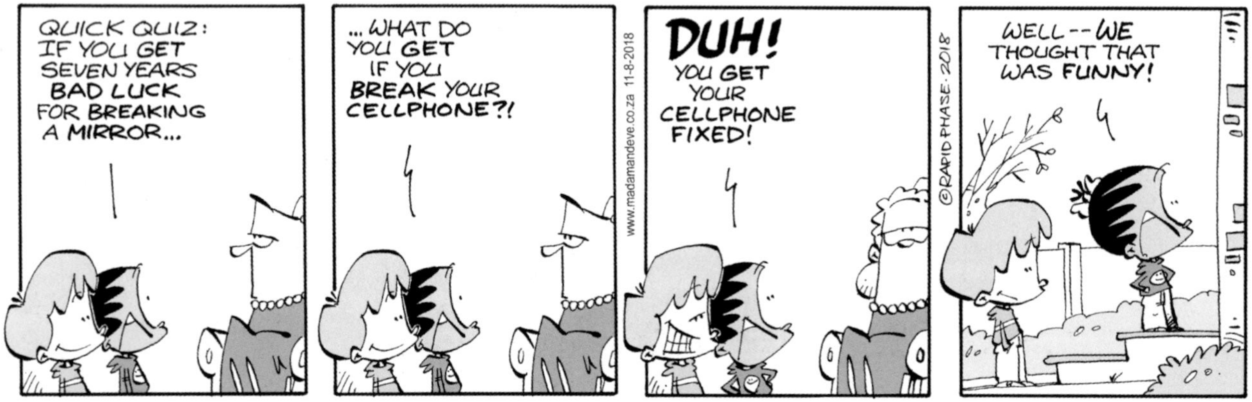
QUICK QUIZ: IF YOU GET SEVEN YEARS BAD LUCK FOR BREAKING A MIRROR...
...WHAT DO YOU GET IF YOU BREAK YOUR CELLPHONE?!
www.madamandeve.co.za 11-8-2018
DUH! YOU GET YOUR CELLPHONE FIXED!
©RAPID PHASE-2018
WELL--WE THOUGHT THAT WAS FUNNY!

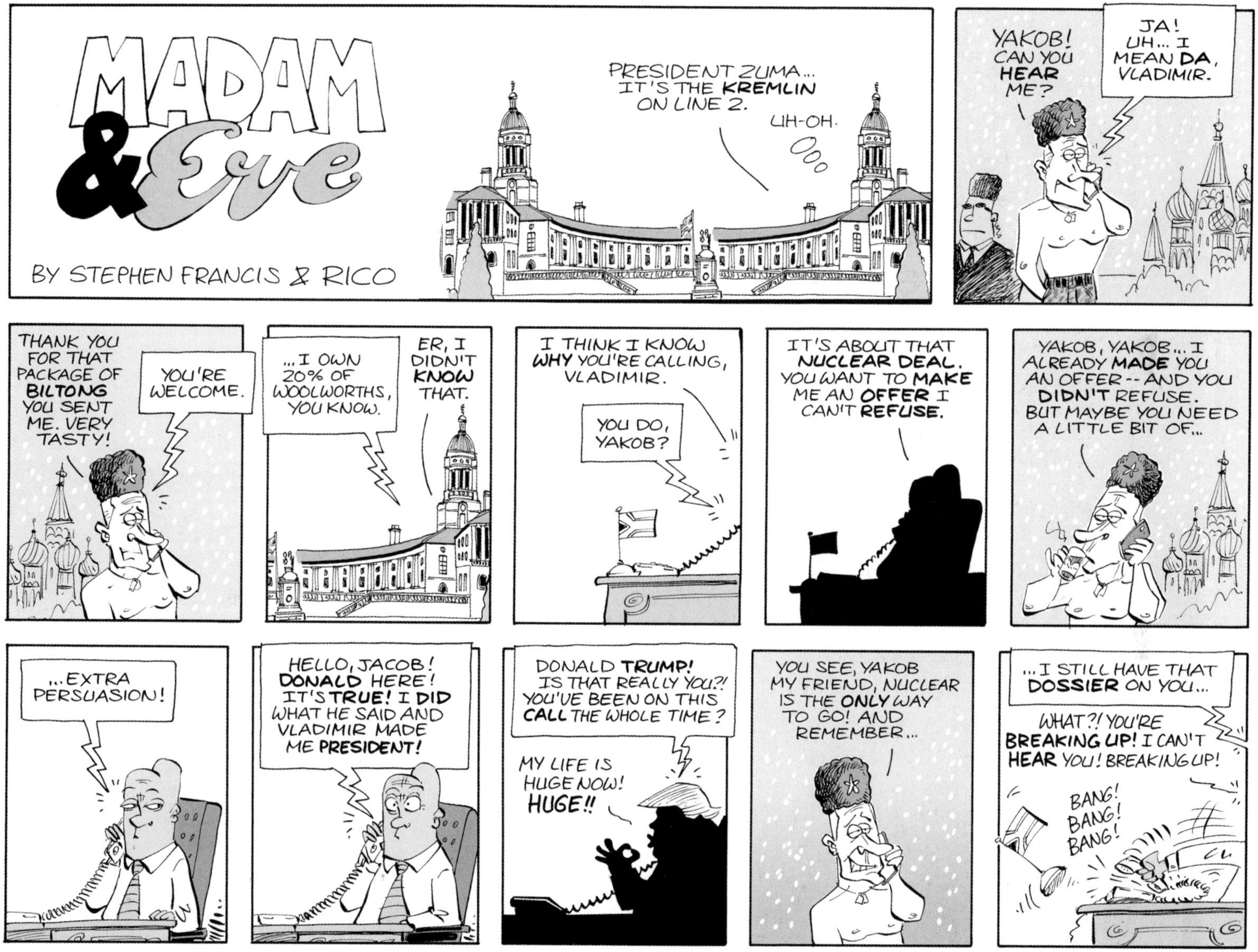
MADAM & Eve
BY STEPHEN FRANCIS & RICO
PRESIDENT ZUMA... IT'S THE **KREMLIN** ON LINE 2.
UH-OH.
YAKOB! CAN YOU **HEAR** ME?
JA! UH... I MEAN **DA**, VLADIMIR.
THANK YOU FOR THAT PACKAGE OF **BILTONG** YOU SENT ME. VERY TASTY!
YOU'RE WELCOME.
...I OWN 20% OF WOOLWORTHS, YOU KNOW.
ER, I DIDN'T **KNOW** THAT.
I THINK I KNOW **WHY** YOU'RE CALLING, VLADIMIR.
YOU DO, YAKOB?
IT'S ABOUT THAT **NUCLEAR DEAL.** YOU WANT TO **MAKE** ME AN **OFFER** I CAN'T **REFUSE.**
YAKOB, YAKOB... I ALREADY **MADE** YOU AN OFFER -- AND YOU **DIDN'T** REFUSE. BUT MAYBE YOU NEED A LITTLE BIT OF...
...EXTRA PERSUASION!
HELLO, JACOB! **DONALD** HERE! IT'S **TRUE! I DID** WHAT HE SAID AND VLADIMIR MADE ME **PRESIDENT!**
DONALD **TRUMP!** IS THAT REALLY YOU?! YOU'VE BEEN ON THIS **CALL** THE WHOLE TIME?
MY LIFE IS HUGE NOW! **HUGE!!**
YOU SEE, YAKOB MY FRIEND, NUCLEAR IS THE **ONLY** WAY TO GO! AND REMEMBER...
...I STILL HAVE THAT **DOSSIER** ON YOU...
WHAT?! YOU'RE **BREAKING UP!** I CAN'T **HEAR** YOU! BREAKING UP!
BANG! BANG! BANG!

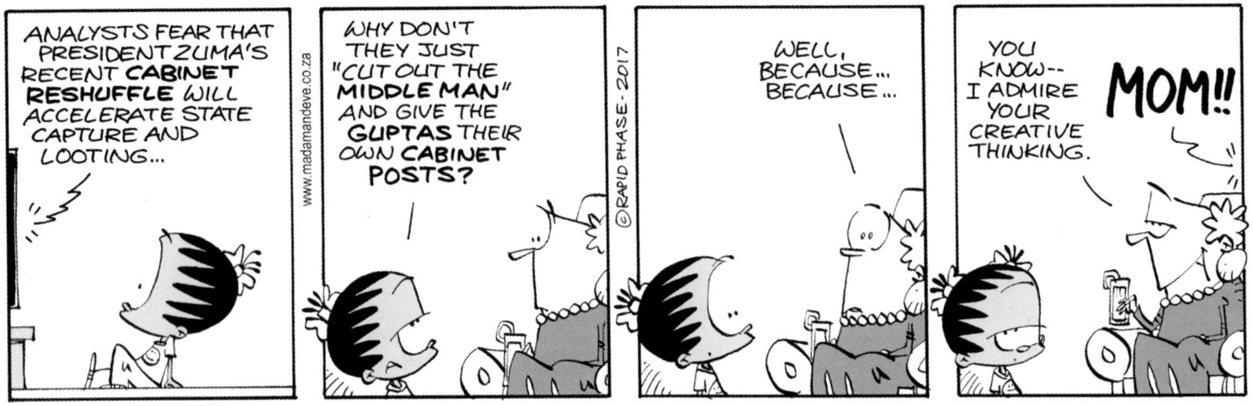
ANALYSTS FEAR THAT PRESIDENT ZUMA'S RECENT **CABINET RESHUFFLE** WILL ACCELERATE STATE CAPTURE AND LOOTING...
www.madamandeve.co.za
WHY DON'T THEY JUST "CUT OUT THE **MIDDLE MAN**" AND GIVE THE **GUPTAS** THEIR OWN **CABINET POSTS?**
©RAPID PHASE - 2017
WELL, BECAUSE... BECAUSE...
YOU KNOW-- I ADMIRE YOUR CREATIVE THINKING.
MOM!!

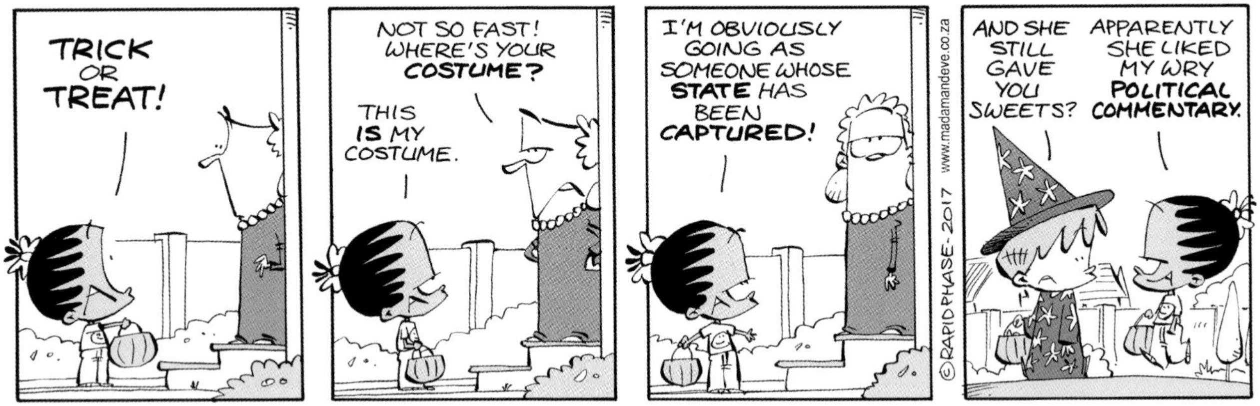
TRICK OR **TREAT!**
NOT SO FAST! WHERE'S YOUR **COSTUME?**
THIS **IS** MY COSTUME.
I'M OBVIOUSLY GOING AS SOMEONE WHOSE **STATE** HAS BEEN **CAPTURED!**
©RAPID PHASE - 2017 www.madamandeve.co.za
AND SHE STILL GAVE YOU SWEETS?
APPARENTLY SHE LIKED MY WRY **POLITICAL COMMENTARY.**

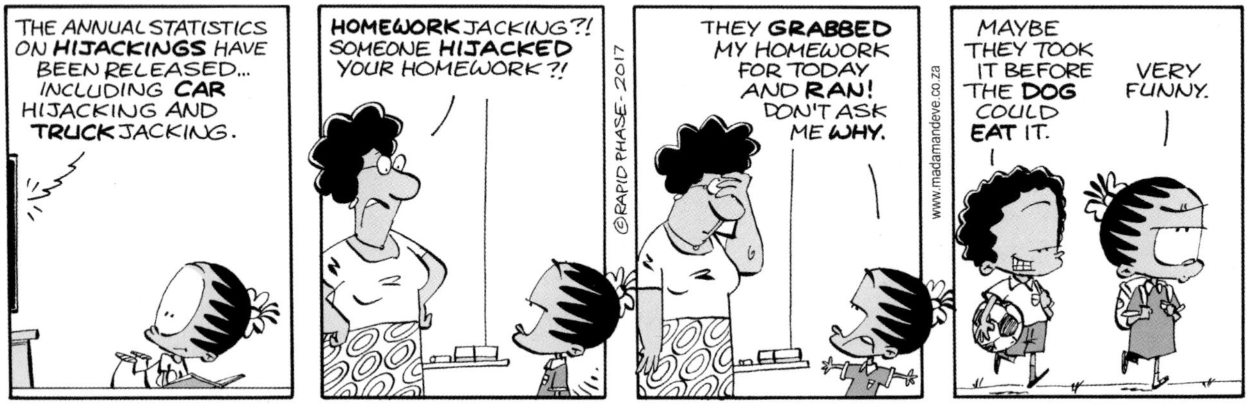
THE ANNUAL STATISTICS ON **HIJACKINGS** HAVE BEEN RELEASED... INCLUDING **CAR** HIJACKING AND **TRUCK**JACKING.
HOMEWORKJACKING?! SOMEONE **HIJACKED** YOUR HOMEWORK?!
©RAPID PHASE - 2017
THEY **GRABBED** MY HOMEWORK FOR TODAY AND **RAN!** DON'T ASK ME **WHY.**
www.madamandeve.co.za
MAYBE THEY TOOK IT BEFORE THE **DOG** COULD **EAT** IT.
VERY FUNNY.

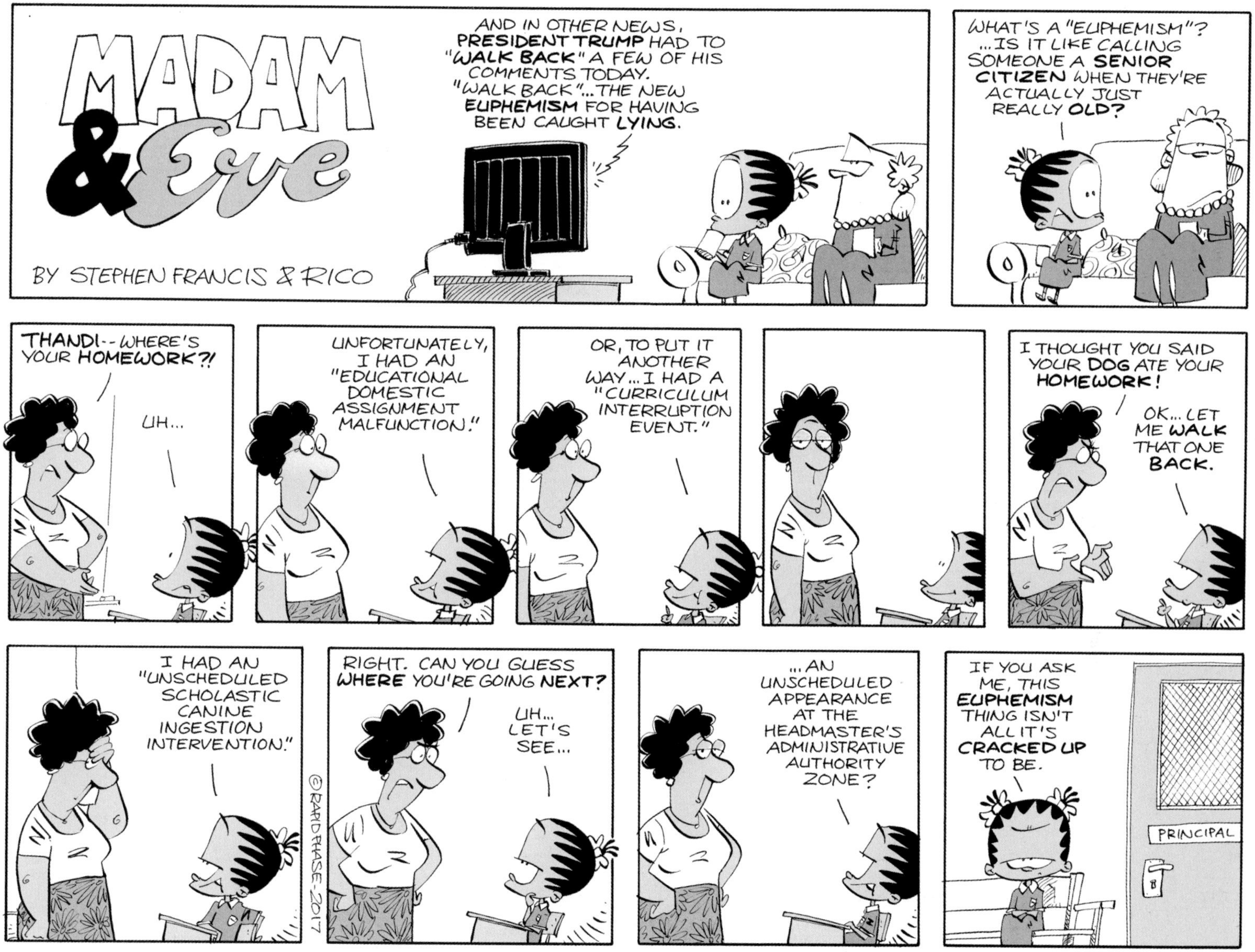
MADAM & Eve
BY STEPHEN FRANCIS & RICO
AND IN OTHER NEWS, PRESIDENT TRUMP HAD TO "WALK BACK" A FEW OF HIS COMMENTS TODAY. "WALK BACK"... THE NEW EUPHEMISM FOR HAVING BEEN CAUGHT LYING.
WHAT'S A "EUPHEMISM"? ...IS IT LIKE CALLING SOMEONE A SENIOR CITIZEN WHEN THEY'RE ACTUALLY JUST REALLY OLD?
THANDI-- WHERE'S YOUR HOMEWORK?!
UH...
UNFORTUNATELY, I HAD AN "EDUCATIONAL DOMESTIC ASSIGNMENT MALFUNCTION."
OR, TO PUT IT ANOTHER WAY... I HAD A "CURRICULUM INTERRUPTION EVENT."
I THOUGHT YOU SAID YOUR DOG ATE YOUR HOMEWORK!
OK... LET ME WALK THAT ONE BACK.
I HAD AN "UNSCHEDULED SCHOLASTIC CANINE INGESTION INTERVENTION."
©RAPID PHASE-2017
RIGHT. CAN YOU GUESS WHERE YOU'RE GOING NEXT?
UH... LET'S SEE...
...AN UNSCHEDULED APPEARANCE AT THE HEADMASTER'S ADMINISTRATIVE AUTHORITY ZONE?
IF YOU ASK ME, THIS EUPHEMISM THING ISN'T ALL IT'S CRACKED UP TO BE.
PRINCIPAL

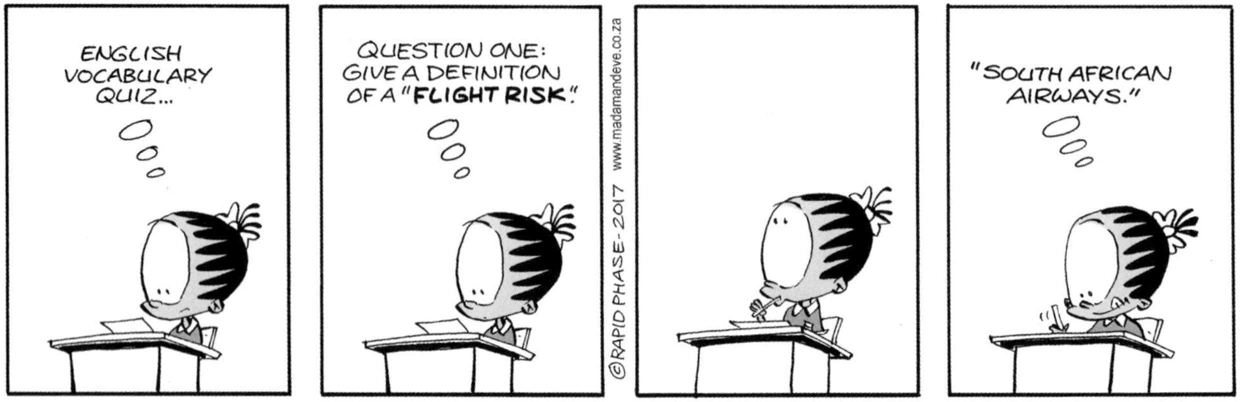
ENGLISH VOCABULARY QUIZ...
QUESTION ONE: GIVE A DEFINITION OF A "**FLIGHT RISK**."
©RAPID PHASE-2017 www.madamandeve.co.za
"SOUTH AFRICAN AIRWAYS."

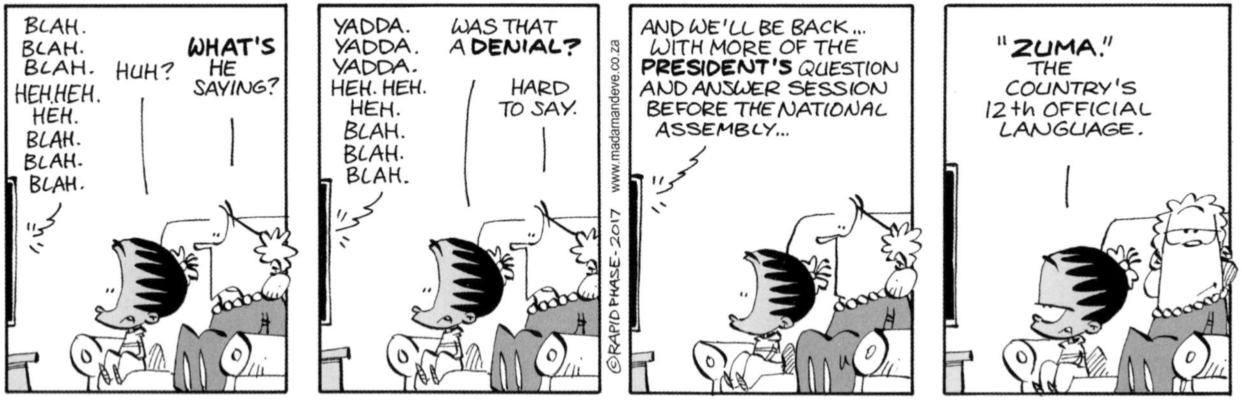
BLAH. BLAH. BLAH. HEH.HEH. HEH. BLAH. BLAH. BLAH.
HUH?
WHAT'S HE SAYING?
YADDA. YADDA. YADDA. HEH. HEH. HEH. BLAH. BLAH. BLAH.
WAS THAT A **DENIAL?**
HARD TO SAY.
©RAPID PHASE-2017 www.madamandeve.co.za
AND WE'LL BE BACK... WITH MORE OF THE **PRESIDENT'S** QUESTION AND ANSWER SESSION BEFORE THE NATIONAL ASSEMBLY...
"**ZUMA.**" THE COUNTRY'S 12th OFFICIAL LANGUAGE.

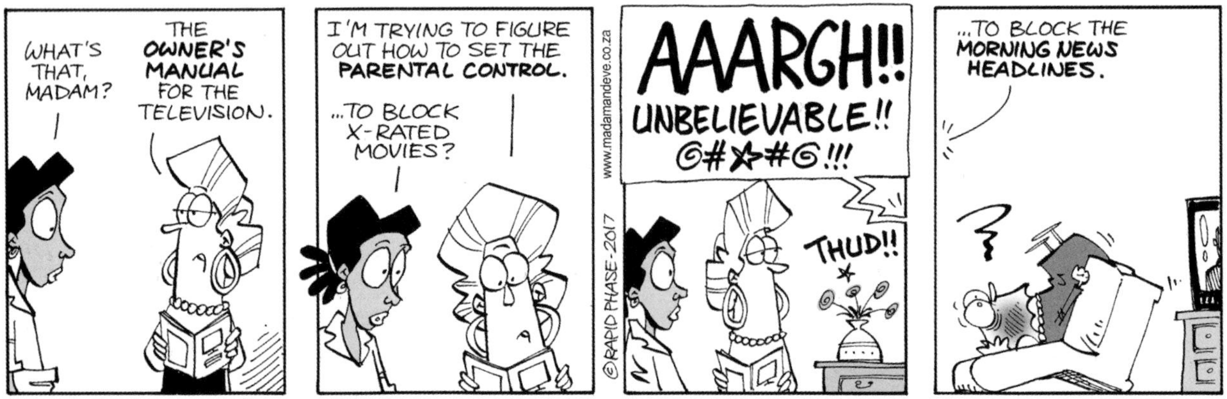
WHAT'S THAT, MADAM?
THE **OWNER'S MANUAL** FOR THE TELEVISION.
I'M TRYING TO FIGURE OUT HOW TO SET THE **PARENTAL CONTROL.**
...TO BLOCK X-RATED MOVIES?
©RAPID PHASE-2017 www.madamandeve.co.za
AAARGH!! UNBELIEVABLE!! @#✩#@!!!
THUD!!
...TO BLOCK THE **MORNING NEWS HEADLINES.**

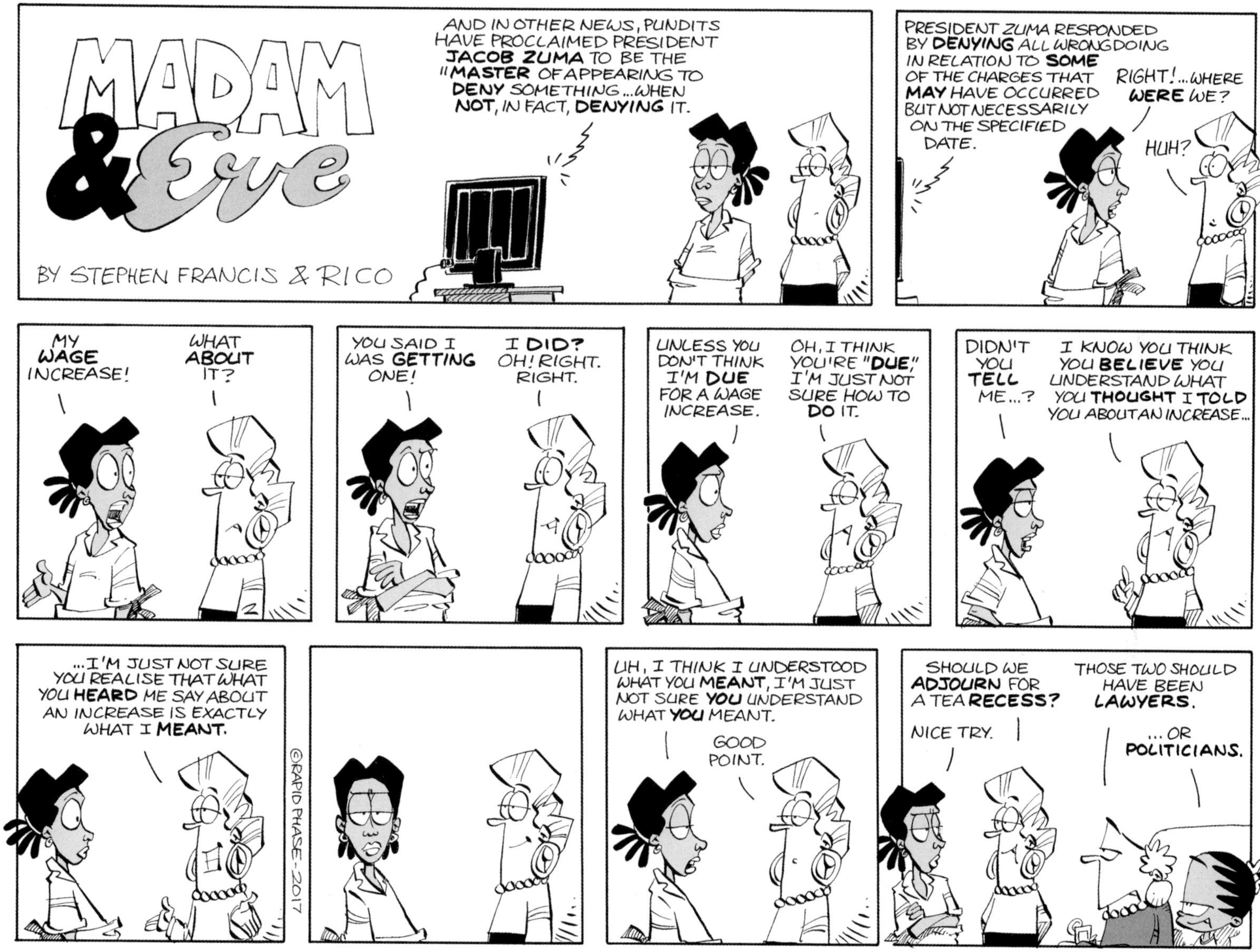
MADAM & Eve
BY STEPHEN FRANCIS & RICO
AND IN OTHER NEWS, PUNDITS HAVE PROCLAIMED PRESIDENT JACOB ZUMA TO BE THE "MASTER OF APPEARING TO DENY SOMETHING... WHEN NOT, IN FACT, DENYING IT.
PRESIDENT ZUMA RESPONDED BY DENYING ALL WRONGDOING IN RELATION TO SOME OF THE CHARGES THAT MAY HAVE OCCURRED BUT NOT NECESSARILY ON THE SPECIFIED DATE.
RIGHT!... WHERE WERE WE?
HUH?
MY WAGE INCREASE!
WHAT ABOUT IT?
YOU SAID I WAS GETTING ONE!
I DID? OH! RIGHT. RIGHT.
UNLESS YOU DON'T THINK I'M DUE FOR A WAGE INCREASE.
OH, I THINK YOU'RE "DUE," I'M JUST NOT SURE HOW TO DO IT.
DIDN'T YOU TELL ME...?
I KNOW YOU THINK YOU BELIEVE YOU UNDERSTAND WHAT YOU THOUGHT I TOLD YOU ABOUT AN INCREASE...
...I'M JUST NOT SURE YOU REALISE THAT WHAT YOU HEARD ME SAY ABOUT AN INCREASE IS EXACTLY WHAT I MEANT.
©RAPID PHASE-2017
UH, I THINK I UNDERSTOOD WHAT YOU MEANT, I'M JUST NOT SURE YOU UNDERSTAND WHAT YOU MEANT.
GOOD POINT.
SHOULD WE ADJOURN FOR A TEA RECESS?
NICE TRY.
THOSE TWO SHOULD HAVE BEEN LAWYERS.
...OR POLITICIANS.

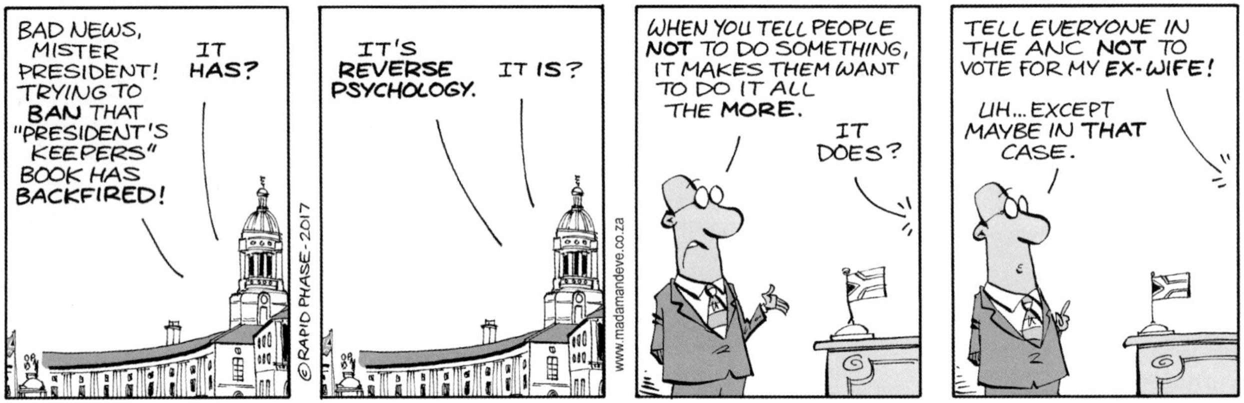
BAD NEWS, MISTER PRESIDENT! TRYING TO BAN THAT "PRESIDENT'S KEEPERS" BOOK HAS BACKFIRED!
IT HAS?
©RAPID PHASE-2017
IT'S REVERSE PSYCHOLOGY.
IT IS?
www.madamandeve.co.za
WHEN YOU TELL PEOPLE NOT TO DO SOMETHING, IT MAKES THEM WANT TO DO IT ALL THE MORE.
IT DOES?
TELL EVERYONE IN THE ANC NOT TO VOTE FOR MY EX-WIFE!
UH... EXCEPT MAYBE IN THAT CASE.

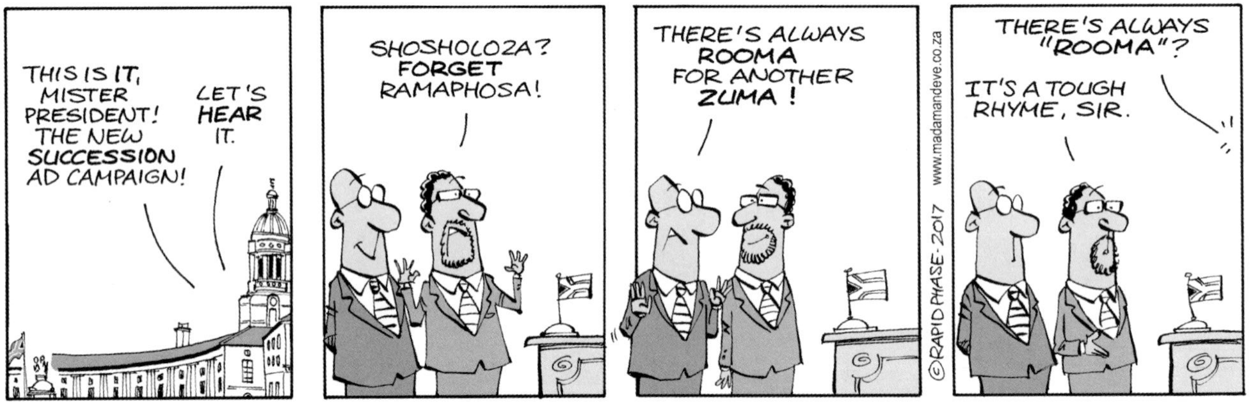
THIS IS IT, MISTER PRESIDENT! THE NEW SUCCESSION AD CAMPAIGN!
LET'S HEAR IT.
SHOSHOLOZA? FORGET RAMAPHOSA!
THERE'S ALWAYS ROOMA FOR ANOTHER ZUMA!
www.madamandeve.co.za
©RAPID PHASE-2017
THERE'S ALWAYS "ROOMA"?
IT'S A TOUGH RHYME, SIR.

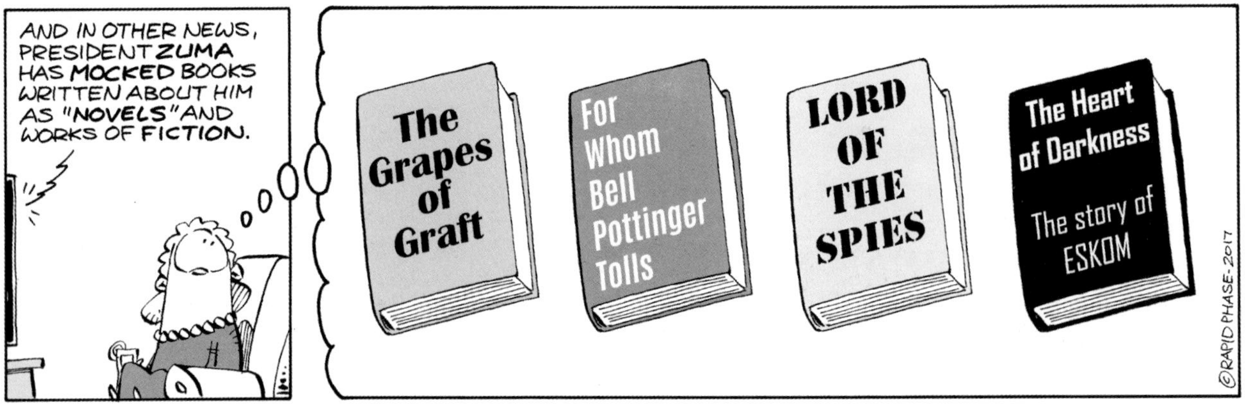
AND IN OTHER NEWS, PRESIDENT ZUMA HAS MOCKED BOOKS WRITTEN ABOUT HIM AS "NOVELS" AND WORKS OF FICTION.
The Grapes of Graft
For Whom Bell Pottinger Tolls
LORD OF THE SPIES
The Heart of Darkness The story of ESKOM
©RAPID PHASE-2017

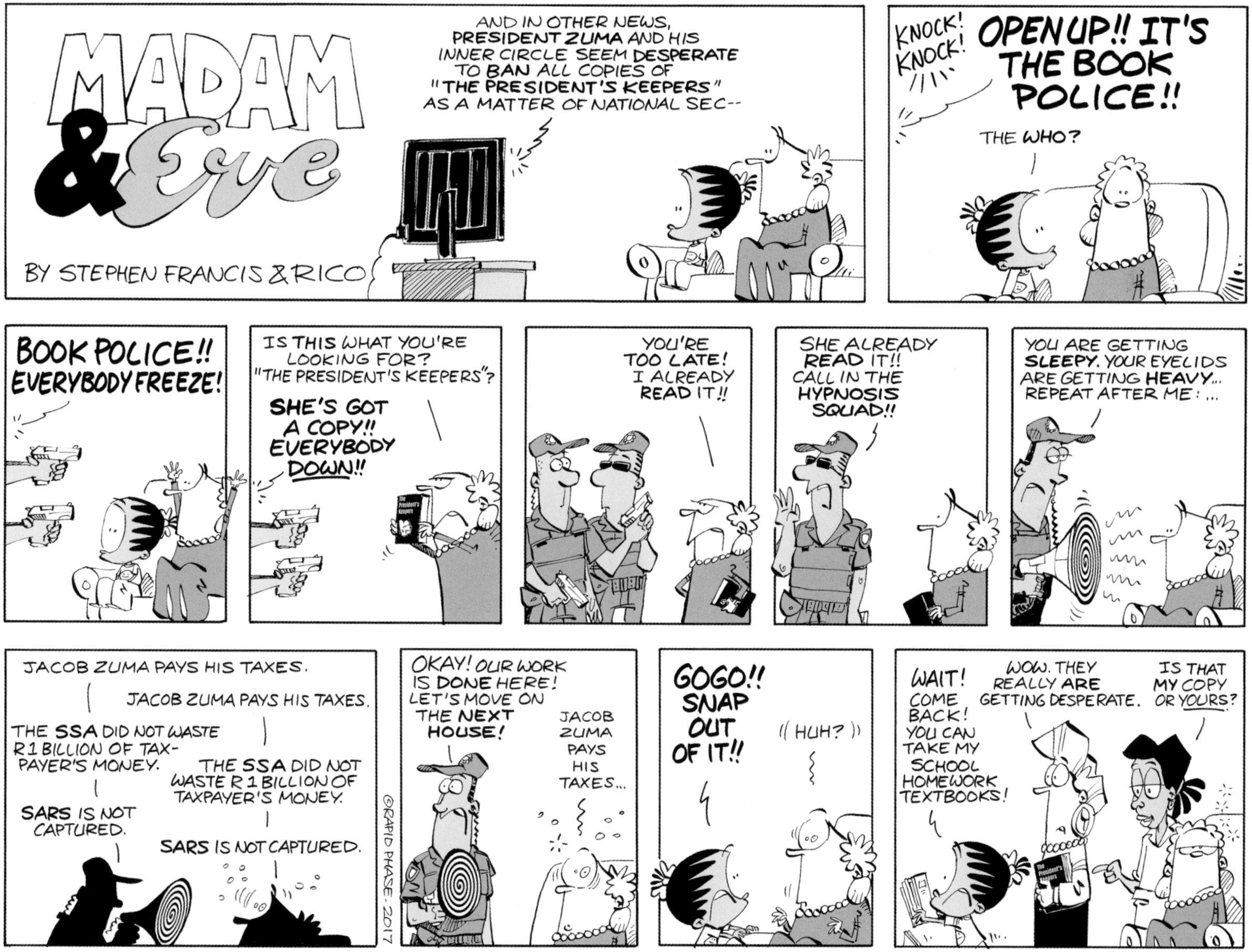
MADAM & Eve
BY STEPHEN FRANCIS & RICO
AND IN OTHER NEWS, PRESIDENT ZUMA AND HIS INNER CIRCLE SEEM DESPERATE TO BAN ALL COPIES OF "THE PRESIDENT'S KEEPERS" AS A MATTER OF NATIONAL SEC--
KNOCK! KNOCK!
OPEN UP!! IT'S THE BOOK POLICE!!
THE WHO?
BOOK POLICE!! EVERYBODY FREEZE!
IS THIS WHAT YOU'RE LOOKING FOR? "THE PRESIDENT'S KEEPERS"?
SHE'S GOT A COPY!! EVERYBODY DOWN!!
YOU'RE TOO LATE! I ALREADY READ IT!!
SHE ALREADY READ IT!! CALL IN THE HYPNOSIS SQUAD!!
YOU ARE GETTING SLEEPY. YOUR EYELIDS ARE GETTING HEAVY... REPEAT AFTER ME: ...
JACOB ZUMA PAYS HIS TAXES.
JACOB ZUMA PAYS HIS TAXES.
THE SSA DID NOT WASTE R 1 BILLION OF TAX-PAYER'S MONEY.
THE SSA DID NOT WASTE R 1 BILLION OF TAXPAYER'S MONEY.
SARS IS NOT CAPTURED.
SARS IS NOT CAPTURED.
©RAPID PHASE 2017
OKAY! OUR WORK IS DONE HERE! LET'S MOVE ON THE NEXT HOUSE!
JACOB ZUMA PAYS HIS TAXES...
GOGO!! SNAP OUT OF IT!!
HUH?
WAIT! COME BACK! YOU CAN TAKE MY SCHOOL HOMEWORK TEXTBOOKS!
WOW. THEY REALLY ARE GETTING DESPERATE.
IS THAT MY COPY OR YOURS?

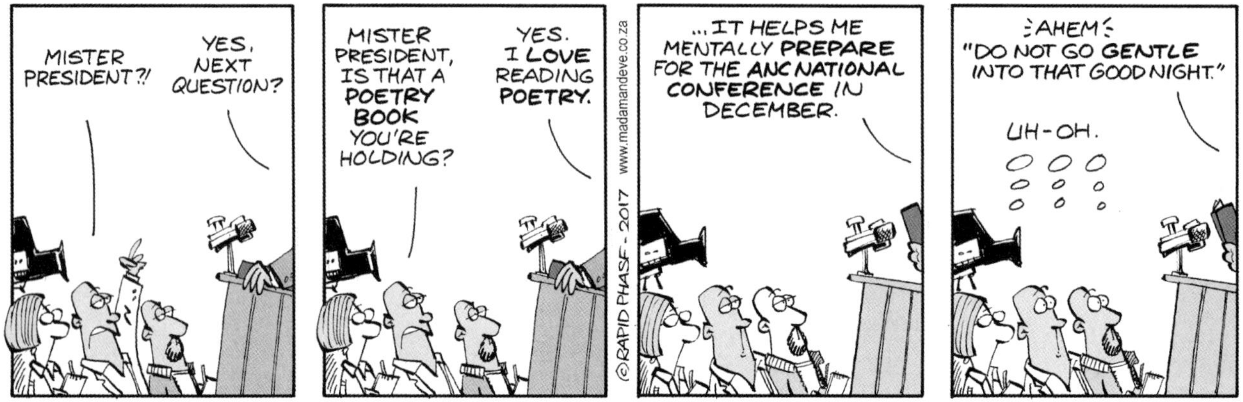
MISTER PRESIDENT?!
YES, NEXT QUESTION?
MISTER PRESIDENT, IS THAT A POETRY BOOK YOU'RE HOLDING?
YES. I LOVE READING POETRY.
©RAPID PHASE - 2017 www.madamandeve.co.za
...IT HELPS ME MENTALLY PREPARE FOR THE ANC NATIONAL CONFERENCE IN DECEMBER.
AHEM
"DO NOT GO GENTLE INTO THAT GOOD NIGHT."
UH-OH.

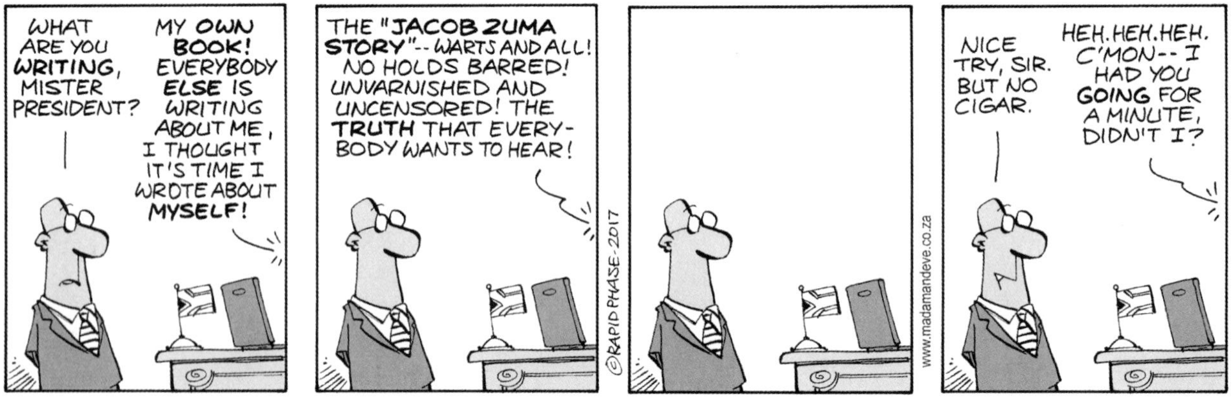
WHAT ARE YOU WRITING, MISTER PRESIDENT?
MY OWN BOOK! EVERYBODY ELSE IS WRITING ABOUT ME, I THOUGHT IT'S TIME I WROTE ABOUT MYSELF!
THE "JACOB ZUMA STORY"-- WARTS AND ALL! NO HOLDS BARRED! UNVARNISHED AND UNCENSORED! THE TRUTH THAT EVERYBODY WANTS TO HEAR!
©RAPID PHASE-2017
www.madamandeve.co.za
NICE TRY, SIR. BUT NO CIGAR.
HEH.HEH.HEH. C'MON-- I HAD YOU GOING FOR A MINUTE, DIDN'T I?

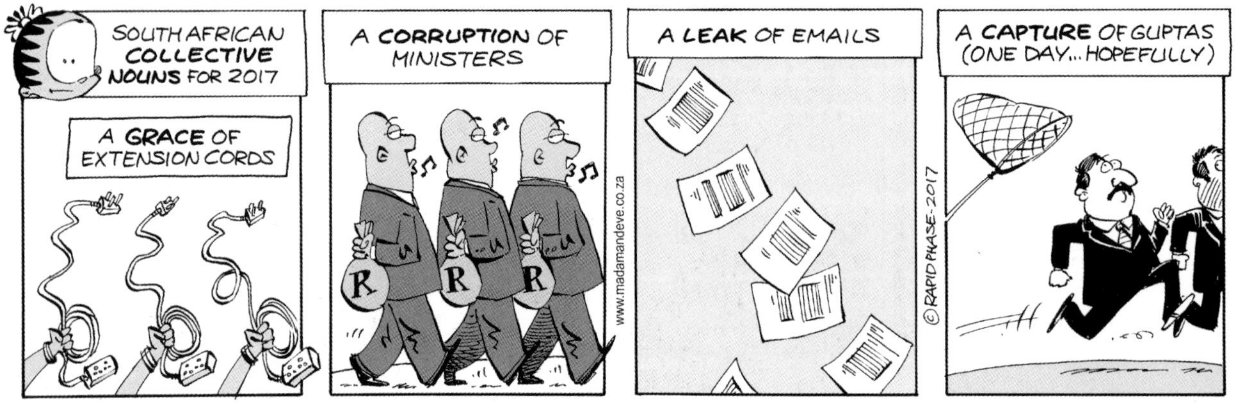
SOUTH AFRICAN COLLECTIVE NOUNS FOR 2017
A GRACE OF EXTENSION CORDS
A CORRUPTION OF MINISTERS
R
R
R
www.madamandeve.co.za
A LEAK OF EMAILS
©RAPID PHASE-2017
A CAPTURE OF GUPTAS (ONE DAY... HOPEFULLY)

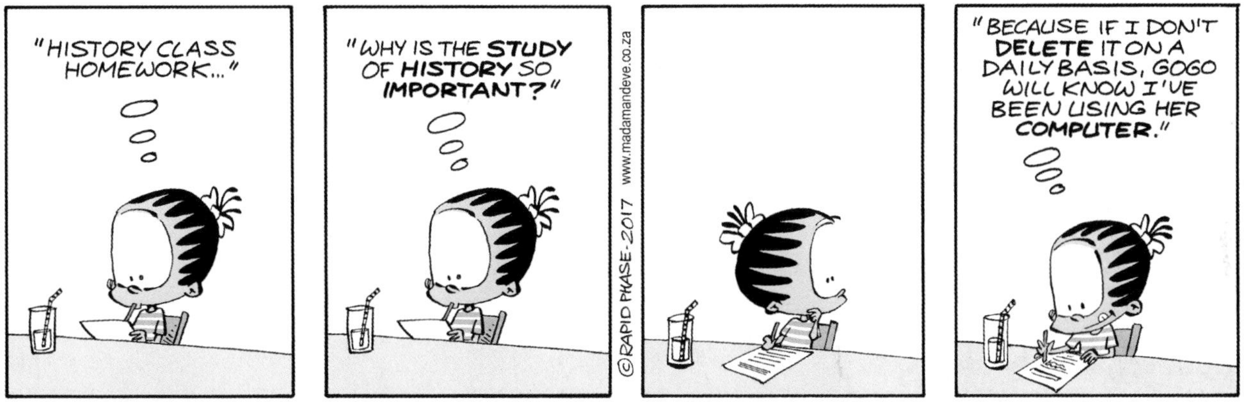
"HISTORY CLASS HOMEWORK..."
"WHY IS THE **STUDY** OF **HISTORY** SO **IMPORTANT?**"
©RAPID PHASE-2017 www.madamandeve.co.za
"BECAUSE IF I DON'T **DELETE** IT ON A DAILY BASIS, GOGO WILL KNOW I'VE BEEN USING HER **COMPUTER**."

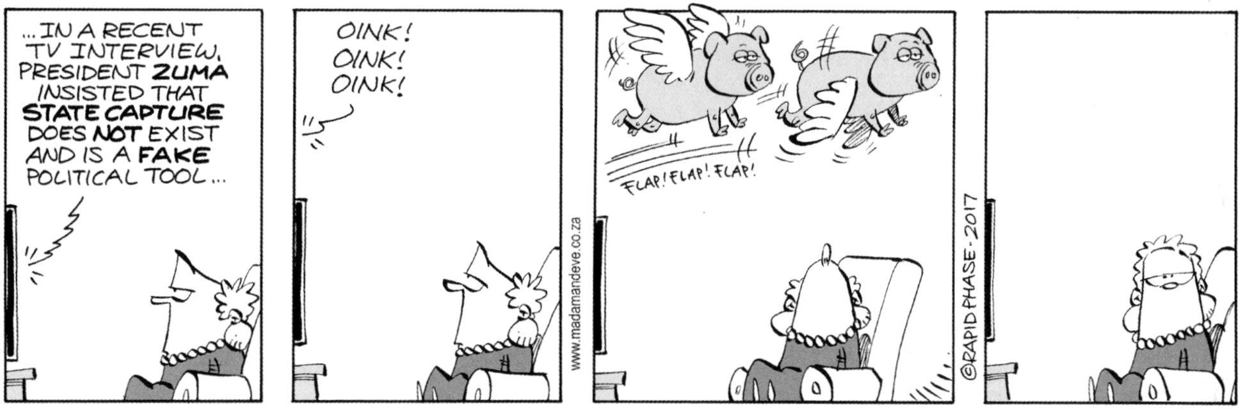
...IN A RECENT TV INTERVIEW, PRESIDENT **ZUMA** INSISTED THAT **STATE CAPTURE** DOES **NOT** EXIST AND IS A **FAKE** POLITICAL TOOL...
OINK! OINK! OINK!
www.madamandeve.co.za
FLAP! FLAP! FLAP!
©RAPID PHASE-2017

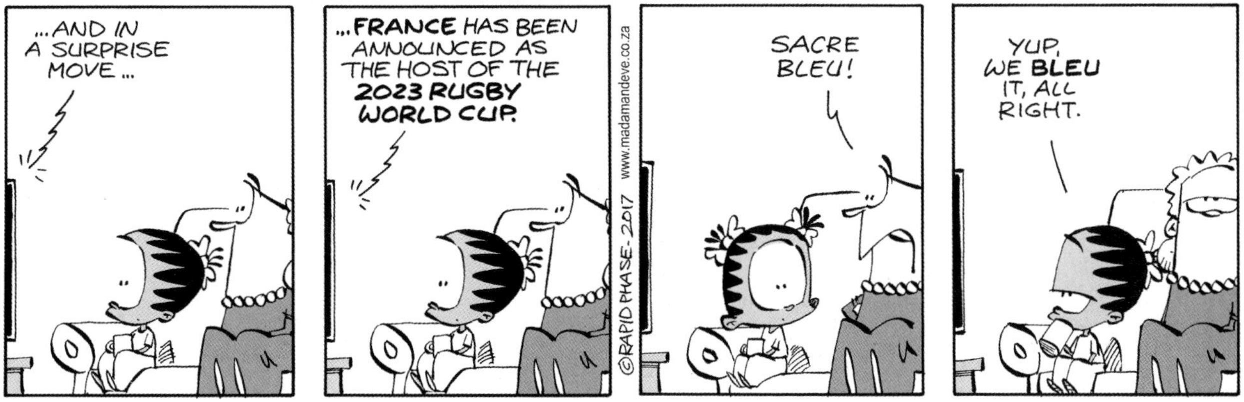
...AND IN A SURPRISE MOVE...
...**FRANCE** HAS BEEN ANNOUNCED AS THE HOST OF THE **2023 RUGBY WORLD CUP**.
©RAPID PHASE-2017 www.madamandeve.co.za
SACRE BLEU!
YUP, WE **BLEU** IT, ALL RIGHT.

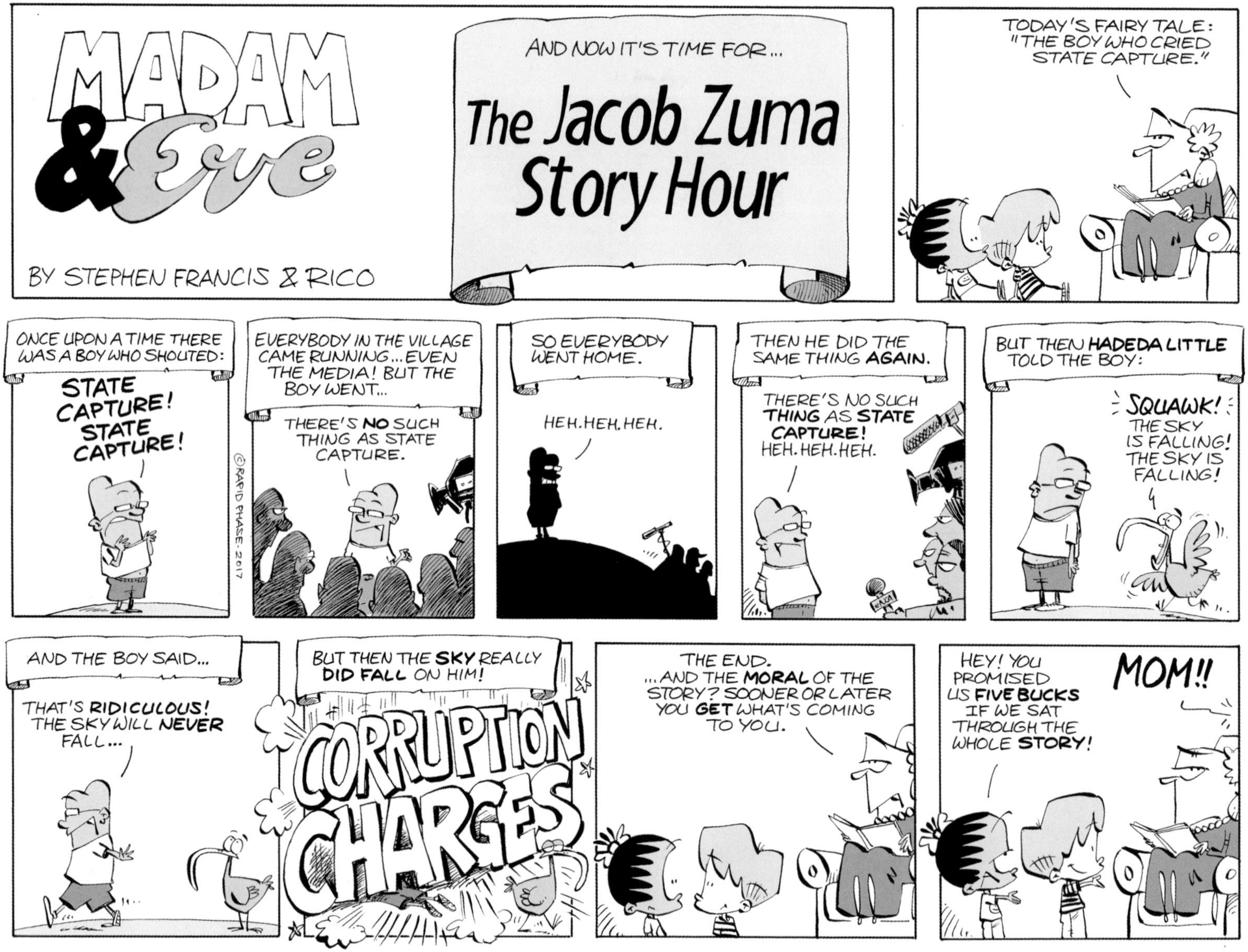
MADAM & Eve
BY STEPHEN FRANCIS & RICO
AND NOW IT'S TIME FOR...
The Jacob Zuma Story Hour
TODAY'S FAIRY TALE: "THE BOY WHO CRIED STATE CAPTURE."
ONCE UPON A TIME THERE WAS A BOY WHO SHOUTED:
STATE CAPTURE! STATE CAPTURE!
© RAPID PHASE · 2017
EVERYBODY IN THE VILLAGE CAME RUNNING... EVEN THE MEDIA! BUT THE BOY WENT...
THERE'S NO SUCH THING AS STATE CAPTURE.
SO EVERYBODY WENT HOME.
HEH. HEH. HEH.
THEN HE DID THE SAME THING AGAIN.
THERE'S NO SUCH THING AS STATE CAPTURE! HEH. HEH. HEH.
BUT THEN HADEDA LITTLE TOLD THE BOY:
SQUAWK! THE SKY IS FALLING! THE SKY IS FALLING!
AND THE BOY SAID...
THAT'S RIDICULOUS! THE SKY WILL NEVER FALL...
BUT THEN THE SKY REALLY DID FALL ON HIM!
CORRUPTION CHARGES
THE END. ...AND THE MORAL OF THE STORY? SOONER OR LATER YOU GET WHAT'S COMING TO YOU.
HEY! YOU PROMISED US FIVE BUCKS IF WE SAT THROUGH THE WHOLE STORY!
MOM!!

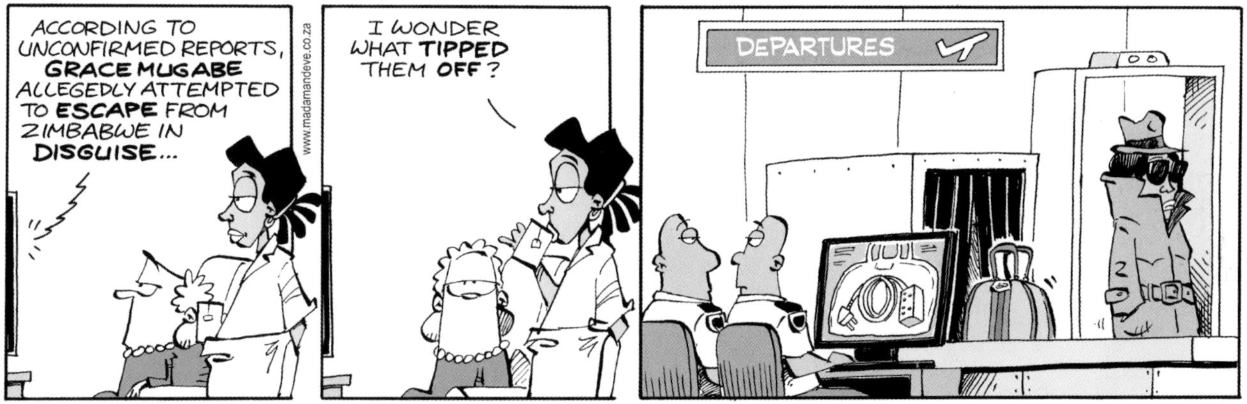
ACCORDING TO UNCONFIRMED REPORTS, GRACE MUGABE ALLEGEDLY ATTEMPTED TO ESCAPE FROM ZIMBABWE IN DISGUISE...
www.madamandeve.co.za
I WONDER WHAT TIPPED THEM OFF?
DEPARTURES

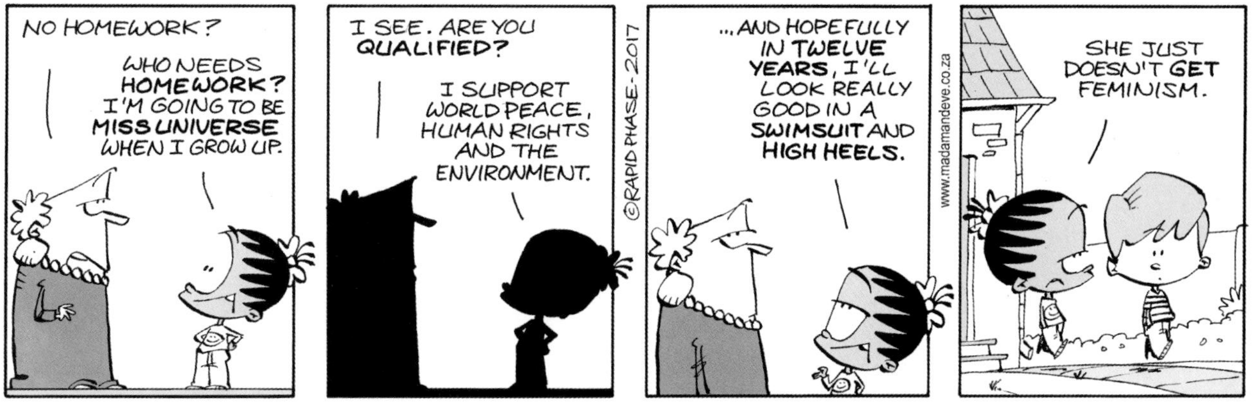
NO HOMEWORK?
WHO NEEDS HOMEWORK? I'M GOING TO BE MISS UNIVERSE WHEN I GROW UP.
I SEE. ARE YOU QUALIFIED?
I SUPPORT WORLD PEACE, HUMAN RIGHTS AND THE ENVIRONMENT.
©RAPID PHASE - 2017
...AND HOPEFULLY IN TWELVE YEARS, I'LL LOOK REALLY GOOD IN A SWIMSUIT AND HIGH HEELS.
www.madamandeve.co.za
SHE JUST DOESN'T GET FEMINISM.

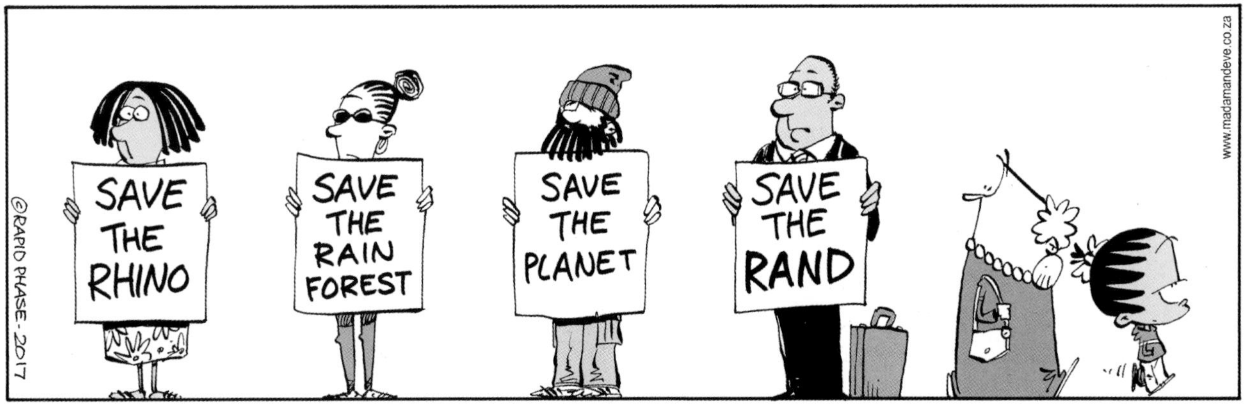
©RAPID PHASE - 2017
SAVE THE RHINO
SAVE THE RAIN FOREST
SAVE THE PLANET
SAVE THE RAND
www.madamandeve.co.za

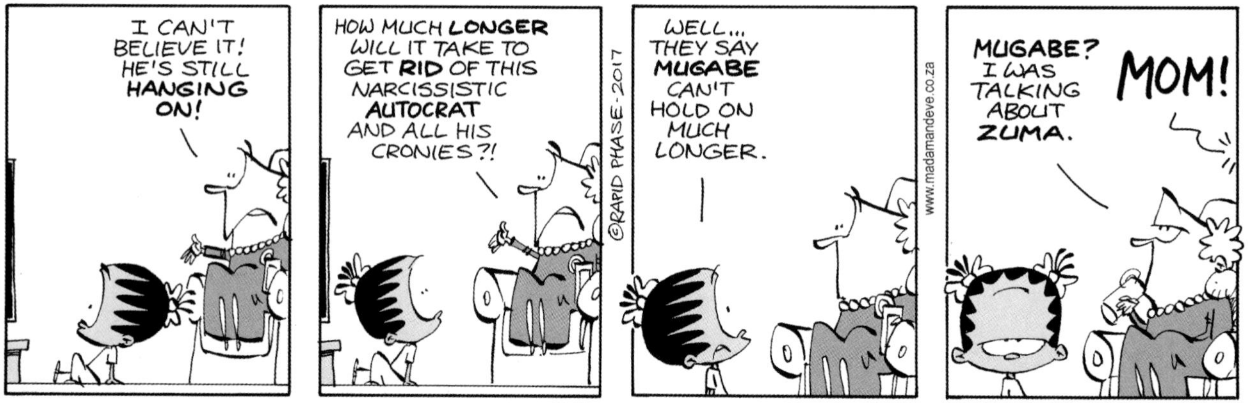
I CAN'T BELIEVE IT! HE'S STILL **HANGING ON!**
HOW MUCH **LONGER** WILL IT TAKE TO GET **RID** OF THIS NARCISSISTIC **AUTOCRAT** AND ALL HIS CRONIES?!
©RAPID PHASE-2017
WELL... THEY SAY **MUGABE** CAN'T HOLD ON MUCH LONGER.
www.madamandeve.co.za
MUGABE? I WAS TALKING ABOUT **ZUMA.**
MOM!

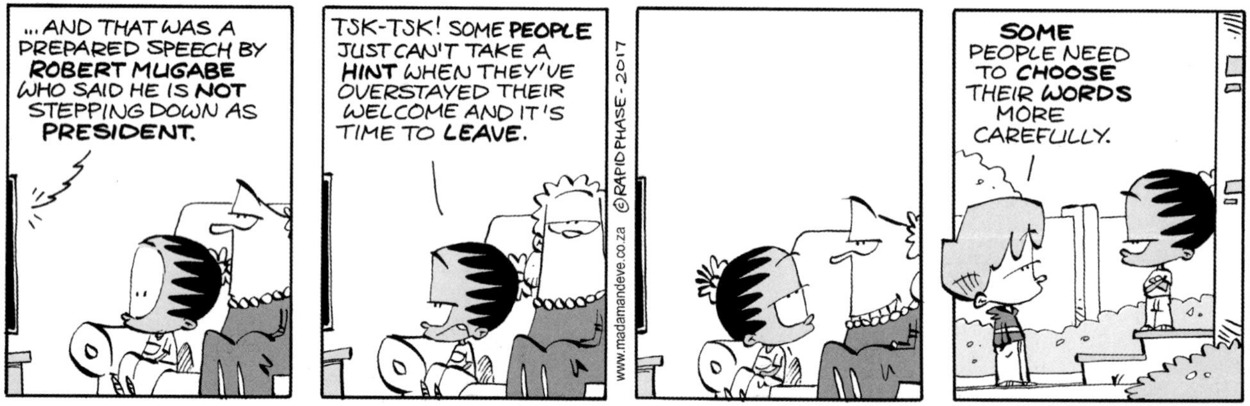
...AND THAT WAS A PREPARED SPEECH BY **ROBERT MUGABE** WHO SAID HE IS **NOT** STEPPING DOWN AS **PRESIDENT.**
TSK-TSK! SOME **PEOPLE** JUST CAN'T TAKE A **HINT** WHEN THEY'VE OVERSTAYED THEIR WELCOME AND IT'S TIME TO **LEAVE.**
©RAPID PHASE-2017
www.madamandeve.co.za
SOME PEOPLE NEED TO **CHOOSE** THEIR **WORDS** MORE CAREFULLY.

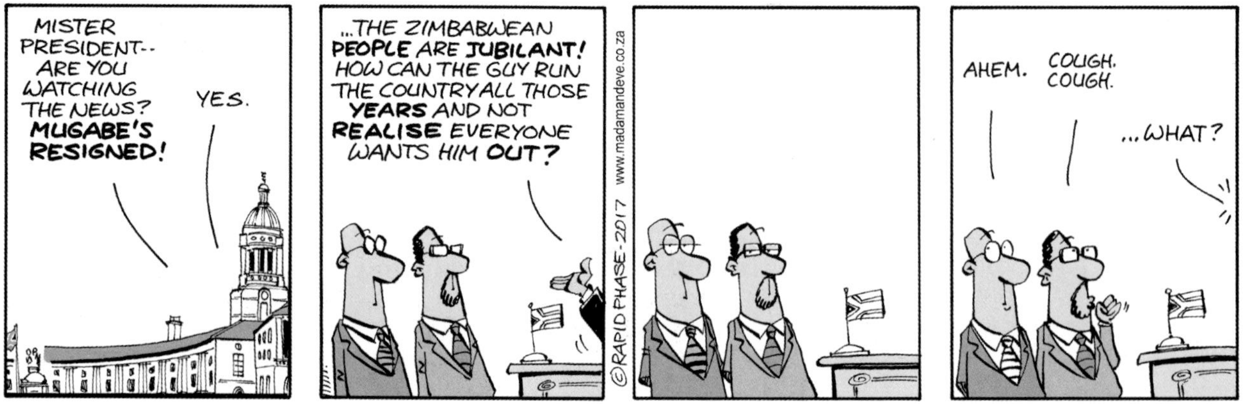
MISTER PRESIDENT-- ARE YOU WATCHING THE NEWS? **MUGABE'S RESIGNED!**
YES.
...THE ZIMBABWEAN **PEOPLE** ARE **JUBILANT!** HOW CAN THE GUY RUN THE COUNTRY ALL THOSE **YEARS** AND NOT **REALISE** EVERYONE WANTS HIM **OUT?**
©RAPID PHASE-2017
www.madamandeve.co.za
AHEM.
COUGH. COUGH.
...WHAT?

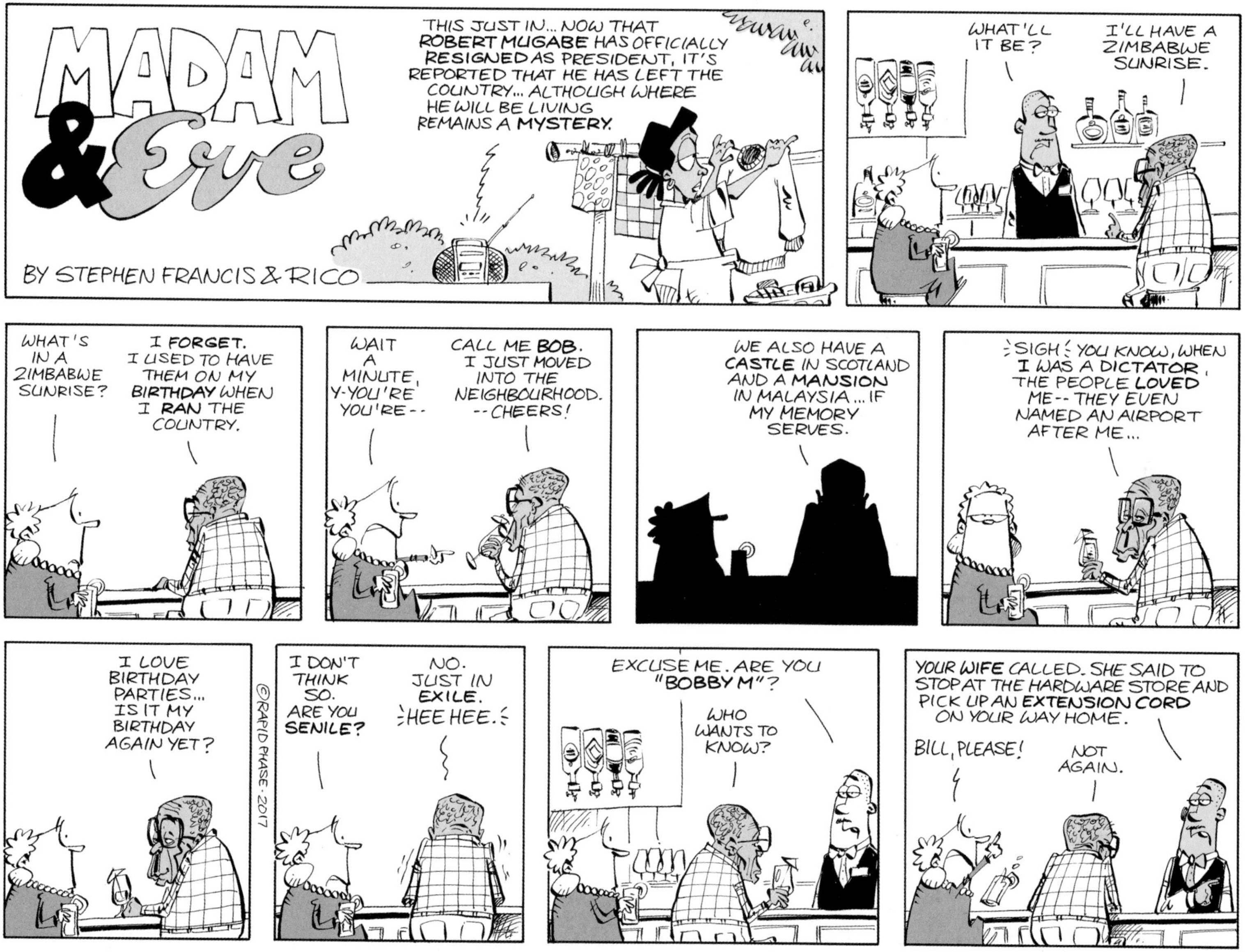
MADAM & Eve
BY STEPHEN FRANCIS & RICO
THIS JUST IN... NOW THAT ROBERT MUGABE HAS OFFICIALLY RESIGNED AS PRESIDENT, IT'S REPORTED THAT HE HAS LEFT THE COUNTRY... ALTHOUGH WHERE HE WILL BE LIVING REMAINS A MYSTERY.
WHAT'LL IT BE?
I'LL HAVE A ZIMBABWE SUNRISE.
WHAT'S IN A ZIMBABWE SUNRISE?
I FORGET. I USED TO HAVE THEM ON MY BIRTHDAY WHEN I RAN THE COUNTRY.
WAIT A MINUTE, Y-YOU'RE YOU'RE--
CALL ME BOB. I JUST MOVED INTO THE NEIGHBOURHOOD. --CHEERS!
WE ALSO HAVE A CASTLE IN SCOTLAND AND A MANSION IN MALAYSIA... IF MY MEMORY SERVES.
SIGH YOU KNOW, WHEN I WAS A DICTATOR, THE PEOPLE LOVED ME-- THEY EVEN NAMED AN AIRPORT AFTER ME...
I LOVE BIRTHDAY PARTIES... IS IT MY BIRTHDAY AGAIN YET?
©RAPID PHASE 2017
I DON'T THINK SO. ARE YOU SENILE?
NO. JUST IN EXILE. HEE HEE.
EXCUSE ME. ARE YOU "BOBBY M"?
WHO WANTS TO KNOW?
YOUR WIFE CALLED. SHE SAID TO STOP AT THE HARDWARE STORE AND PICK UP AN EXTENSION CORD ON YOUR WAY HOME.
BILL, PLEASE!
NOT AGAIN.

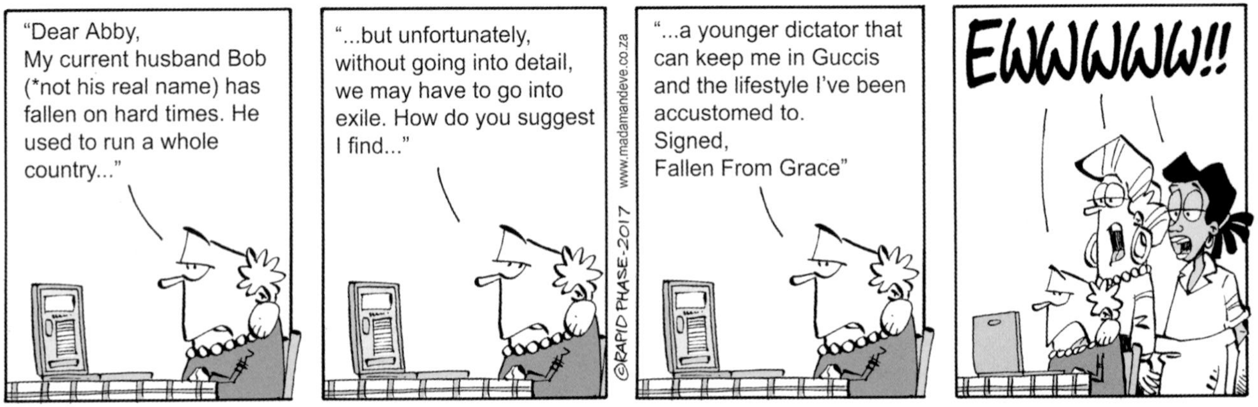
"Dear Abby,
My current husband Bob (*not his real name) has fallen on hard times. He used to run a whole country..."
"...but unfortunately, without going into detail, we may have to go into exile. How do you suggest I find..."
©RAPID PHASE-2017 www.madamandeve.co.za
"...a younger dictator that can keep me in Guccis and the lifestyle I've been accustomed to.
Signed,
Fallen From Grace"
EWWWWW!!

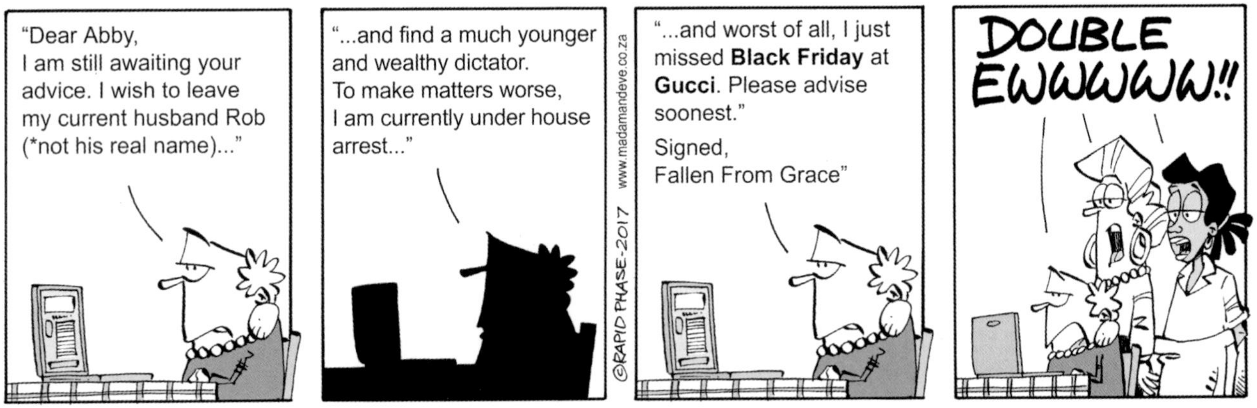
"Dear Abby,
I am still awaiting your advice. I wish to leave my current husband Rob (*not his real name)..."
"...and find a much younger and wealthy dictator.
To make matters worse, I am currently under house arrest..."
©RAPID PHASE-2017 www.madamandeve.co.za
"...and worst of all, I just missed **Black Friday** at **Gucci**. Please advise soonest."
Signed,
Fallen From Grace"
DOUBLE EWWWWW!!

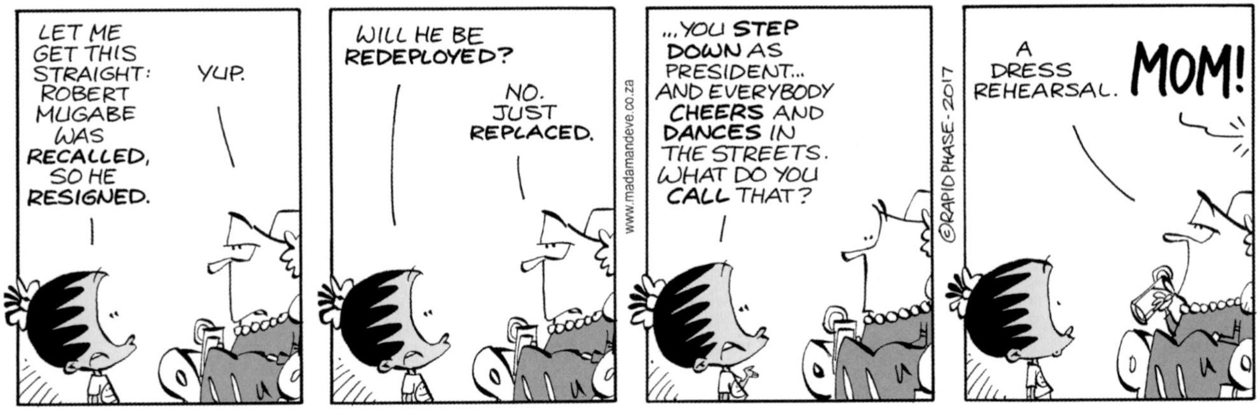
LET ME GET THIS STRAIGHT: ROBERT MUGABE WAS **RECALLED**, SO HE **RESIGNED**.
YUP.
WILL HE BE **REDEPLOYED?**
NO. JUST **REPLACED**.
www.madamandeve.co.za
...YOU **STEP DOWN** AS PRESIDENT... AND EVERYBODY **CHEERS** AND **DANCES** IN THE STREETS. WHAT DO YOU **CALL** THAT?
©RAPID PHASE-2017
A DRESS REHEARSAL.
MOM!

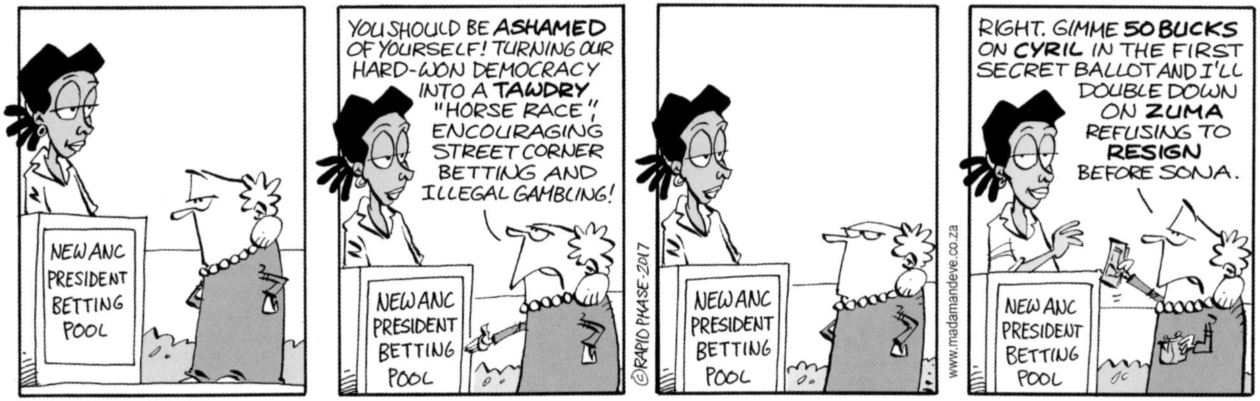
NEW ANC PRESIDENT BETTING POOL
YOU SHOULD BE **ASHAMED** OF YOURSELF! TURNING OUR HARD-WON DEMOCRACY INTO A **TAWDRY** "HORSE RACE", ENCOURAGING STREET CORNER BETTING AND ILLEGAL GAMBLING!
NEW ANC PRESIDENT BETTING POOL
©RAPID PHASE-2017
NEW ANC PRESIDENT BETTING POOL
www.madamandeve.co.za
RIGHT. GIMME **50 BUCKS** ON **CYRIL** IN THE FIRST SECRET BALLOT AND I'LL DOUBLE DOWN ON **ZUMA** REFUSING TO **RESIGN** BEFORE SONA.
NEW ANC PRESIDENT BETTING POOL

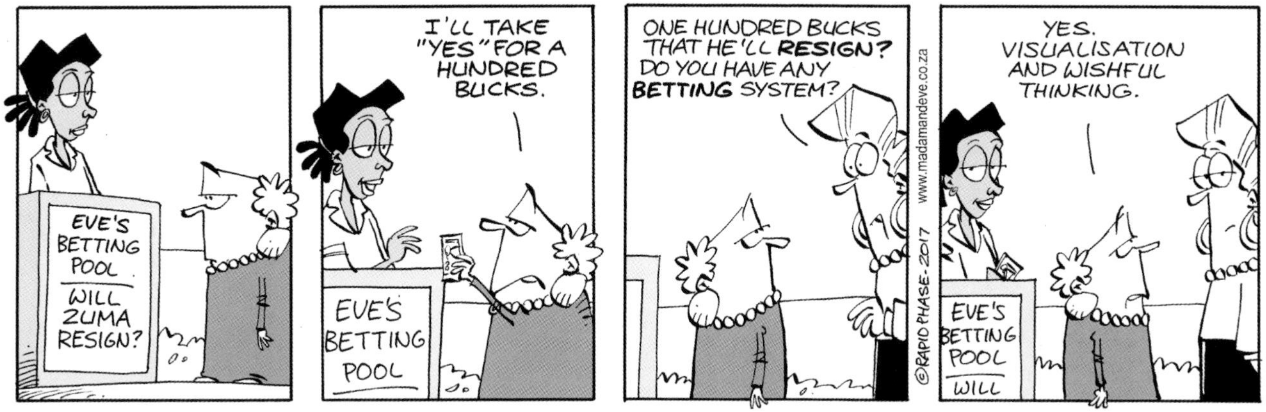
EVE'S BETTING POOL
WILL ZUMA RESIGN?
I'LL TAKE "**YES**" FOR A HUNDRED BUCKS.
EVE'S BETTING POOL
ONE HUNDRED BUCKS THAT HE'LL **RESIGN?** DO YOU HAVE ANY **BETTING** SYSTEM?
www.madamandeve.co.za
©RAPID PHASE-2017
YES. VISUALISATION AND WISHFUL THINKING.
EVE'S BETTING POOL
WILL

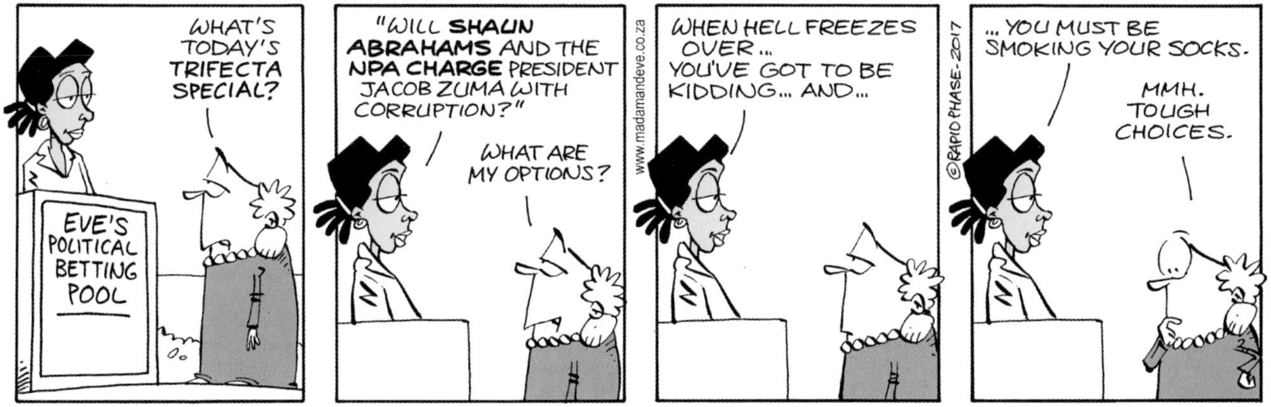
WHAT'S TODAY'S **TRIFECTA SPECIAL?**
EVE'S POLITICAL BETTING POOL
"WILL **SHAUN ABRAHAMS** AND THE **NPA CHARGE** PRESIDENT JACOB ZUMA WITH CORRUPTION?"
WHAT ARE MY OPTIONS?
www.madamandeve.co.za
WHEN HELL FREEZES OVER... YOU'VE GOT TO BE KIDDING... AND...
©RAPID PHASE-2017
...YOU MUST BE SMOKING YOUR SOCKS.
MMH. TOUGH CHOICES.

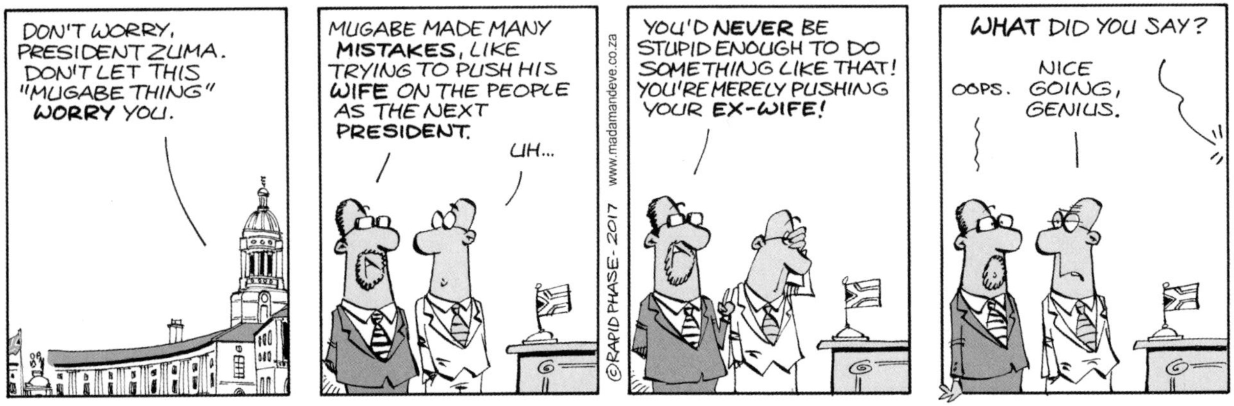
DON'T WORRY, PRESIDENT ZUMA. DON'T LET THIS "MUGABE THING" **WORRY** YOU.
MUGABE MADE MANY **MISTAKES**, LIKE TRYING TO PUSH HIS **WIFE** ON THE PEOPLE AS THE NEXT **PRESIDENT**.
UH...
©RAPID PHASE · 2017 www.madamandeve.co.za
YOU'D **NEVER** BE STUPID ENOUGH TO DO SOMETHING LIKE THAT! YOU'RE MERELY PUSHING YOUR **EX-WIFE**!
WHAT DID YOU SAY?
OOPS.
NICE GOING, GENIUS.

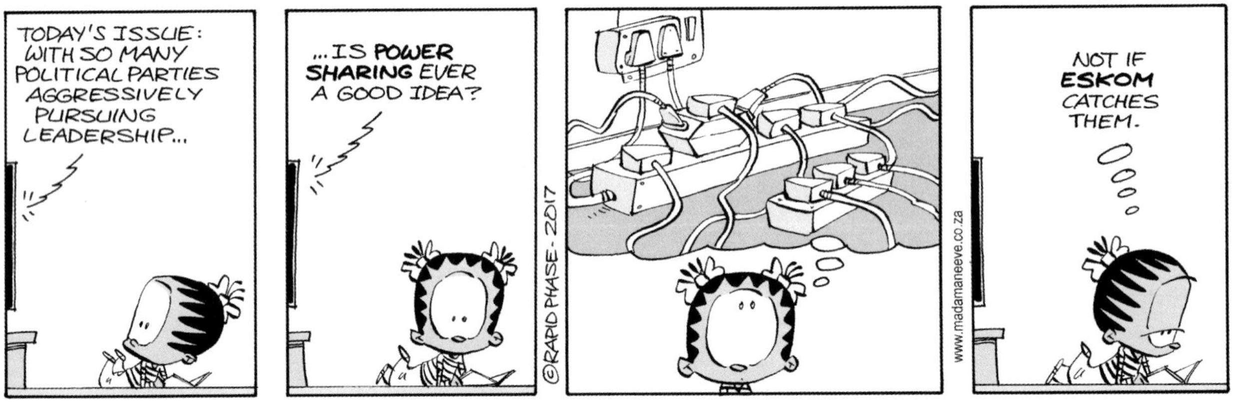
TODAY'S ISSUE: WITH SO MANY POLITICAL PARTIES AGGRESSIVELY PURSUING LEADERSHIP...
...IS **POWER SHARING** EVER A GOOD IDEA?
©RAPID PHASE · 2017
www.madamandeve.co.za
NOT IF **ESKOM** CATCHES THEM.

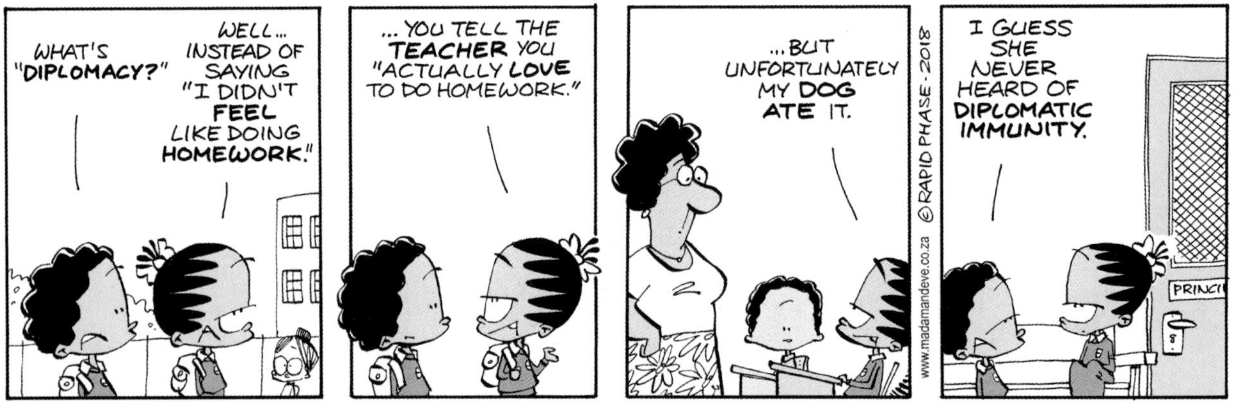
WHAT'S "**DIPLOMACY?**"
WELL... INSTEAD OF SAYING "I DIDN'T **FEEL** LIKE DOING **HOMEWORK**."
...YOU TELL THE **TEACHER** YOU "ACTUALLY **LOVE** TO DO HOMEWORK."
...BUT UNFORTUNATELY MY **DOG ATE** IT.
©RAPID PHASE · 2018 www.madamandeve.co.za
I GUESS SHE NEVER HEARD OF **DIPLOMATIC IMMUNITY**.
PRINCI

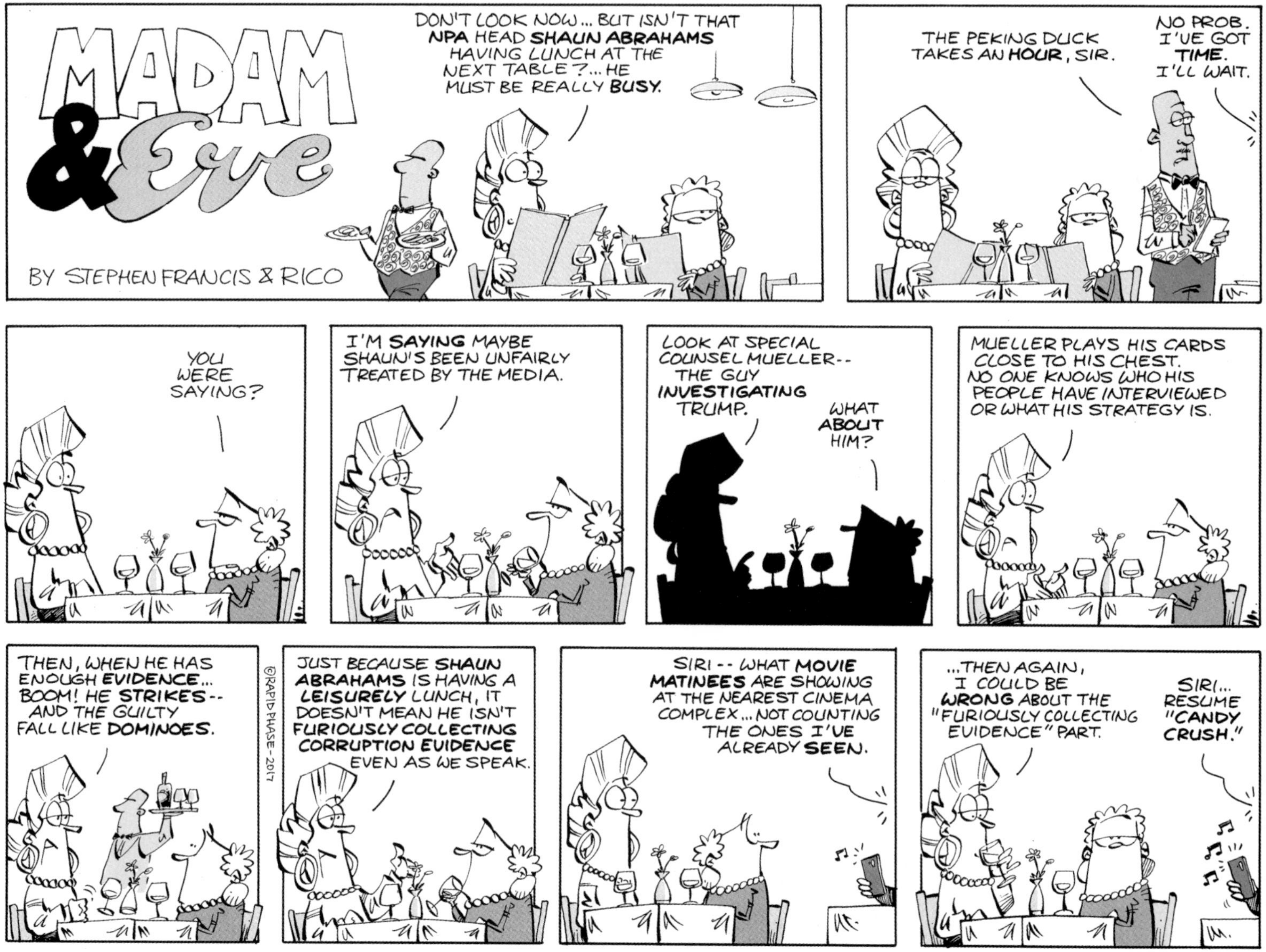
MADAM & Eve
BY STEPHEN FRANCIS & RICO
DON'T LOOK NOW... BUT ISN'T THAT NPA HEAD SHAUN ABRAHAMS HAVING LUNCH AT THE NEXT TABLE?... HE MUST BE REALLY BUSY.
THE PEKING DUCK TAKES AN HOUR, SIR.
NO PROB. I'VE GOT TIME. I'LL WAIT.
YOU WERE SAYING?
I'M SAYING MAYBE SHAUN'S BEEN UNFAIRLY TREATED BY THE MEDIA.
LOOK AT SPECIAL COUNSEL MUELLER-- THE GUY INVESTIGATING TRUMP.
WHAT ABOUT HIM?
MUELLER PLAYS HIS CARDS CLOSE TO HIS CHEST. NO ONE KNOWS WHO HIS PEOPLE HAVE INTERVIEWED OR WHAT HIS STRATEGY IS.
THEN, WHEN HE HAS ENOUGH EVIDENCE... BOOM! HE STRIKES-- AND THE GUILTY FALL LIKE DOMINOES.
©RAPID PHASE-2017
JUST BECAUSE SHAUN ABRAHAMS IS HAVING A LEISURELY LUNCH, IT DOESN'T MEAN HE ISN'T FURIOUSLY COLLECTING CORRUPTION EVIDENCE EVEN AS WE SPEAK.
SIRI -- WHAT MOVIE MATINEES ARE SHOWING AT THE NEAREST CINEMA COMPLEX... NOT COUNTING THE ONES I'VE ALREADY SEEN.
...THEN AGAIN, I COULD BE WRONG ABOUT THE "FURIOUSLY COLLECTING EVIDENCE" PART.
SIRI... RESUME "CANDY CRUSH."

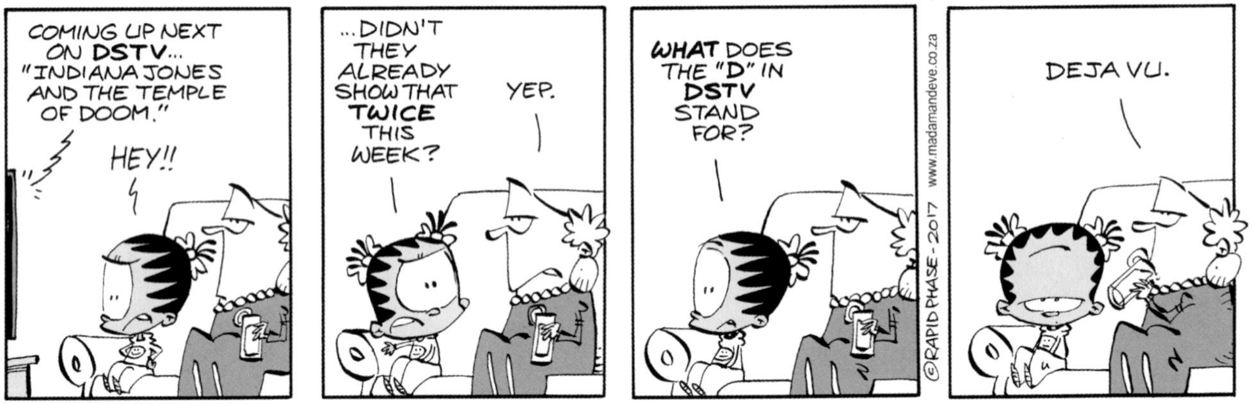
COMING UP NEXT ON DSTV... "INDIANA JONES AND THE TEMPLE OF DOOM."
HEY!!
...DIDN'T THEY ALREADY SHOW THAT TWICE THIS WEEK?
YEP.
WHAT DOES THE "D" IN DSTV STAND FOR?
©RAPID PHASE-2017 www.madamandeve.co.za
DEJA VU.

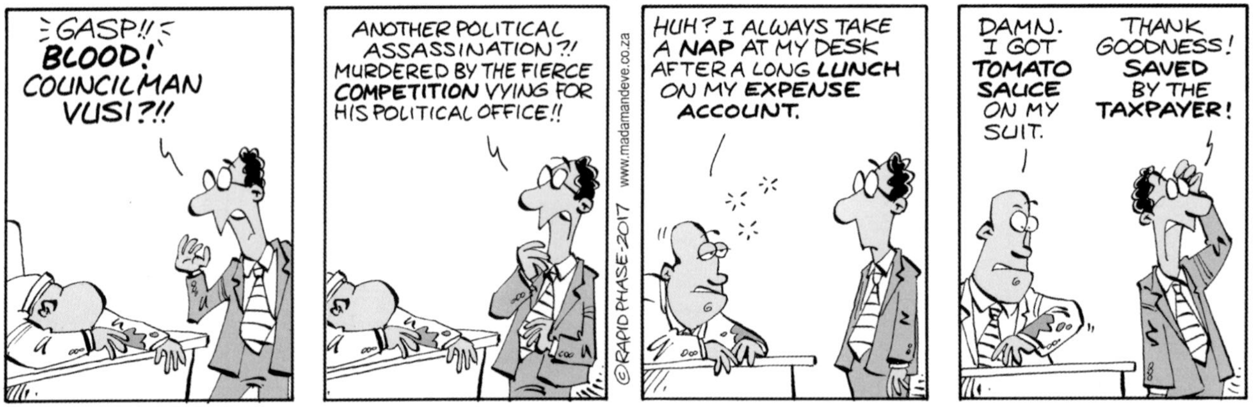
GASP!! BLOOD! COUNCILMAN VUSI?!!
ANOTHER POLITICAL ASSASSINATION?! MURDERED BY THE FIERCE COMPETITION VYING FOR HIS POLITICAL OFFICE!!
©RAPID PHASE-2017 www.madamandeve.co.za
HUH? I ALWAYS TAKE A NAP AT MY DESK AFTER A LONG LUNCH ON MY EXPENSE ACCOUNT.
DAMN. I GOT TOMATO SAUCE ON MY SUIT.
THANK GOODNESS! SAVED BY THE TAXPAYER!

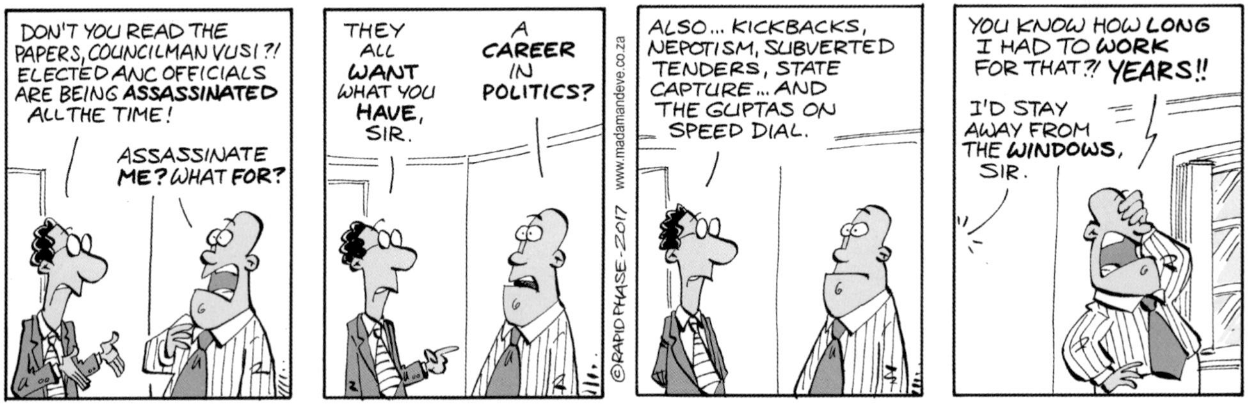
DON'T YOU READ THE PAPERS, COUNCILMAN VUSI?! ELECTED ANC OFFICIALS ARE BEING ASSASSINATED ALL THE TIME!
ASSASSINATE ME? WHAT FOR?
THEY ALL WANT WHAT YOU HAVE, SIR.
A CAREER IN POLITICS?
©RAPID PHASE-2017 www.madamandeve.co.za
ALSO... KICKBACKS, NEPOTISM, SUBVERTED TENDERS, STATE CAPTURE... AND THE GUPTAS ON SPEED DIAL.
YOU KNOW HOW LONG I HAD TO WORK FOR THAT?! YEARS!!
I'D STAY AWAY FROM THE WINDOWS, SIR.

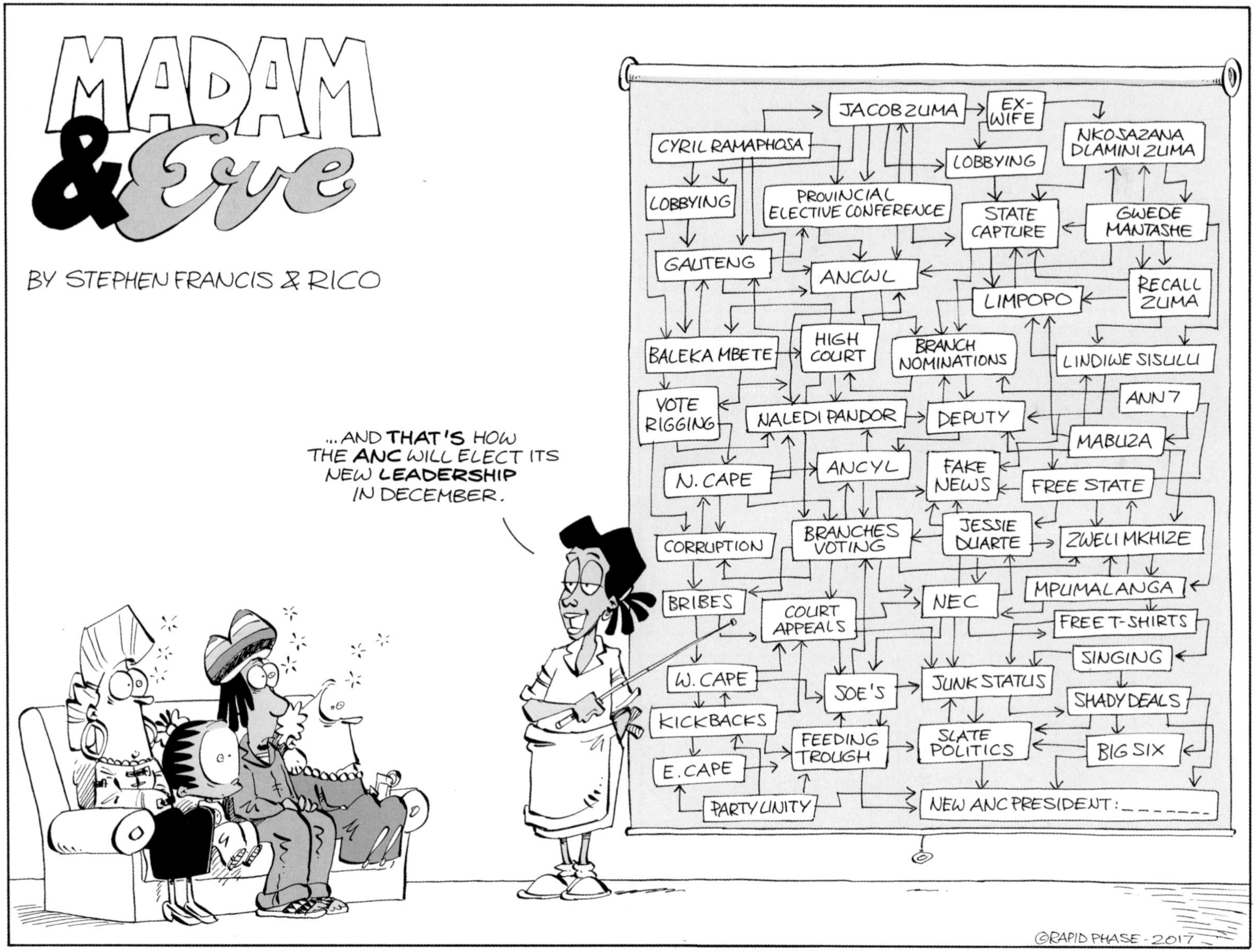
MADAM & Eve
BY STEPHEN FRANCIS & RICO
...AND THAT'S HOW THE ANC WILL ELECT ITS NEW LEADERSHIP IN DECEMBER.
JACOB ZUMA
EX-WIFE
CYRIL RAMAPHOSA
LOBBYING
NKOSAZANA DLAMINI ZUMA
LOBBYING
PROVINCIAL ELECTIVE CONFERENCE
STATE CAPTURE
GWEDE MANTASHE
GAUTENG
ANCWL
RECALL ZUMA
LIMPOPO
BALEKA MBETE
HIGH COURT
BRANCH NOMINATIONS
LINDIWE SISULU
ANN7
VOTE RIGGING
NALEDI PANDOR
DEPUTY
MABUZA
N. CAPE
ANCYL
FAKE NEWS
FREE STATE
CORRUPTION
BRANCHES VOTING
JESSIE DUARTE
ZWELI MKHIZE
BRIBES
COURT APPEALS
NEC
MPUMALANGA
FREE T-SHIRTS
SINGING
W. CAPE
SOE'S
JUNK STATUS
SHADY DEALS
KICKBACKS
FEEDING TROUGH
SLATE POLITICS
BIG SIX
E. CAPE
PARTY UNITY
NEW ANC PRESIDENT: _______
©RAPID PHASE - 2017

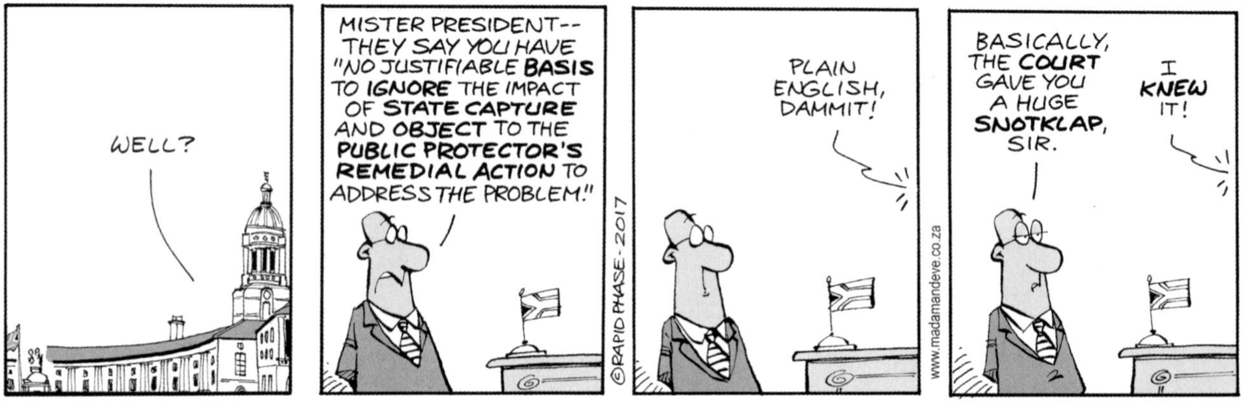
WELL?
MISTER PRESIDENT-- THEY SAY YOU HAVE "NO JUSTIFIABLE BASIS TO IGNORE THE IMPACT OF STATE CAPTURE AND OBJECT TO THE PUBLIC PROTECTOR'S REMEDIAL ACTION TO ADDRESS THE PROBLEM!"
©RAPID PHASE · 2017
PLAIN ENGLISH, DAMMIT!
www.madamandeve.co.za
BASICALLY, THE COURT GAVE YOU A HUGE SNOTKLAP, SIR.
I KNEW IT!

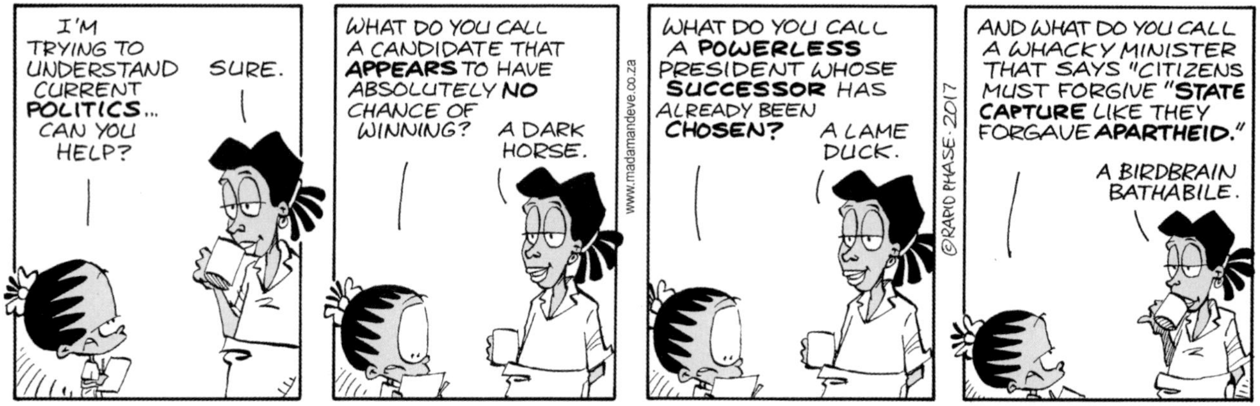
I'M TRYING TO UNDERSTAND CURRENT POLITICS... CAN YOU HELP?
SURE.
WHAT DO YOU CALL A CANDIDATE THAT APPEARS TO HAVE ABSOLUTELY NO CHANCE OF WINNING?
A DARK HORSE.
www.madamandeve.co.za
WHAT DO YOU CALL A POWERLESS PRESIDENT WHOSE SUCCESSOR HAS ALREADY BEEN CHOSEN?
A LAME DUCK.
©RAPID PHASE · 2017
AND WHAT DO YOU CALL A WHACKY MINISTER THAT SAYS "CITIZENS MUST FORGIVE "STATE CAPTURE LIKE THEY FORGAVE APARTHEID."
A BIRDBRAIN BATHABILE.

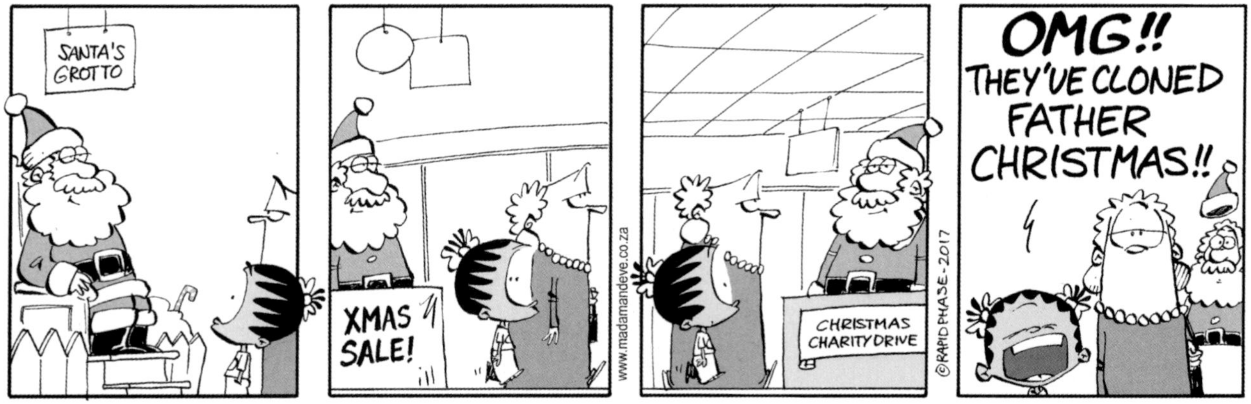
SANTA'S GROTTO
XMAS SALE!
www.madamandeve.co.za
CHRISTMAS CHARITY DRIVE
©RAPID PHASE · 2017
OMG!! THEY'VE CLONED FATHER CHRISTMAS!!

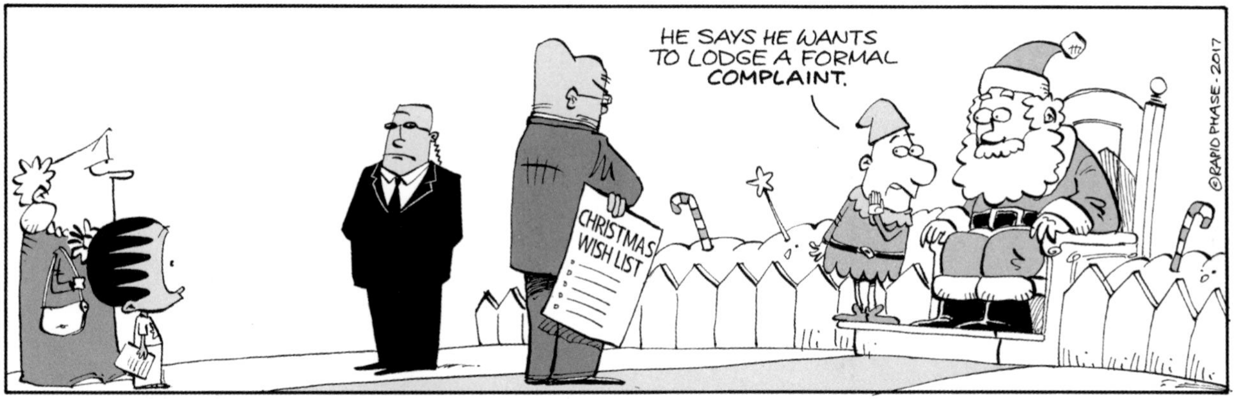

HE SAYS HE WANTS TO LODGE A FORMAL **COMPLAINT.**
CHRISTMAS WISH LIST
©RAPID PHASE·2017

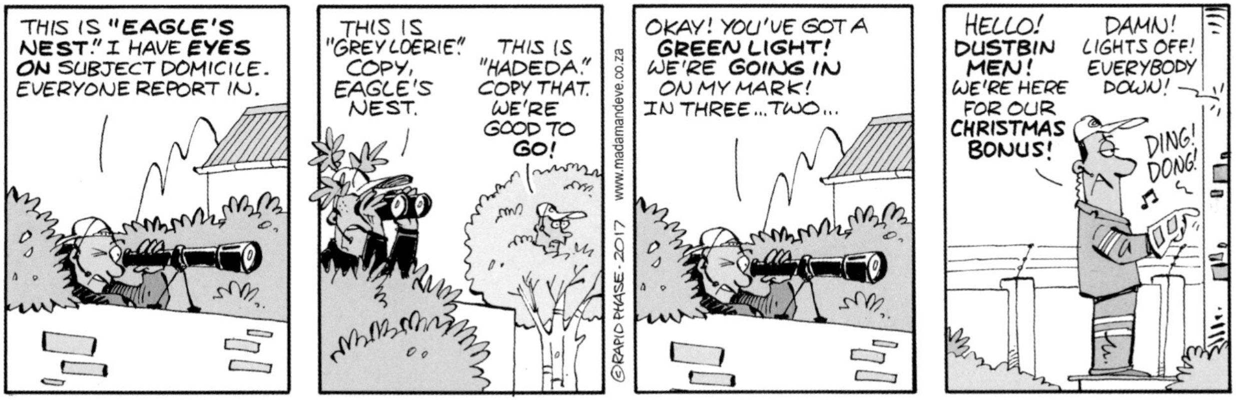

THIS IS **"EAGLE'S NEST."** I HAVE **EYES ON** SUBJECT DOMICILE. EVERYONE REPORT IN.
THIS IS "GREY LOERIE." COPY, EAGLE'S NEST.
THIS IS "HADEDA." COPY THAT. WE'RE GOOD TO **GO!**
©RAPID PHASE·2017 www.madamandeve.co.za
OKAY! YOU'VE GOT A **GREEN LIGHT!** WE'RE **GOING IN** ON MY MARK! IN THREE... TWO...
HELLO! **DUSTBIN MEN!** WE'RE HERE FOR OUR **CHRISTMAS BONUS!**
DAMN! LIGHTS OFF! EVERYBODY DOWN!
DING! DONG!

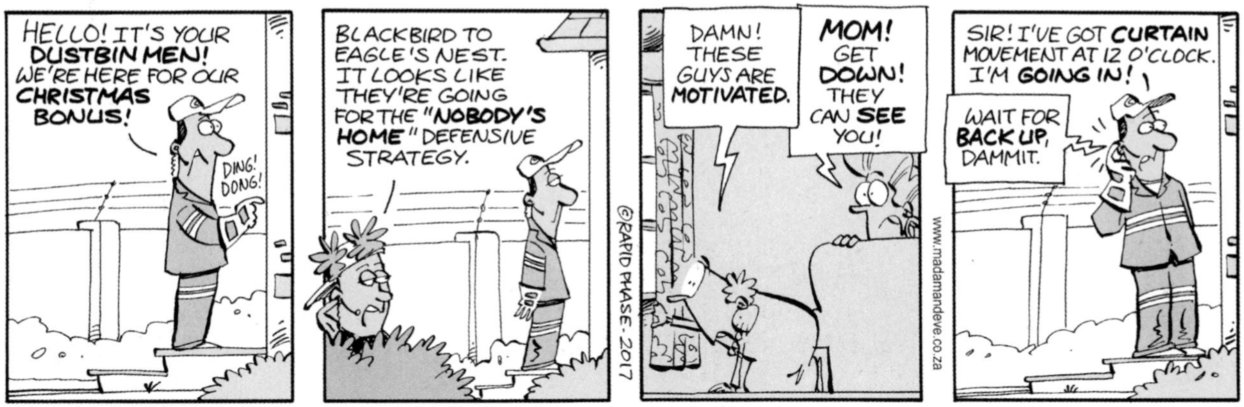

HELLO! IT'S YOUR **DUSTBIN MEN!** WE'RE HERE FOR OUR **CHRISTMAS BONUS!**
DING! DONG!
BLACKBIRD TO EAGLE'S NEST. IT LOOKS LIKE THEY'RE GOING FOR THE **"NOBODY'S HOME"** DEFENSIVE STRATEGY.
©RAPID PHASE·2017
DAMN! THESE GUYS ARE **MOTIVATED.**
MOM! GET **DOWN!** THEY CAN **SEE** YOU!
www.madamandeve.co.za
SIR! I'VE GOT **CURTAIN** MOVEMENT AT 12 O'CLOCK. I'M **GOING IN!**
WAIT FOR **BACK UP,** DAMMIT.

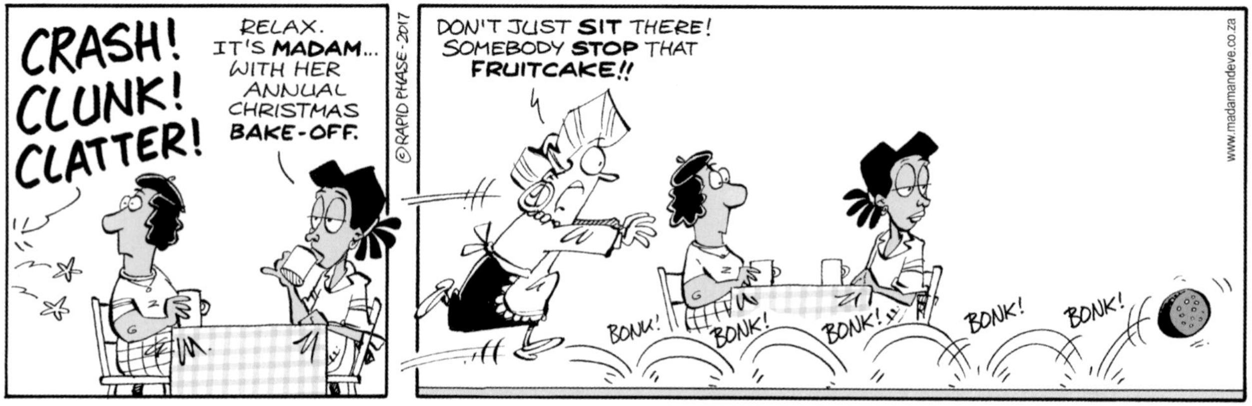
CRASH! CLUNK! CLATTER!
RELAX. IT'S **MADAM**... WITH HER ANNUAL CHRISTMAS **BAKE-OFF.**
© RAPID PHASE · 2017
DON'T JUST **SIT** THERE! SOMEBODY **STOP** THAT **FRUITCAKE!!**
BONK!
BONK!
BONK!
BONK!
BONK!
www.madamandeve.co.za

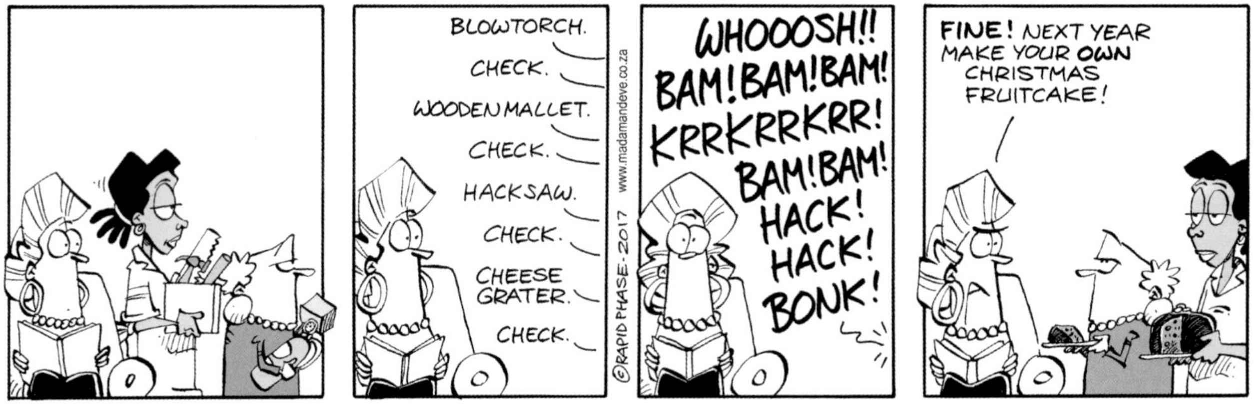
BLOWTORCH.
CHECK.
WOODEN MALLET.
CHECK.
HACKSAW.
CHECK.
CHEESE GRATER.
CHECK.
www.madamandeve.co.za
© RAPID PHASE · 2017
WHOOOSH!! BAM!BAM!BAM! KRRKRRKRR! BAM!BAM! HACK! HACK! BONK!
FINE! NEXT YEAR MAKE YOUR **OWN** CHRISTMAS FRUITCAKE!

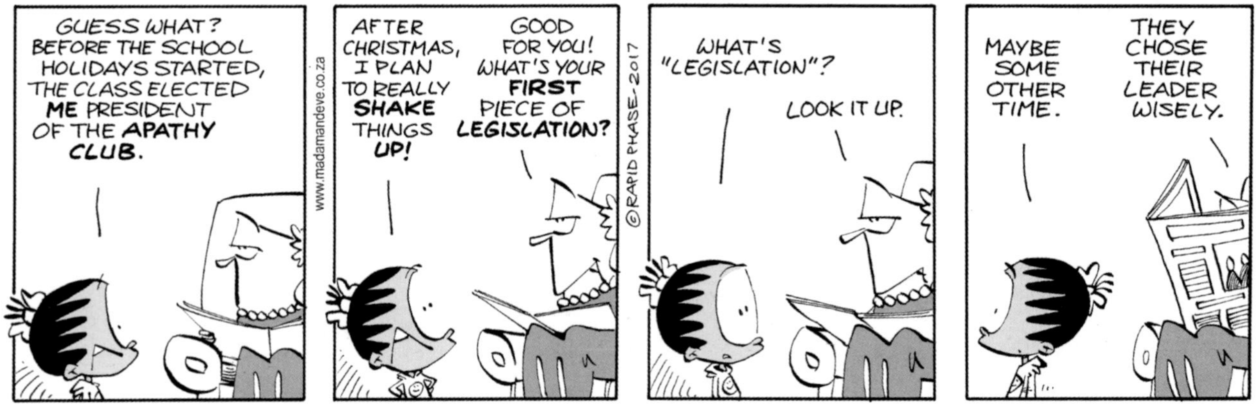
GUESS WHAT? BEFORE THE SCHOOL HOLIDAYS STARTED, THE CLASS ELECTED **ME** PRESIDENT OF THE **APATHY CLUB.**
www.madamandeve.co.za
AFTER CHRISTMAS, I PLAN TO REALLY **SHAKE** THINGS **UP!**
GOOD FOR YOU! WHAT'S YOUR **FIRST** PIECE OF **LEGISLATION?**
© RAPID PHASE · 2017
WHAT'S "LEGISLATION"?
LOOK IT UP.
MAYBE SOME OTHER TIME.
THEY CHOSE THEIR LEADER WISELY.

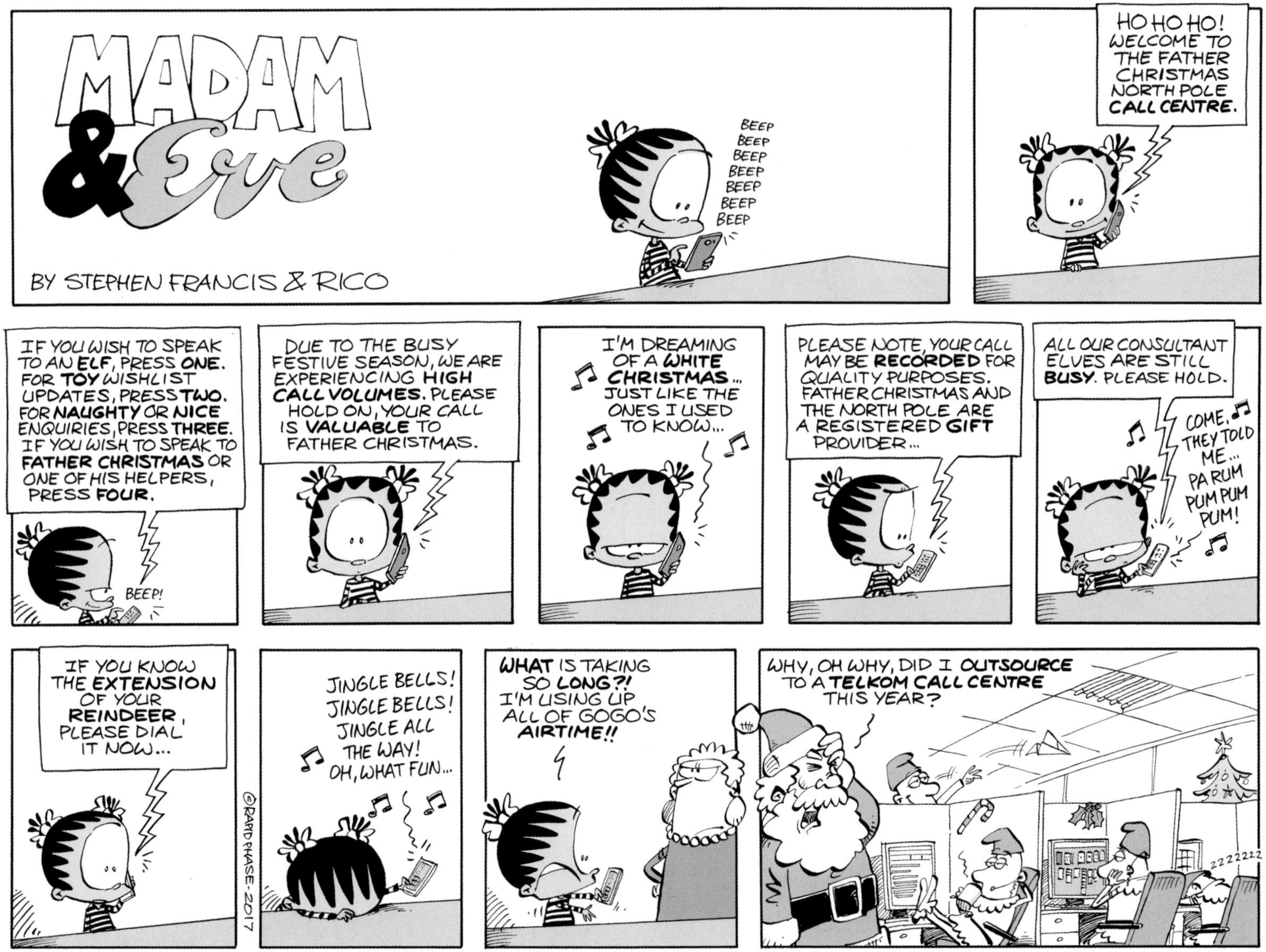
MADAM & Eve
BY STEPHEN FRANCIS & RICO
BEEP BEEP BEEP BEEP BEEP BEEP BEEP
HO HO HO! WELCOME TO THE FATHER CHRISTMAS NORTH POLE **CALL CENTRE**.
IF YOU WISH TO SPEAK TO AN **ELF**, PRESS **ONE**. FOR **TOY** WISHLIST UPDATES, PRESS **TWO**. FOR **NAUGHTY** OR **NICE** ENQUIRIES, PRESS **THREE**. IF YOU WISH TO SPEAK TO **FATHER CHRISTMAS** OR ONE OF HIS HELPERS, PRESS **FOUR**.
BEEP!
DUE TO THE BUSY FESTIVE SEASON, WE ARE EXPERIENCING **HIGH CALL VOLUMES**. PLEASE HOLD ON, YOUR CALL IS **VALUABLE** TO FATHER CHRISTMAS.
I'M DREAMING OF A **WHITE CHRISTMAS**... JUST LIKE THE ONES I USED TO KNOW...
PLEASE NOTE, YOUR CALL MAY BE **RECORDED** FOR QUALITY PURPOSES. FATHER CHRISTMAS AND THE NORTH POLE ARE A REGISTERED **GIFT** PROVIDER...
ALL OUR CONSULTANT ELVES ARE STILL **BUSY**. PLEASE HOLD.
COME, THEY TOLD ME... PA RUM PUM PUM PUM!
IF YOU KNOW THE **EXTENSION** OF YOUR **REINDEER**, PLEASE DIAL IT NOW...
©RAPID PHASE · 2017
JINGLE BELLS! JINGLE BELLS! JINGLE ALL THE WAY! OH, WHAT FUN...
WHAT IS TAKING SO **LONG?!** I'M USING UP ALL OF GOGO'S **AIRTIME!!**
WHY, OH WHY, DID I **OUTSOURCE** TO A **TELKOM CALL CENTRE** THIS YEAR?
ZZZZZZZ

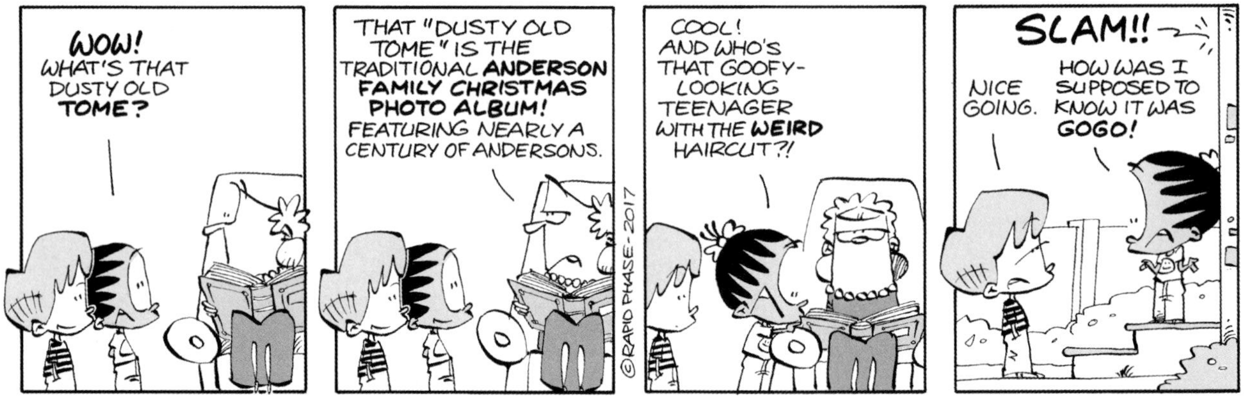
WOW! WHAT'S THAT DUSTY OLD TOME?
THAT "DUSTY OLD TOME" IS THE TRADITIONAL ANDERSON FAMILY CHRISTMAS PHOTO ALBUM! FEATURING NEARLY A CENTURY OF ANDERSONS.
©RAPID PHASE-2017
COOL! AND WHO'S THAT GOOFY-LOOKING TEENAGER WITH THE WEIRD HAIRCUT?!
SLAM!!
NICE GOING.
HOW WAS I SUPPOSED TO KNOW IT WAS GOGO!

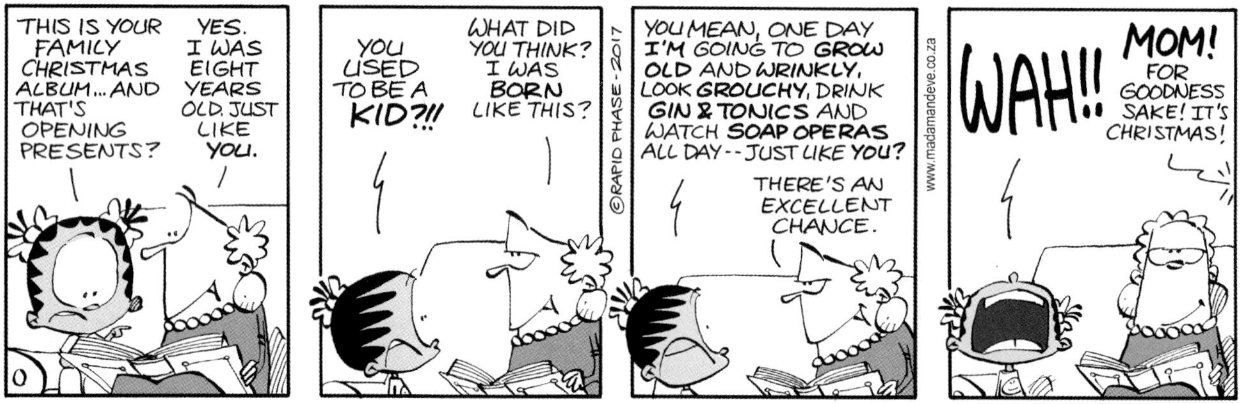
THIS IS YOUR FAMILY CHRISTMAS ALBUM... AND THAT'S OPENING PRESENTS?
YES. I WAS EIGHT YEARS OLD. JUST LIKE YOU.
YOU USED TO BE A KID?!!
WHAT DID YOU THINK? I WAS BORN LIKE THIS?
©RAPID PHASE-2017
YOU MEAN, ONE DAY I'M GOING TO GROW OLD AND WRINKLY, LOOK GROUCHY, DRINK GIN & TONICS AND WATCH SOAP OPERAS ALL DAY--JUST LIKE YOU?
THERE'S AN EXCELLENT CHANCE.
www.madamandeve.co.za
WAH!!
MOM! FOR GOODNESS SAKE! IT'S CHRISTMAS!

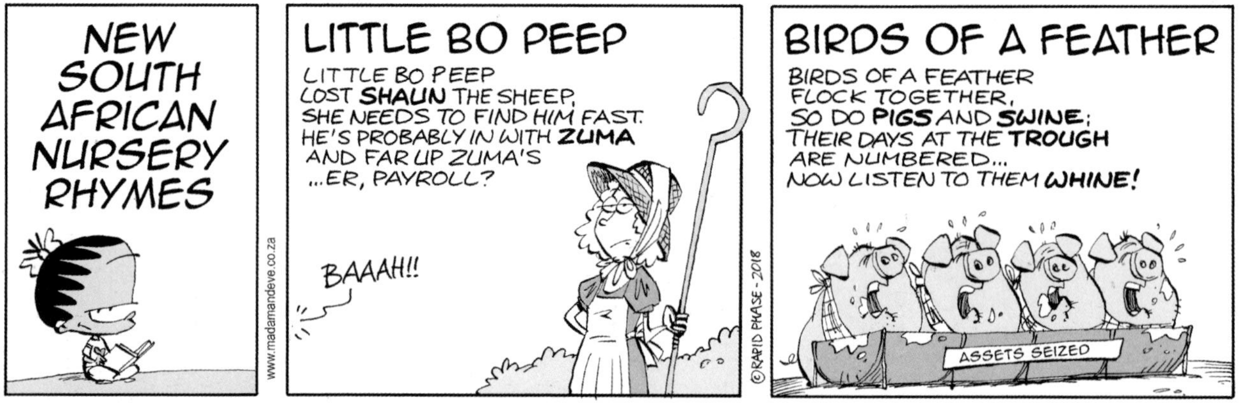
NEW SOUTH AFRICAN NURSERY RHYMES
www.madamandeve.co.za
LITTLE BO PEEP
LITTLE BO PEEP LOST SHAUN THE SHEEP, SHE NEEDS TO FIND HIM FAST. HE'S PROBABLY IN WITH ZUMA AND FAR UP ZUMA'S ...ER, PAYROLL?
BAAAH!!
©RAPID PHASE-2018
BIRDS OF A FEATHER
BIRDS OF A FEATHER FLOCK TOGETHER, SO DO PIGS AND SWINE; THEIR DAYS AT THE TROUGH ARE NUMBERED... NOW LISTEN TO THEM WHINE!
ASSETS SEIZED

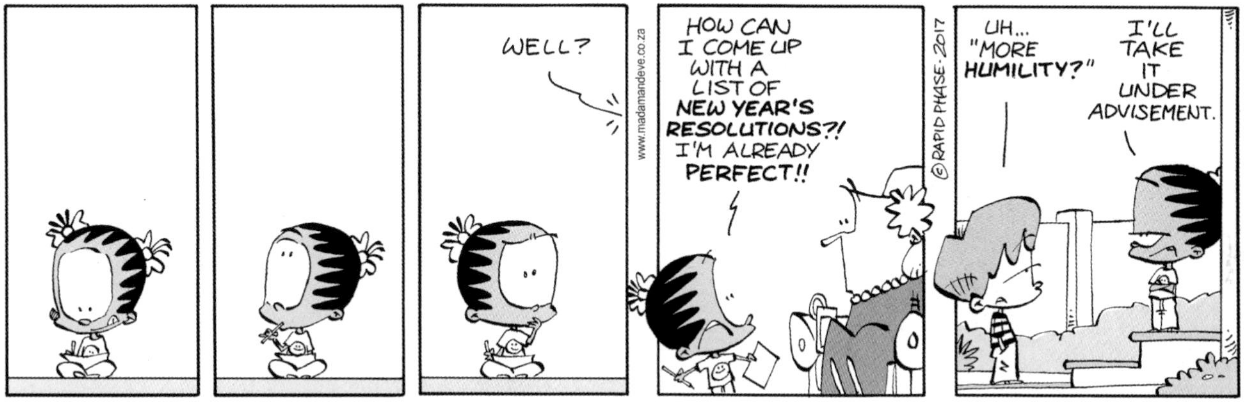
WELL?
www.madamandeve.co.za
HOW CAN I COME UP WITH A LIST OF NEW YEAR'S RESOLUTIONS?! I'M ALREADY PERFECT!!
© RAPID PHASE - 2017
UH... "MORE HUMILITY?"
I'LL TAKE IT UNDER ADVISEMENT.

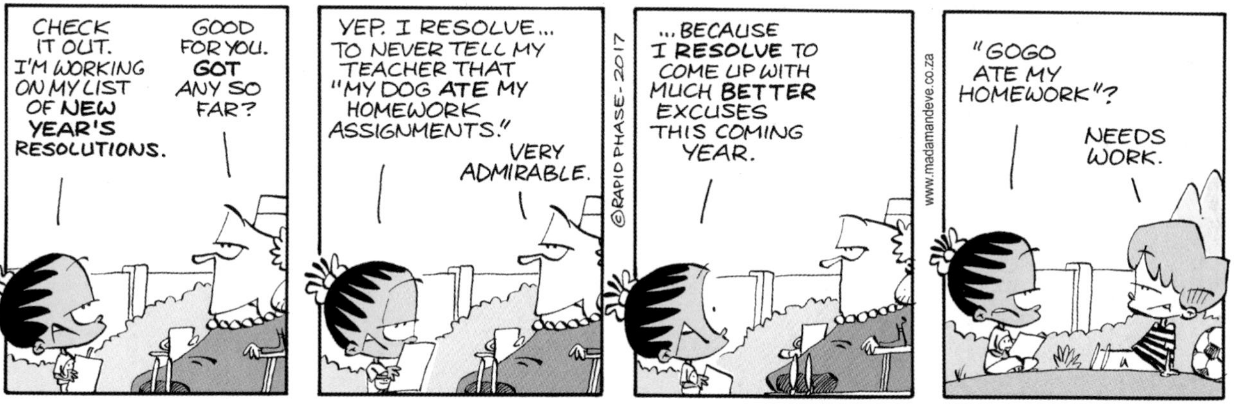
CHECK IT OUT. I'M WORKING ON MY LIST OF NEW YEAR'S RESOLUTIONS.
GOOD FOR YOU. GOT ANY SO FAR?
YEP. I RESOLVE... TO NEVER TELL MY TEACHER THAT "MY DOG ATE MY HOMEWORK ASSIGNMENTS."
VERY ADMIRABLE.
© RAPID PHASE - 2017
...BECAUSE I RESOLVE TO COME UP WITH MUCH BETTER EXCUSES THIS COMING YEAR.
www.madamandeve.co.za
"GOGO ATE MY HOMEWORK"?
NEEDS WORK.

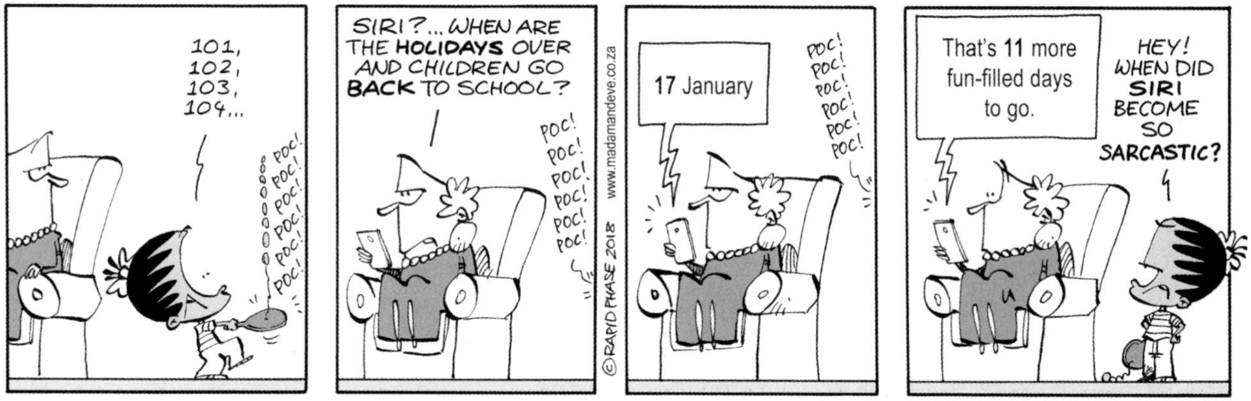
101, 102, 103, 104...
POC! POC! POC! POC! POC! POC!
SIRI?... WHEN ARE THE HOLIDAYS OVER AND CHILDREN GO BACK TO SCHOOL?
POC! POC! POC! POC! POC! POC!
www.madamandeve.co.za
© RAPID PHASE 2018
17 January
POC! POC! POC! POC! POC! POC!
That's 11 more fun-filled days to go.
HEY! WHEN DID SIRI BECOME SO SARCASTIC?

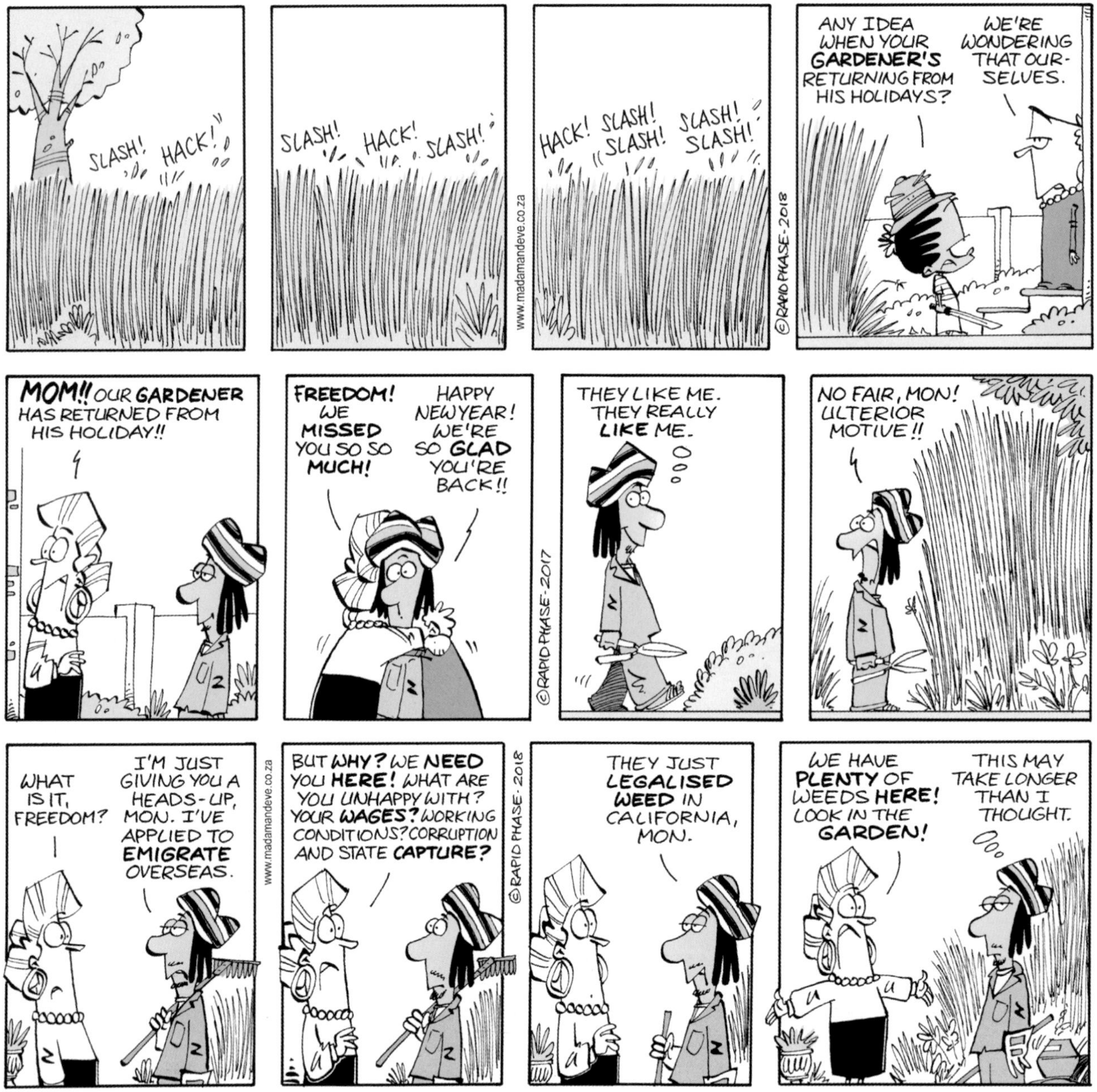
SLASH! HACK!
SLASH! HACK! SLASH!
HACK! SLASH! SLASH! SLASH! SLASH!
ANY IDEA WHEN YOUR GARDENER'S RETURNING FROM HIS HOLIDAYS?
WE'RE WONDERING THAT OURSELVES.
www.madamandeve.co.za
© RAPID PHASE · 2018
MOM!! OUR GARDENER HAS RETURNED FROM HIS HOLIDAY!!
FREEDOM! WE MISSED YOU SO SO MUCH!
HAPPY NEW YEAR! WE'RE SO GLAD YOU'RE BACK!!
THEY LIKE ME. THEY REALLY LIKE ME.
NO FAIR, MON! ULTERIOR MOTIVE!!
© RAPID PHASE · 2017
WHAT IS IT, FREEDOM?
I'M JUST GIVING YOU A HEADS-UP, MON. I'VE APPLIED TO EMIGRATE OVERSEAS.
BUT WHY? WE NEED YOU HERE! WHAT ARE YOU UNHAPPY WITH? YOUR WAGES? WORKING CONDITIONS? CORRUPTION AND STATE CAPTURE?
THEY JUST LEGALISED WEED IN CALIFORNIA, MON.
WE HAVE PLENTY OF WEEDS HERE! LOOK IN THE GARDEN!
THIS MAY TAKE LONGER THAN I THOUGHT.
www.madamandeve.co.za
© RAPID PHASE · 2018

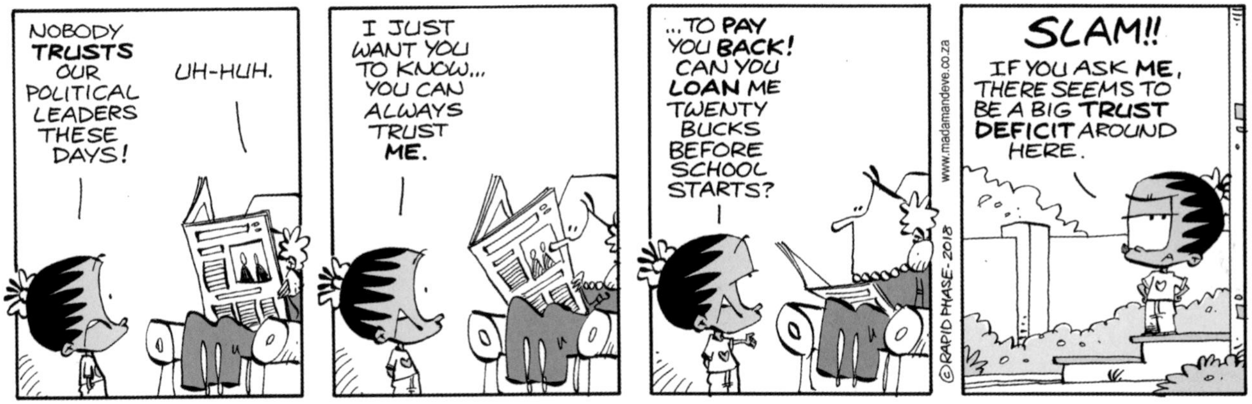
NOBODY TRUSTS OUR POLITICAL LEADERS THESE DAYS!
UH-HUH.
I JUST WANT YOU TO KNOW... YOU CAN ALWAYS TRUST ME.
...TO PAY YOU BACK! CAN YOU LOAN ME TWENTY BUCKS BEFORE SCHOOL STARTS?
www.madamandeve.co.za
©RAPID PHASE-2018
SLAM!!
IF YOU ASK ME, THERE SEEMS TO BE A BIG TRUST DEFICIT AROUND HERE.

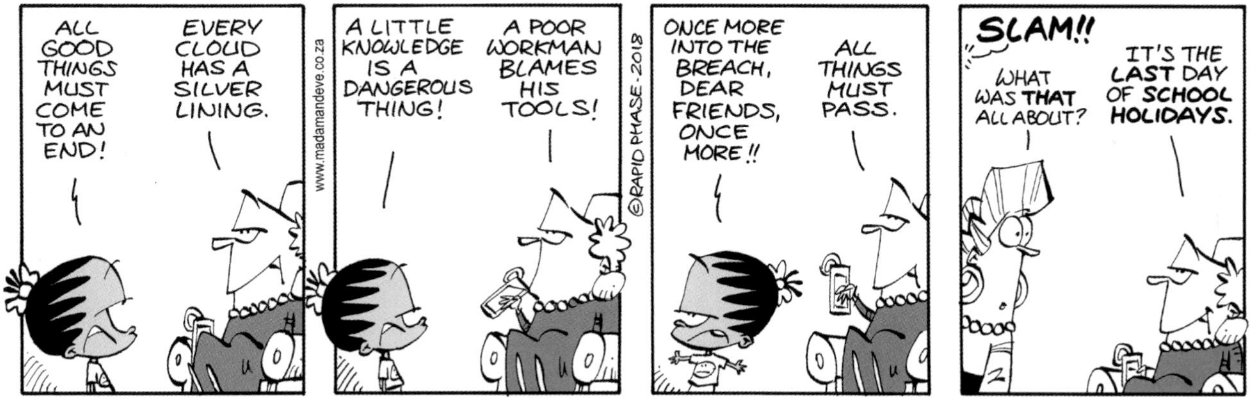
ALL GOOD THINGS MUST COME TO AN END!
EVERY CLOUD HAS A SILVER LINING.
www.madamandeve.co.za
A LITTLE KNOWLEDGE IS A DANGEROUS THING!
A POOR WORKMAN BLAMES HIS TOOLS!
©RAPID PHASE-2018
ONCE MORE INTO THE BREACH, DEAR FRIENDS, ONCE MORE!!
ALL THINGS MUST PASS.
SLAM!!
WHAT WAS THAT ALL ABOUT?
IT'S THE LAST DAY OF SCHOOL HOLIDAYS.

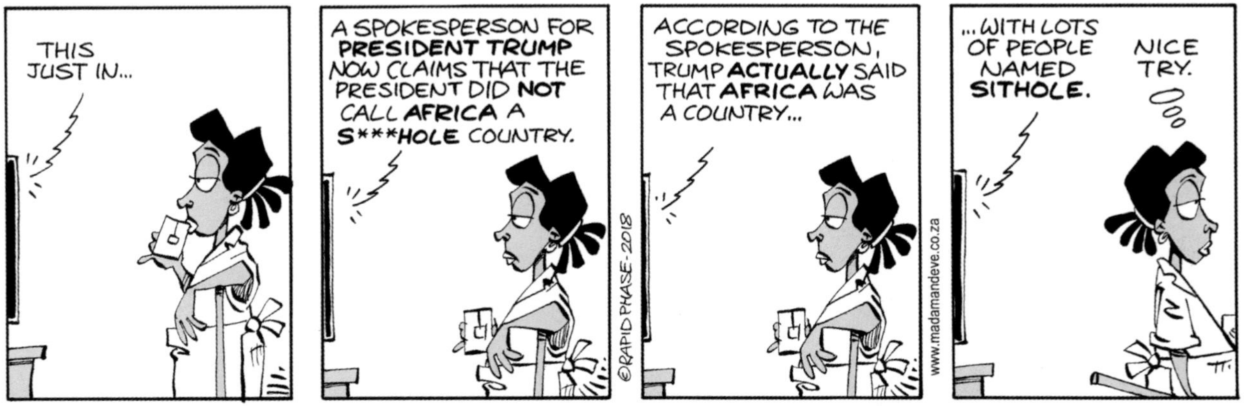
THIS JUST IN...
A SPOKESPERSON FOR PRESIDENT TRUMP NOW CLAIMS THAT THE PRESIDENT DID NOT CALL AFRICA A S***HOLE COUNTRY.
©RAPID PHASE-2018
ACCORDING TO THE SPOKESPERSON, TRUMP ACTUALLY SAID THAT AFRICA WAS A COUNTRY...
www.madamandeve.co.za
...WITH LOTS OF PEOPLE NAMED SITHOLE.
NICE TRY.

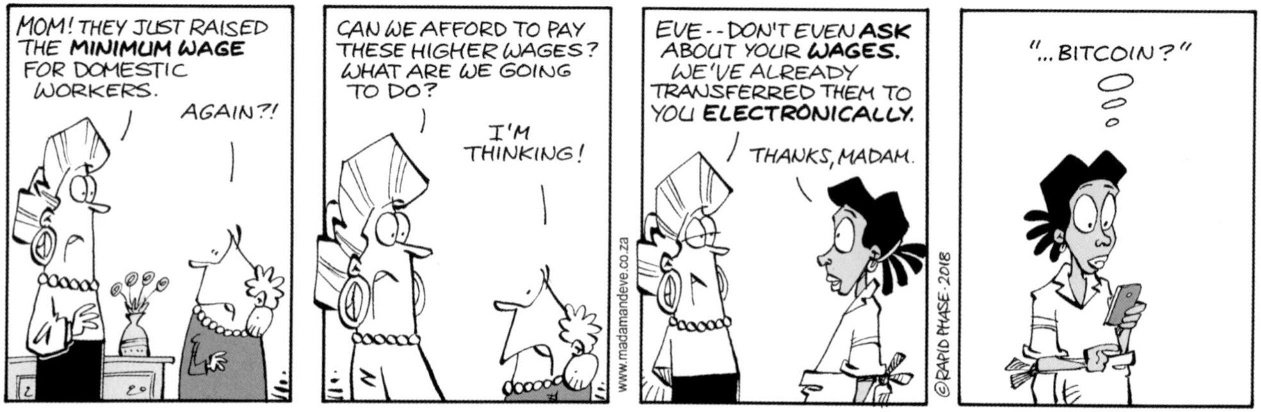
MOM! THEY JUST RAISED THE **MINIMUM WAGE** FOR DOMESTIC WORKERS.
AGAIN?!
CAN WE AFFORD TO PAY THESE HIGHER WAGES? WHAT ARE WE GOING TO DO?
I'M THINKING!
www.madamandeve.co.za
EVE--DON'T EVEN **ASK** ABOUT YOUR **WAGES.** WE'VE ALREADY TRANSFERRED THEM TO YOU **ELECTRONICALLY.**
THANKS, MADAM.
©RAPID PHASE · 2018
"...BITCOIN?"

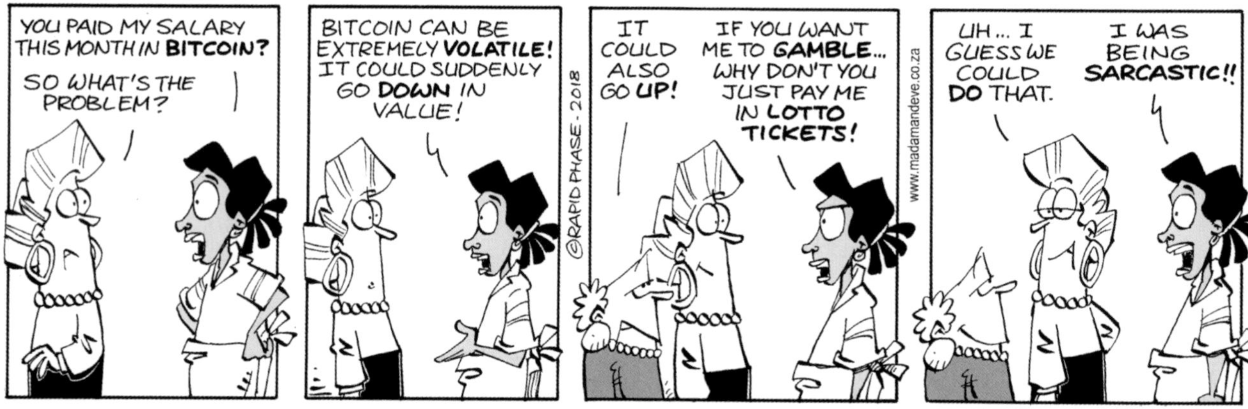
YOU PAID MY SALARY THIS MONTH IN **BITCOIN?**
SO WHAT'S THE PROBLEM?
BITCOIN CAN BE EXTREMELY **VOLATILE!** IT COULD SUDDENLY GO **DOWN** IN VALUE!
©RAPID PHASE · 2018
IT COULD ALSO GO **UP!**
IF YOU WANT ME TO **GAMBLE...** WHY DON'T YOU JUST PAY ME IN **LOTTO TICKETS!**
www.madamandeve.co.za
UH... I GUESS WE COULD **DO** THAT.
I WAS BEING **SARCASTIC!!**

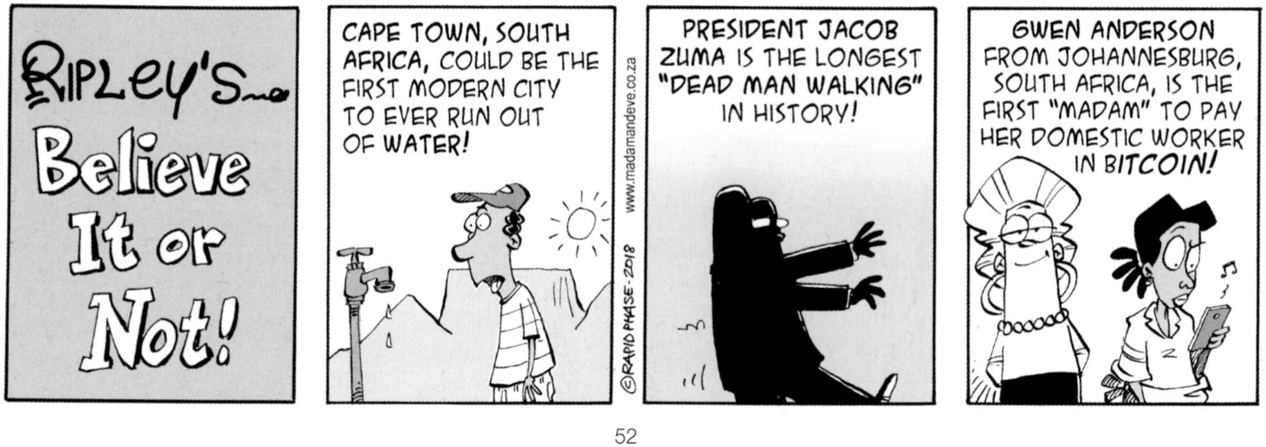
RIPLEY'S
Believe It or Not!
CAPE TOWN, SOUTH AFRICA, COULD BE THE FIRST MODERN CITY TO EVER RUN OUT OF WATER!
www.madamandeve.co.za
©RAPID PHASE · 2018
PRESIDENT JACOB ZUMA IS THE LONGEST "DEAD MAN WALKING" IN HISTORY!
GWEN ANDERSON FROM JOHANNESBURG, SOUTH AFRICA, IS THE FIRST "MADAM" TO PAY HER DOMESTIC WORKER IN BITCOIN!

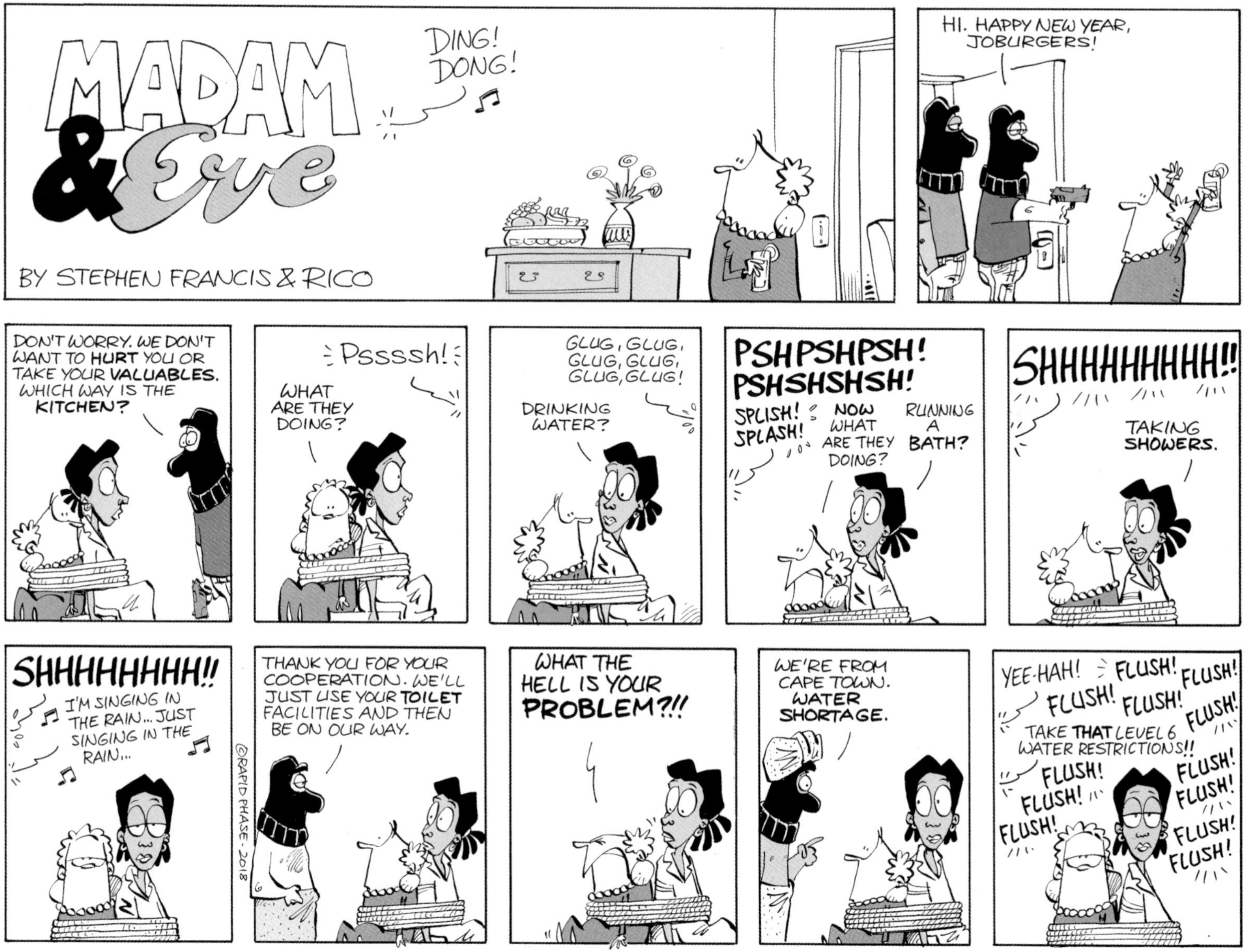
MADAM & Eve
BY STEPHEN FRANCIS & RICO
DING! DONG!
HI. HAPPY NEW YEAR, JOBURGERS!
DON'T WORRY. WE DON'T WANT TO HURT YOU OR TAKE YOUR VALUABLES. WHICH WAY IS THE KITCHEN?
Psssssh!
WHAT ARE THEY DOING?
GLUG, GLUG, GLUG, GLUG, GLUG, GLUG!
DRINKING WATER?
PSHPSHPSH! PSHSHSHSH!
SPLISH! SPLASH!
NOW WHAT ARE THEY DOING?
RUNNING A BATH?
SHHHHHHHHH!!
TAKING SHOWERS.
SHHHHHHHH!!
I'M SINGING IN THE RAIN... JUST SINGING IN THE RAIN...
©RAPID PHASE · 2018
THANK YOU FOR YOUR COOPERATION. WE'LL JUST USE YOUR TOILET FACILITIES AND THEN BE ON OUR WAY.
WHAT THE HELL IS YOUR PROBLEM?!!
WE'RE FROM CAPE TOWN. WATER SHORTAGE.
YEE-HAH!
FLUSH! FLUSH! FLUSH! FLUSH! FLUSH!
TAKE THAT LEVEL 6 WATER RESTRICTIONS!!
FLUSH! FLUSH! FLUSH! FLUSH! FLUSH! FLUSH! FLUSH!

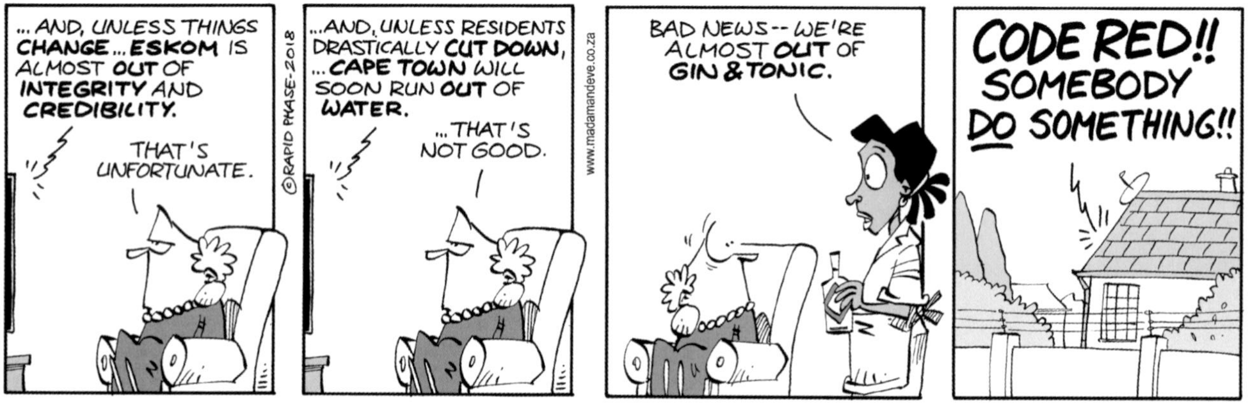
...AND, UNLESS THINGS **CHANGE**... **ESKOM** IS ALMOST **OUT** OF **INTEGRITY** AND **CREDIBILITY.**
THAT'S UNFORTUNATE.
©RAPID PHASE-2018
...AND, UNLESS RESIDENTS DRASTICALLY **CUT DOWN**, ... **CAPE TOWN** WILL SOON RUN **OUT** OF **WATER.**
... THAT'S NOT GOOD.
www.madamandeve.co.za
BAD NEWS -- WE'RE ALMOST **OUT** OF **GIN & TONIC.**
CODE RED!! SOMEBODY DO SOMETHING!!

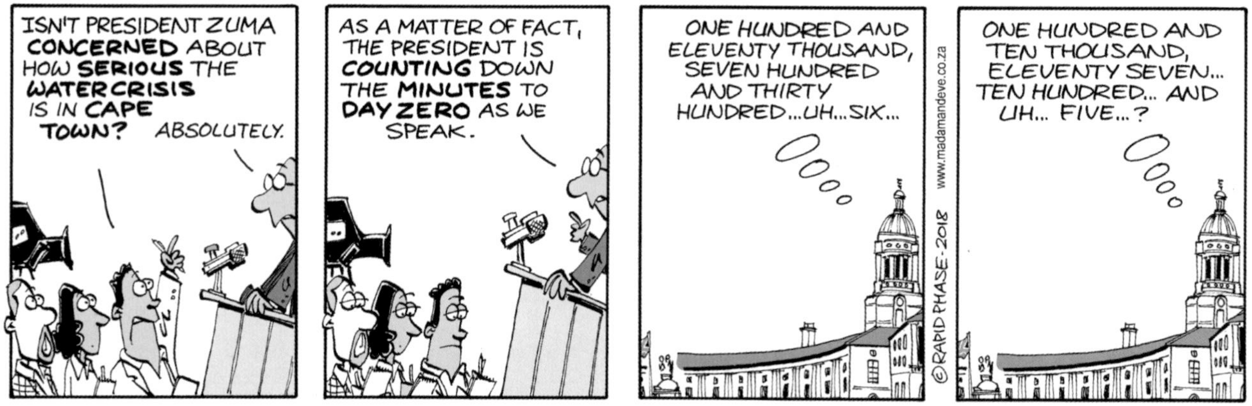
ISN'T PRESIDENT ZUMA **CONCERNED** ABOUT HOW **SERIOUS** THE **WATER CRISIS** IS IN **CAPE TOWN?**
ABSOLUTELY.
AS A MATTER OF FACT, THE PRESIDENT IS **COUNTING** DOWN THE **MINUTES** TO **DAY ZERO** AS WE SPEAK.
ONE HUNDRED AND ELEVENTY THOUSAND, SEVEN HUNDRED AND THIRTY HUNDRED...UH...SIX...
©RAPID PHASE-2018
www.madamandeve.co.za
ONE HUNDRED AND TEN THOUSAND, ELEVENTY SEVEN... TEN HUNDRED... AND UH... FIVE...?

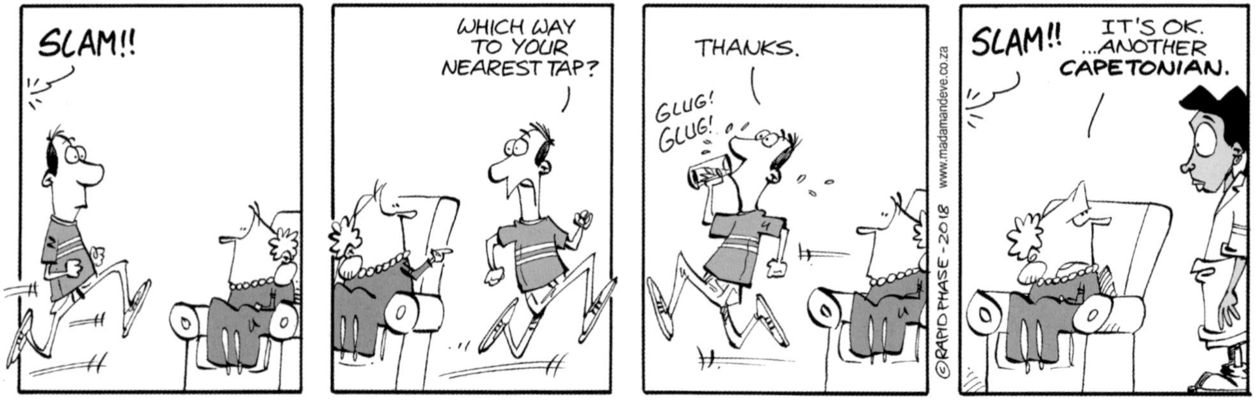
SLAM!!
WHICH WAY TO YOUR NEAREST TAP?
THANKS.
GLUG! GLUG!
©RAPID PHASE-2018
www.madamandeve.co.za
SLAM!!
IT'S OK. ...ANOTHER **CAPETONIAN.**

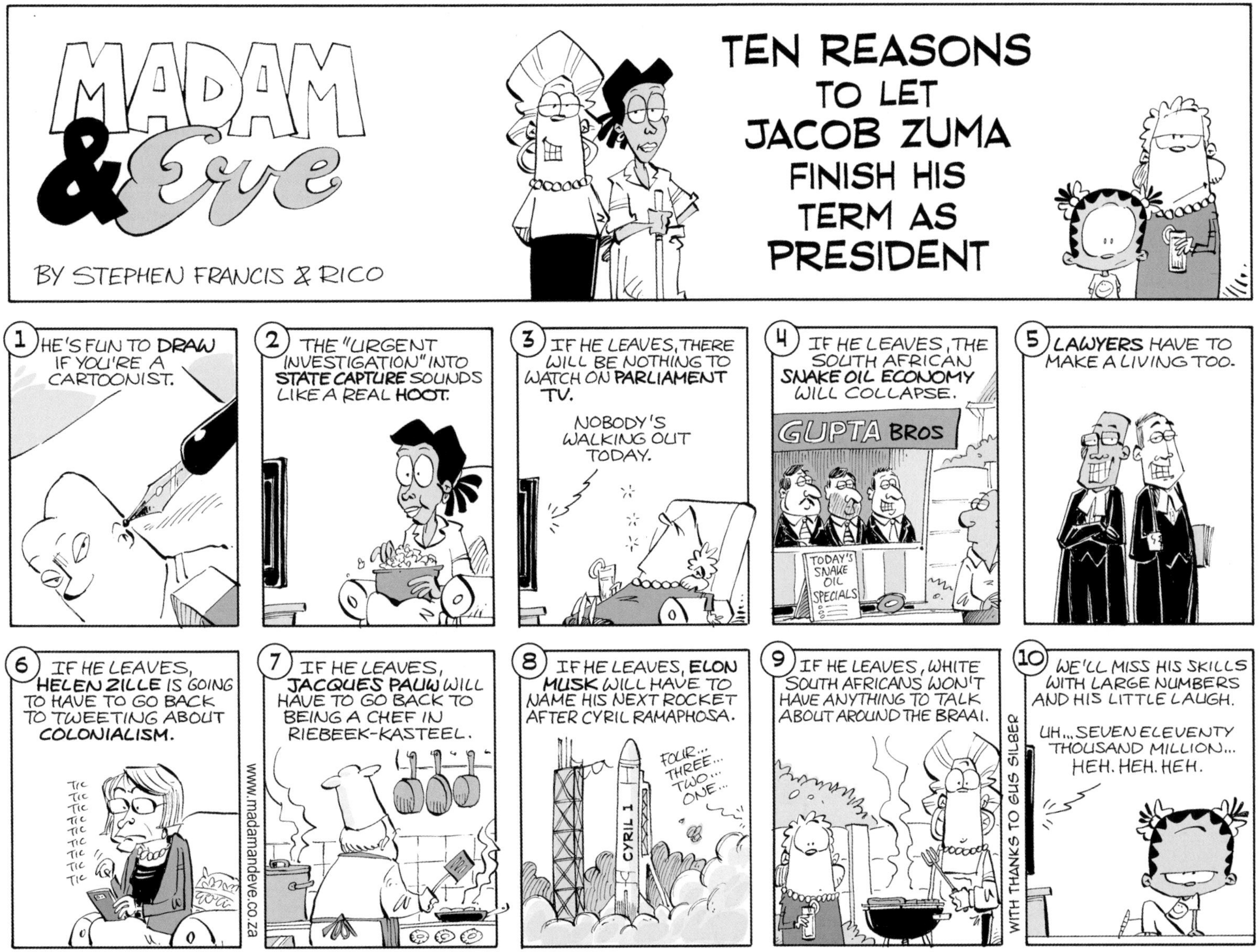
MADAM & Eve
BY STEPHEN FRANCIS & RICO
TEN REASONS TO LET JACOB ZUMA FINISH HIS TERM AS PRESIDENT
1 HE'S FUN TO DRAW IF YOU'RE A CARTOONIST.
2 THE "URGENT INVESTIGATION" INTO STATE CAPTURE SOUNDS LIKE A REAL HOOT.
3 IF HE LEAVES, THERE WILL BE NOTHING TO WATCH ON PARLIAMENT TV.
NOBODY'S WALKING OUT TODAY.
4 IF HE LEAVES, THE SOUTH AFRICAN SNAKE OIL ECONOMY WILL COLLAPSE.
GUPTA BROS
TODAY'S SNAKE OIL SPECIALS
5 LAWYERS HAVE TO MAKE A LIVING TOO.
6 IF HE LEAVES, HELEN ZILLE IS GOING TO HAVE TO GO BACK TO TWEETING ABOUT COLONIALISM.
TIC TIC TIC TIC TIC TIC TIC TIC TIC
www.madamandeve.co.za
7 IF HE LEAVES, JACQUES PAUW WILL HAVE TO GO BACK TO BEING A CHEF IN RIEBEEK-KASTEEL.
8 IF HE LEAVES, ELON MUSK WILL HAVE TO NAME HIS NEXT ROCKET AFTER CYRIL RAMAPHOSA.
FOUR... THREE... TWO... ONE...
CYRIL 1
9 IF HE LEAVES, WHITE SOUTH AFRICANS WON'T HAVE ANYTHING TO TALK ABOUT AROUND THE BRAAI.
WITH THANKS TO GUS SILBER
10 WE'LL MISS HIS SKILLS WITH LARGE NUMBERS AND HIS LITTLE LAUGH.
UH... SEVEN ELEVENTY THOUSAND MILLION... HEH. HEH. HEH.

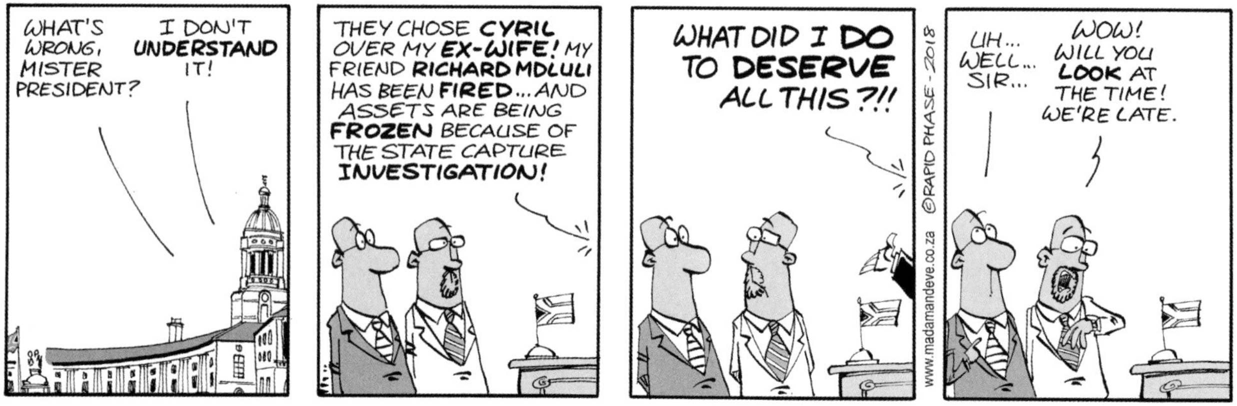
WHAT'S WRONG, MISTER PRESIDENT?
I DON'T UNDERSTAND IT!
THEY CHOSE CYRIL OVER MY EX-WIFE! MY FRIEND RICHARD MDLULI HAS BEEN FIRED... AND ASSETS ARE BEING FROZEN BECAUSE OF THE STATE CAPTURE INVESTIGATION!
WHAT DID I DO TO DESERVE ALL THIS?!!
©RAPID PHASE-2018
www.madamandeve.co.za
UH... WELL... SIR...
WOW! WILL YOU LOOK AT THE TIME! WE'RE LATE.

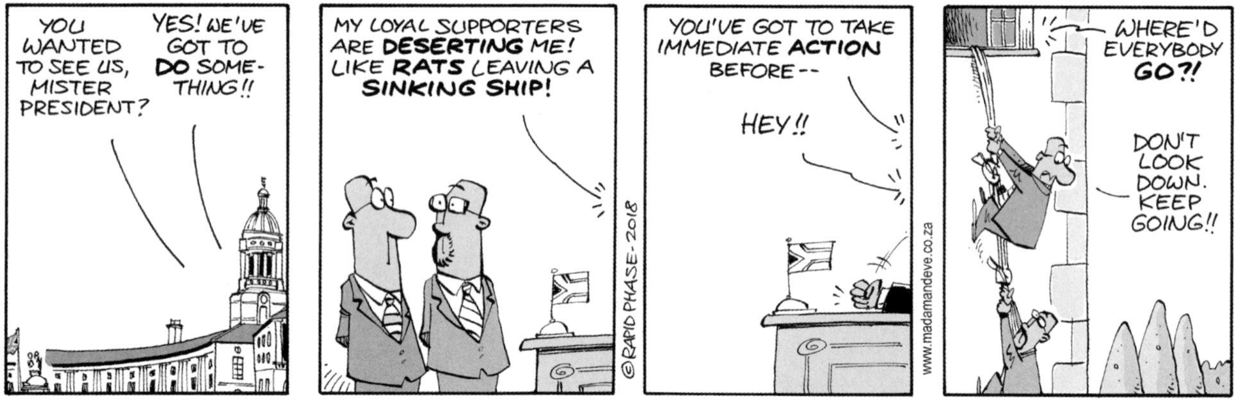
YOU WANTED TO SEE US, MISTER PRESIDENT?
YES! WE'VE GOT TO DO SOME-THING!!
MY LOYAL SUPPORTERS ARE DESERTING ME! LIKE RATS LEAVING A SINKING SHIP!
©RAPID PHASE-2018
YOU'VE GOT TO TAKE IMMEDIATE ACTION BEFORE--
HEY!!
www.madamandeve.co.za
WHERE'D EVERYBODY GO?!
DON'T LOOK DOWN. KEEP GOING!!

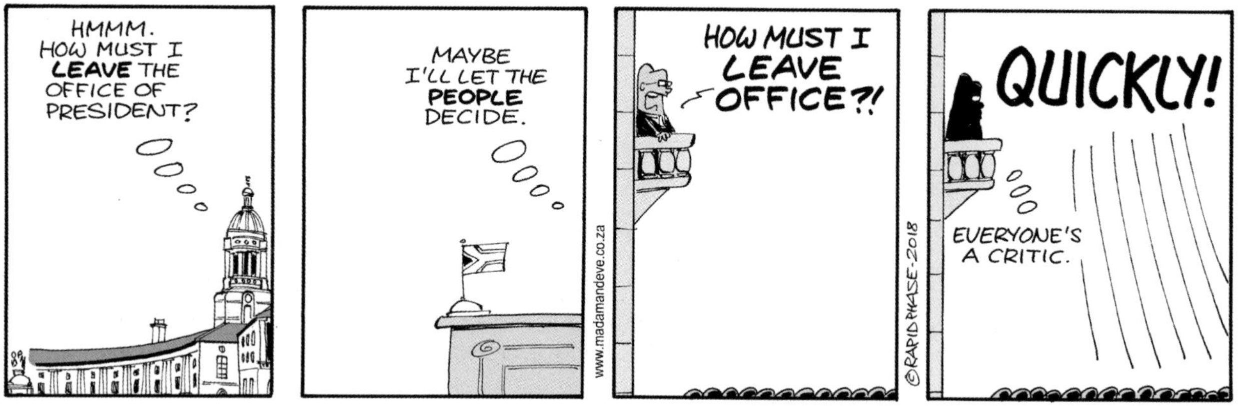
HMMM. HOW MUST I LEAVE THE OFFICE OF PRESIDENT?
MAYBE I'LL LET THE PEOPLE DECIDE.
www.madamandeve.co.za
HOW MUST I LEAVE OFFICE?!
©RAPID PHASE-2018
QUICKLY!
EVERYONE'S A CRITIC.

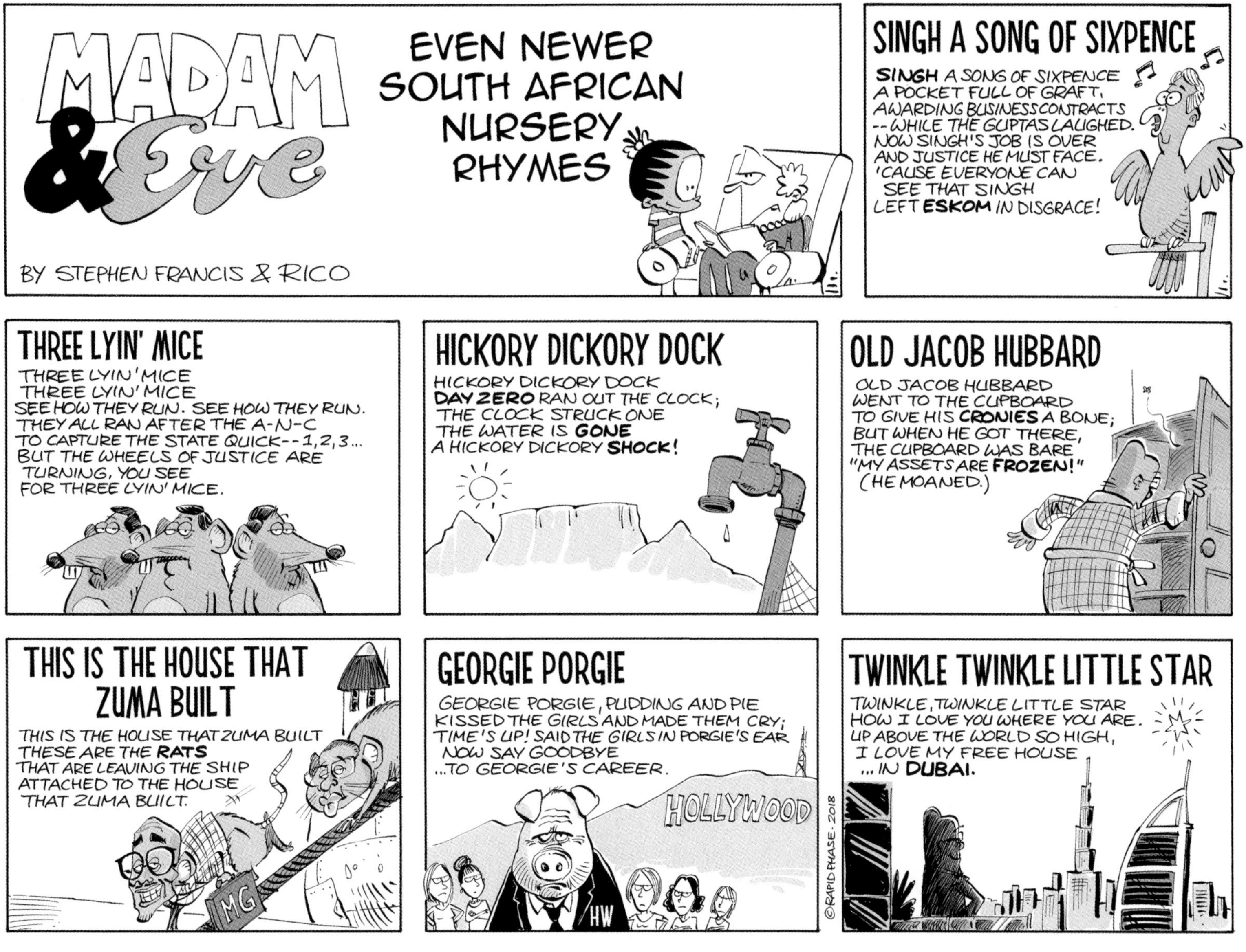
MADAM & Eve
EVEN NEWER SOUTH AFRICAN NURSERY RHYMES
BY STEPHEN FRANCIS & RICO
SINGH A SONG OF SIXPENCE
SINGH A SONG OF SIXPENCE A POCKET FULL OF GRAFT, AWARDING BUSINESS CONTRACTS --WHILE THE GUPTAS LAUGHED. NOW SINGH'S JOB IS OVER AND JUSTICE HE MUST FACE. 'CAUSE EVERYONE CAN SEE THAT SINGH LEFT ESKOM IN DISGRACE!
THREE LYIN' MICE
THREE LYIN' MICE THREE LYIN' MICE SEE HOW THEY RUN. SEE HOW THEY RUN. THEY ALL RAN AFTER THE A-N-C TO CAPTURE THE STATE QUICK--1,2,3... BUT THE WHEELS OF JUSTICE ARE TURNING, YOU SEE FOR THREE LYIN' MICE.
HICKORY DICKORY DOCK
HICKORY DICKORY DOCK DAY ZERO RAN OUT THE CLOCK; THE CLOCK STRUCK ONE THE WATER IS GONE A HICKORY DICKORY SHOCK!
OLD JACOB HUBBARD
OLD JACOB HUBBARD WENT TO THE CUPBOARD TO GIVE HIS CRONIES A BONE; BUT WHEN HE GOT THERE, THE CUPBOARD WAS BARE "MY ASSETS ARE FROZEN!" (HE MOANED.)
THIS IS THE HOUSE THAT ZUMA BUILT
THIS IS THE HOUSE THAT ZUMA BUILT THESE ARE THE RATS THAT ARE LEAVING THE SHIP ATTACHED TO THE HOUSE THAT ZUMA BUILT.
MG
GEORGIE PORGIE
GEORGIE PORGIE, PUDDING AND PIE KISSED THE GIRLS AND MADE THEM CRY; TIME'S UP! SAID THE GIRLS IN PORGIE'S EAR NOW SAY GOODBYE ...TO GEORGIE'S CAREER.
HOLLYWOOD
HW
©RAPID PHASE · 2018
TWINKLE TWINKLE LITTLE STAR
TWINKLE, TWINKLE LITTLE STAR HOW I LOVE YOU WHERE YOU ARE. UP ABOVE THE WORLD SO HIGH, I LOVE MY FREE HOUSE ... IN DUBAI.

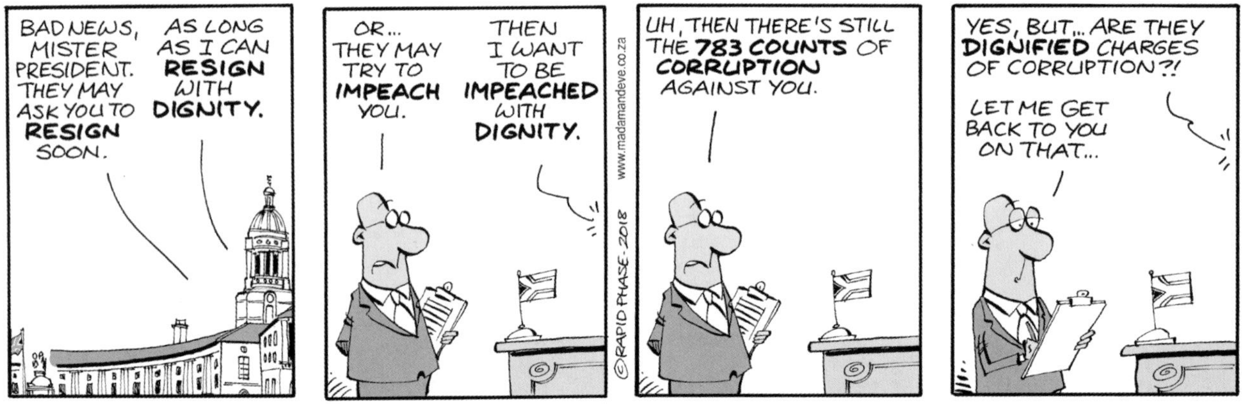
BAD NEWS, MISTER PRESIDENT. THEY MAY ASK YOU TO **RESIGN** SOON.
AS LONG AS I CAN **RESIGN** WITH **DIGNITY**.
OR... THEY MAY TRY TO **IMPEACH** YOU.
THEN I WANT TO BE **IMPEACHED** WITH **DIGNITY**.
www.madamandeve.co.za
©RAPID PHASE-2018
UH, THEN THERE'S STILL THE **783 COUNTS** OF **CORRUPTION** AGAINST YOU.
YES, BUT... ARE THEY **DIGNIFIED** CHARGES OF CORRUPTION?!
LET ME GET BACK TO YOU ON THAT...

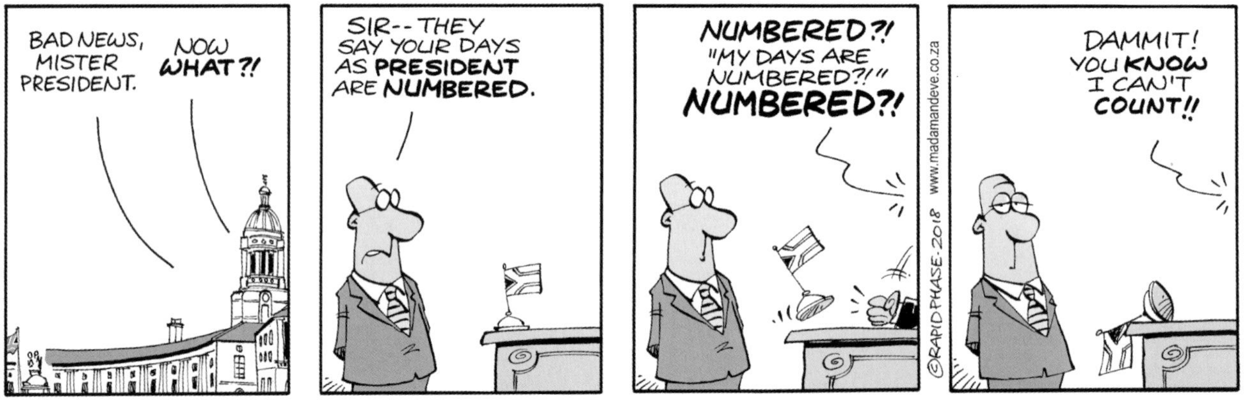
BAD NEWS, MISTER PRESIDENT.
NOW **WHAT**?!
SIR--THEY SAY YOUR DAYS AS **PRESIDENT** ARE **NUMBERED**.
NUMBERED?! "MY DAYS ARE NUMBERED?!" **NUMBERED?!**
www.madamandeve.co.za
©RAPID PHASE-2018
DAMMIT! YOU **KNOW** I CAN'T **COUNT!!**

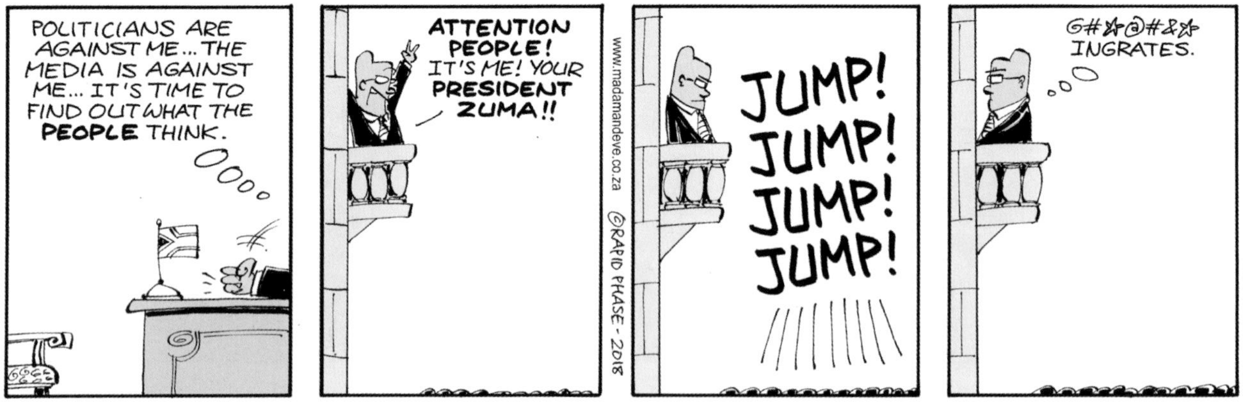
POLITICIANS ARE AGAINST ME... THE MEDIA IS AGAINST ME... IT'S TIME TO FIND OUT WHAT THE **PEOPLE** THINK.
ATTENTION PEOPLE! IT'S ME! YOUR **PRESIDENT ZUMA!!**
www.madamandeve.co.za
©RAPID PHASE-2018
JUMP! JUMP! JUMP! JUMP!
G#✩@#&✩ INGRATES.

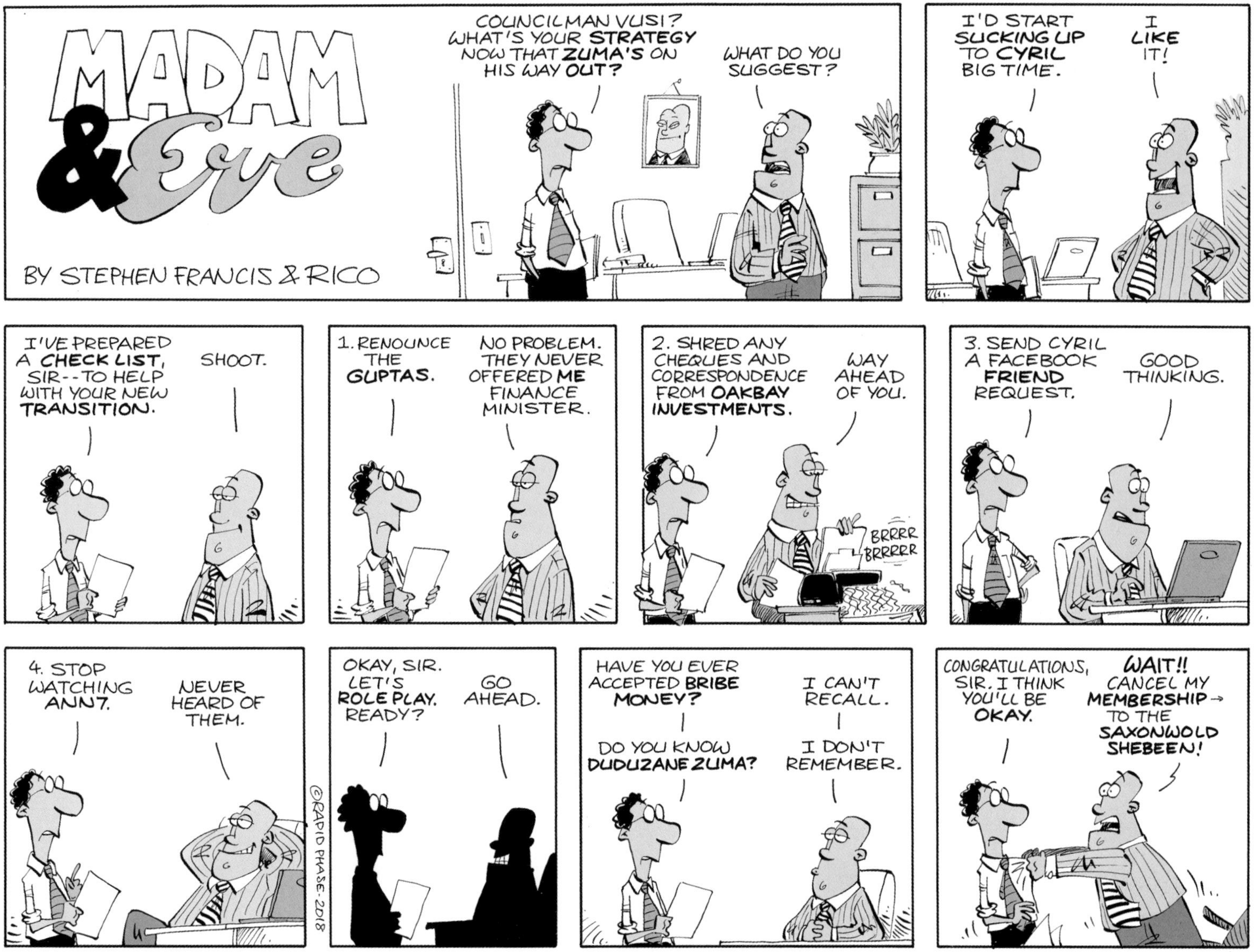
MADAM & Eve
BY STEPHEN FRANCIS & RICO
COUNCILMAN VUSI? WHAT'S YOUR STRATEGY NOW THAT ZUMA'S ON HIS WAY OUT?
WHAT DO YOU SUGGEST?
I'D START SUCKING UP TO CYRIL BIG TIME.
I LIKE IT!
I'VE PREPARED A CHECK LIST, SIR--TO HELP WITH YOUR NEW TRANSITION.
SHOOT.
1. RENOUNCE THE GUPTAS.
NO PROBLEM. THEY NEVER OFFERED ME FINANCE MINISTER.
2. SHRED ANY CHEQUES AND CORRESPONDENCE FROM OAKBAY INVESTMENTS.
WAY AHEAD OF YOU.
BRRRR BRRRRR
3. SEND CYRIL A FACEBOOK FRIEND REQUEST.
GOOD THINKING.
4. STOP WATCHING ANN7.
NEVER HEARD OF THEM.
©RAPID PHASE·2018
OKAY, SIR. LET'S ROLE PLAY. READY?
GO AHEAD.
HAVE YOU EVER ACCEPTED BRIBE MONEY?
I CAN'T RECALL.
DO YOU KNOW DUDUZANE ZUMA?
I DON'T REMEMBER.
CONGRATULATIONS, SIR. I THINK YOU'LL BE OKAY.
WAIT!! CANCEL MY MEMBERSHIP TO THE SAXONWOLD SHEBEEN!

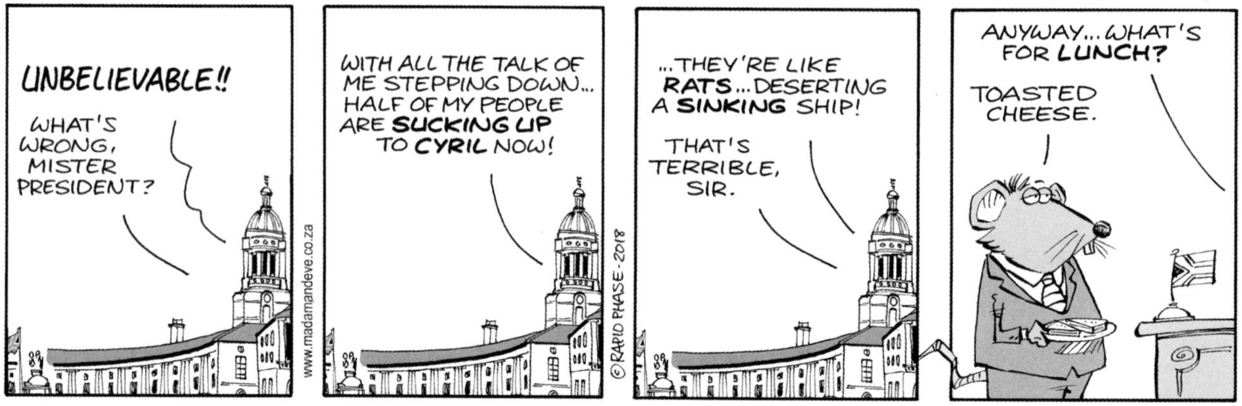
UNBELIEVABLE!!
WHAT'S WRONG, MISTER PRESIDENT?
WITH ALL THE TALK OF ME STEPPING DOWN... HALF OF MY PEOPLE ARE **SUCKING UP** TO **CYRIL** NOW!
...THEY'RE LIKE **RATS**...DESERTING A **SINKING** SHIP!
THAT'S TERRIBLE, SIR.
ANYWAY... WHAT'S FOR **LUNCH?**
TOASTED CHEESE.
www.madamandeve.co.za
©RAPID PHASE-2018

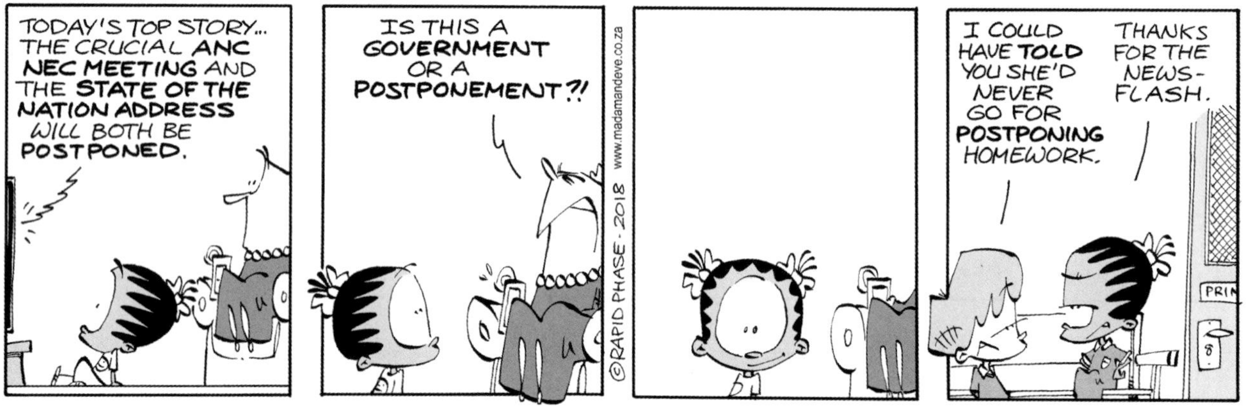
TODAY'S TOP STORY... THE CRUCIAL **ANC NEC MEETING** AND THE **STATE OF THE NATION ADDRESS** WILL BOTH BE **POSTPONED**.
IS THIS A **GOVERNMENT** OR A **POSTPONEMENT?!**
I COULD HAVE **TOLD** YOU SHE'D NEVER GO FOR **POSTPONING** HOMEWORK.
THANKS FOR THE NEWS-FLASH.
PRIN
www.madamandeve.co.za
©RAPID PHASE · 2018

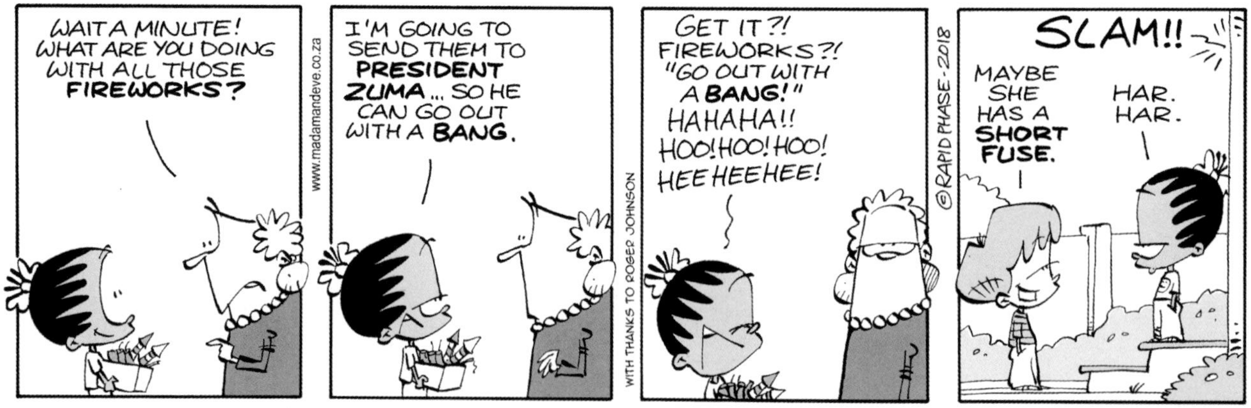
WAIT A MINUTE! WHAT ARE YOU DOING WITH ALL THOSE **FIREWORKS?**
I'M GOING TO SEND THEM TO **PRESIDENT ZUMA**... SO HE CAN GO OUT WITH A **BANG**.
GET IT?! FIREWORKS?! "GO OUT WITH A **BANG!**"
HAHAHA!! HOO! HOO! HOO! HEE HEE HEE!
SLAM!!
MAYBE SHE HAS A **SHORT FUSE.**
HAR. HAR.
www.madamandeve.co.za
WITH THANKS TO ROGER JOHNSON
©RAPID PHASE-2018

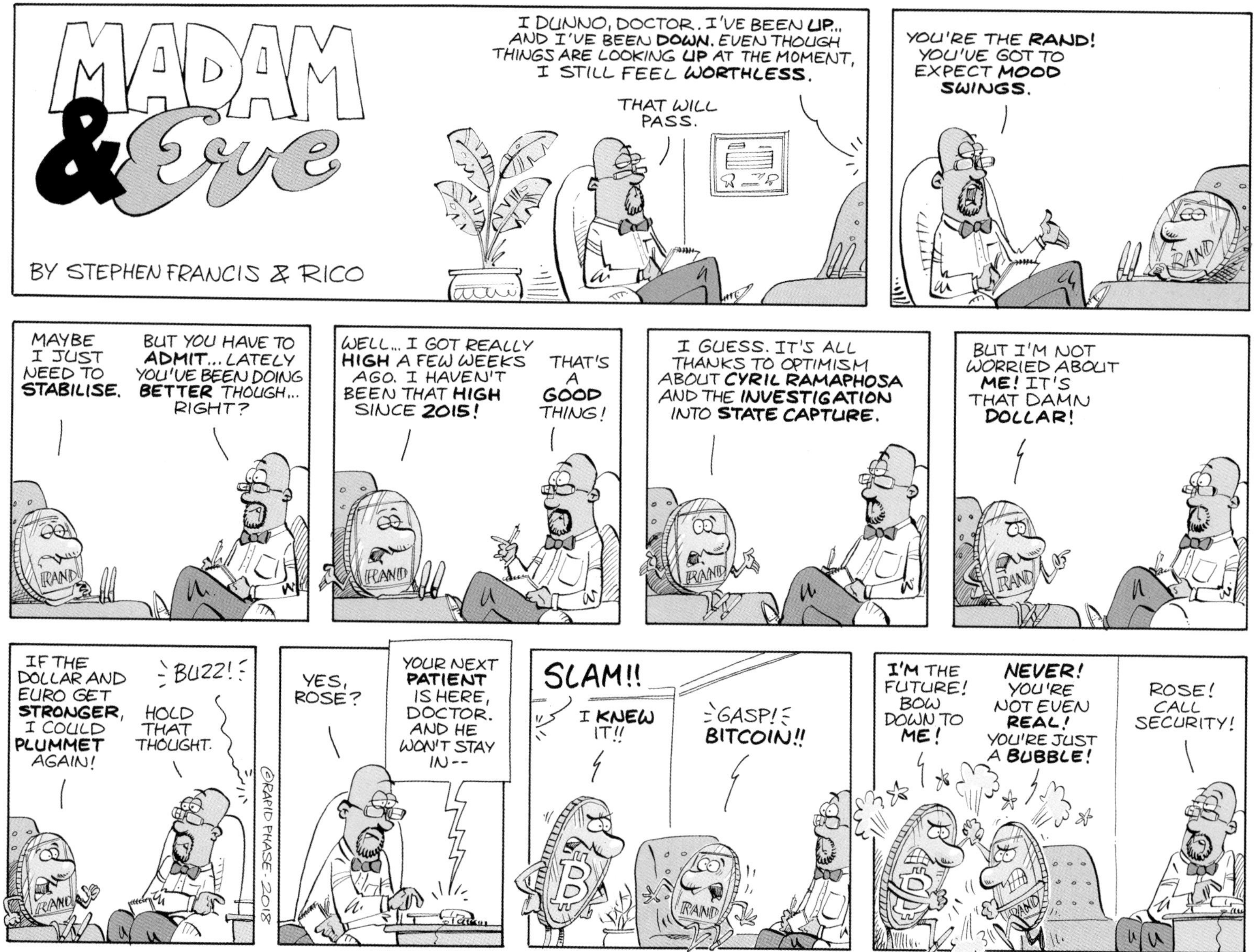
MADAM & Eve
BY STEPHEN FRANCIS & RICO
I DUNNO, DOCTOR. I'VE BEEN **UP**... AND I'VE BEEN **DOWN**. EVEN THOUGH THINGS ARE LOOKING **UP** AT THE MOMENT, I STILL FEEL **WORTHLESS**.
THAT WILL PASS.
YOU'RE THE **RAND**! YOU'VE GOT TO EXPECT **MOOD SWINGS**.
RAND
MAYBE I JUST NEED TO **STABILISE**.
BUT YOU HAVE TO **ADMIT**... LATELY YOU'VE BEEN DOING **BETTER** THOUGH... RIGHT?
RAND
WELL... I GOT REALLY **HIGH** A FEW WEEKS AGO. I HAVEN'T BEEN THAT **HIGH** SINCE **2015**!
THAT'S A **GOOD** THING!
RAND
I GUESS. IT'S ALL THANKS TO OPTIMISM ABOUT **CYRIL RAMAPHOSA** AND THE **INVESTIGATION** INTO **STATE CAPTURE**.
RAND
BUT I'M NOT WORRIED ABOUT **ME**! IT'S THAT DAMN **DOLLAR**!
RAND
IF THE DOLLAR AND EURO GET **STRONGER**, I COULD **PLUMMET** AGAIN!
BUZZ!
HOLD THAT THOUGHT.
RAND
©RAPID PHASE · 2018
YES, ROSE?
YOUR NEXT **PATIENT** IS HERE, DOCTOR. AND HE WON'T STAY IN--
SLAM!!
I **KNEW** IT!!
GASP! **BITCOIN**!!
RAND
I'M THE FUTURE! BOW DOWN TO **ME**!
NEVER! YOU'RE NOT EVEN **REAL**! YOU'RE JUST A **BUBBLE**!
RAND
ROSE! CALL SECURITY!

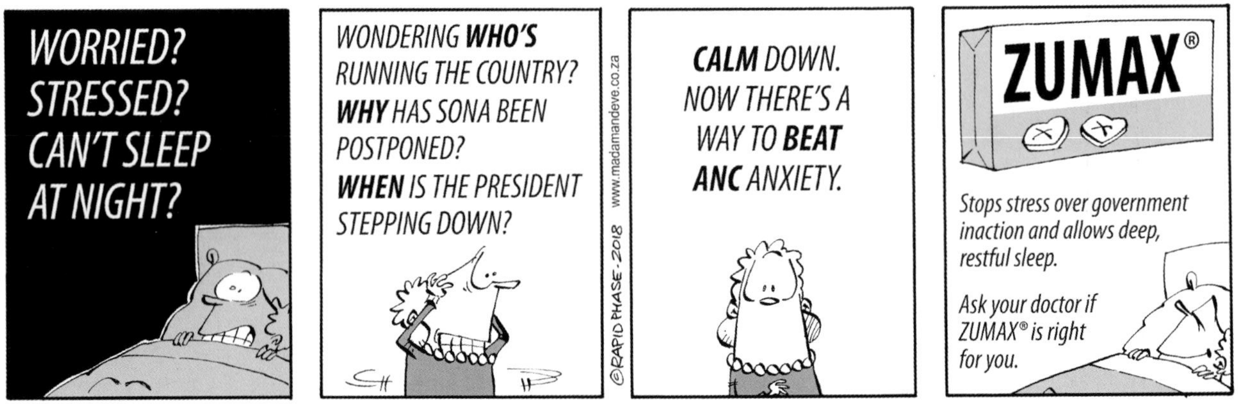
WORRIED? STRESSED? CAN'T SLEEP AT NIGHT?
WONDERING **WHO'S** RUNNING THE COUNTRY? **WHY** HAS SONA BEEN POSTPONED? **WHEN** IS THE PRESIDENT STEPPING DOWN?
©RAPID PHASE-2018 www.madamandeve.co.za
CALM DOWN. NOW THERE'S A WAY TO **BEAT ANC** ANXIETY.
ZUMAX®
Stops stress over government inaction and allows deep, restful sleep.
Ask your doctor if ZUMAX® is right for you.

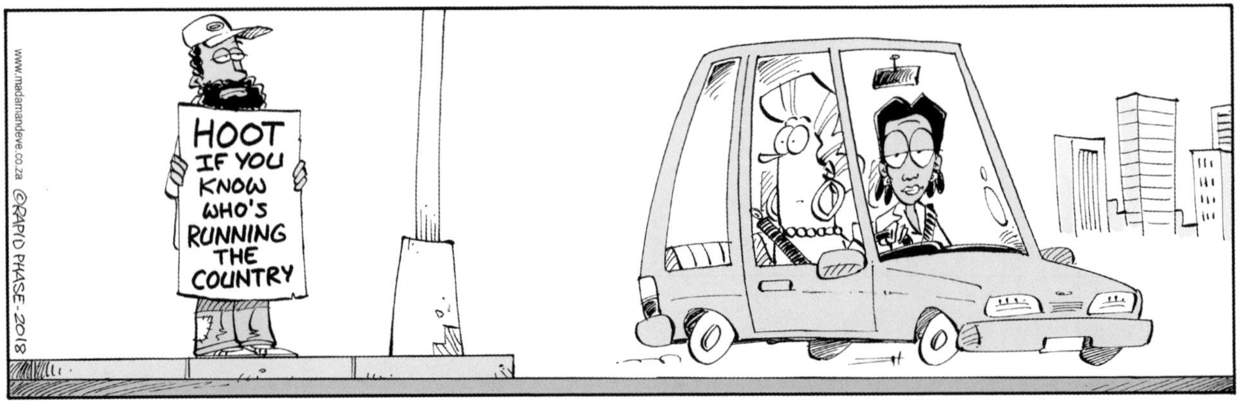
www.madamandeve.co.za ©RAPID PHASE-2018
HOOT IF YOU KNOW WHO'S RUNNING THE COUNTRY

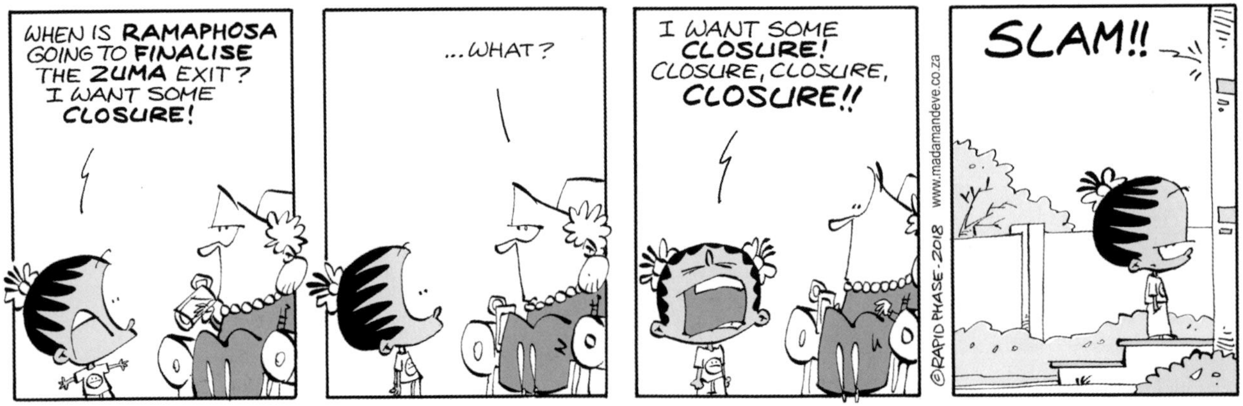
WHEN IS **RAMAPHOSA** GOING TO **FINALISE** THE **ZUMA** EXIT? I WANT SOME **CLOSURE**!
...WHAT?
I WANT SOME **CLOSURE!** CLOSURE, CLOSURE, **CLOSURE!!**
©RAPID PHASE-2018 www.madamandeve.co.za
SLAM!!

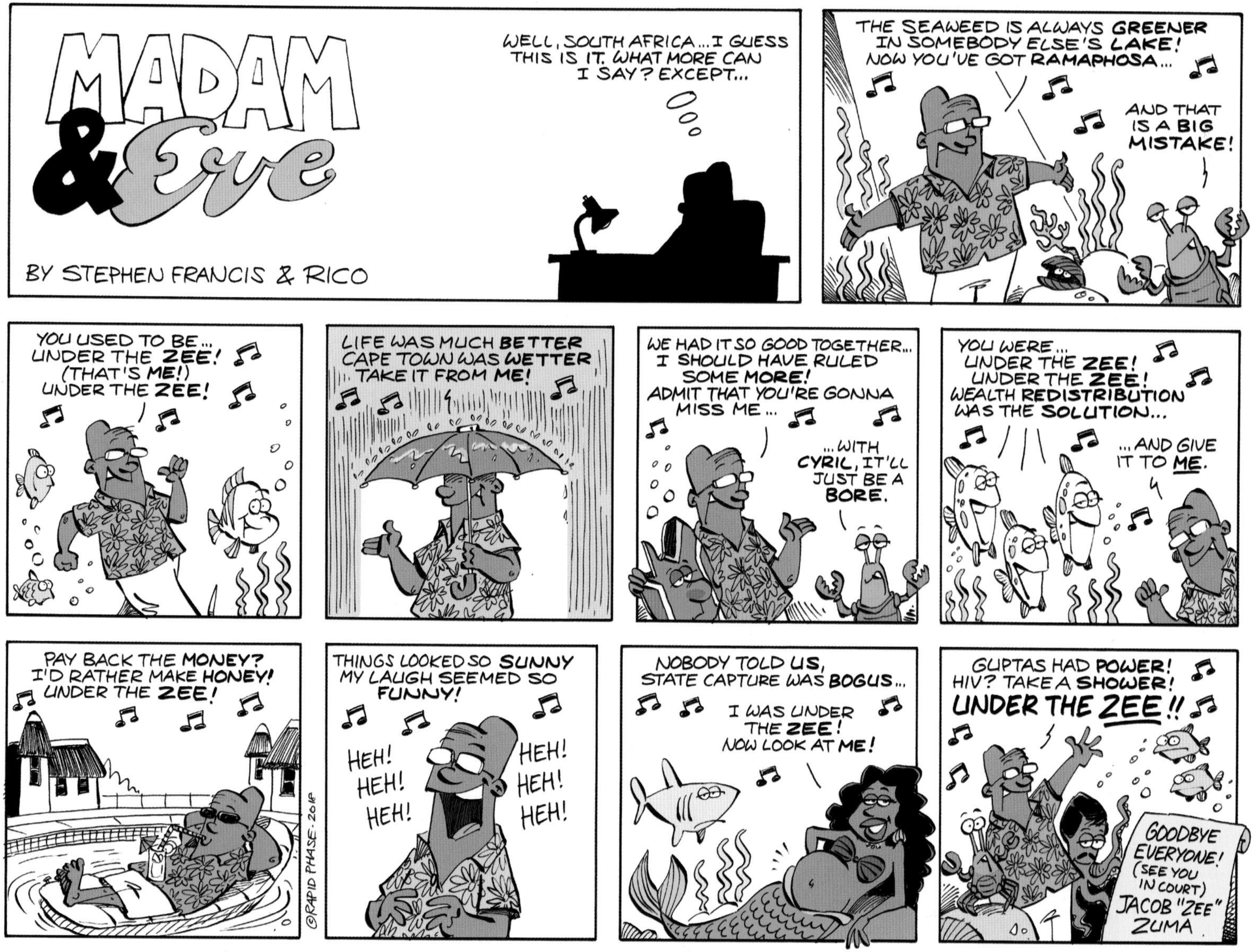
MADAM & Eve
BY STEPHEN FRANCIS & RICO
WELL, SOUTH AFRICA... I GUESS THIS IS IT. WHAT MORE CAN I SAY? EXCEPT...
THE SEAWEED IS ALWAYS GREENER IN SOMEBODY ELSE'S LAKE! NOW YOU'VE GOT RAMAPHOSA...
AND THAT IS A BIG MISTAKE!
YOU USED TO BE... UNDER THE ZEE! (THAT'S ME!) UNDER THE ZEE!
LIFE WAS MUCH BETTER CAPE TOWN WAS WETTER TAKE IT FROM ME!
WE HAD IT SO GOOD TOGETHER... I SHOULD HAVE RULED SOME MORE! ADMIT THAT YOU'RE GONNA MISS ME...
...WITH CYRIL, IT'LL JUST BE A BORE.
YOU WERE... UNDER THE ZEE! UNDER THE ZEE! WEALTH REDISTRIBUTION WAS THE SOLUTION...
...AND GIVE IT TO ME.
PAY BACK THE MONEY? I'D RATHER MAKE HONEY! UNDER THE ZEE!
©RAPID PHASE · 2018
THINGS LOOKED SO SUNNY MY LAUGH SEEMED SO FUNNY!
HEH! HEH! HEH!
HEH! HEH! HEH!
NOBODY TOLD US, STATE CAPTURE WAS BOGUS...
I WAS UNDER THE ZEE! NOW LOOK AT ME!
GUPTAS HAD POWER! HIV? TAKE A SHOWER! UNDER THE ZEE!!
GOODBYE EVERYONE! (SEE YOU IN COURT) JACOB "ZEE" ZUMA

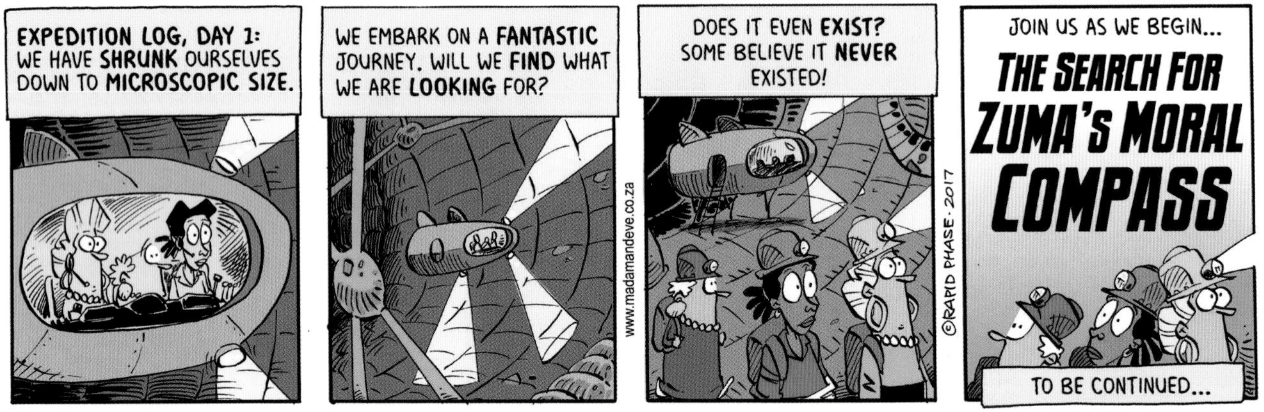
EXPEDITION LOG, DAY 1: WE HAVE SHRUNK OURSELVES DOWN TO MICROSCOPIC SIZE.
WE EMBARK ON A FANTASTIC JOURNEY. WILL WE FIND WHAT WE ARE LOOKING FOR?
www.madamandeve.co.za
DOES IT EVEN EXIST? SOME BELIEVE IT NEVER EXISTED!
©RAPID PHASE-2017
JOIN US AS WE BEGIN...
THE SEARCH FOR ZUMA's MORAL COMPASS
TO BE CONTINUED...

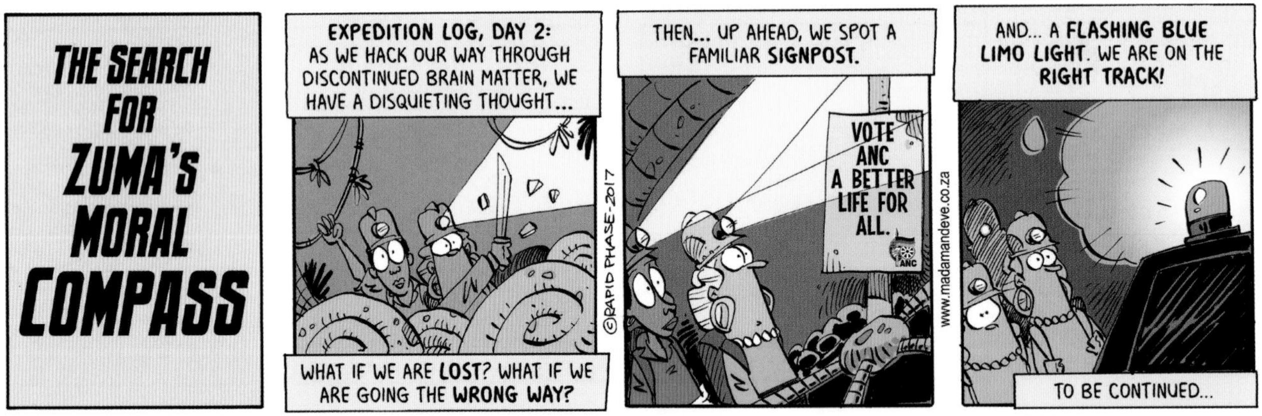
THE SEARCH FOR ZUMA's MORAL COMPASS
EXPEDITION LOG, DAY 2: AS WE HACK OUR WAY THROUGH DISCONTINUED BRAIN MATTER, WE HAVE A DISQUIETING THOUGHT...
WHAT IF WE ARE LOST? WHAT IF WE ARE GOING THE WRONG WAY?
©RAPID PHASE-2017
THEN... UP AHEAD, WE SPOT A FAMILIAR SIGNPOST.
VOTE ANC A BETTER LIFE FOR ALL.
ANC
www.madamandeve.co.za
AND... A FLASHING BLUE LIMO LIGHT. WE ARE ON THE RIGHT TRACK!
TO BE CONTINUED...

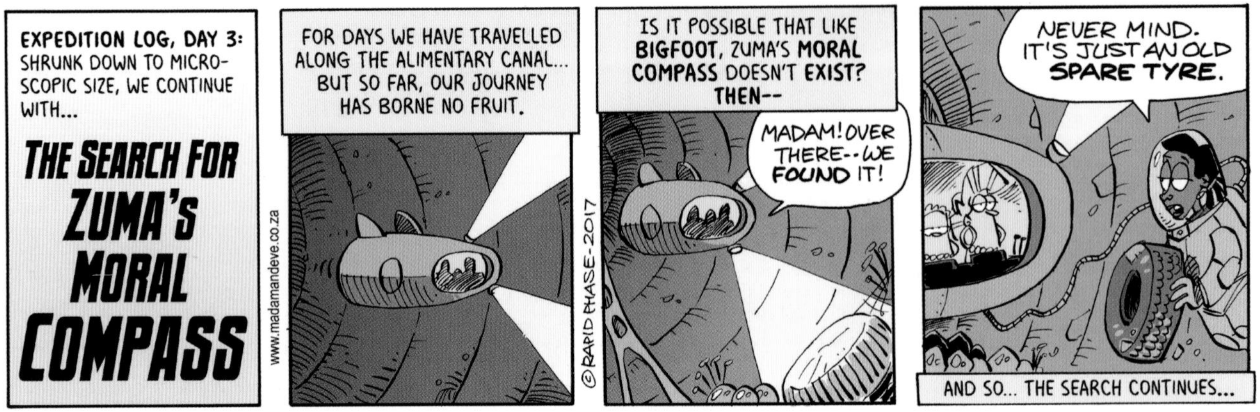
EXPEDITION LOG, DAY 3: SHRUNK DOWN TO MICRO-SCOPIC SIZE, WE CONTINUE WITH...
THE SEARCH FOR ZUMA's MORAL COMPASS
www.madamandeve.co.za
FOR DAYS WE HAVE TRAVELLED ALONG THE ALIMENTARY CANAL... BUT SO FAR, OUR JOURNEY HAS BORNE NO FRUIT.
©RAPID PHASE-2017
IS IT POSSIBLE THAT LIKE BIGFOOT, ZUMA'S MORAL COMPASS DOESN'T EXIST? THEN--
MADAM! OVER THERE--WE FOUND IT!
NEVER MIND. IT'S JUST AN OLD SPARE TYRE.
AND SO... THE SEARCH CONTINUES...

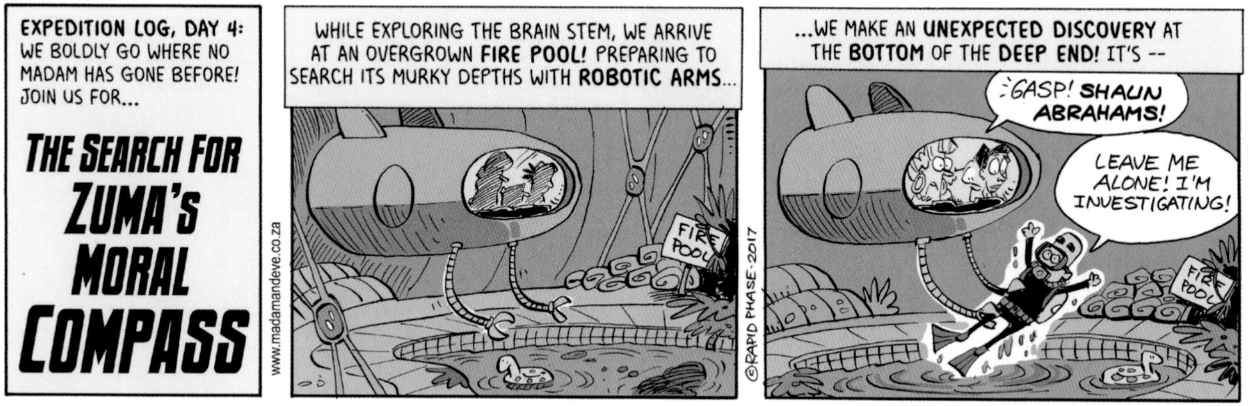
EXPEDITION LOG, DAY 4: WE BOLDLY GO WHERE NO MADAM HAS GONE BEFORE! JOIN US FOR...
THE SEARCH FOR ZUMA's MORAL COMPASS
WHILE EXPLORING THE BRAIN STEM, WE ARRIVE AT AN OVERGROWN FIRE POOL! PREPARING TO SEARCH ITS MURKY DEPTHS WITH ROBOTIC ARMS...
www.madamandeve.co.za
FIRE POOL
©RAPID PHASE·2017
...WE MAKE AN UNEXPECTED DISCOVERY AT THE BOTTOM OF THE DEEP END! IT'S --
GASP! SHAUN ABRAHAMS!
LEAVE ME ALONE! I'M INVESTIGATING!
FIRE POOL

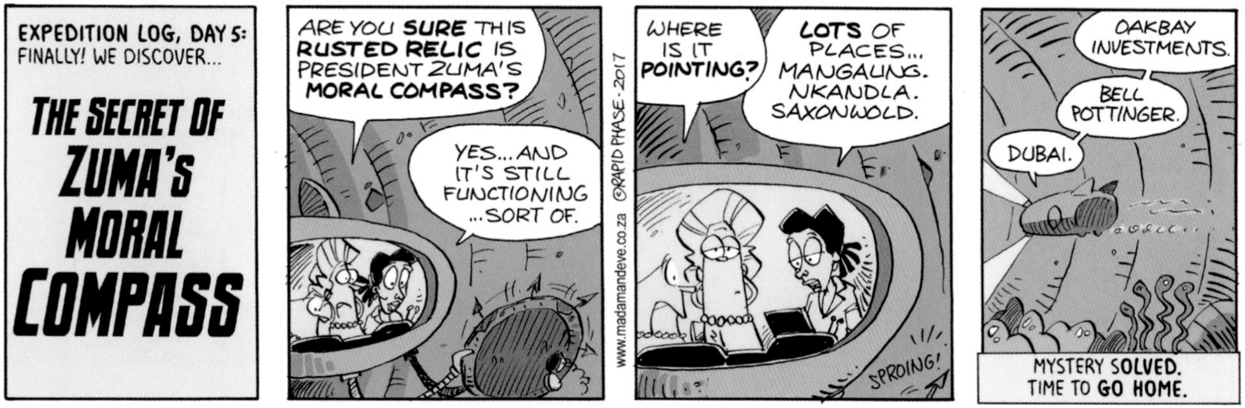
EXPEDITION LOG, DAY 5: FINALLY! WE DISCOVER...
THE SECRET OF ZUMA's MORAL COMPASS
ARE YOU SURE THIS RUSTED RELIC IS PRESIDENT ZUMA'S MORAL COMPASS?
YES... AND IT'S STILL FUNCTIONING ...SORT OF.
www.madamandeve.co.za ©RAPID PHASE·2017
WHERE IS IT POINTING?
LOTS OF PLACES... MANGAUNG. NKANDLA. SAXONWOLD.
SPROING!
OAKBAY INVESTMENTS.
BELL POTTINGER.
DUBAI.
MYSTERY SOLVED. TIME TO GO HOME.

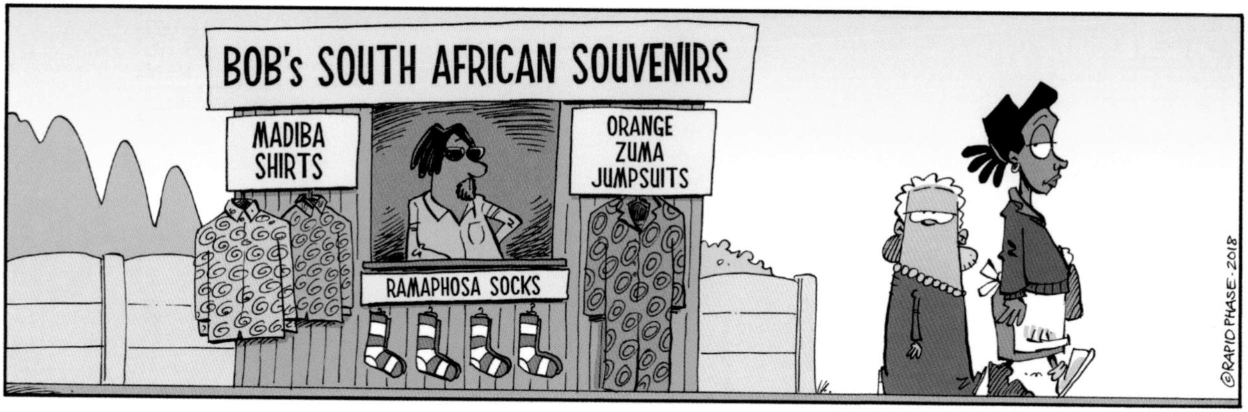
BOB's SOUTH AFRICAN SOUVENIRS
MADIBA SHIRTS
ORANGE ZUMA JUMPSUITS
RAMAPHOSA SOCKS
©RAPID PHASE·2018

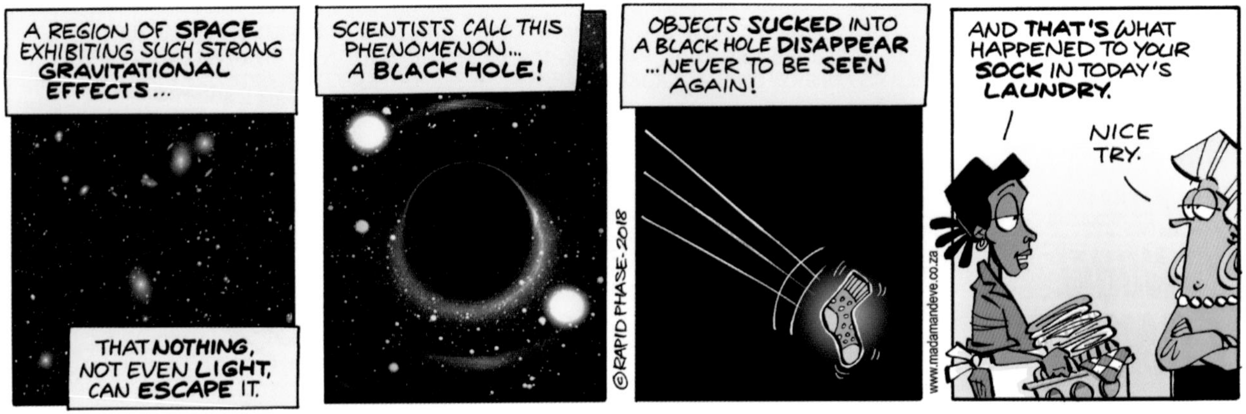
A REGION OF SPACE EXHIBITING SUCH STRONG GRAVITATIONAL EFFECTS...
THAT NOTHING, NOT EVEN LIGHT, CAN ESCAPE IT.
SCIENTISTS CALL THIS PHENOMENON... A BLACK HOLE!
©RAPID PHASE-2018
OBJECTS SUCKED INTO A BLACK HOLE DISAPPEAR ...NEVER TO BE SEEN AGAIN!
www.madamandeve.co.za
AND THAT'S WHAT HAPPENED TO YOUR SOCK IN TODAY'S LAUNDRY.
NICE TRY.

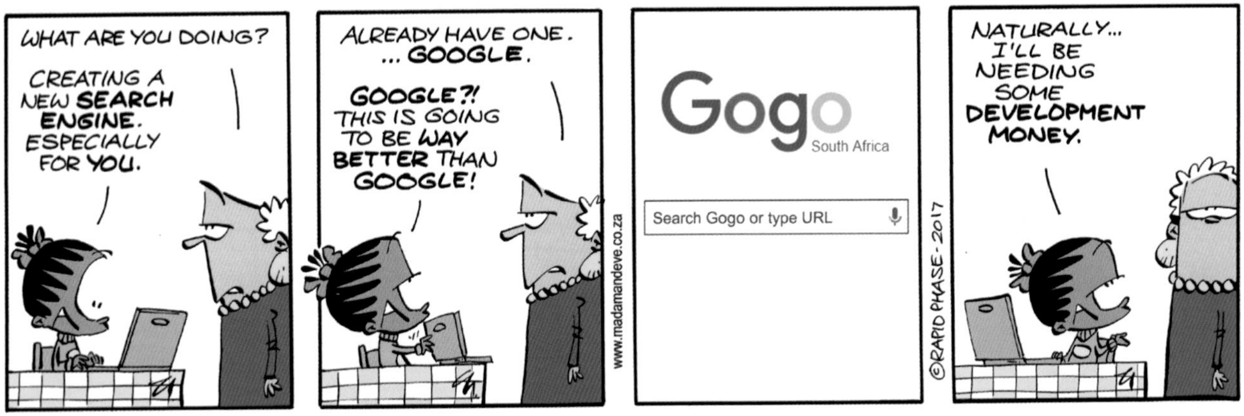
WHAT ARE YOU DOING?
CREATING A NEW SEARCH ENGINE. ESPECIALLY FOR YOU.
ALREADY HAVE ONE. ...GOOGLE.
GOOGLE?! THIS IS GOING TO BE WAY BETTER THAN GOOGLE!
www.madamandeve.co.za
Gogo
South Africa
Search Gogo or type URL
©RAPID PHASE-2017
NATURALLY... I'LL BE NEEDING SOME DEVELOPMENT MONEY.

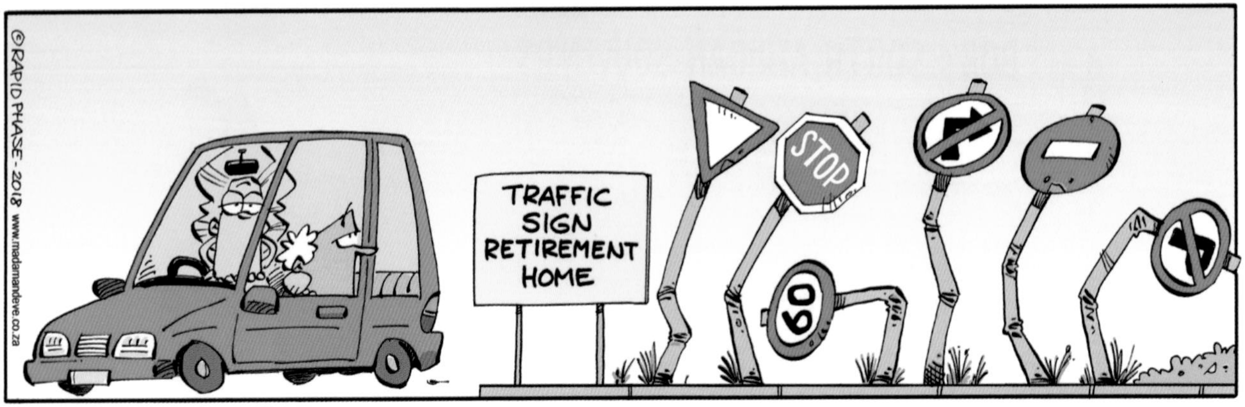
©RAPID PHASE-2018
www.madamandeve.co.za
TRAFFIC SIGN RETIREMENT HOME
STOP
60

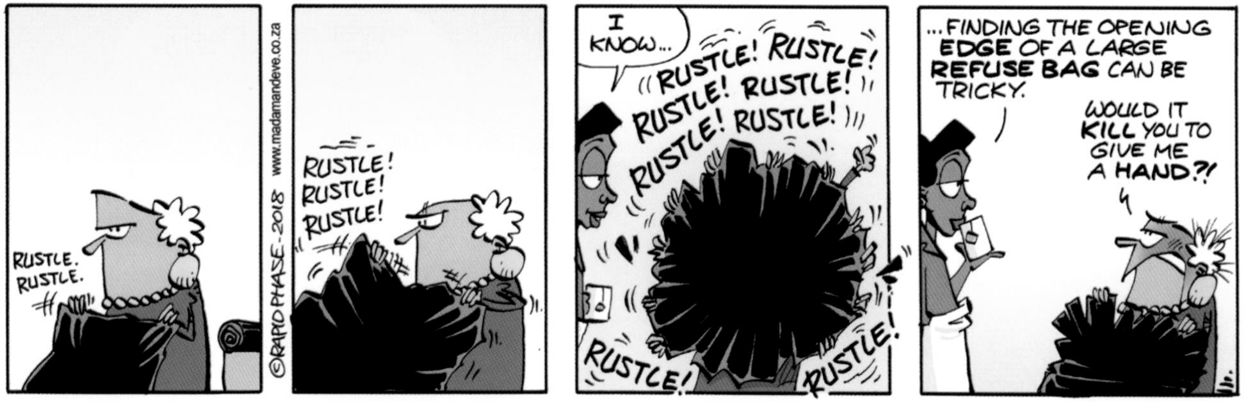
RUSTLE. RUSTLE.
©RAPID PHASE - 2018 www.madamandeve.co.za
RUSTLE! RUSTLE! RUSTLE!
I KNOW...
RUSTLE! RUSTLE! RUSTLE! RUSTLE! RUSTLE! RUSTLE!
RUSTLE! RUSTLE!
...FINDING THE OPENING EDGE OF A LARGE REFUSE BAG CAN BE TRICKY.
WOULD IT KILL YOU TO GIVE ME A HAND?!

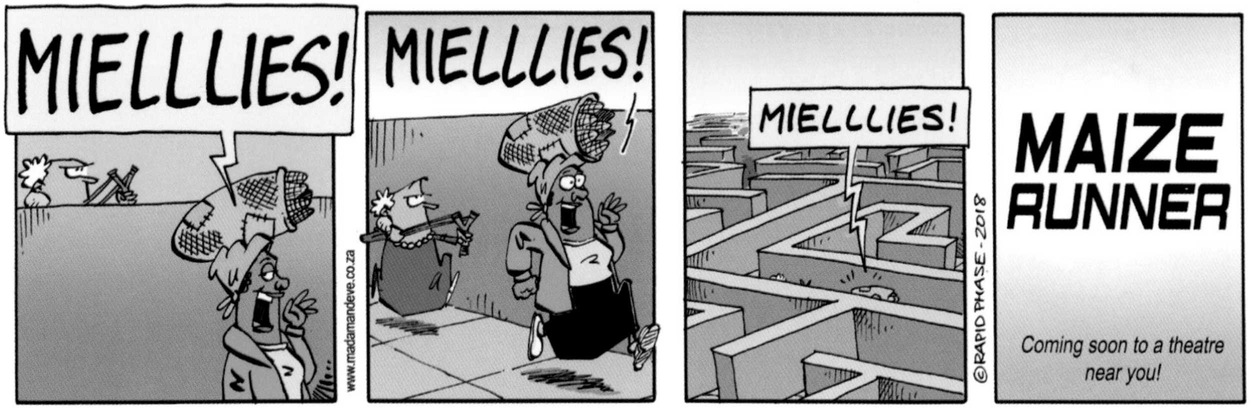
MIELLIES!
www.madamandeve.co.za
MIELLLIES!
MIELLLIES!
©RAPID PHASE - 2018
MAIZE RUNNER
Coming soon to a theatre near you!

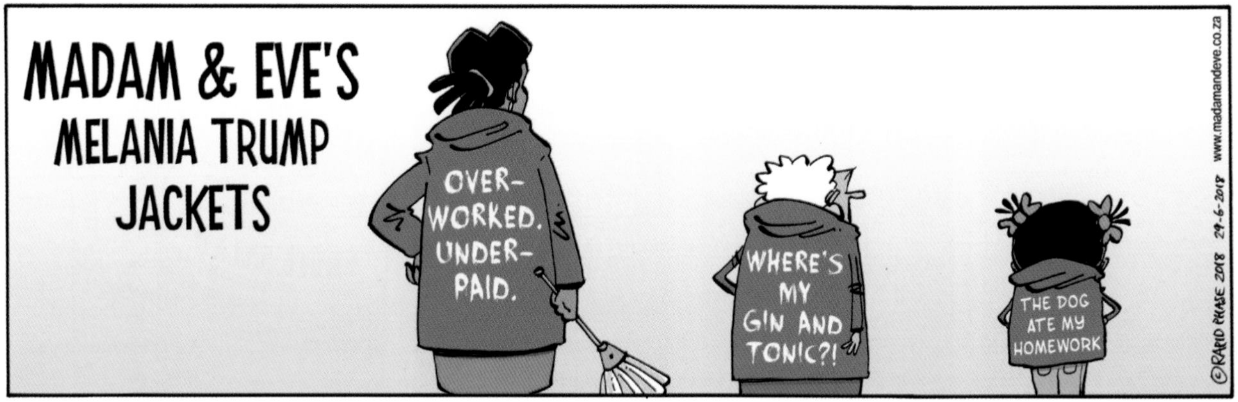
MADAM & EVE'S MELANIA TRUMP JACKETS
OVER-WORKED. UNDER-PAID.
WHERE'S MY GIN AND TONIC?!
THE DOG ATE MY HOMEWORK
©RAPID PHASE 2018 29-6-2018 www.madamandeve.co.za

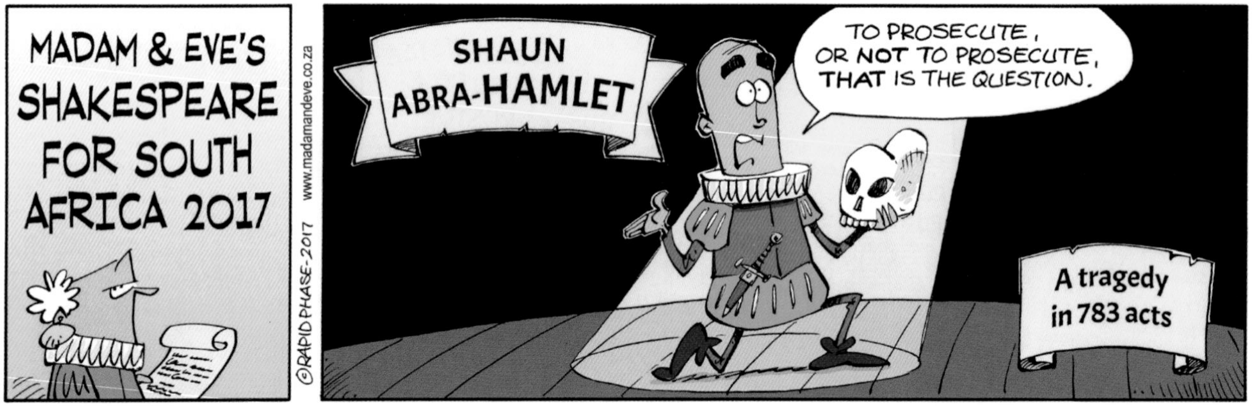
MADAM & EVE'S SHAKESPEARE FOR SOUTH AFRICA 2017
www.madamandeve.co.za
©RAPID PHASE-2017
SHAUN ABRA-HAMLET
TO PROSECUTE, OR NOT TO PROSECUTE, THAT IS THE QUESTION.
A tragedy in 783 acts

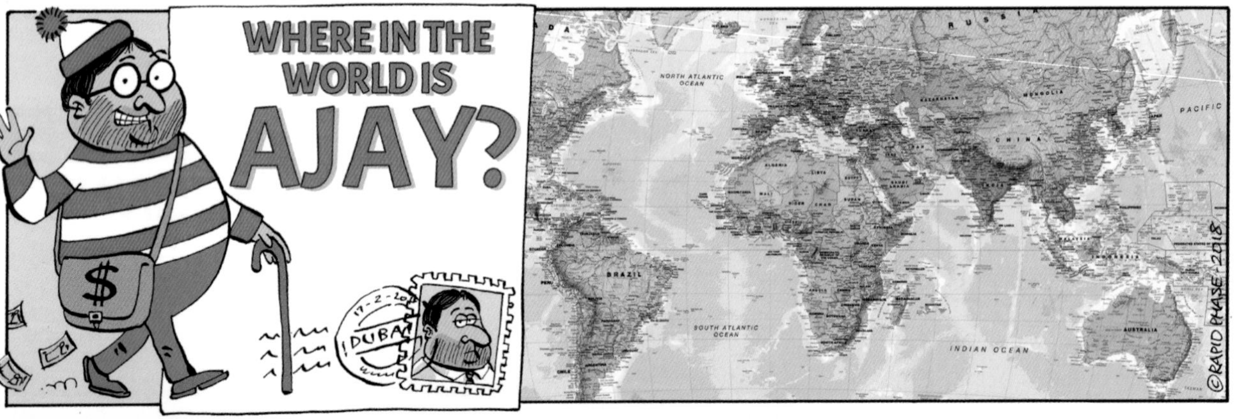
WHERE IN THE WORLD IS AJAY?
DUBAI
INDIAN OCEAN
©RAPID PHASE-2018

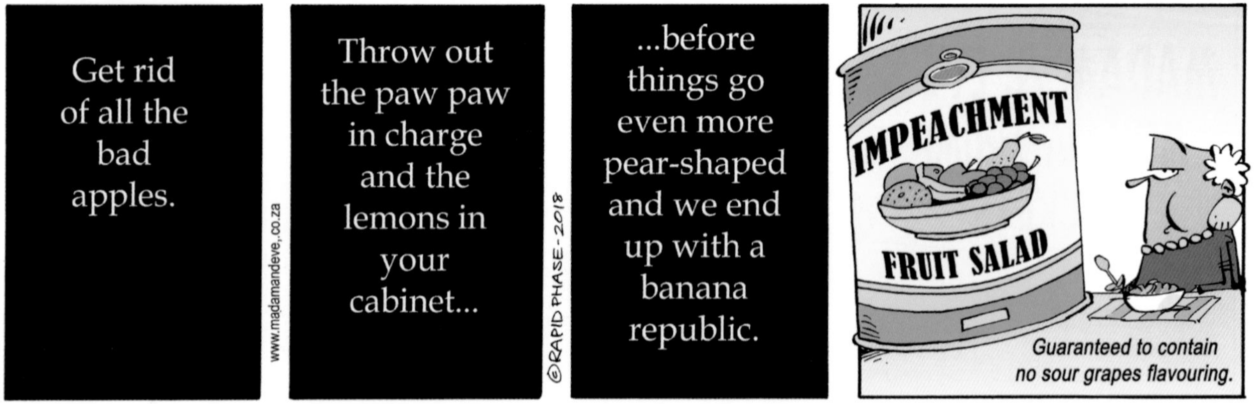
Get rid of all the bad apples.
www.madamandeve.co.za
Throw out the paw paw in charge and the lemons in your cabinet...
©RAPID PHASE-2018
...before things go even more pear-shaped and we end up with a banana republic.
IMPEACHMENT
FRUIT SALAD
Guaranteed to contain no sour grapes flavouring.

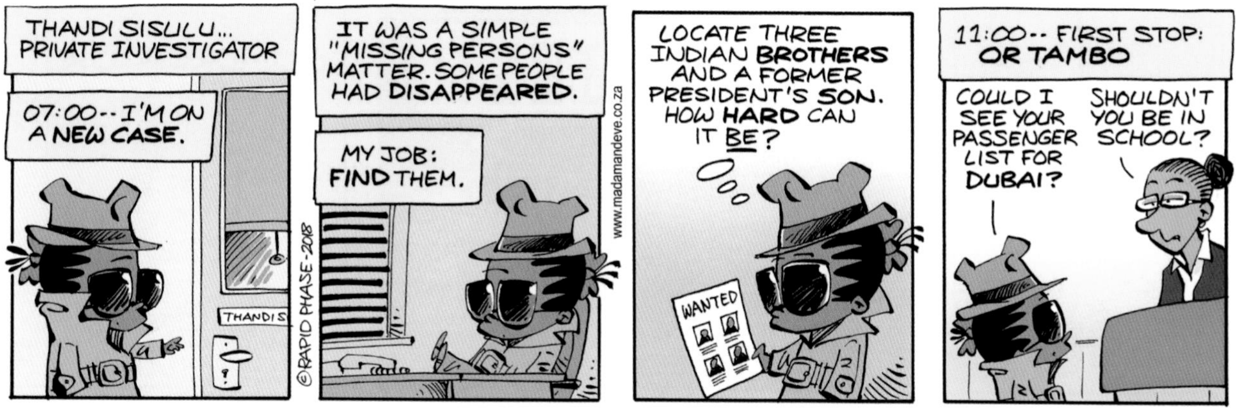
THANDI SISULU...
PRIVATE INVESTIGATOR
07:00-- I'M ON A **NEW CASE**.
THANDI S
©RAPID PHASE-2018
IT WAS A SIMPLE "MISSING PERSONS" MATTER. SOME PEOPLE HAD **DISAPPEARED**.
MY JOB: **FIND** THEM.
www.madamandeve.co.za
LOCATE THREE INDIAN **BROTHERS** AND A FORMER PRESIDENT'S **SON**. HOW **HARD** CAN IT BE?
WANTED
11:00-- FIRST STOP: **OR TAMBO**
COULD I SEE YOUR PASSENGER LIST FOR **DUBAI**?
SHOULDN'T YOU BE IN SCHOOL?

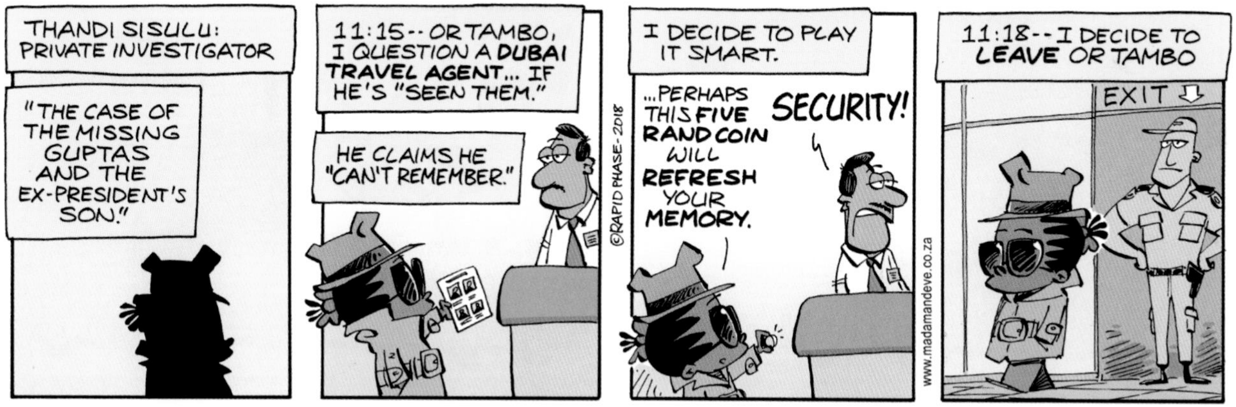
THANDI SISULU:
PRIVATE INVESTIGATOR
"THE CASE OF THE MISSING GUPTAS AND THE EX-PRESIDENT'S SON."
11:15-- OR TAMBO, I QUESTION A **DUBAI TRAVEL AGENT**... IF HE'S "SEEN THEM."
HE CLAIMS HE "CAN'T REMEMBER."
©RAPID PHASE-2018
I DECIDE TO PLAY IT SMART.
...PERHAPS THIS **FIVE RAND COIN** WILL **REFRESH** YOUR **MEMORY**.
SECURITY!
www.madamandeve.co.za
11:18-- I DECIDE TO **LEAVE** OR TAMBO
EXIT

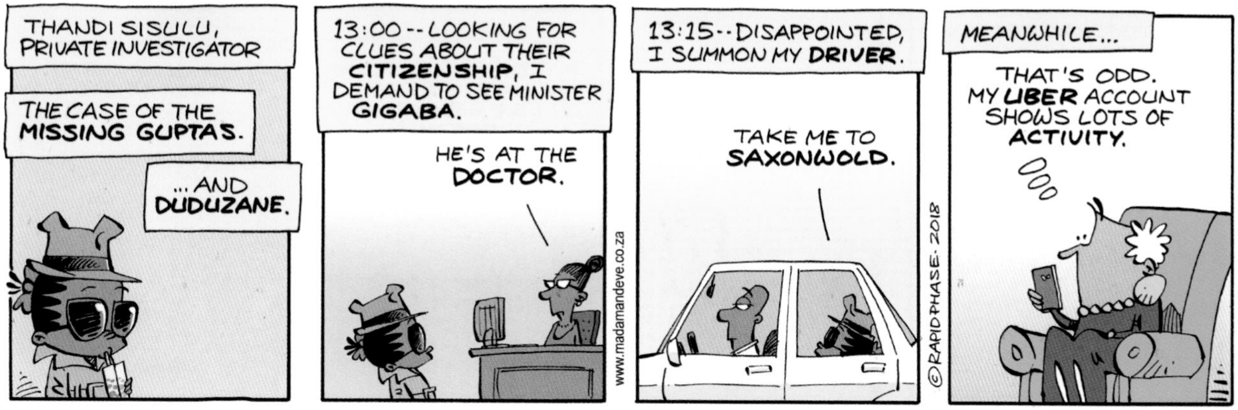
THANDI SISULU,
PRIVATE INVESTIGATOR
THE CASE OF THE **MISSING GUPTAS**.
...AND **DUDUZANE**.
13:00-- LOOKING FOR CLUES ABOUT THEIR **CITIZENSHIP**, I DEMAND TO SEE MINISTER **GIGABA**.
HE'S AT THE **DOCTOR**.
www.madamandeve.co.za
13:15-- DISAPPOINTED, I SUMMON MY **DRIVER**.
TAKE ME TO **SAXONWOLD**.
©RAPID PHASE-2018
MEANWHILE...
THAT'S ODD. MY **UBER** ACCOUNT SHOWS LOTS OF **ACTIVITY**.

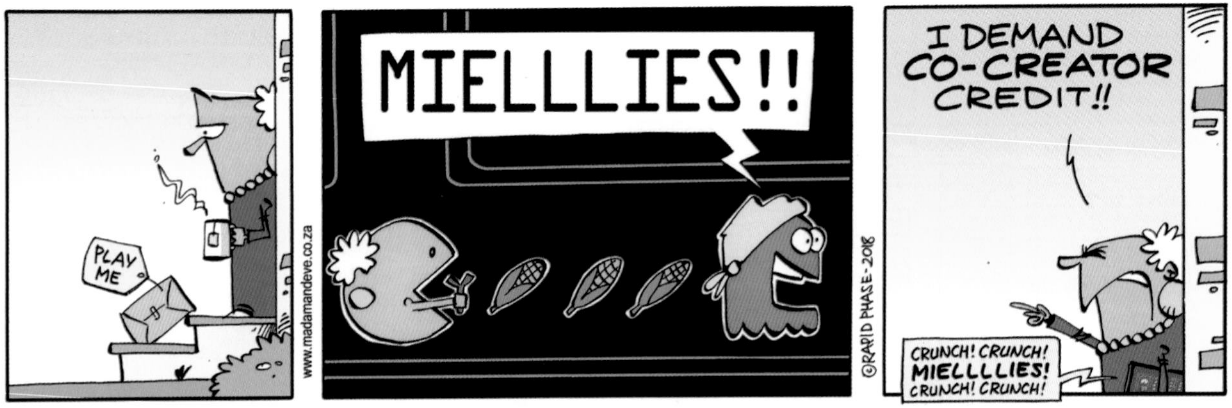
PLAY ME
www.madamandeve.co.za
MIELLLIES!!
©RAPID PHASE-2018
I DEMAND CO-CREATOR CREDIT!!
CRUNCH! CRUNCH! MIELLLIES! CRUNCH! CRUNCH!

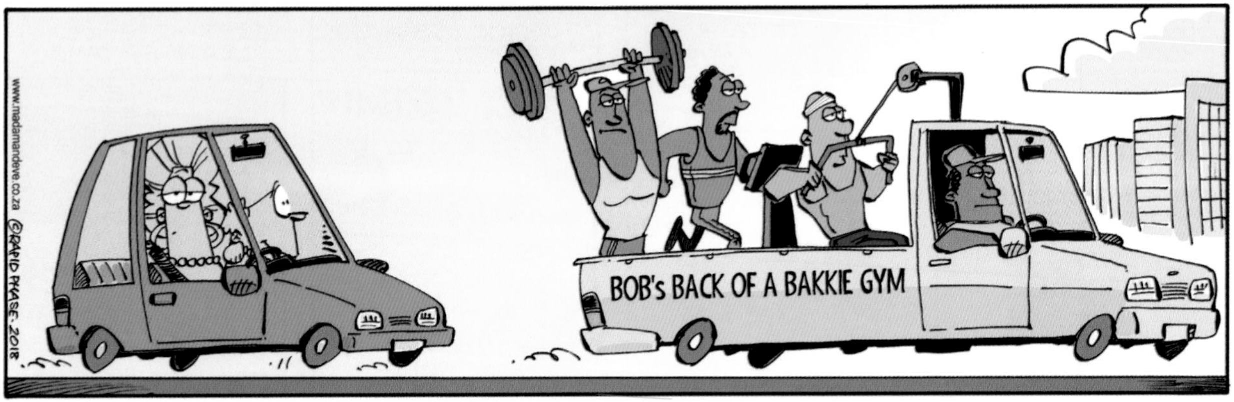
www.madamandeve.co.za
©RAPID PHASE-2018
BOB's BACK OF A BAKKIE GYM

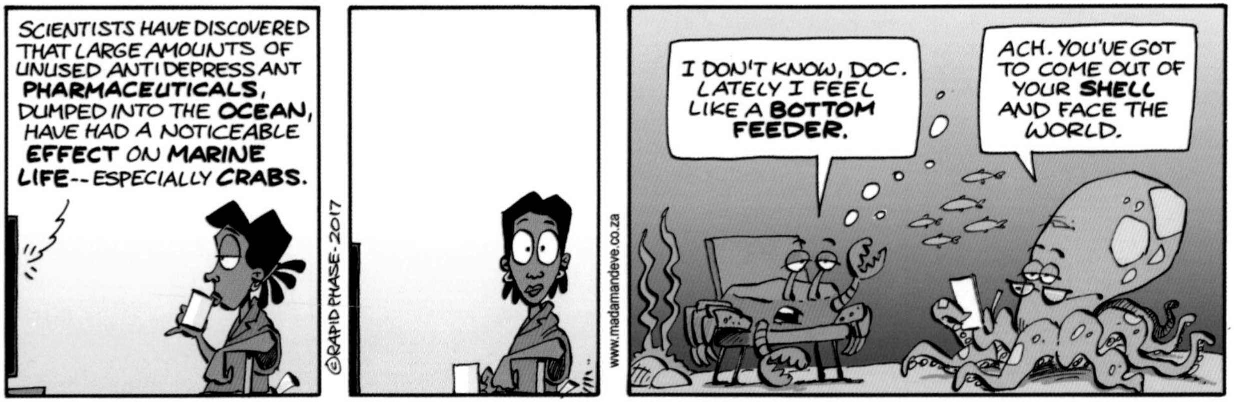
SCIENTISTS HAVE DISCOVERED THAT LARGE AMOUNTS OF UNUSED ANTIDEPRESSANT PHARMACEUTICALS, DUMPED INTO THE OCEAN, HAVE HAD A NOTICEABLE EFFECT ON MARINE LIFE--ESPECIALLY CRABS.
©RAPID PHASE-2017
www.madamandeve.co.za
I DON'T KNOW, DOC. LATELY I FEEL LIKE A BOTTOM FEEDER.
ACH. YOU'VE GOT TO COME OUT OF YOUR SHELL AND FACE THE WORLD.

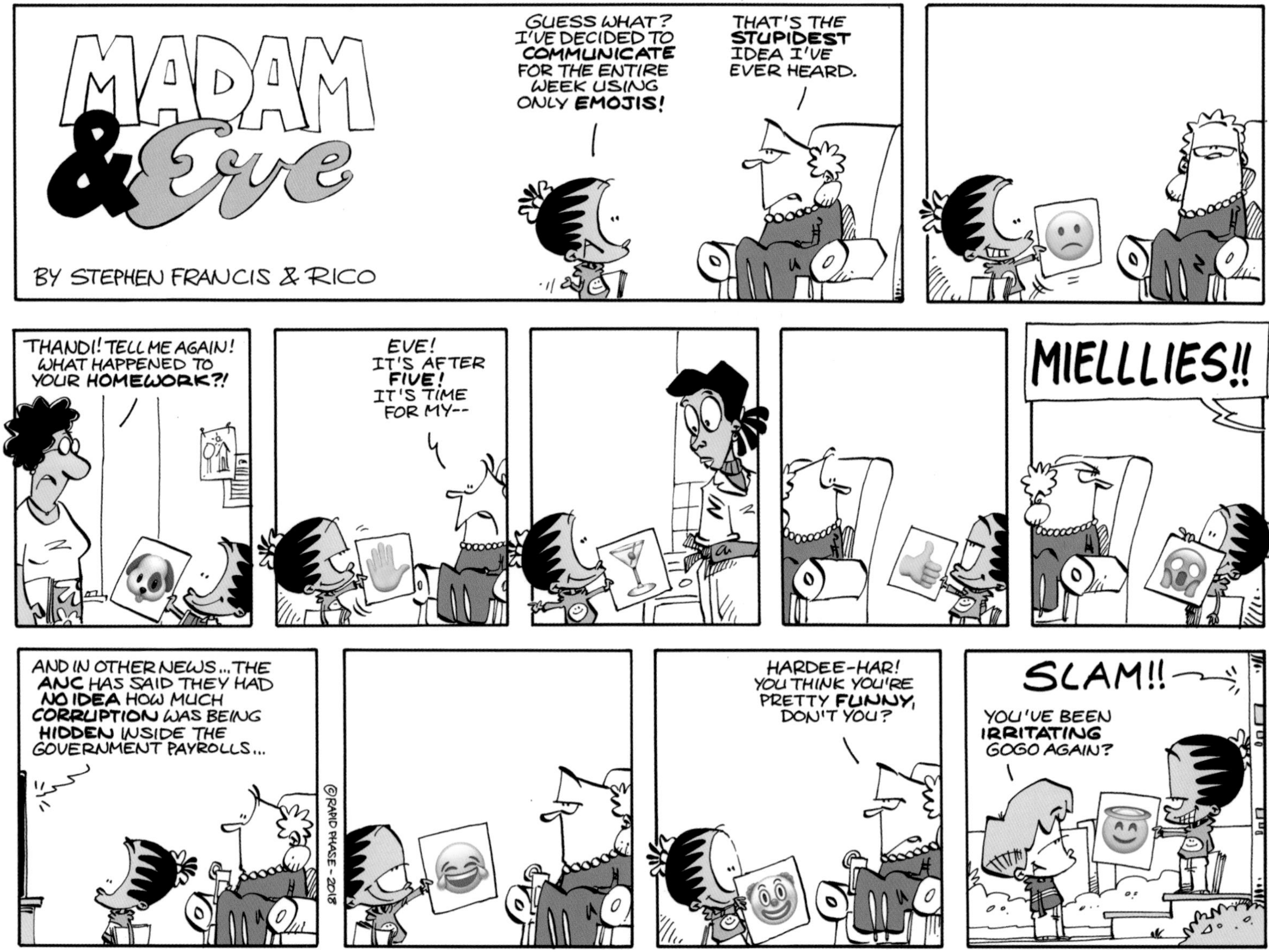
MADAM & Eve
BY STEPHEN FRANCIS & RICO
GUESS WHAT? I'VE DECIDED TO COMMUNICATE FOR THE ENTIRE WEEK USING ONLY EMOJIS!
THAT'S THE STUPIDEST IDEA I'VE EVER HEARD.
THANDI! TELL ME AGAIN! WHAT HAPPENED TO YOUR HOMEWORK?!
EVE! IT'S AFTER FIVE! IT'S TIME FOR MY--
MIELLLIES!!
AND IN OTHER NEWS... THE ANC HAS SAID THEY HAD NO IDEA HOW MUCH CORRUPTION WAS BEING HIDDEN INSIDE THE GOVERNMENT PAYROLLS...
©RAPID PHASE - 2018
HARDEE-HAR! YOU THINK YOU'RE PRETTY FUNNY, DON'T YOU?
SLAM!!
YOU'VE BEEN IRRITATING GOGO AGAIN?

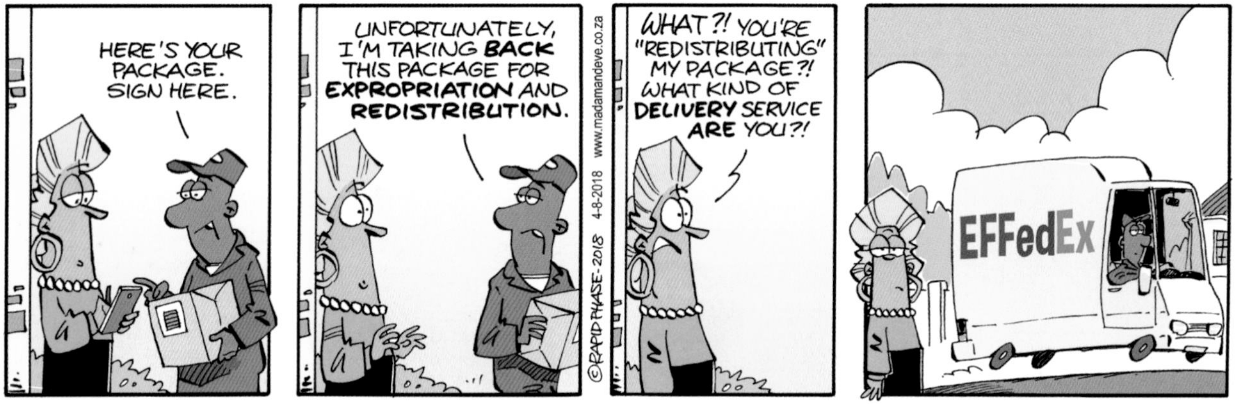
HERE'S YOUR PACKAGE. SIGN HERE.
UNFORTUNATELY, I'M TAKING BACK THIS PACKAGE FOR EXPROPRIATION AND REDISTRIBUTION.
©RAPID PHASE-2018 4-8-2018 www.madamandeve.co.za
WHAT?! YOU'RE "REDISTRIBUTING" MY PACKAGE?! WHAT KIND OF DELIVERY SERVICE ARE YOU?!
EFFedEx

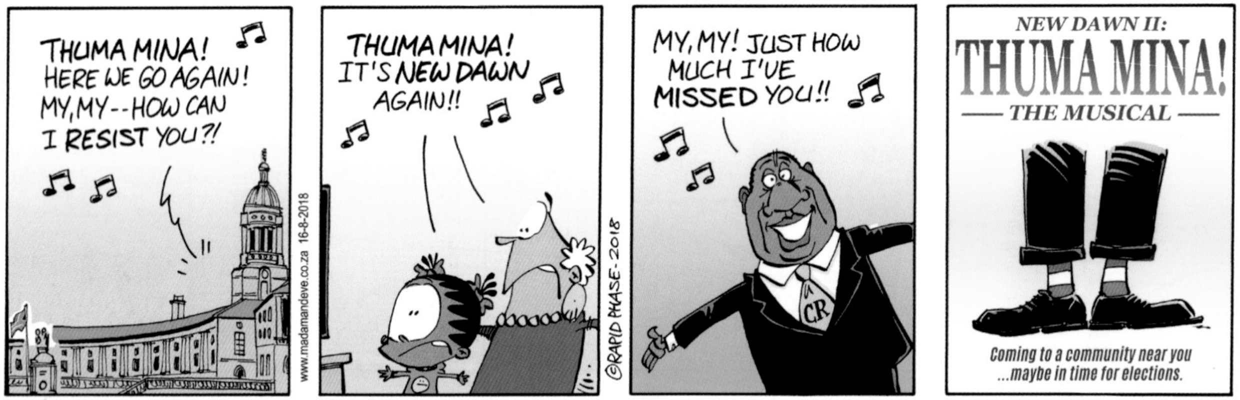
THUMA MINA! HERE WE GO AGAIN! MY, MY--HOW CAN I RESIST YOU?!
www.madamandeve.co.za 16-8-2018
THUMA MINA! IT'S NEW DAWN AGAIN!!
©RAPID PHASE-2018
MY, MY! JUST HOW MUCH I'VE MISSED YOU!!
CR
NEW DAWN II:
THUMA MINA!
— THE MUSICAL —
Coming to a community near you
...maybe in time for elections.

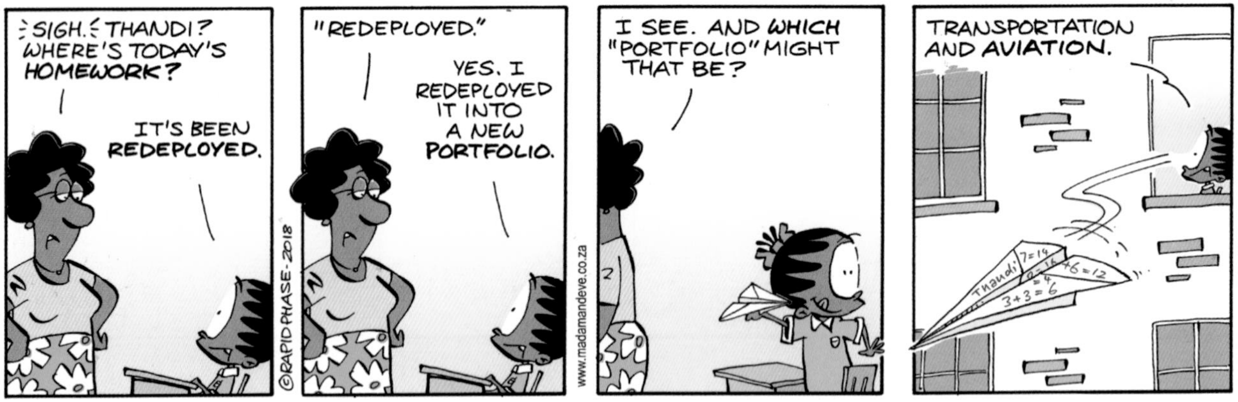
SIGH. THANDI? WHERE'S TODAY'S HOMEWORK?
IT'S BEEN REDEPLOYED.
©RAPID PHASE-2018
"REDEPLOYED."
YES. I REDEPLOYED IT INTO A NEW PORTFOLIO.
www.madamandeve.co.za
I SEE. AND WHICH "PORTFOLIO" MIGHT THAT BE?
TRANSPORTATION AND AVIATION.

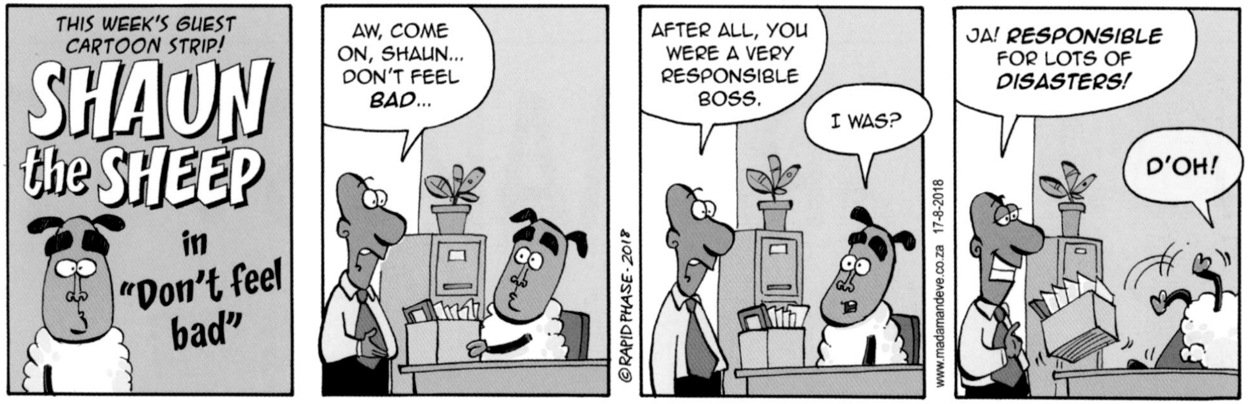
THIS WEEK'S GUEST CARTOON STRIP!
SHAUN the SHEEP
in "Don't feel bad"
AW, COME ON, SHAUN... DON'T FEEL **BAD**...
©RAPID PHASE-2018
AFTER ALL, YOU WERE A VERY RESPONSIBLE BOSS.
I WAS?
www.madamandeve.co.za 17-8-2018
JA! **RESPONSIBLE** FOR LOTS OF **DISASTERS!**
D'OH!

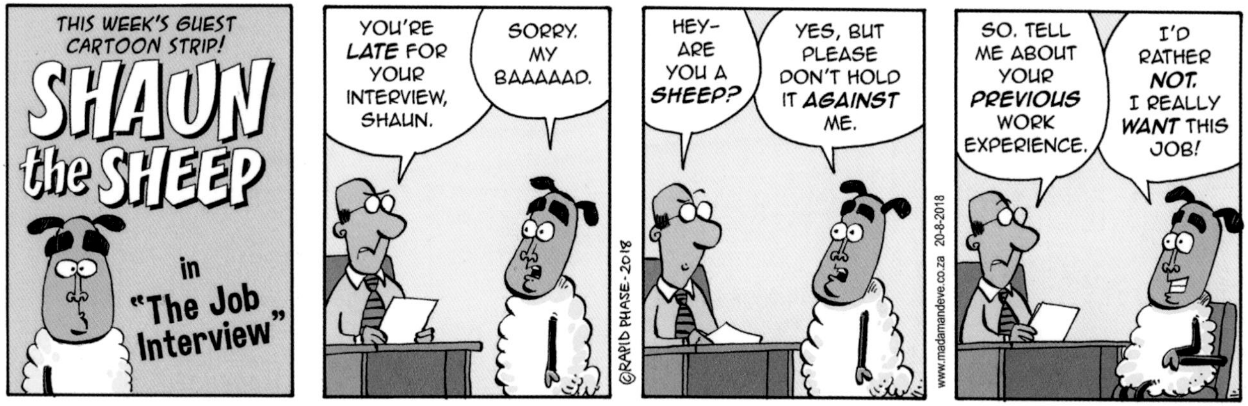
THIS WEEK'S GUEST CARTOON STRIP!
SHAUN the SHEEP
in "The Job Interview"
YOU'RE **LATE** FOR YOUR INTERVIEW, SHAUN.
SORRY. MY BAAAAAD.
©RAPID PHASE-2018
HEY- ARE YOU A **SHEEP?**
YES, BUT PLEASE DON'T HOLD IT **AGAINST** ME.
www.madamandeve.co.za 20-8-2018
SO. TELL ME ABOUT YOUR **PREVIOUS** WORK EXPERIENCE.
I'D RATHER **NOT.** I REALLY **WANT** THIS JOB!

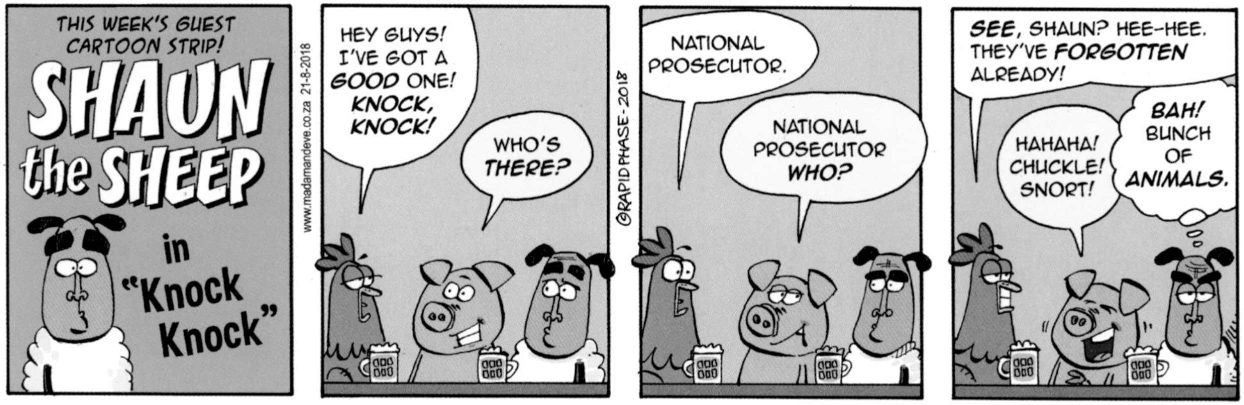
THIS WEEK'S GUEST CARTOON STRIP!
SHAUN the SHEEP
in "Knock Knock"
www.madamandeve.co.za 21-8-2018
HEY GUYS! I'VE GOT A **GOOD** ONE! **KNOCK, KNOCK!**
WHO'S **THERE?**
©RAPID PHASE-2018
NATIONAL PROSECUTOR.
NATIONAL PROSECUTOR **WHO?**
SEE, SHAUN? HEE-HEE. THEY'VE **FORGOTTEN** ALREADY!
HAHAHA! CHUCKLE! SNORT!
BAH! BUNCH OF **ANIMALS.**

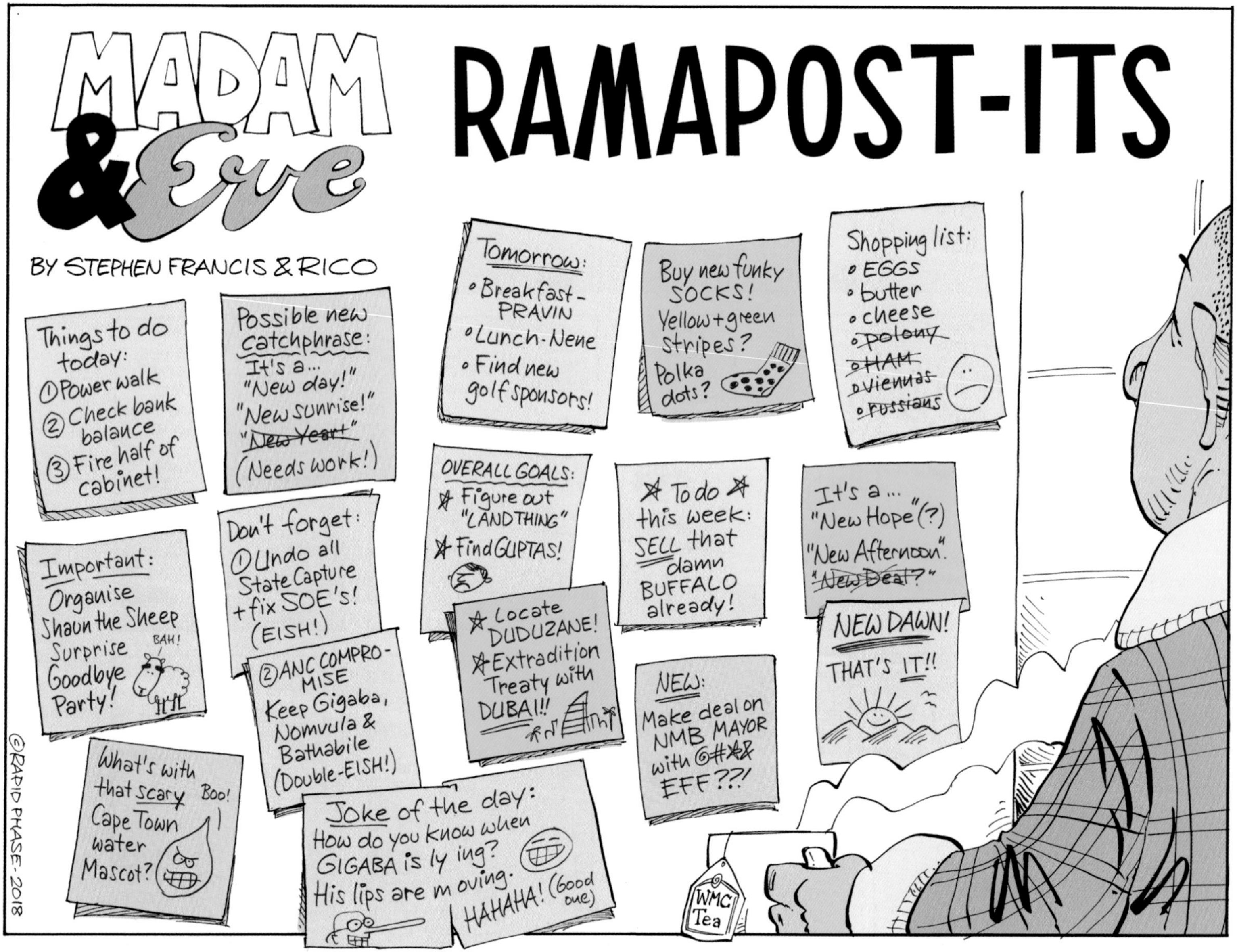

MADAM & Eve
RAMAPOST-ITS
BY STEPHEN FRANCIS & RICO
Tomorrow: • Breakfast - PRAVIN • Lunch - Nene • Find new golf sponsors!
Buy new funky SOCKS! Yellow + green stripes? Polka dots?
Shopping list: • EGGS • butter • cheese • polony • HAM • viennas • russians
Things to do today: ① Power walk ② Check bank balance ③ Fire half of cabinet!
Possible new catchphrase: It's a... "New day!" "New sunrise!" "New Year!" (Needs work!)
OVERALL GOALS: ✯ Figure out "LANDTHING" ✯ Find GUPTAS!
✯ To do ✯ this week: SELL that damn BUFFALO already!
It's a... "New Hope"(?) "New Afternoon". "New Deal?"
Important: Organise Shaun the Sheep Surprise Goodbye Party!
BAH!
Don't forget: ① Undo all State Capture + fix SOE's! (EISH!)
✯ Locate DUDUZANE! ✯ Extradition Treaty with DUBAI!!
NEW DAWN! THAT'S IT!!
② ANC COMPRO-MISE Keep Gigaba, Nomvula & Bathabile (Double-EISH!)
NEW: Make deal on NMB MAYOR with @#✯& EFF??!
What's with that scary Cape Town water Mascot?
Boo!
Joke of the day: How do you know when GIGABA is lying? His lips are moving.
HAHAHA! (Good one)
WMC Tea
© RAPID PHASE - 2018

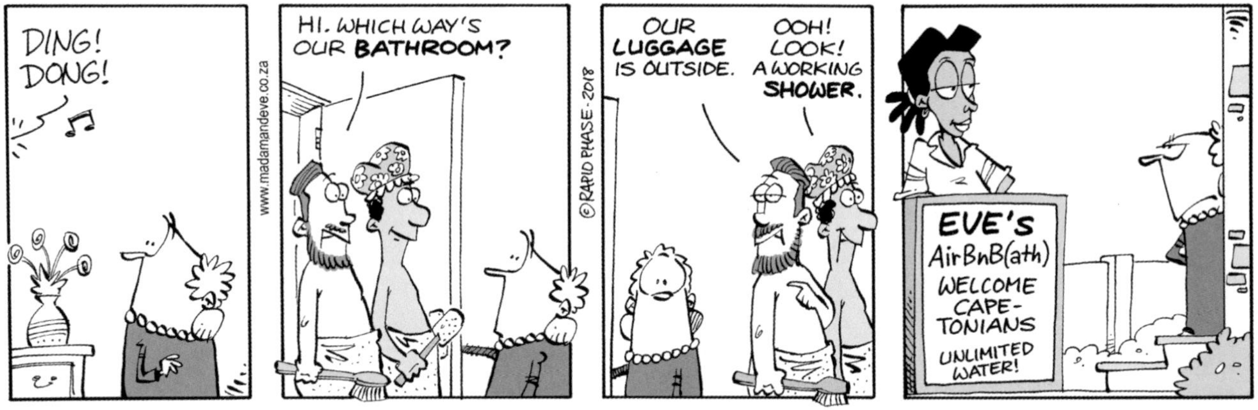
DING! DONG!
HI. WHICH WAY'S OUR **BATHROOM?**
www.madamandeve.co.za
OUR **LUGGAGE** IS OUTSIDE.
OOH! LOOK! A WORKING **SHOWER.**
©RAPID PHASE · 2018
EVE'S AirBnB(ath) WELCOME CAPE-TONIANS UNLIMITED WATER!

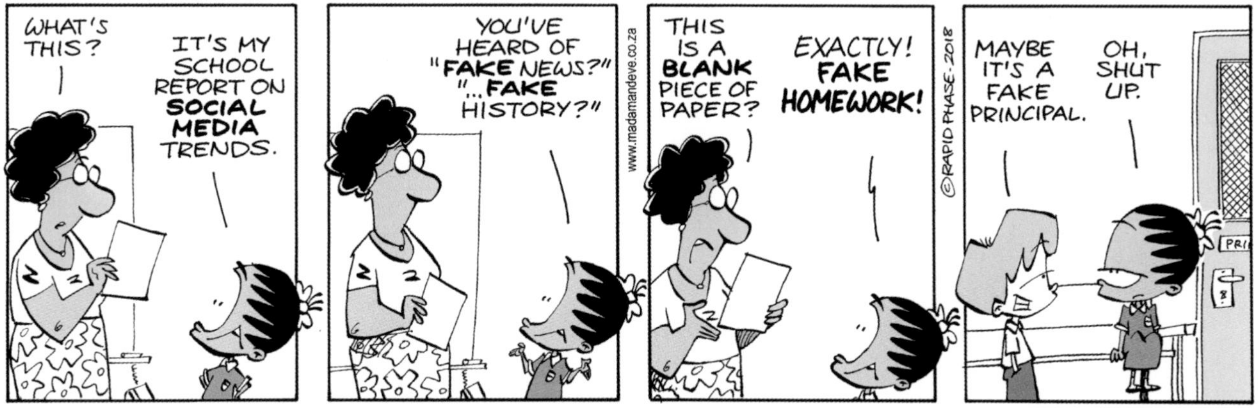
WHAT'S THIS?
IT'S MY SCHOOL REPORT ON **SOCIAL MEDIA** TRENDS.
YOU'VE HEARD OF "**FAKE** NEWS?" "...**FAKE** HISTORY?"
www.madamandeve.co.za
THIS IS A **BLANK** PIECE OF PAPER?
EXACTLY! **FAKE HOMEWORK!**
©RAPID PHASE · 2018
MAYBE IT'S A FAKE PRINCIPAL.
OH, SHUT UP.

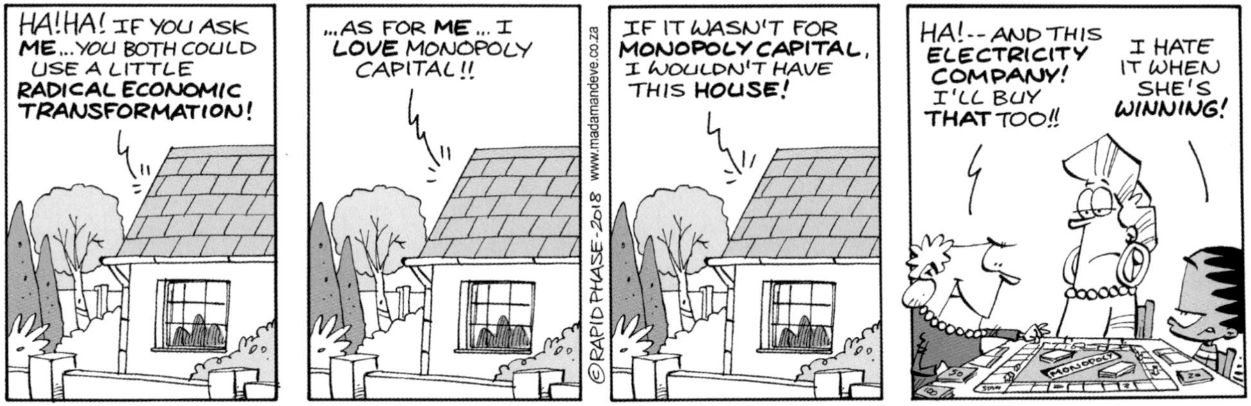
HA!HA! IF YOU ASK **ME**...YOU BOTH COULD USE A LITTLE **RADICAL ECONOMIC TRANSFORMATION!**
...AS FOR **ME**... I **LOVE** MONOPOLY CAPITAL!!
©RAPID PHASE · 2018 www.madamandeve.co.za
IF IT WASN'T FOR **MONOPOLY CAPITAL**, I WOULDN'T HAVE THIS **HOUSE!**
HA!-- AND THIS **ELECTRICITY COMPANY!** I'LL BUY **THAT** TOO!!
I HATE IT WHEN SHE'S **WINNING!**

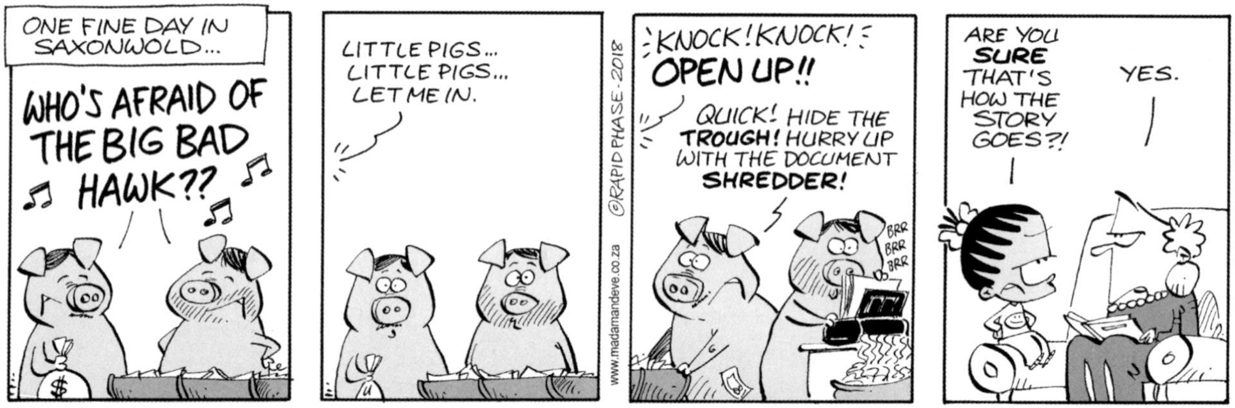
ONE FINE DAY IN SAXONWOLD...
WHO'S AFRAID OF THE BIG BAD HAWK??
LITTLE PIGS... LITTLE PIGS... LET ME IN.
©RAPID PHASE-2018
www.madamandeve.co.za
KNOCK! KNOCK!
OPEN UP!!
QUICK! HIDE THE TROUGH! HURRY UP WITH THE DOCUMENT SHREDDER!
BRR BRR BRR
ARE YOU SURE THAT'S HOW THE STORY GOES?!
YES.

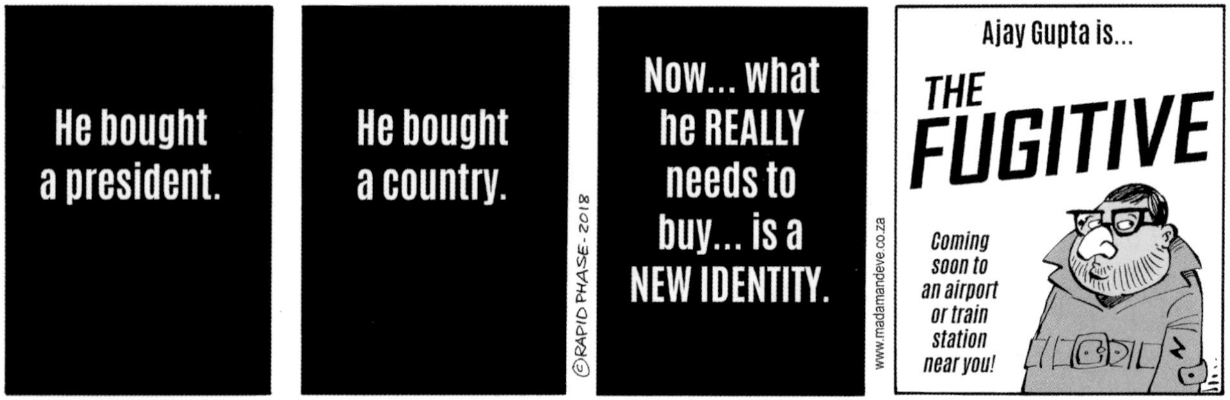
He bought a president.
He bought a country.
©RAPID PHASE-2018
Now... what he REALLY needs to buy... is a NEW IDENTITY.
www.madamandeve.co.za
Ajay Gupta is...
THE FUGITIVE
Coming soon to an airport or train station near you!

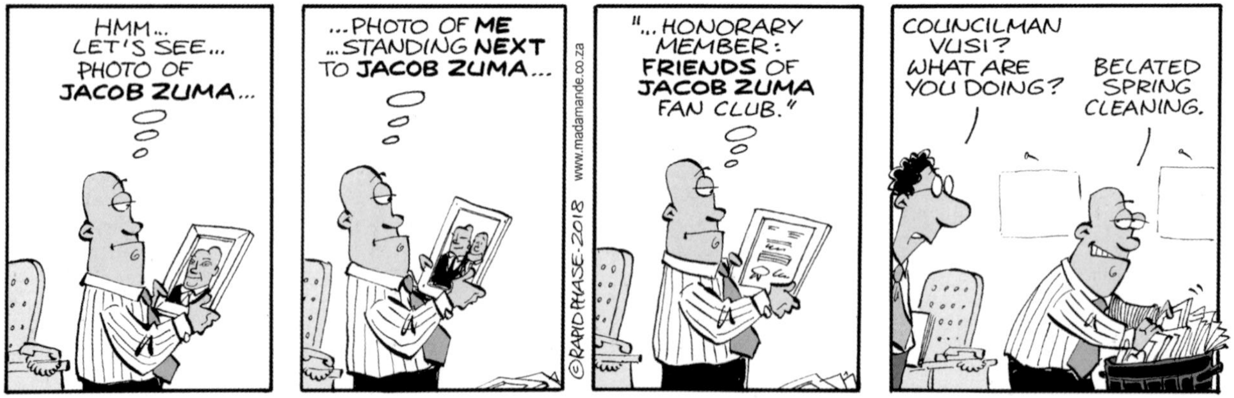
HMM... LET'S SEE... PHOTO OF JACOB ZUMA...
...PHOTO OF ME ...STANDING NEXT TO JACOB ZUMA...
www.madamande.co.za
©RAPID PHASE-2018
"...HONORARY MEMBER: FRIENDS OF JACOB ZUMA FAN CLUB."
COUNCILMAN VUSI? WHAT ARE YOU DOING?
BELATED SPRING CLEANING.

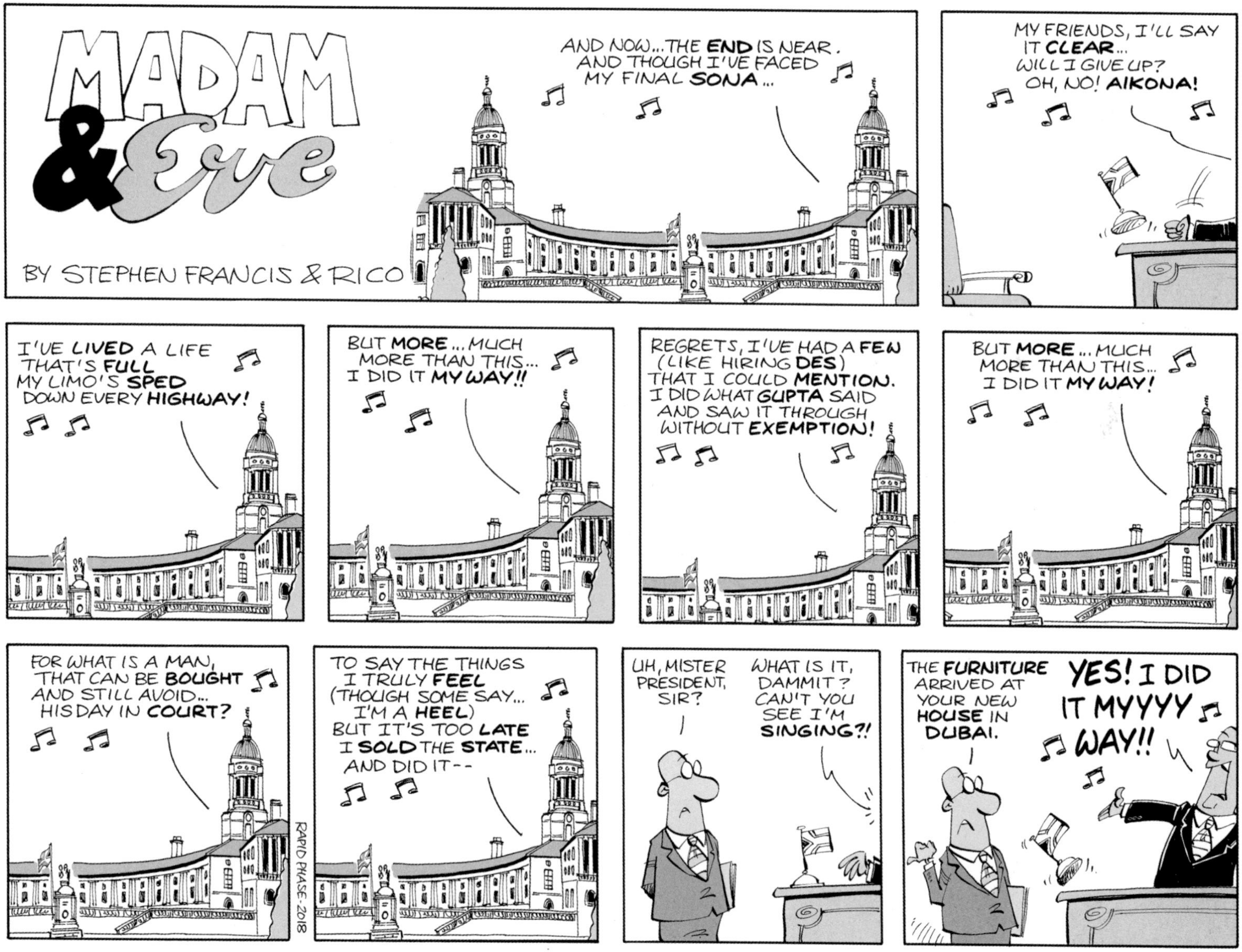
MADAM & Eve
BY STEPHEN FRANCIS & RICO
AND NOW... THE END IS NEAR. AND THOUGH I'VE FACED MY FINAL SONA...
MY FRIENDS, I'LL SAY IT CLEAR... WILL I GIVE UP? OH, NO! AIKONA!
I'VE LIVED A LIFE THAT'S FULL MY LIMO'S SPED DOWN EVERY HIGHWAY!
BUT MORE... MUCH MORE THAN THIS... I DID IT MY WAY!!
REGRETS, I'VE HAD A FEW (LIKE HIRING DES) THAT I COULD MENTION. I DID WHAT GUPTA SAID AND SAW IT THROUGH WITHOUT EXEMPTION!
BUT MORE... MUCH MORE THAN THIS... I DID IT MY WAY!
FOR WHAT IS A MAN, THAT CAN BE BOUGHT AND STILL AVOID... HIS DAY IN COURT?
RAPID PHASE · 2018
TO SAY THE THINGS I TRULY FEEL (THOUGH SOME SAY... I'M A HEEL) BUT IT'S TOO LATE I SOLD THE STATE... AND DID IT--
UH, MISTER PRESIDENT, SIR?
WHAT IS IT, DAMMIT? CAN'T YOU SEE I'M SINGING?!
THE FURNITURE ARRIVED AT YOUR NEW HOUSE IN DUBAI.
YES! I DID IT MYYYY WAY!!

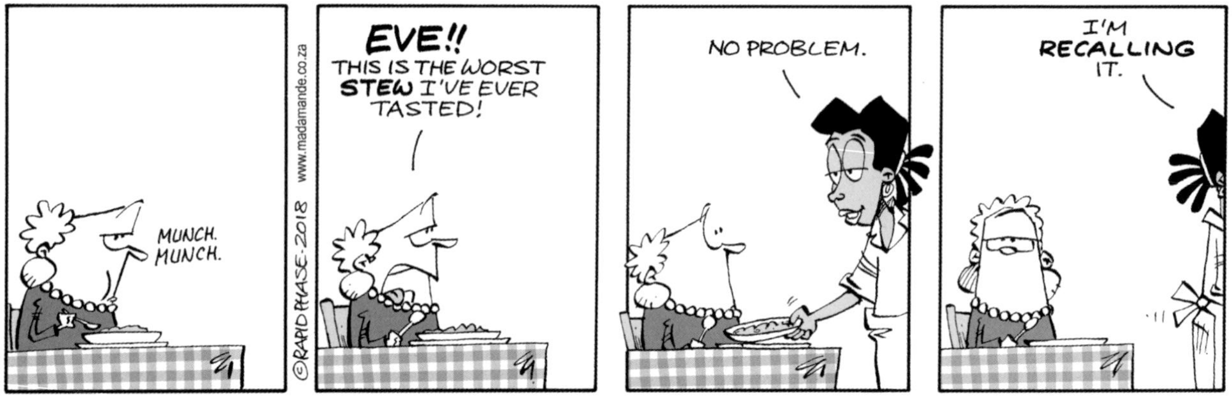
MUNCH. MUNCH.
©RAPID PHASE-2018
www.madamandeve.co.za
EVE!! THIS IS THE WORST STEW I'VE EVER TASTED!
NO PROBLEM.
I'M RECALLING IT.

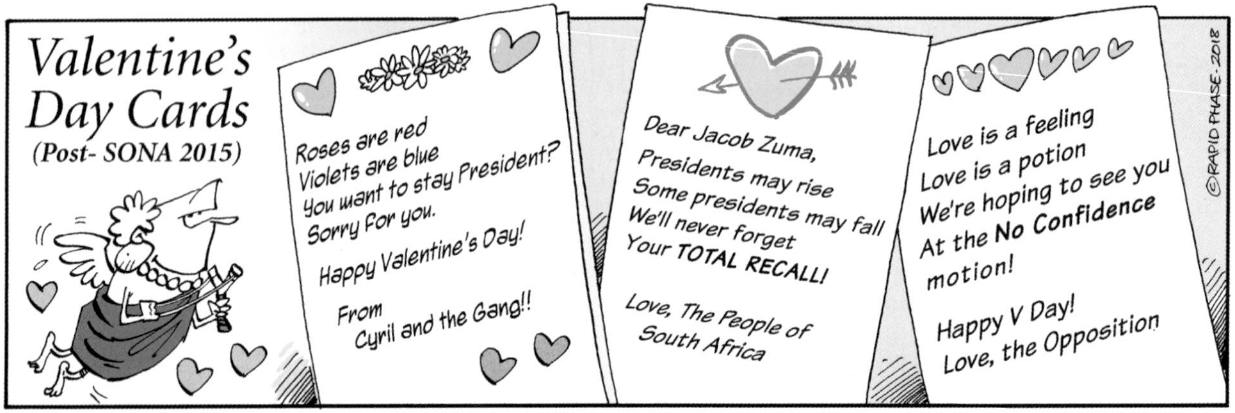
Valentine's Day Cards (Post- SONA 2015)
Roses are red
Violets are blue
You want to stay President?
Sorry for you.
Happy Valentine's Day!
From Cyril and the Gang!!
Dear Jacob Zuma,
Presidents may rise
Some presidents may fall
We'll never forget
Your TOTAL RECALL!
Love, The People of South Africa
Love is a feeling
Love is a potion
We're hoping to see you
At the No Confidence motion!
Happy V Day!
Love, the Opposition
©RAPID PHASE-2018

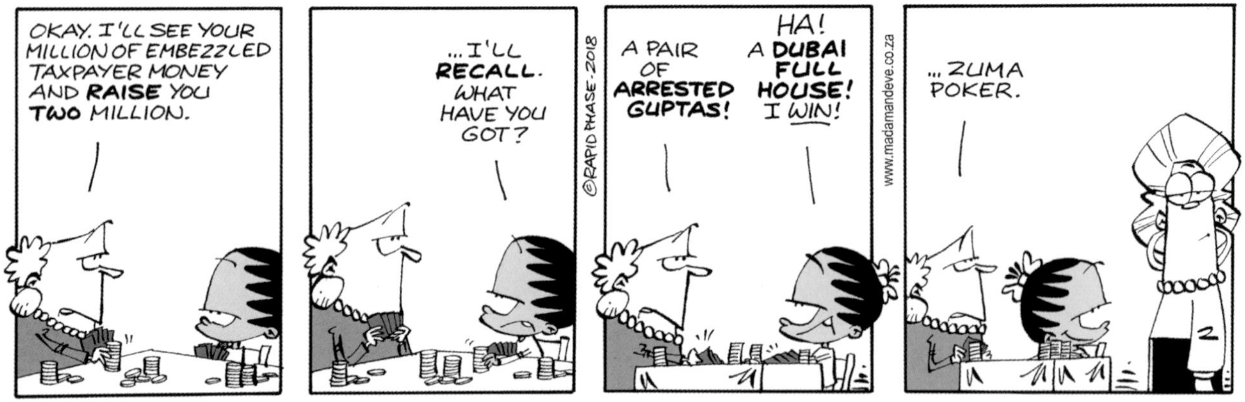
OKAY. I'LL SEE YOUR MILLION OF EMBEZZLED TAXPAYER MONEY AND RAISE YOU TWO MILLION.
...I'LL RECALL. WHAT HAVE YOU GOT?
©RAPID PHASE-2018
A PAIR OF ARRESTED GUPTAS!
HA! A DUBAI FULL HOUSE! I WIN!
www.madamandeve.co.za
...ZUMA POKER.

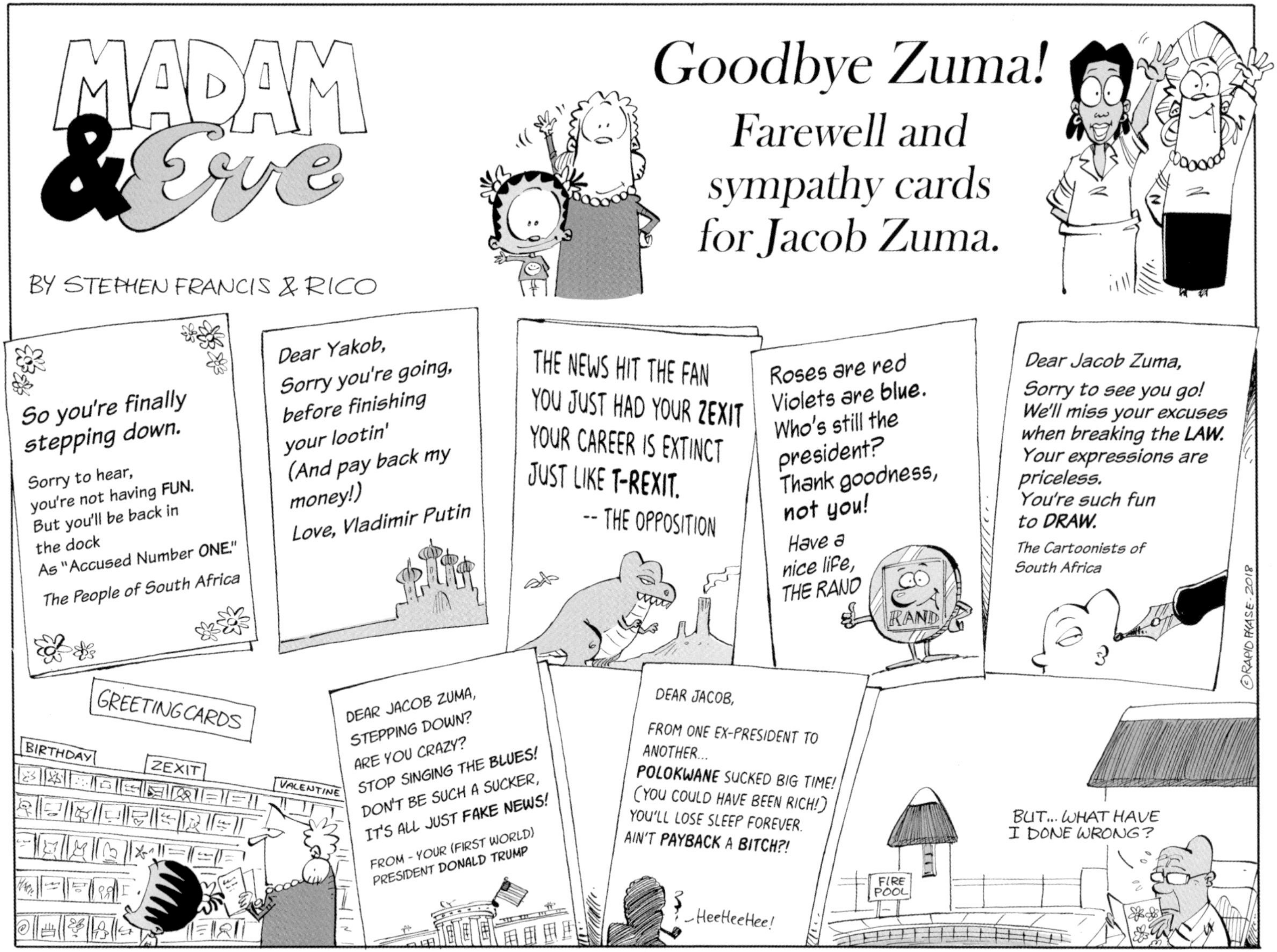
MADAM & Eve
BY STEPHEN FRANCIS & RICO
Goodbye Zuma!
Farewell and sympathy cards for Jacob Zuma.
So you're finally stepping down.
Sorry to hear, you're not having FUN. But you'll be back in the dock As "Accused Number ONE."
The People of South Africa
Dear Yakob, Sorry you're going, before finishing your lootin' (And pay back my money!) Love, Vladimir Putin
THE NEWS HIT THE FAN YOU JUST HAD YOUR ZEXIT YOUR CAREER IS EXTINCT JUST LIKE T-REXIT.
-- THE OPPOSITION
Roses are red Violets are blue. Who's still the president? Thank goodness, not you!
Have a nice life, THE RAND
RAND
Dear Jacob Zuma, Sorry to see you go! We'll miss your excuses when breaking the LAW. Your expressions are priceless. You're such fun to DRAW.
The Cartoonists of South Africa
©RAPID PHASE · 2018
GREETING CARDS
BIRTHDAY
ZEXIT
VALENTINE
DEAR JACOB ZUMA, STEPPING DOWN? ARE YOU CRAZY? STOP SINGING THE BLUES! DON'T BE SUCH A SUCKER, IT'S ALL JUST FAKE NEWS!
FROM - YOUR (FIRST WORLD) PRESIDENT DONALD TRUMP
DEAR JACOB,
FROM ONE EX-PRESIDENT TO ANOTHER...
POLOKWANE SUCKED BIG TIME! (YOU COULD HAVE BEEN RICH!) YOU'LL LOSE SLEEP FOREVER. AIN'T PAYBACK A BITCH?!
HeeHeeHee!
FIRE POOL
BUT... WHAT HAVE I DONE WRONG?

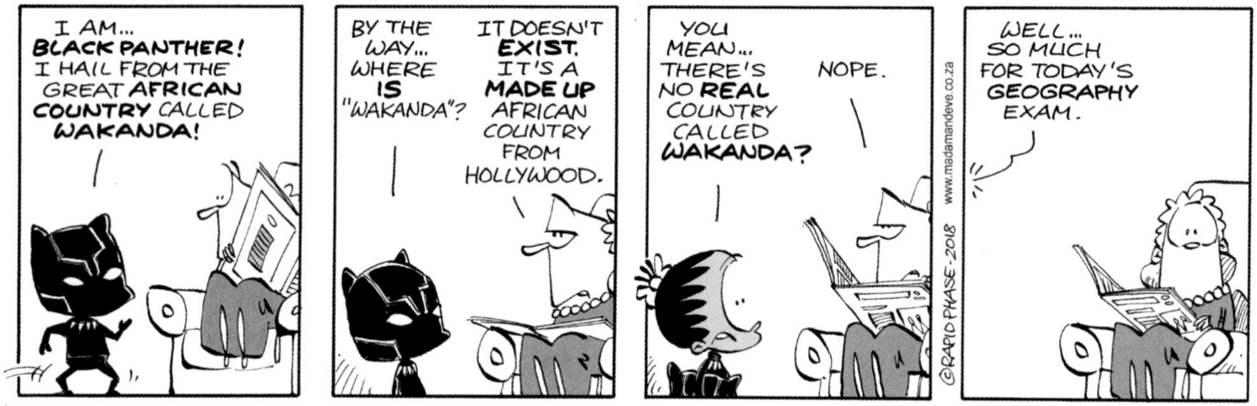
I AM... **BLACK PANTHER!** I HAIL FROM THE GREAT **AFRICAN COUNTRY** CALLED **WAKANDA!**
BY THE WAY... WHERE **IS** "WAKANDA"?
IT DOESN'T **EXIST.** IT'S A **MADE UP** AFRICAN COUNTRY FROM HOLLYWOOD.
YOU MEAN... THERE'S NO **REAL** COUNTRY CALLED **WAKANDA?**
NOPE.
©RAPID PHASE-2018 www.madamandeve.co.za
WELL... SO MUCH FOR TODAY'S **GEOGRAPHY** EXAM.

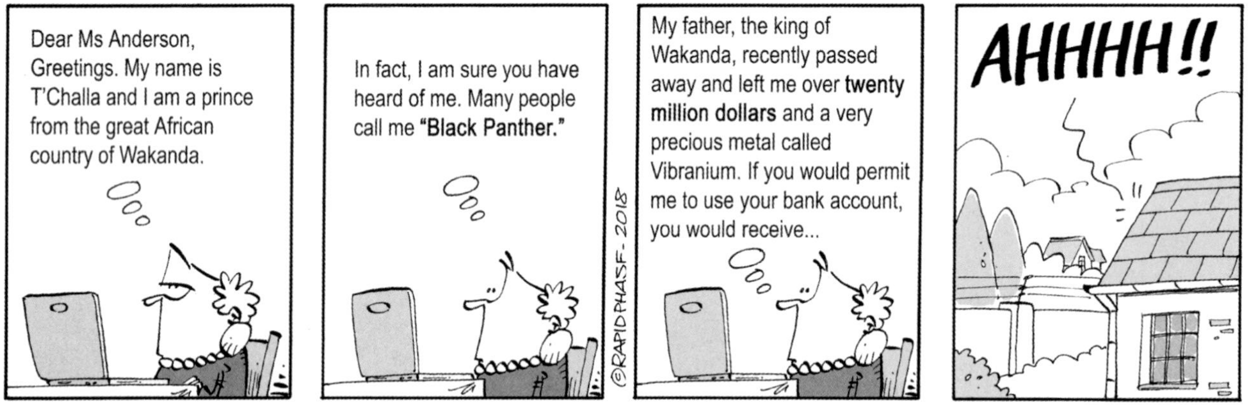
Dear Ms Anderson,
Greetings. My name is T'Challa and I am a prince from the great African country of Wakanda.
In fact, I am sure you have heard of me. Many people call me **"Black Panther."**
©RAPID PHASE-2018
My father, the king of Wakanda, recently passed away and left me over **twenty million dollars** and a very precious metal called Vibranium. If you would permit me to use your bank account, you would receive...
AHHHH!!

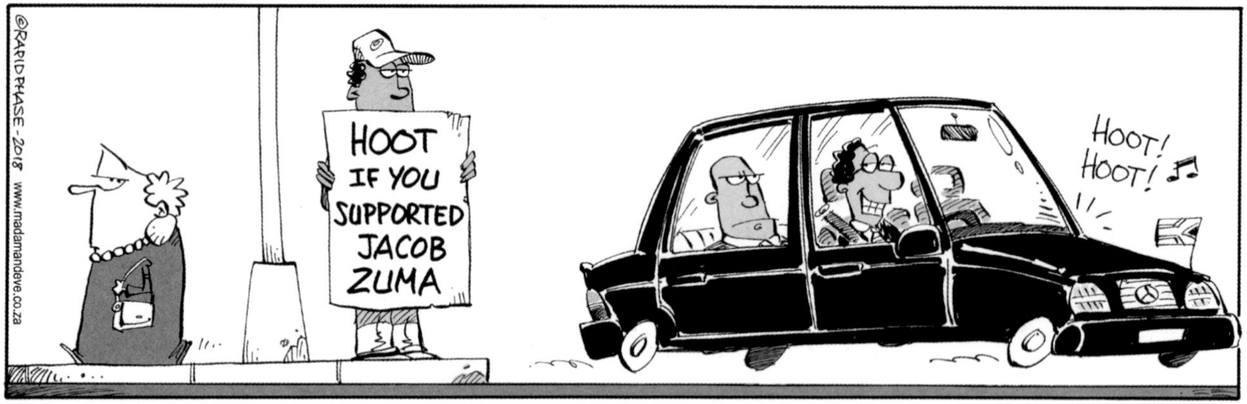
©RAPID PHASE-2018 www.madamandeve.co.za
HOOT IF YOU SUPPORTED JACOB ZUMA
HOOT! HOOT!

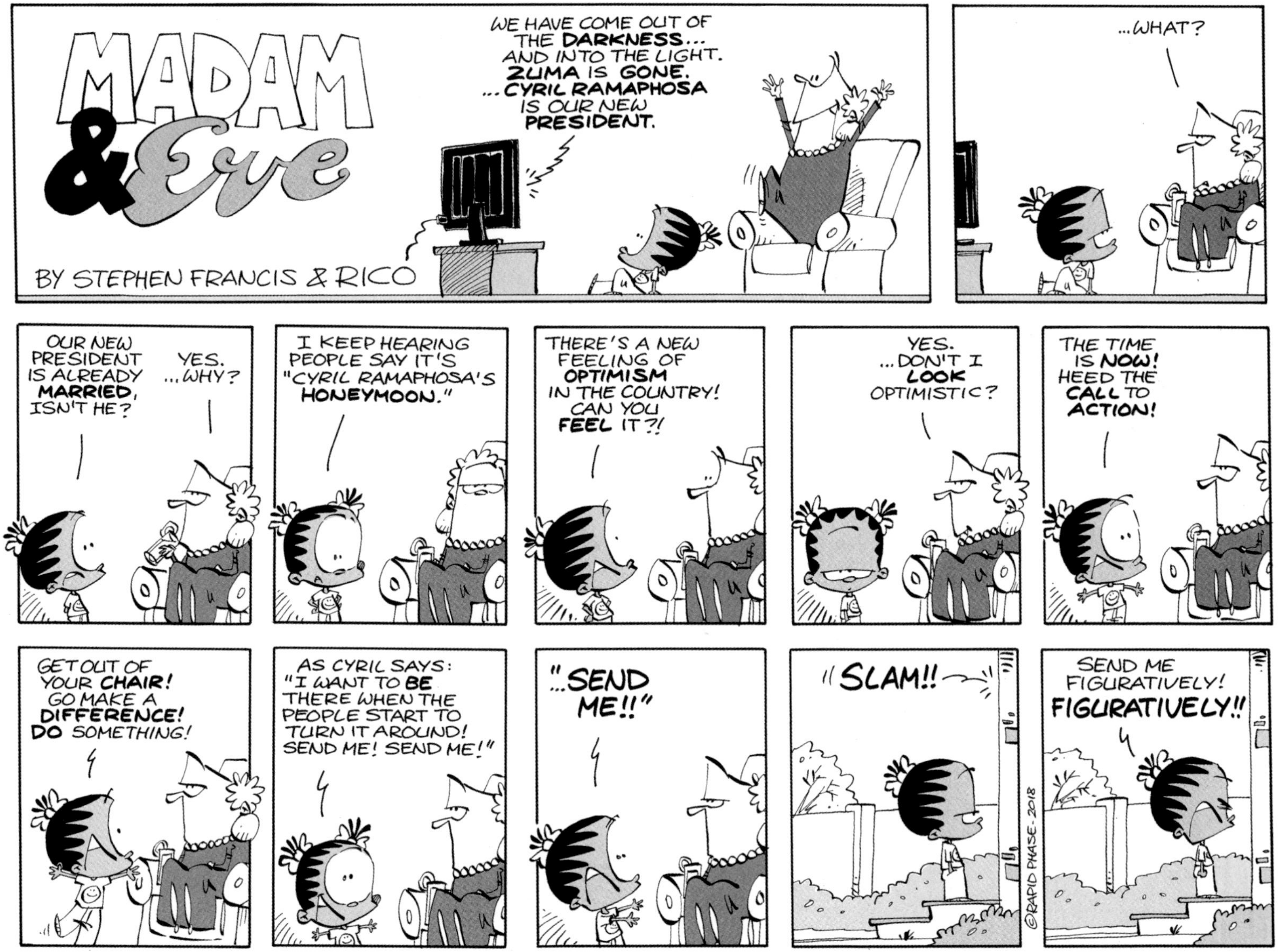
MADAM & Eve
BY STEPHEN FRANCIS & RICO
WE HAVE COME OUT OF THE DARKNESS... AND INTO THE LIGHT. ZUMA IS GONE. ...CYRIL RAMAPHOSA IS OUR NEW PRESIDENT.
...WHAT?
OUR NEW PRESIDENT IS ALREADY MARRIED, ISN'T HE?
YES. ...WHY?
I KEEP HEARING PEOPLE SAY IT'S "CYRIL RAMAPHOSA'S HONEYMOON."
THERE'S A NEW FEELING OF OPTIMISM IN THE COUNTRY! CAN YOU FEEL IT?!
YES. ...DON'T I LOOK OPTIMISTIC?
THE TIME IS NOW! HEED THE CALL TO ACTION!
GET OUT OF YOUR CHAIR! GO MAKE A DIFFERENCE! DO SOMETHING!
AS CYRIL SAYS: "I WANT TO BE THERE WHEN THE PEOPLE START TO TURN IT AROUND! SEND ME! SEND ME!"
"...SEND ME!!"
SLAM!!
©RAPID PHASE - 2018
SEND ME FIGURATIVELY! FIGURATIVELY!!

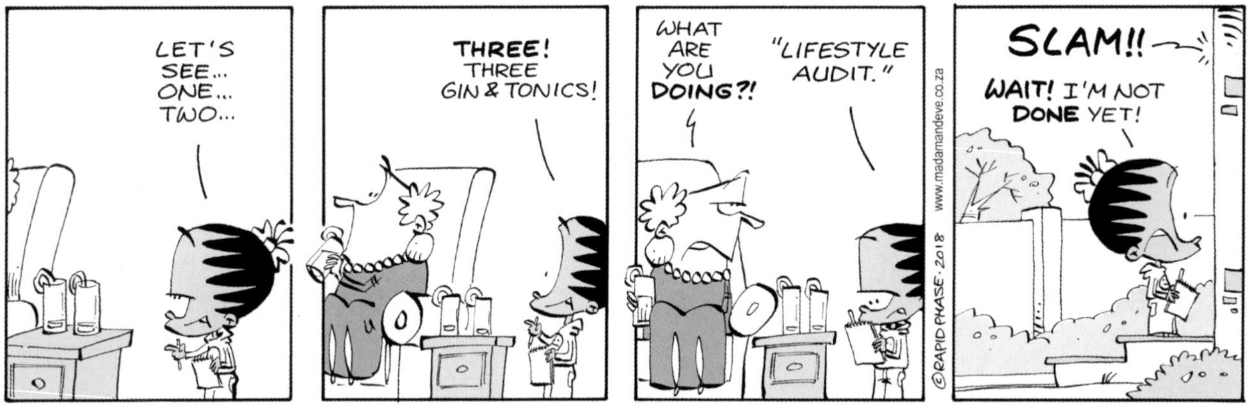
LET'S SEE... ONE... TWO...
THREE! THREE GIN & TONICS!
WHAT ARE YOU DOING?!
"LIFESTYLE AUDIT."
©RAPID PHASE-2018 www.madamandeve.co.za
SLAM!!
WAIT! I'M NOT DONE YET!

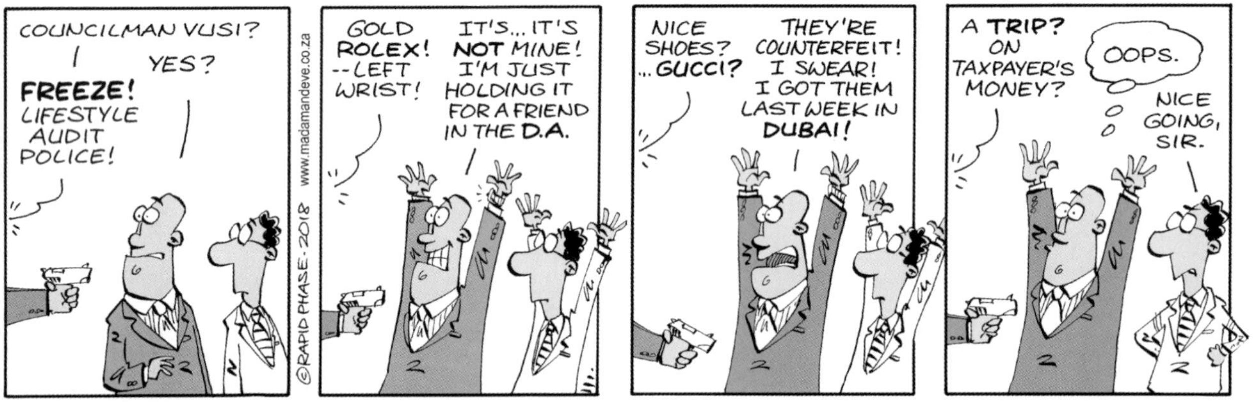
COUNCILMAN VUSI?
YES?
FREEZE! LIFESTYLE AUDIT POLICE!
©RAPID PHASE-2018 www.madamandeve.co.za
GOLD ROLEX! --LEFT WRIST!
IT'S... IT'S NOT MINE! I'M JUST HOLDING IT FOR A FRIEND IN THE D.A.
NICE SHOES? ...GUCCI?
THEY'RE COUNTERFEIT! I SWEAR! I GOT THEM LAST WEEK IN DUBAI!
A TRIP? ON TAXPAYER'S MONEY?
OOPS.
NICE GOING, SIR.

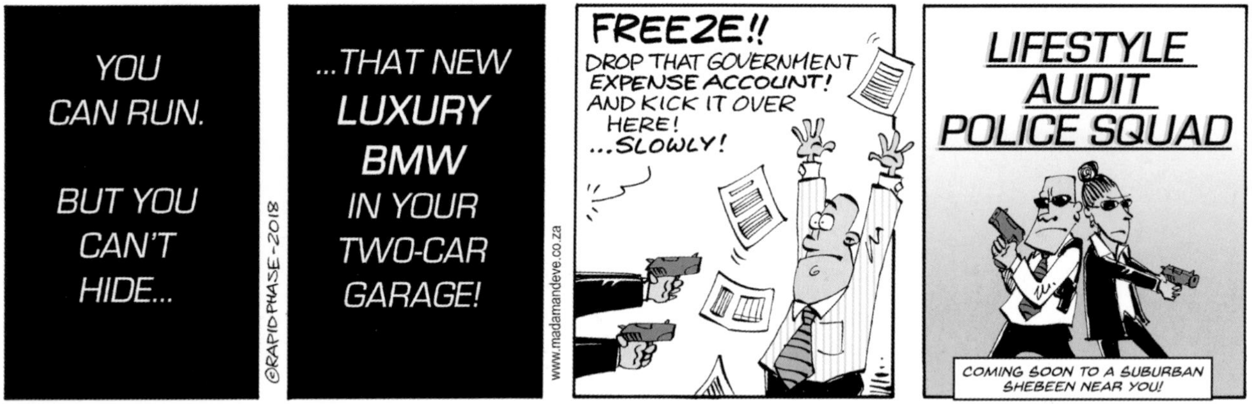
YOU CAN RUN.
BUT YOU CAN'T HIDE...
©RAPID PHASE-2018
...THAT NEW LUXURY BMW IN YOUR TWO-CAR GARAGE!
www.madamandeve.co.za
FREEZE!!
DROP THAT GOVERNMENT EXPENSE ACCOUNT! AND KICK IT OVER HERE! ...SLOWLY!
LIFESTYLE AUDIT POLICE SQUAD
COMING SOON TO A SUBURBAN SHEBEEN NEAR YOU!

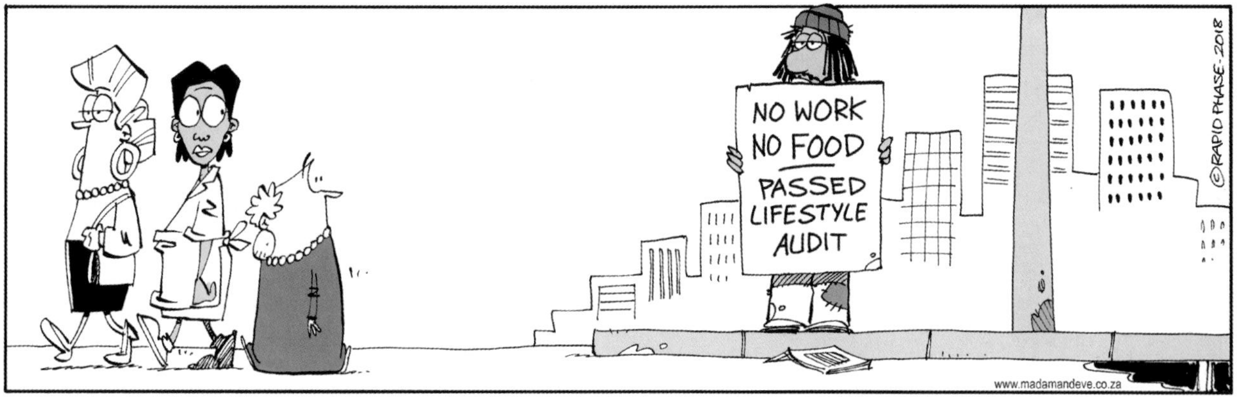
NO WORK
NO FOOD
PASSED LIFESTYLE AUDIT
©RAPID PHASE·2018
www.madamandeve.co.za

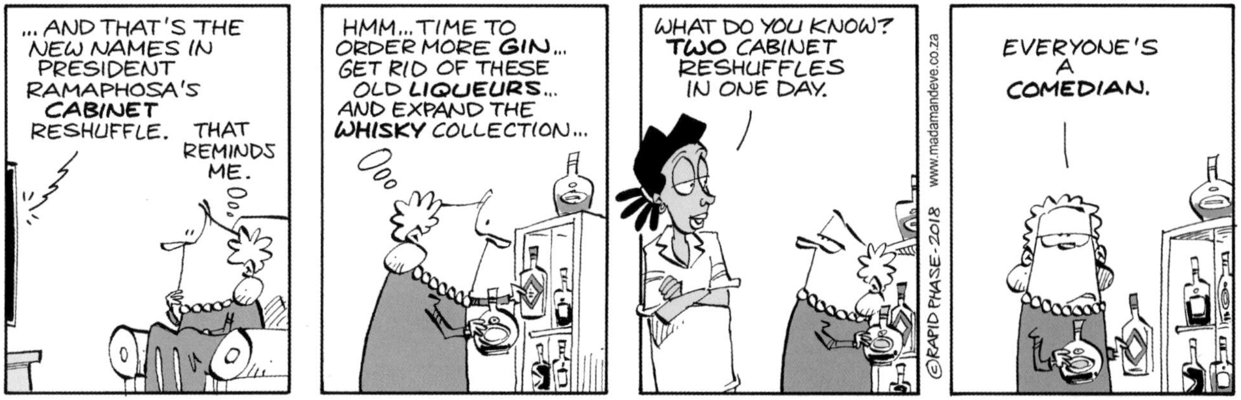
...AND THAT'S THE NEW NAMES IN PRESIDENT RAMAPHOSA'S **CABINET** RESHUFFLE.
THAT REMINDS ME.
HMM... TIME TO ORDER MORE **GIN**... GET RID OF THESE OLD **LIQUEURS**... AND EXPAND THE **WHISKY** COLLECTION...
WHAT DO YOU KNOW? **TWO** CABINET RESHUFFLES IN ONE DAY.
EVERYONE'S A **COMEDIAN**.
©RAPID PHASE·2018
www.madamandeve.co.za

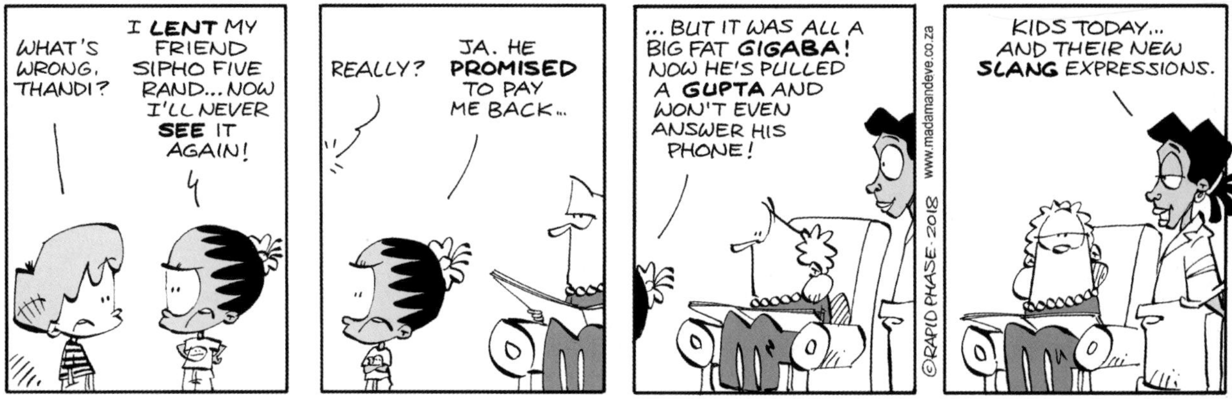
WHAT'S WRONG, THANDI?
I **LENT** MY FRIEND SIPHO FIVE RAND... NOW I'LL NEVER **SEE** IT AGAIN!
REALLY?
JA. HE **PROMISED** TO PAY ME BACK...
...BUT IT WAS ALL A BIG FAT **GIGABA**! NOW HE'S PULLED A **GUPTA** AND WON'T EVEN ANSWER HIS PHONE!
KIDS TODAY... AND THEIR NEW **SLANG** EXPRESSIONS.
©RAPID PHASE·2018
www.madamandeve.co.za

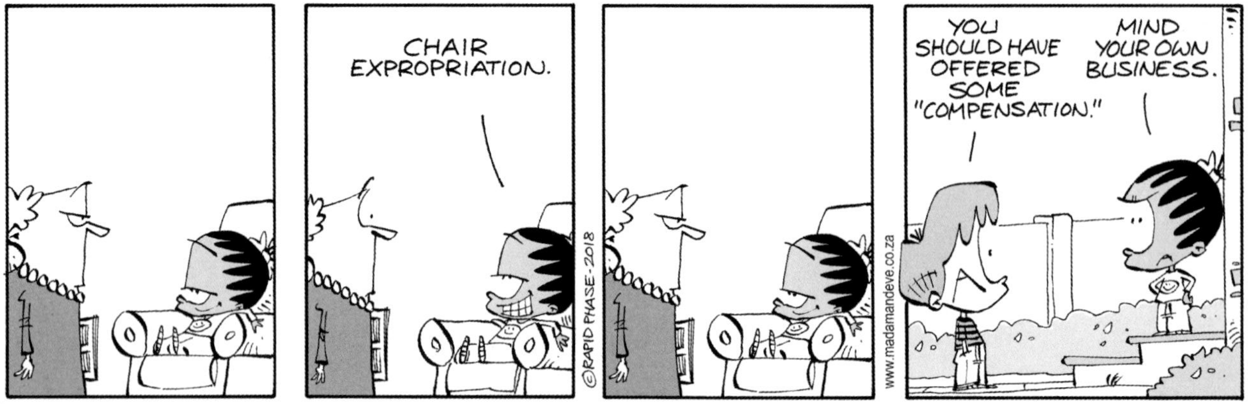
CHAIR EXPROPRIATION.
©RAPID PHASE·2018
YOU SHOULD HAVE OFFERED SOME "COMPENSATION."
MIND YOUR OWN BUSINESS.
www.madamandeve.co.za

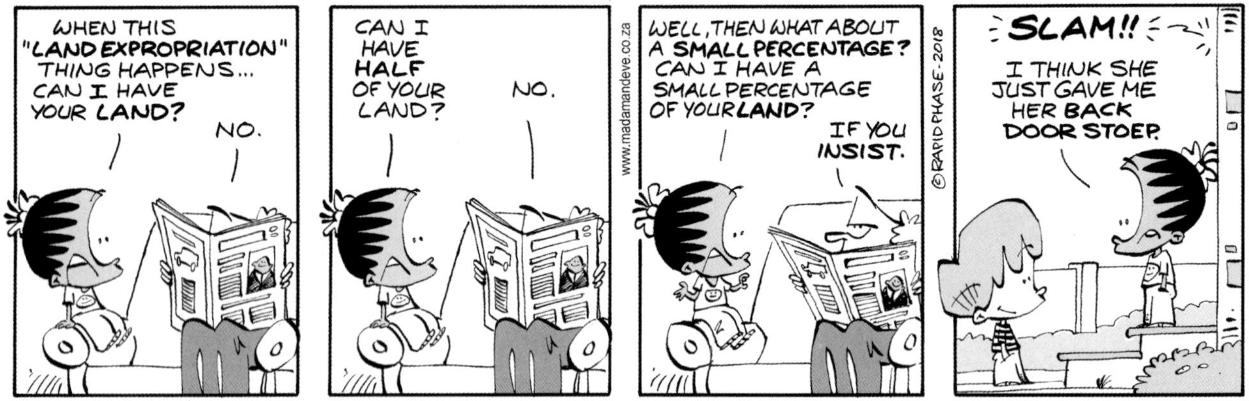
WHEN THIS "LAND EXPROPRIATION" THING HAPPENS... CAN I HAVE YOUR LAND?
NO.
CAN I HAVE HALF OF YOUR LAND?
NO.
www.madamandeve.co.za
WELL, THEN WHAT ABOUT A SMALL PERCENTAGE? CAN I HAVE A SMALL PERCENTAGE OF YOUR LAND?
IF YOU INSIST.
©RAPID PHASE·2018
SLAM!!
I THINK SHE JUST GAVE ME HER BACK DOOR STOEP.

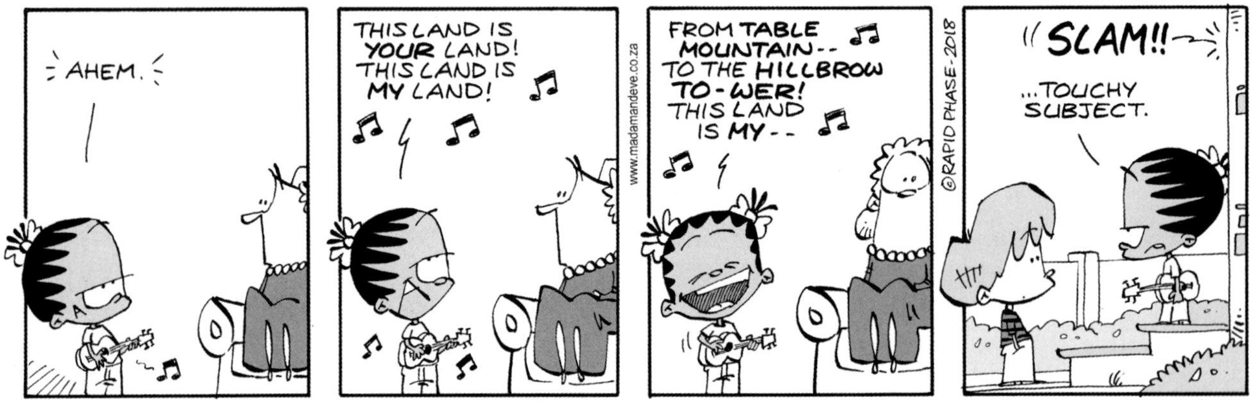
AHEM.
THIS LAND IS YOUR LAND! THIS LAND IS MY LAND!
www.madamandeve.co.za
FROM TABLE MOUNTAIN-- TO THE HILLBROW TO-WER! THIS LAND IS MY--
©RAPID PHASE·2018
SLAM!!
...TOUCHY SUBJECT.

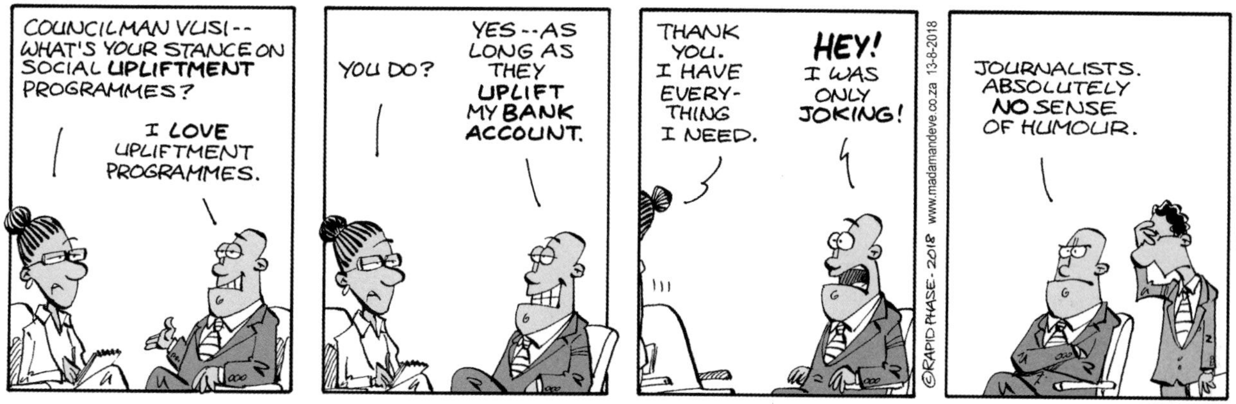

COUNCILMAN VUSI-- WHAT'S YOUR STANCE ON SOCIAL **UPLIFTMENT** PROGRAMMES?
I **LOVE** UPLIFTMENT PROGRAMMES.
YOU DO?
YES--AS LONG AS THEY **UPLIFT** MY **BANK ACCOUNT**.
THANK YOU. I HAVE EVERY-THING I NEED.
HEY! I WAS ONLY **JOKING!**
©RAPID PHASE-2018 www.madamandeve.co.za 13-8-2018
JOURNALISTS. ABSOLUTELY **NO** SENSE OF HUMOUR.

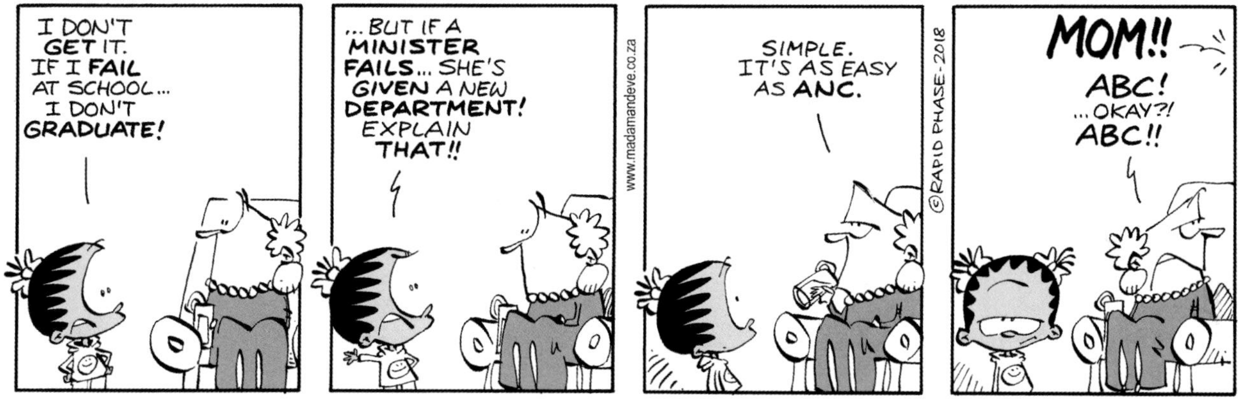

I DON'T **GET** IT. IF I **FAIL** AT SCHOOL... I DON'T **GRADUATE!**
...BUT IF A **MINISTER FAILS**... SHE'S **GIVEN** A NEW **DEPARTMENT!** EXPLAIN **THAT!!**
www.madamandeve.co.za
SIMPLE. IT'S AS EASY AS **ANC.**
©RAPID PHASE-2018
MOM!!
ABC! ...OKAY?! **ABC!!**

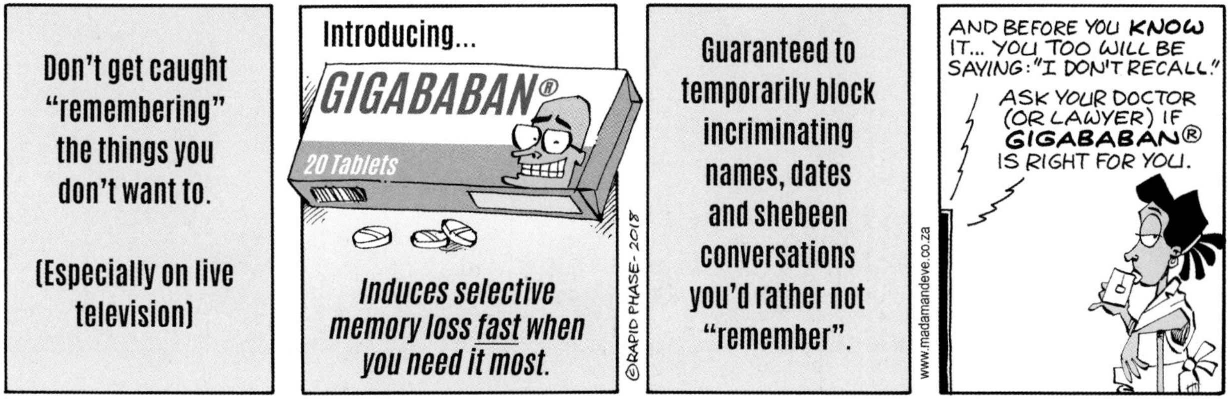

Don't get caught "remembering" the things you don't want to.
(Especially on live television)
Introducing...
GIGABABAN®
20 Tablets
Induces selective memory loss fast when you need it most.
©RAPID PHASE-2018
Guaranteed to temporarily block incriminating names, dates and shebeen conversations you'd rather not "remember".
www.madamandeve.co.za
AND BEFORE YOU **KNOW** IT... YOU TOO WILL BE SAYING: "I DON'T RECALL."
ASK YOUR DOCTOR (OR LAWYER) IF **GIGABABAN®** IS RIGHT FOR YOU.

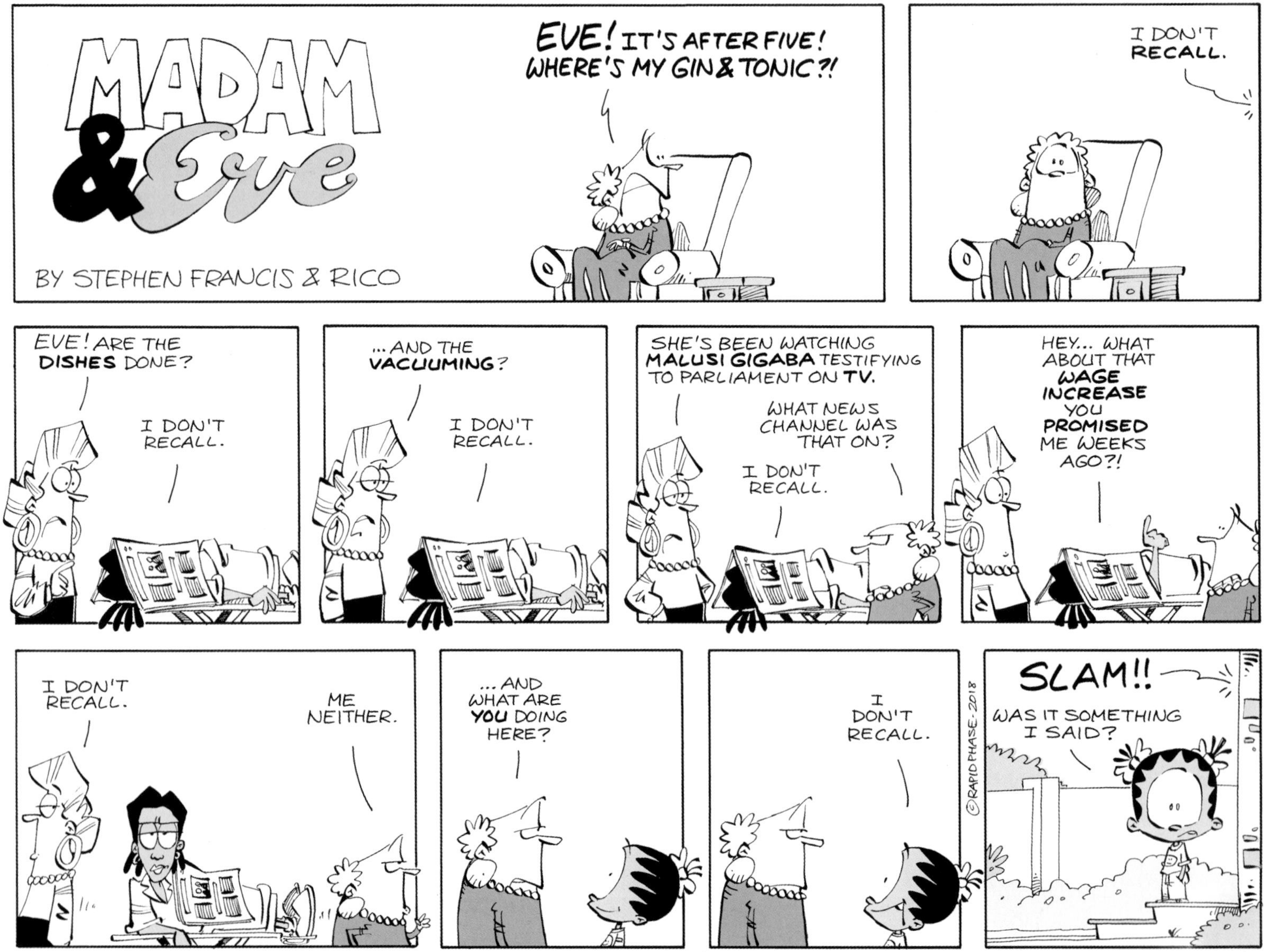
MADAM & Eve
BY STEPHEN FRANCIS & RICO
EVE! IT'S AFTER FIVE! WHERE'S MY GIN & TONIC?!
I DON'T RECALL.
EVE! ARE THE DISHES DONE?
I DON'T RECALL.
...AND THE VACUUMING?
I DON'T RECALL.
SHE'S BEEN WATCHING MALUSI GIGABA TESTIFYING TO PARLIAMENT ON TV.
WHAT NEWS CHANNEL WAS THAT ON?
I DON'T RECALL.
HEY... WHAT ABOUT THAT WAGE INCREASE YOU PROMISED ME WEEKS AGO?!
I DON'T RECALL.
ME NEITHER.
...AND WHAT ARE YOU DOING HERE?
I DON'T RECALL.
©RAPID PHASE·2018
SLAM!!
WAS IT SOMETHING I SAID?

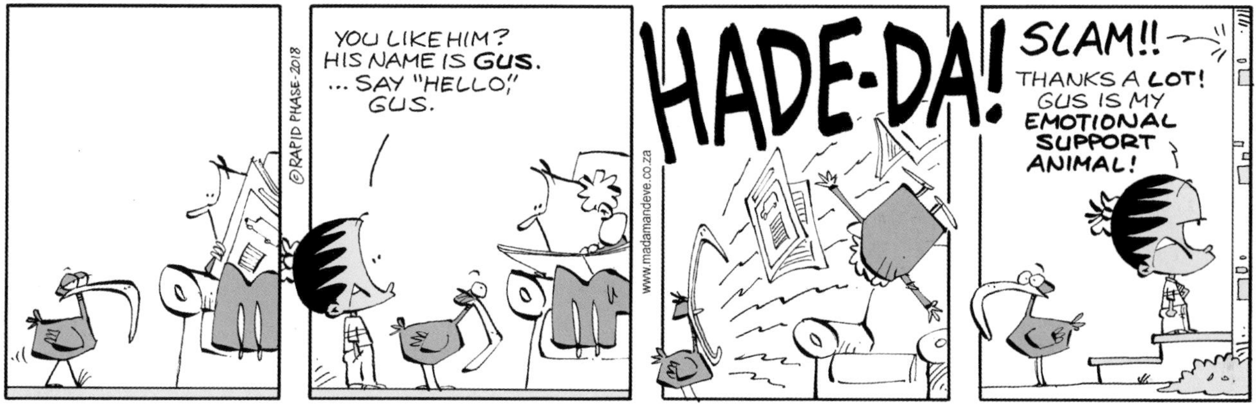
©RAPID PHASE-2018
YOU LIKE HIM? HIS NAME IS **GUS**. ... SAY "HELLO," GUS.
www.madamandeve.co.za
HADE-DA!
SLAM!!
THANKS A **LOT**! GUS IS MY **EMOTIONAL SUPPORT ANIMAL!**

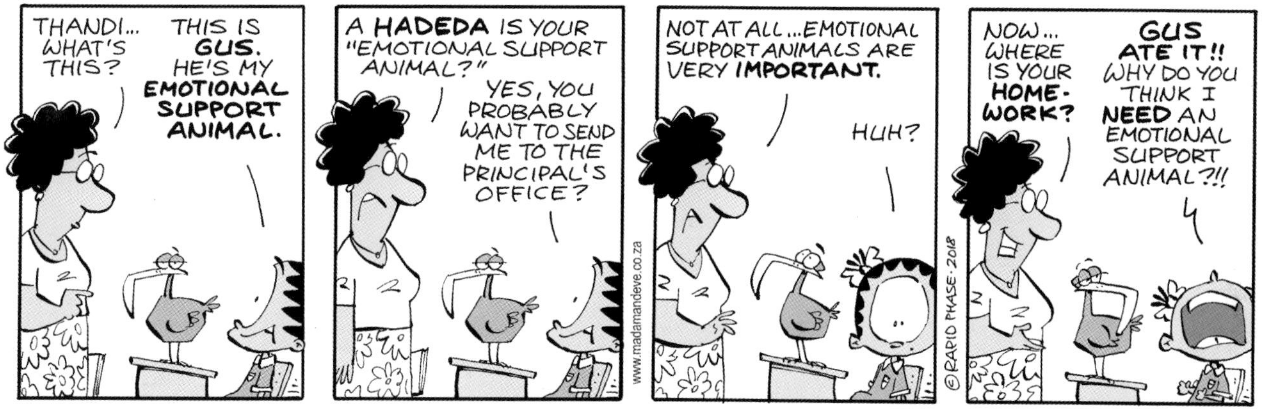
THANDI... WHAT'S THIS?
THIS IS **GUS.** HE'S MY **EMOTIONAL SUPPORT ANIMAL.**
A **HADEDA** IS YOUR "EMOTIONAL SUPPORT ANIMAL?"
YES, YOU PROBABLY WANT TO SEND ME TO THE PRINCIPAL'S OFFICE?
www.madamandeve.co.za
NOT AT ALL ...EMOTIONAL SUPPORT ANIMALS ARE VERY **IMPORTANT**.
HUH?
©RAPID PHASE-2018
NOW... WHERE IS YOUR **HOME-WORK?**
GUS ATE IT!! WHY DO YOU THINK I **NEED** AN EMOTIONAL SUPPORT ANIMAL?!!

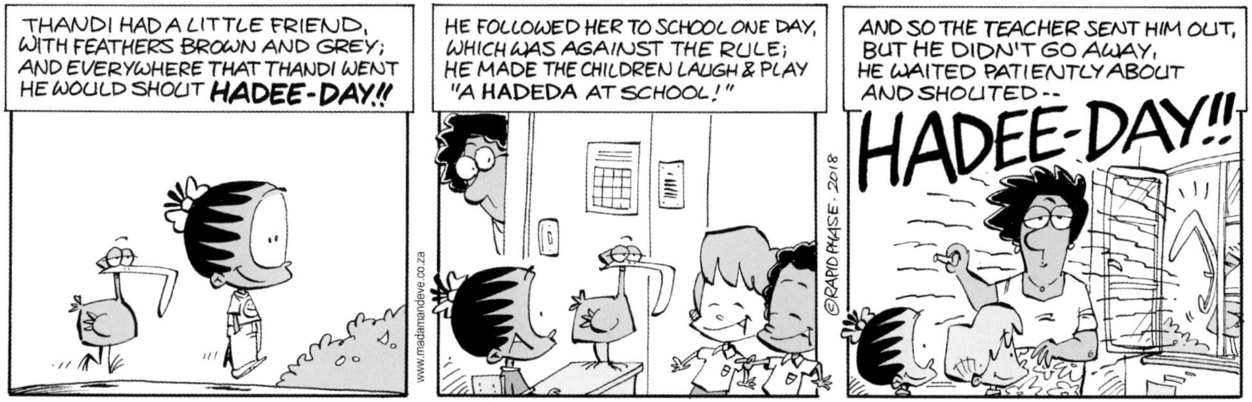
THANDI HAD A LITTLE FRIEND, WITH FEATHERS BROWN AND GREY; AND EVERYWHERE THAT THANDI WENT HE WOULD SHOUT **HADEE-DAY!!**
www.madamandeve.co.za
HE FOLLOWED HER TO SCHOOL ONE DAY, WHICH WAS AGAINST THE RULE; HE MADE THE CHILDREN LAUGH & PLAY "**A HADEDA AT SCHOOL!**"
©RAPID PHASE-2018
AND SO THE TEACHER SENT HIM OUT, BUT HE DIDN'T GO AWAY, HE WAITED PATIENTLY ABOUT AND SHOUTED--
HADEE-DAY!!

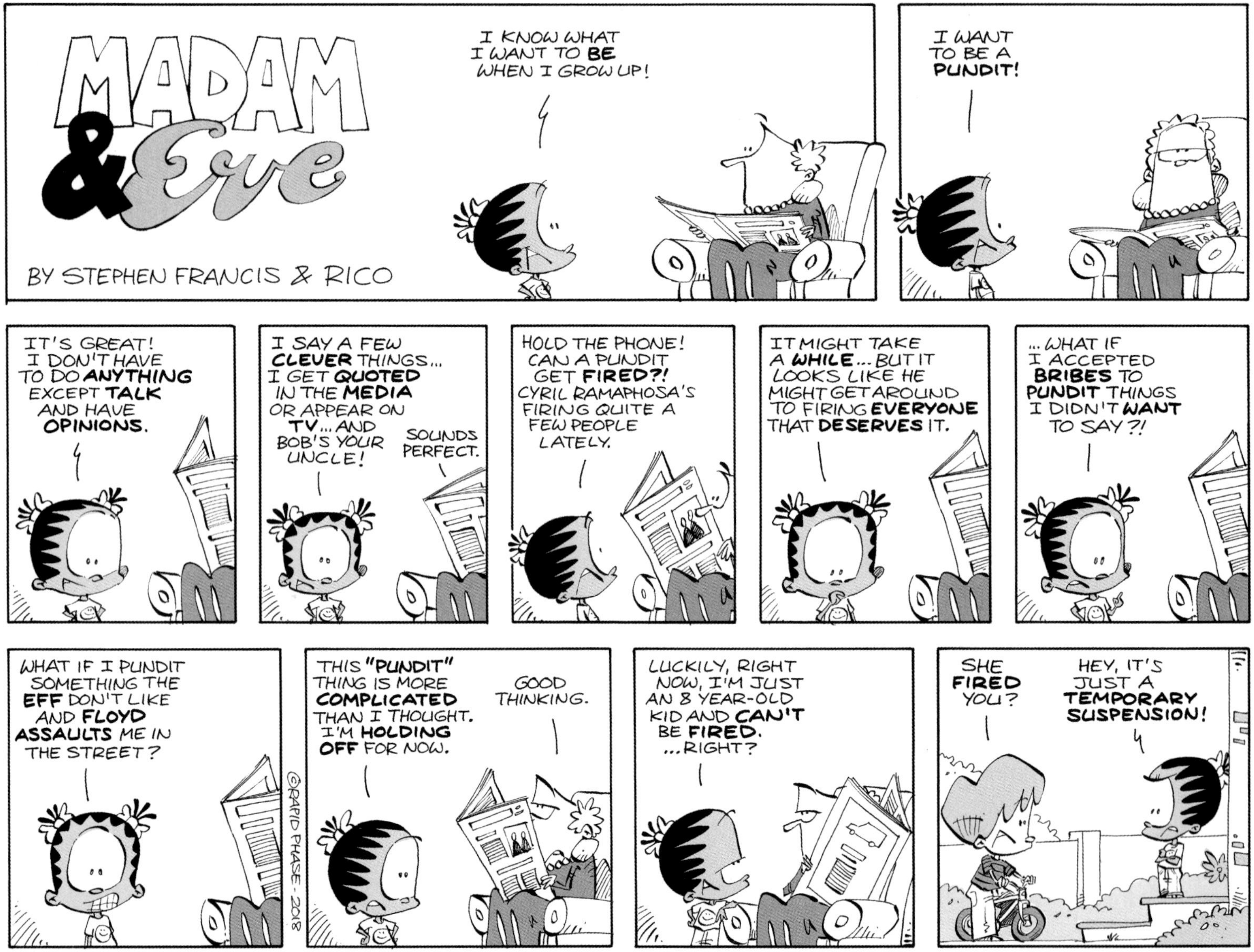
MADAM & Eve
BY STEPHEN FRANCIS & RICO
I KNOW WHAT I WANT TO **BE** WHEN I GROW UP!
I WANT TO BE A **PUNDIT!**
IT'S GREAT! I DON'T HAVE TO DO **ANYTHING** EXCEPT **TALK** AND HAVE **OPINIONS.**
I SAY A FEW **CLEVER** THINGS... I GET **QUOTED** IN THE **MEDIA** OR APPEAR ON **TV**... AND BOB'S YOUR UNCLE!
SOUNDS PERFECT.
HOLD THE PHONE! CAN A PUNDIT GET **FIRED?!** CYRIL RAMAPHOSA'S FIRING QUITE A FEW PEOPLE LATELY.
IT MIGHT TAKE A **WHILE**... BUT IT LOOKS LIKE HE MIGHT GET AROUND TO FIRING **EVERYONE** THAT **DESERVES** IT.
...WHAT IF I ACCEPTED **BRIBES** TO **PUNDIT** THINGS I DIDN'T **WANT** TO SAY?!
WHAT IF I PUNDIT SOMETHING THE **EFF** DON'T LIKE AND **FLOYD ASSAULTS** ME IN THE STREET?
©RAPID PHASE - 2018
THIS **"PUNDIT"** THING IS MORE **COMPLICATED** THAN I THOUGHT. I'M **HOLDING OFF** FOR NOW.
GOOD THINKING.
LUCKILY, RIGHT NOW, I'M JUST AN 8 YEAR-OLD KID AND **CAN'T** BE **FIRED.** ...RIGHT?
SHE **FIRED** YOU?
HEY, IT'S JUST A **TEMPORARY SUSPENSION!**

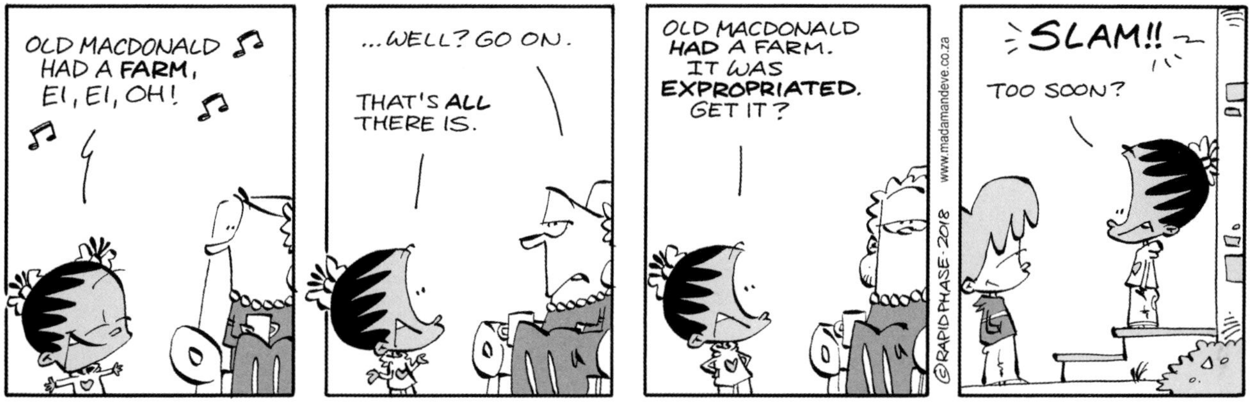
OLD MACDONALD HAD A FARM, EI, EI, OH!
...WELL? GO ON.
THAT'S ALL THERE IS.
OLD MACDONALD HAD A FARM. IT WAS EXPROPRIATED. GET IT?
©RAPID PHASE · 2018 www.madamandeve.co.za
SLAM!!
TOO SOON?

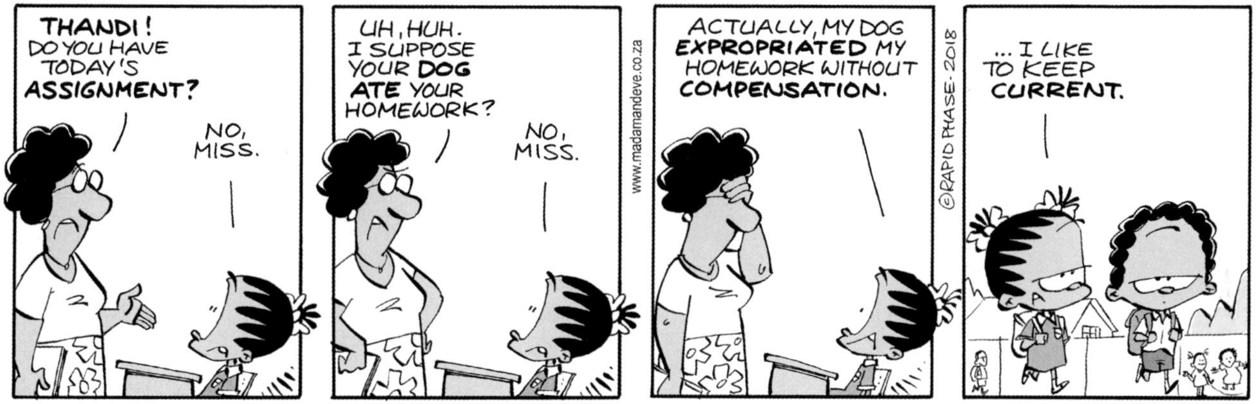
THANDI! DO YOU HAVE TODAY'S ASSIGNMENT?
NO, MISS.
UH, HUH. I SUPPOSE YOUR DOG ATE YOUR HOMEWORK?
NO, MISS.
www.madamandeve.co.za
ACTUALLY, MY DOG EXPROPRIATED MY HOMEWORK WITHOUT COMPENSATION.
©RAPID PHASE · 2018
... I LIKE TO KEEP CURRENT.

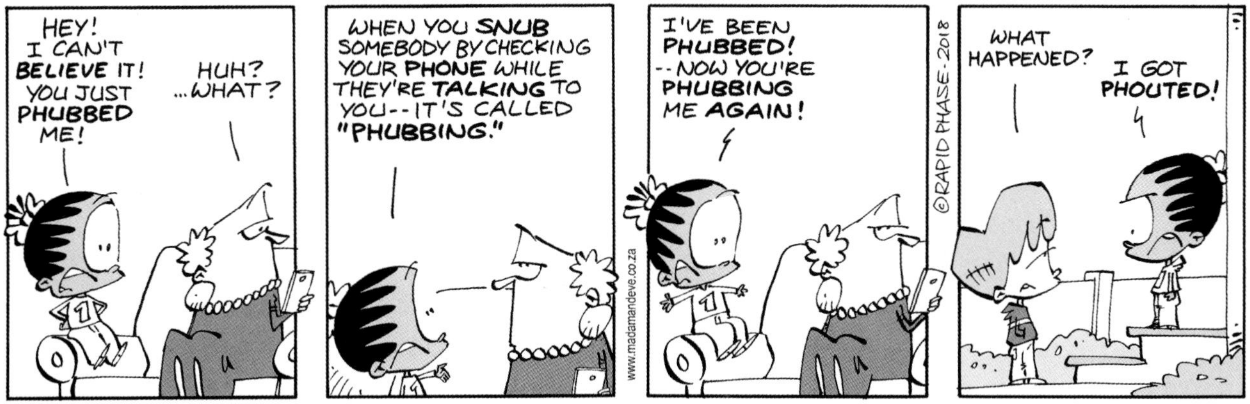
HEY! I CAN'T BELIEVE IT! YOU JUST PHUBBED ME!
HUH? ...WHAT?
WHEN YOU SNUB SOMEBODY BY CHECKING YOUR PHONE WHILE THEY'RE TALKING TO YOU--IT'S CALLED "PHUBBING."
www.madamandeve.co.za
I'VE BEEN PHUBBED! --NOW YOU'RE PHUBBING ME AGAIN!
©RAPID PHASE · 2018
WHAT HAPPENED?
I GOT PHOUTED!

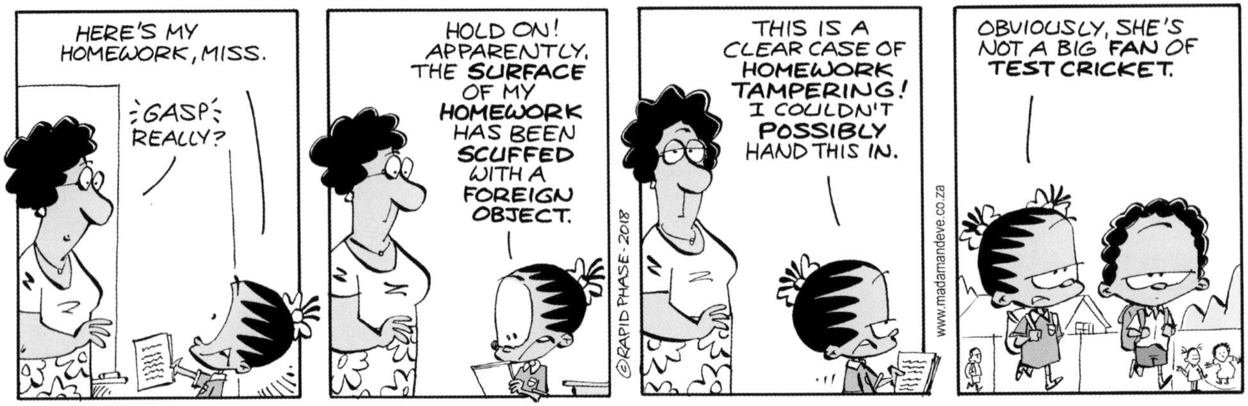
HERE'S MY HOMEWORK, MISS.
GASP REALLY?
HOLD ON! APPARENTLY, THE SURFACE OF MY HOMEWORK HAS BEEN SCUFFED WITH A FOREIGN OBJECT.
©RAPID PHASE-2018
THIS IS A CLEAR CASE OF HOMEWORK TAMPERING! I COULDN'T POSSIBLY HAND THIS IN.
www.madamandeve.co.za
OBVIOUSLY, SHE'S NOT A BIG FAN OF TEST CRICKET.

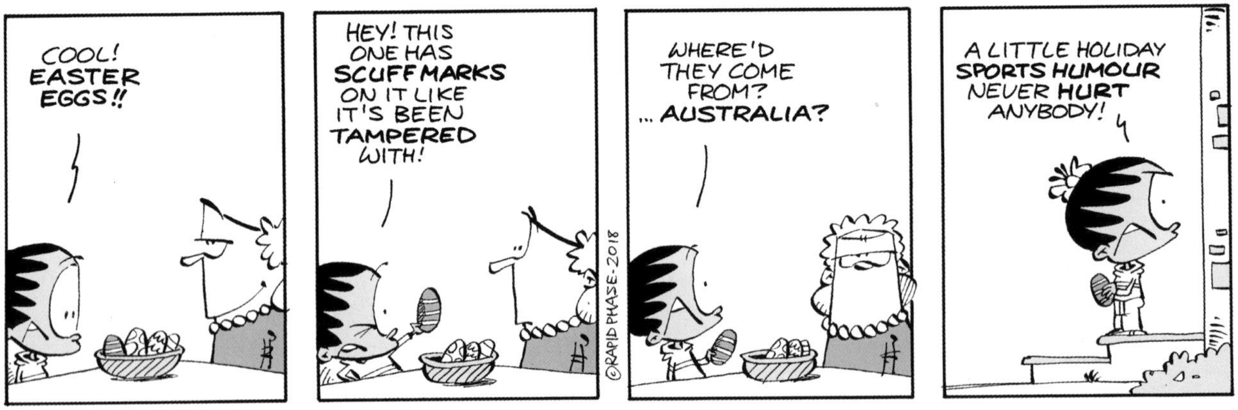
COOL! EASTER EGGS!!
HEY! THIS ONE HAS SCUFF MARKS ON IT LIKE IT'S BEEN TAMPERED WITH!
©RAPID PHASE-2018
WHERE'D THEY COME FROM? ... AUSTRALIA?
A LITTLE HOLIDAY SPORTS HUMOUR NEVER HURT ANYBODY!

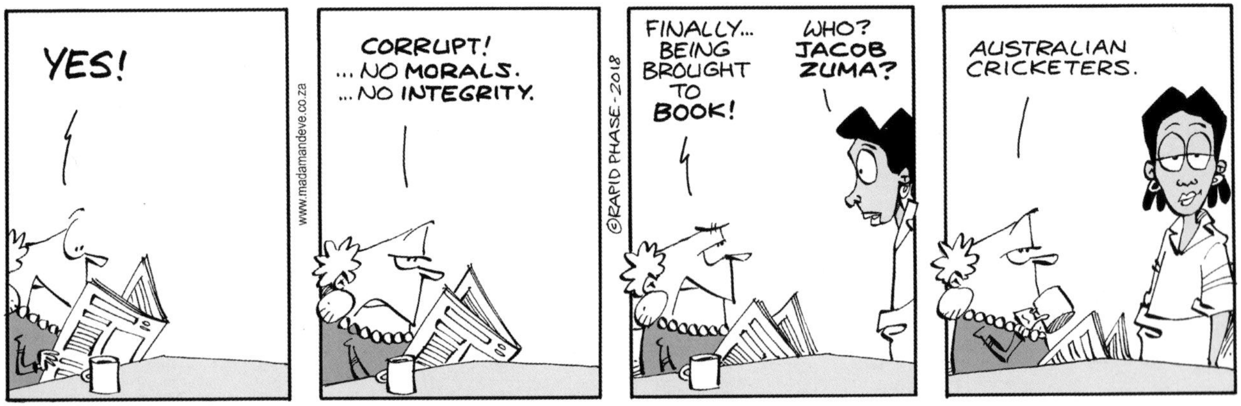
YES!
www.madamandeve.co.za
CORRUPT! ... NO MORALS. ... NO INTEGRITY.
©RAPID PHASE-2018
FINALLY... BEING BROUGHT TO BOOK!
WHO? JACOB ZUMA?
AUSTRALIAN CRICKETERS.

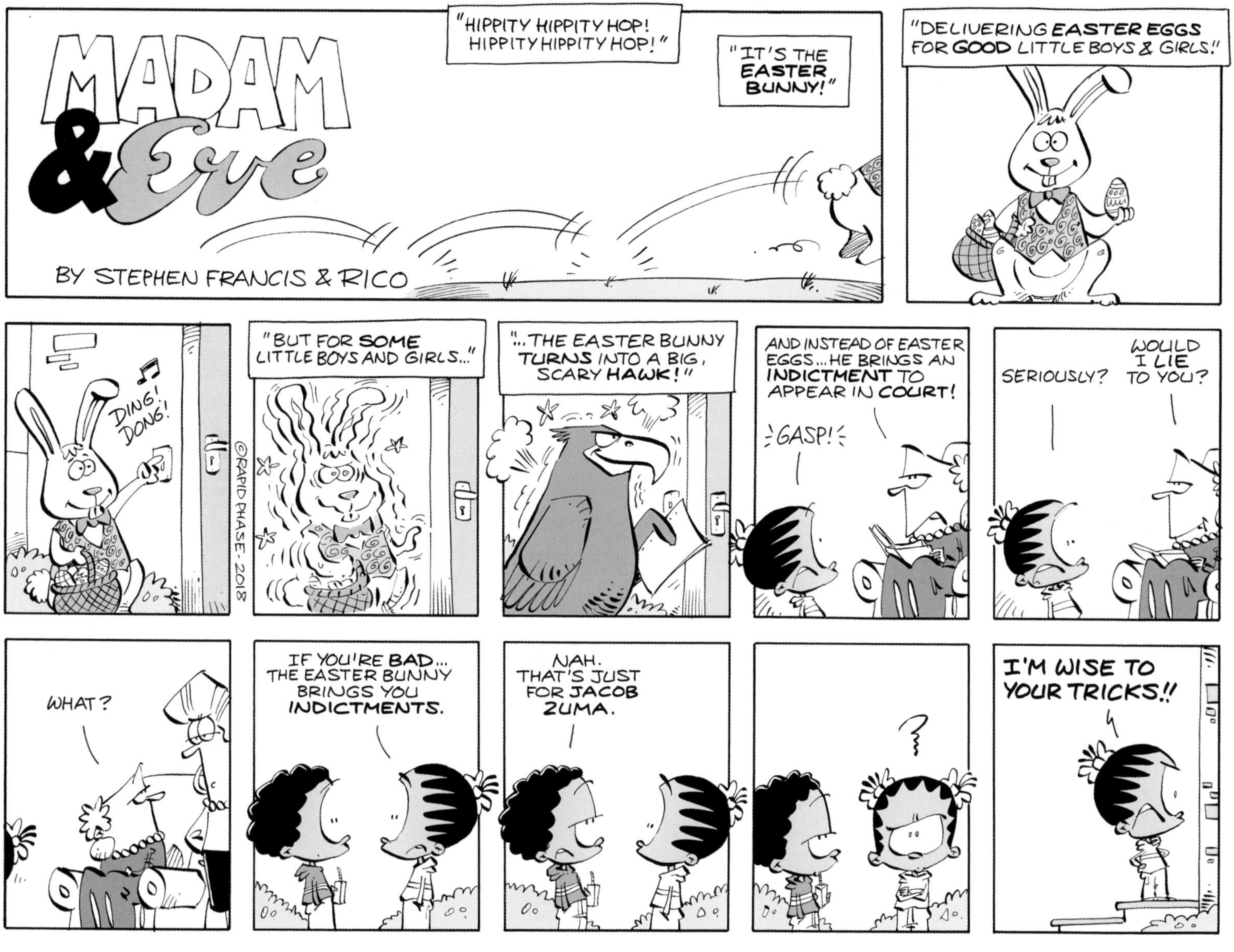
MADAM & Eve
BY STEPHEN FRANCIS & RICO
"HIPPITY HIPPITY HOP! HIPPITY HIPPITY HOP!"
"IT'S THE EASTER BUNNY!"
"DELIVERING EASTER EGGS FOR GOOD LITTLE BOYS & GIRLS!"
DING! DONG!
©RAPID PHASE · 2018
"BUT FOR SOME LITTLE BOYS AND GIRLS..."
"...THE EASTER BUNNY TURNS INTO A BIG, SCARY HAWK!"
AND INSTEAD OF EASTER EGGS... HE BRINGS AN INDICTMENT TO APPEAR IN COURT!
GASP!
SERIOUSLY?
WOULD I LIE TO YOU?
WHAT?
IF YOU'RE BAD... THE EASTER BUNNY BRINGS YOU INDICTMENTS.
NAH. THAT'S JUST FOR JACOB ZUMA.
?
I'M WISE TO YOUR TRICKS!!

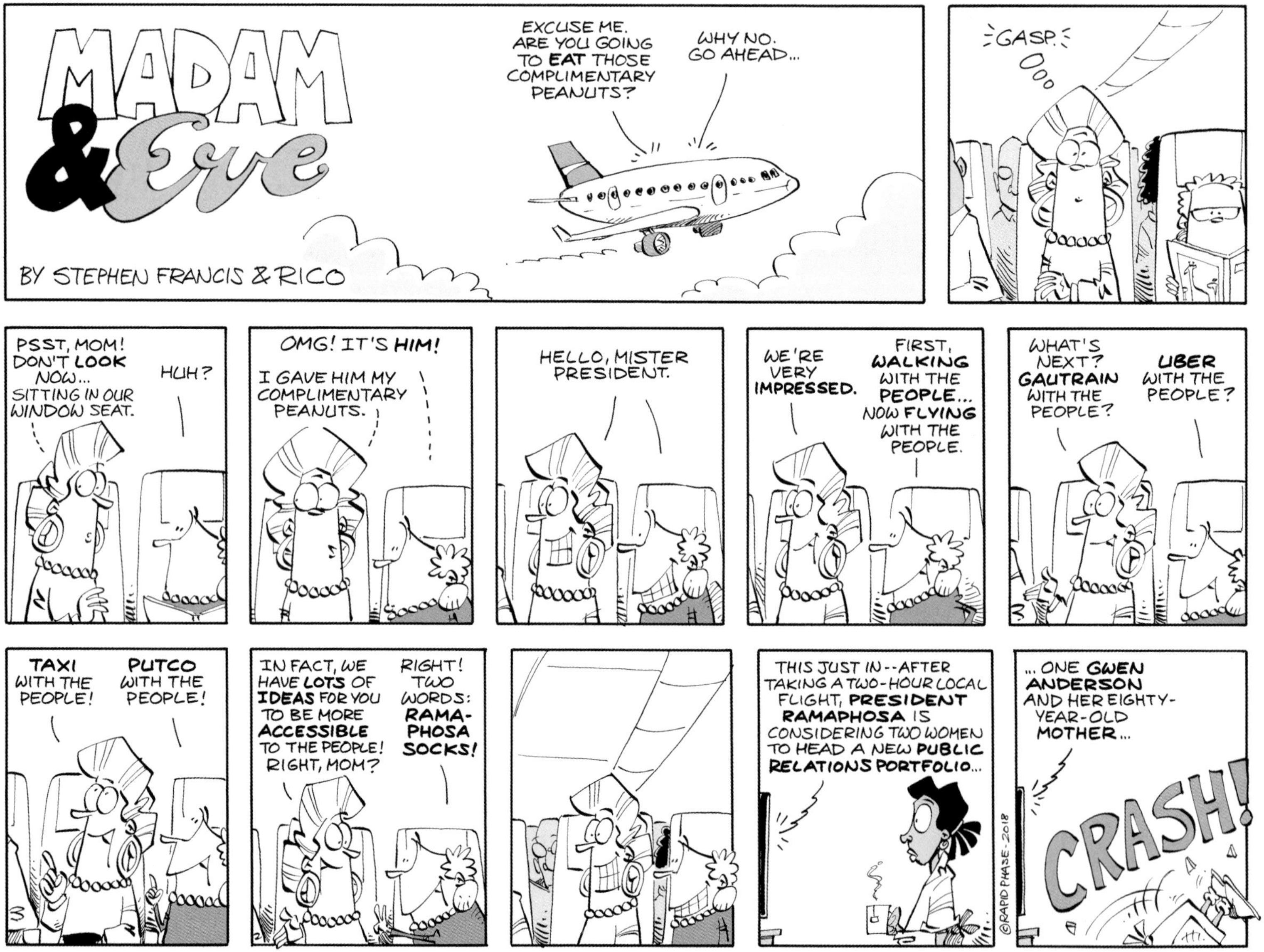
MADAM & Eve
BY STEPHEN FRANCIS & RICO
EXCUSE ME. ARE YOU GOING TO EAT THOSE COMPLIMENTARY PEANUTS?
WHY NO. GO AHEAD...
GASP
PSST, MOM! DON'T LOOK NOW... SITTING IN OUR WINDOW SEAT.
HUH?
OMG! IT'S HIM!
I GAVE HIM MY COMPLIMENTARY PEANUTS.
HELLO, MISTER PRESIDENT.
WE'RE VERY IMPRESSED.
FIRST, WALKING WITH THE PEOPLE... NOW FLYING WITH THE PEOPLE.
WHAT'S NEXT? GAUTRAIN WITH THE PEOPLE?
UBER WITH THE PEOPLE?
TAXI WITH THE PEOPLE!
PUTCO WITH THE PEOPLE!
IN FACT, WE HAVE LOTS OF IDEAS FOR YOU TO BE MORE ACCESSIBLE TO THE PEOPLE! RIGHT, MOM?
RIGHT! TWO WORDS: RAMAPHOSA SOCKS!
THIS JUST IN--AFTER TAKING A TWO-HOUR LOCAL FLIGHT, PRESIDENT RAMAPHOSA IS CONSIDERING TWO WOMEN TO HEAD A NEW PUBLIC RELATIONS PORTFOLIO...
©RAPID PHASE · 2018
... ONE GWEN ANDERSON AND HER EIGHTY-YEAR-OLD MOTHER...
CRASH!

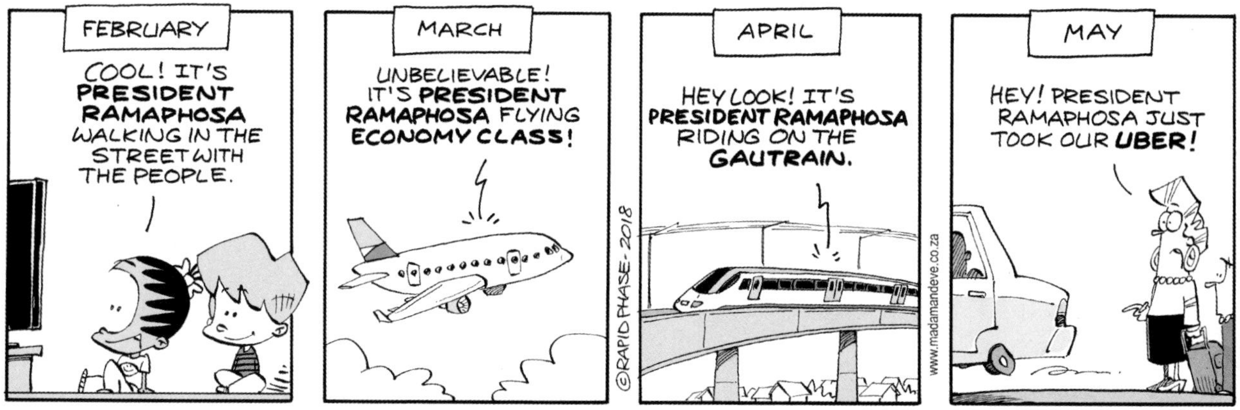
FEBRUARY
COOL! IT'S **PRESIDENT RAMAPHOSA** WALKING IN THE STREET WITH THE PEOPLE.
MARCH
UNBELIEVABLE! IT'S **PRESIDENT RAMAPHOSA** FLYING **ECONOMY CLASS!**
©RAPID PHASE - 2018
APRIL
HEY LOOK! IT'S **PRESIDENT RAMAPHOSA** RIDING ON THE **GAUTRAIN.**
www.madamandeve.co.za
MAY
HEY! PRESIDENT RAMAPHOSA JUST TOOK OUR **UBER!**

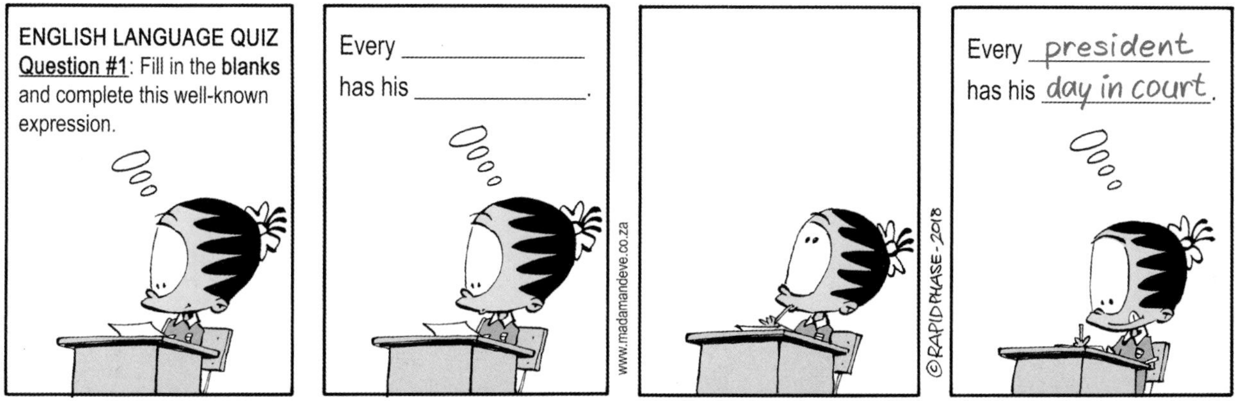
ENGLISH LANGUAGE QUIZ
Question #1: Fill in the **blanks** and complete this well-known expression.
Every ______________
has his ______________.
www.madamandeve.co.za
©RAPID PHASE - 2018
Every president
has his day in court.

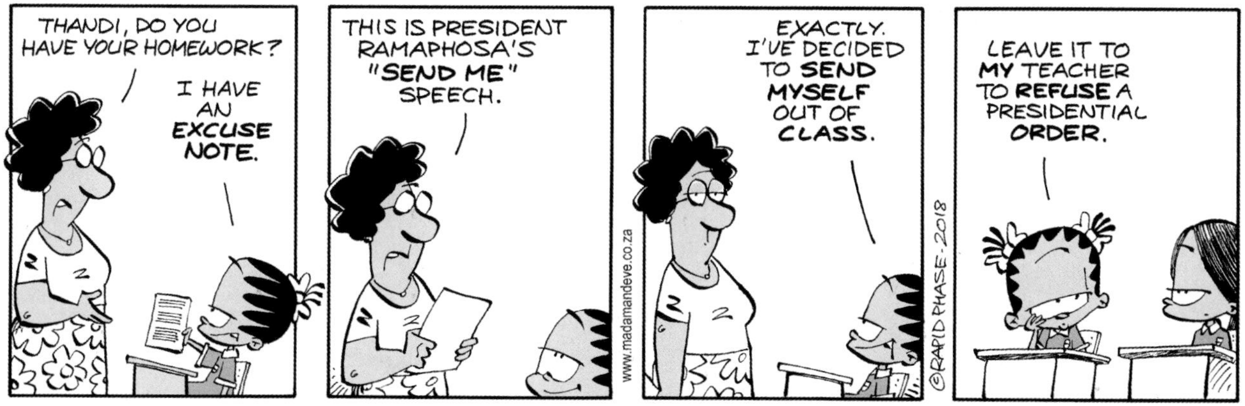
THANDI, DO YOU HAVE YOUR HOMEWORK?
I HAVE AN **EXCUSE NOTE.**
THIS IS PRESIDENT RAMAPHOSA'S **"SEND ME"** SPEECH.
www.madamandeve.co.za
EXACTLY. I'VE DECIDED TO **SEND MYSELF** OUT OF **CLASS.**
©RAPID PHASE - 2018
LEAVE IT TO **MY** TEACHER TO **REFUSE** A PRESIDENTIAL **ORDER.**

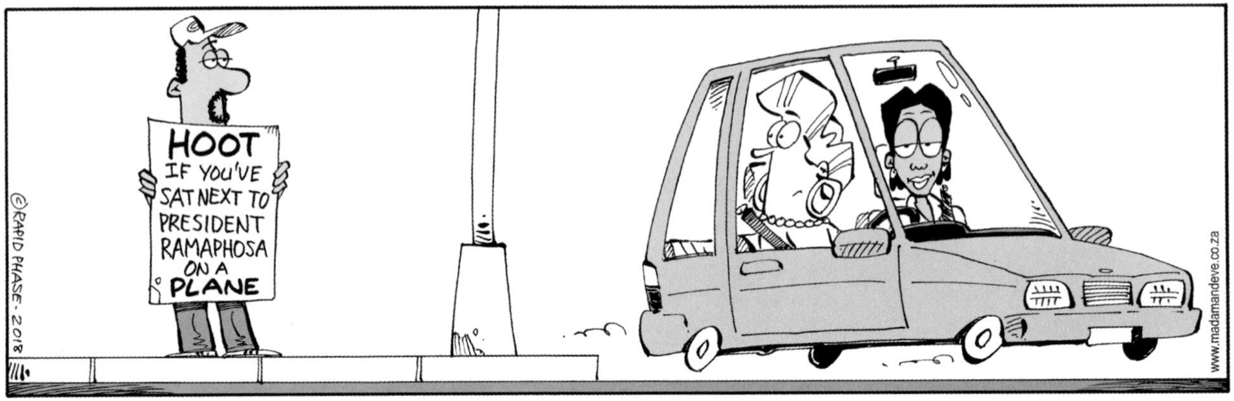
HOOT IF YOU'VE SAT NEXT TO PRESIDENT RAMAPHOSA ON A PLANE
©RAPID PHASE · 2018
www.madamandeve.co.za

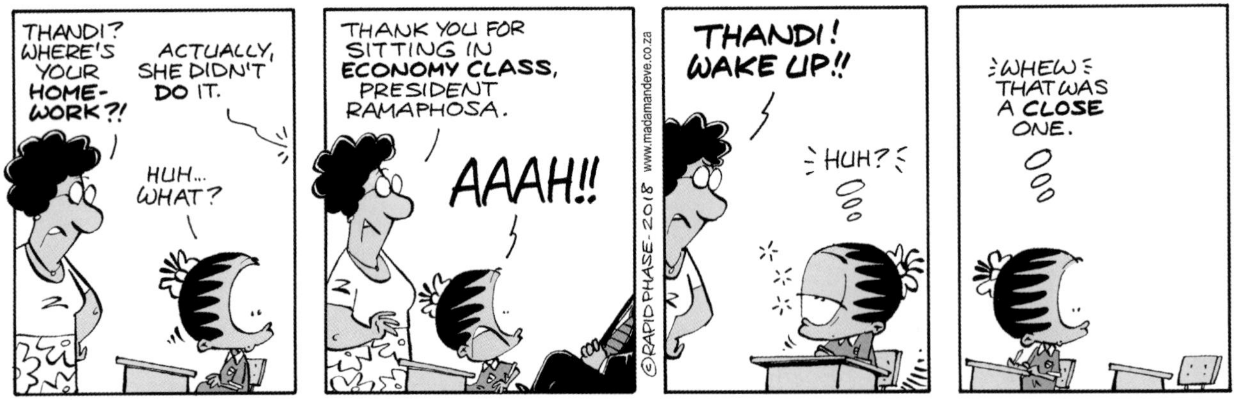
THANDI? WHERE'S YOUR HOME-WORK?!
ACTUALLY, SHE DIDN'T DO IT.
HUH... WHAT?
THANK YOU FOR SITTING IN ECONOMY CLASS, PRESIDENT RAMAPHOSA.
AAAH!!
©RAPID PHASE · 2018 www.madamandeve.co.za
THANDI! WAKE UP!!
HUH?
WHEW THAT WAS A CLOSE ONE.

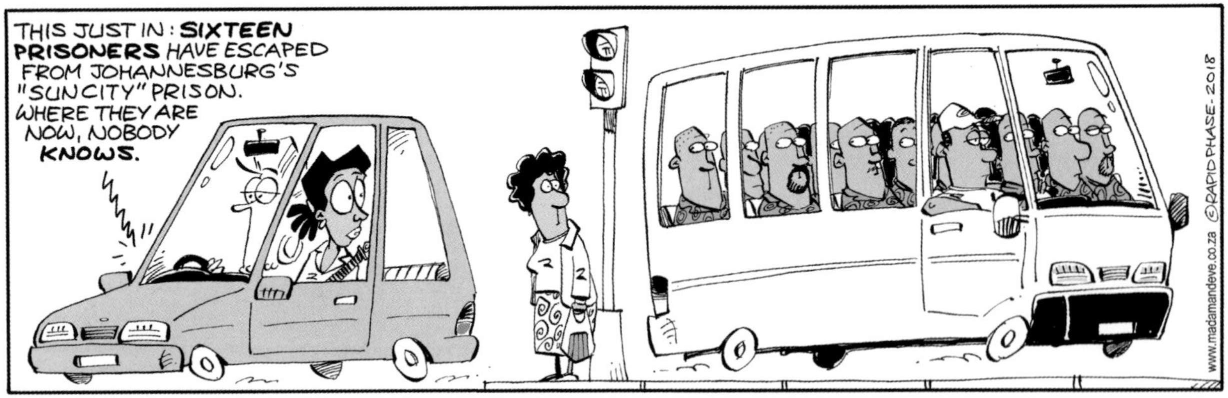
THIS JUST IN: SIXTEEN PRISONERS HAVE ESCAPED FROM JOHANNESBURG'S "SUN CITY" PRISON. WHERE THEY ARE NOW, NOBODY KNOWS.
©RAPID PHASE · 2018
www.madamandeve.co.za

MADAM & Eve

BY STEPHEN FRANCIS & RICO

In the jungle,
the economic jungle...

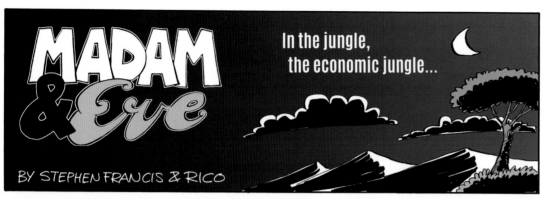

The lions don't sleep tonight.

Untethered.

Unleashed.

Unstoppable.

The worldwide hunt has begun...

...for $100 billion of investments in South Africa over the next five years!

Trevor *"Howlin' Mad"* Manuel

Trudi *"The Adviser"* Makhaya

Jacko *"The Banker"* Maree

Mcebisi *"The Whistleblower"* Jonas

...and President Cyril *"The Buffalo"* Ramaphosa in...

I LOVE IT WHEN A PLAN COMES TOGETHER.

THE C-TEAM

COMING SOON TO AN INVESTMENT HOUSE NEAR YOU.

I JUST HOPE THEY'RE FLYING ECONOMY CLASS.

LOOKS BORING.

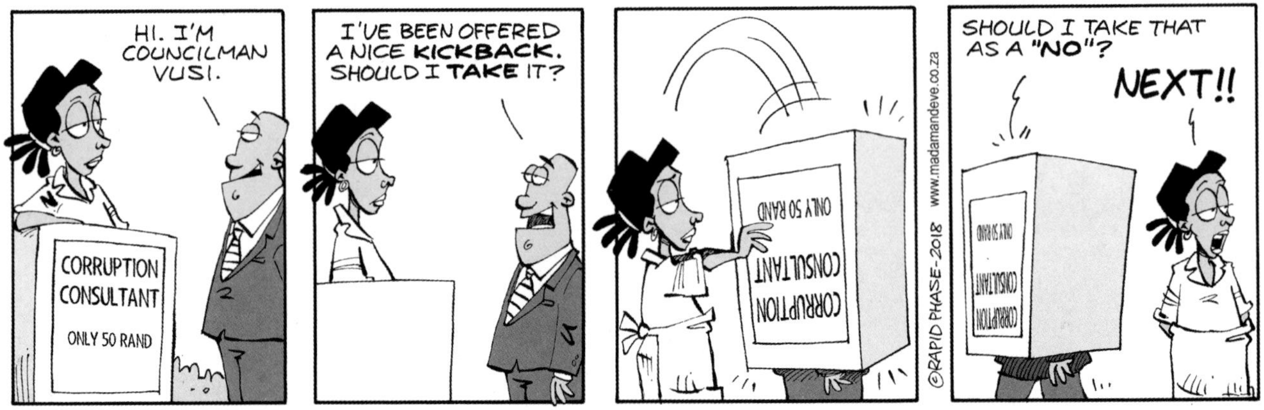
HI. I'M COUNCILMAN VUSI.
CORRUPTION CONSULTANT
ONLY 50 RAND
I'VE BEEN OFFERED A NICE **KICKBACK.** SHOULD I **TAKE** IT?
©RAPID PHASE-2018 www.madamandeve.co.za
SHOULD I TAKE THAT AS A **"NO"**?
NEXT!!

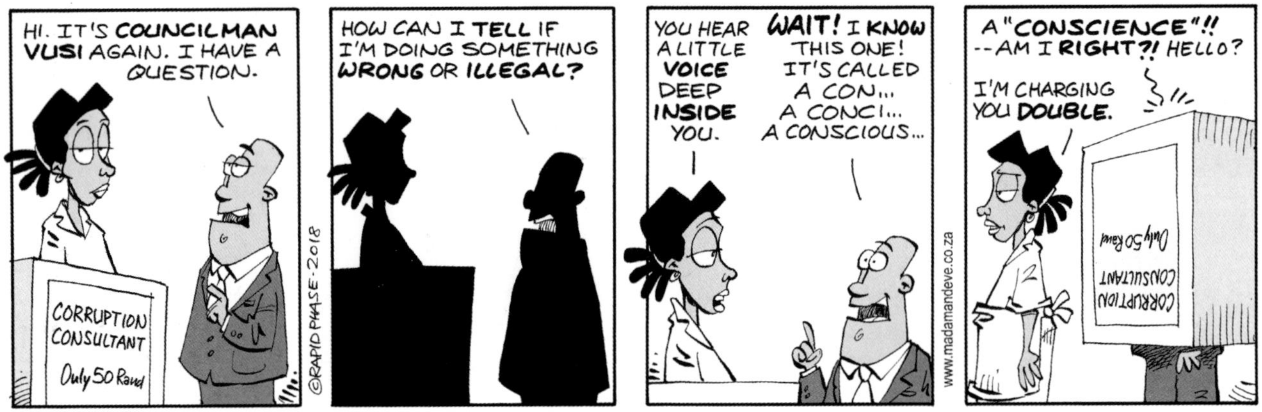
HI. IT'S **COUNCILMAN VUSI** AGAIN. I HAVE A QUESTION.
CORRUPTION CONSULTANT
Only 50 Rand
HOW CAN I **TELL** IF I'M DOING SOMETHING **WRONG** OR **ILLEGAL?**
©RAPID PHASE-2018
YOU HEAR A LITTLE **VOICE** DEEP **INSIDE** YOU.
WAIT! I **KNOW** THIS ONE! IT'S CALLED A CON... A CONCI... A CONSCIOUS...
www.madamandeve.co.za
A "**CONSCIENCE**"!! --AM I **RIGHT?!** HELLO?
I'M CHARGING YOU **DOUBLE.**

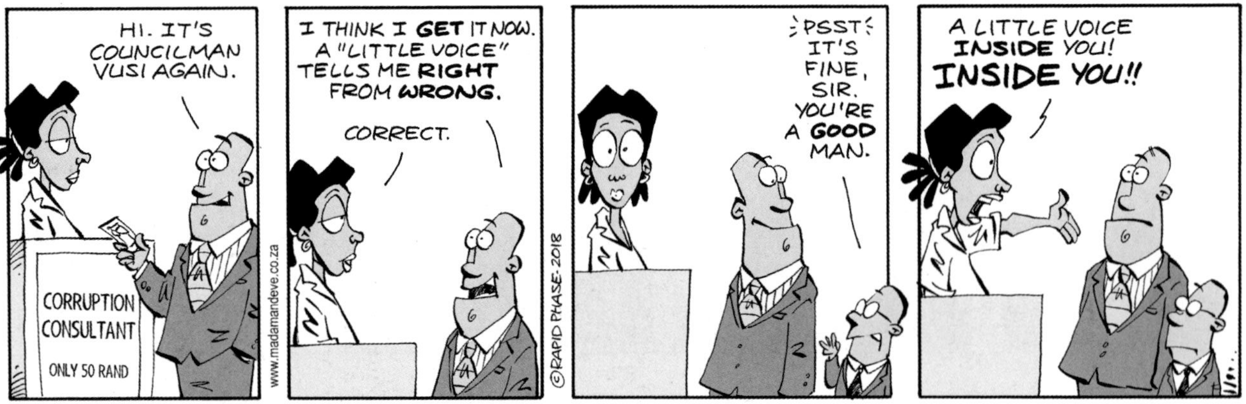
HI. IT'S COUNCILMAN VUSI AGAIN.
CORRUPTION CONSULTANT
ONLY 50 RAND
www.madamandeve.co.za
I THINK I **GET** IT NOW. A "LITTLE VOICE" TELLS ME **RIGHT** FROM **WRONG.**
CORRECT.
©RAPID PHASE-2018
PSST IT'S FINE, SIR. YOU'RE A **GOOD** MAN.
A LITTLE VOICE **INSIDE** YOU! **INSIDE YOU!!**

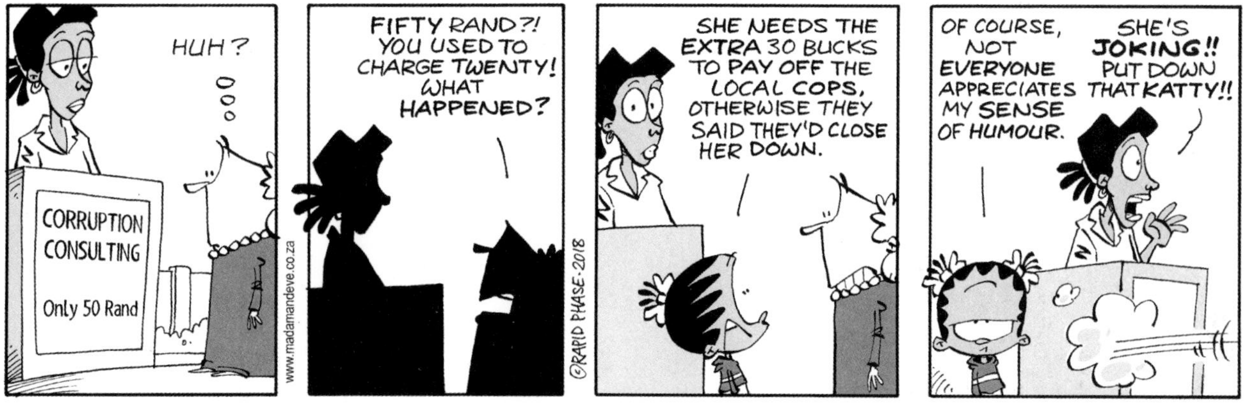
CORRUPTION CONSULTING Only 50 Rand
HUH?
www.madamandeve.co.za
FIFTY RAND?! YOU USED TO CHARGE TWENTY! WHAT HAPPENED?
©RAPID PHASE·2018
SHE NEEDS THE EXTRA 30 BUCKS TO PAY OFF THE LOCAL COPS, OTHERWISE THEY SAID THEY'D CLOSE HER DOWN.
OF COURSE, NOT EVERYONE APPRECIATES MY SENSE OF HUMOUR.
SHE'S JOKING!! PUT DOWN THAT KATTY!!

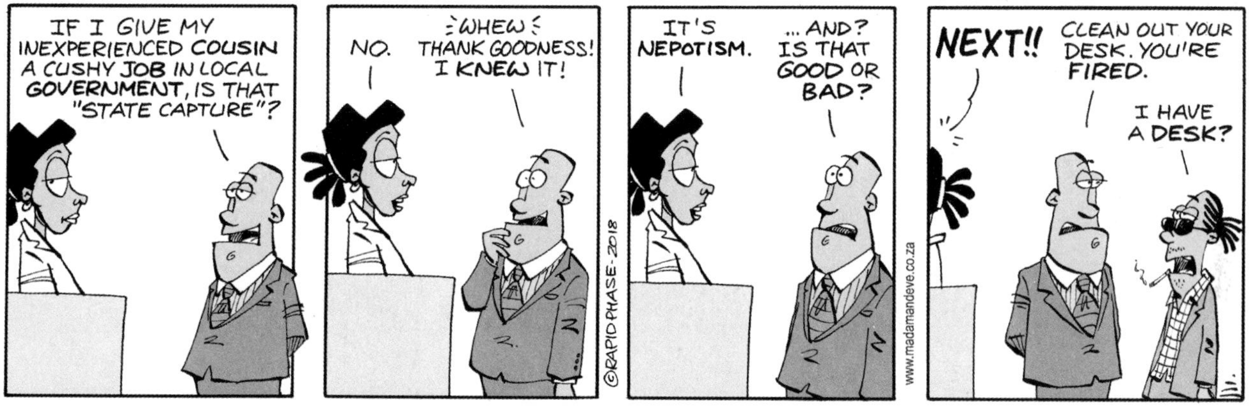
IF I GIVE MY INEXPERIENCED COUSIN A CUSHY JOB IN LOCAL GOVERNMENT, IS THAT "STATE CAPTURE"?
NO.
WHEW THANK GOODNESS! I KNEW IT!
©RAPID PHASE·2018
IT'S NEPOTISM.
... AND? IS THAT GOOD OR BAD?
www.madamandeve.co.za
NEXT!!
CLEAN OUT YOUR DESK. YOU'RE FIRED.
I HAVE A DESK?

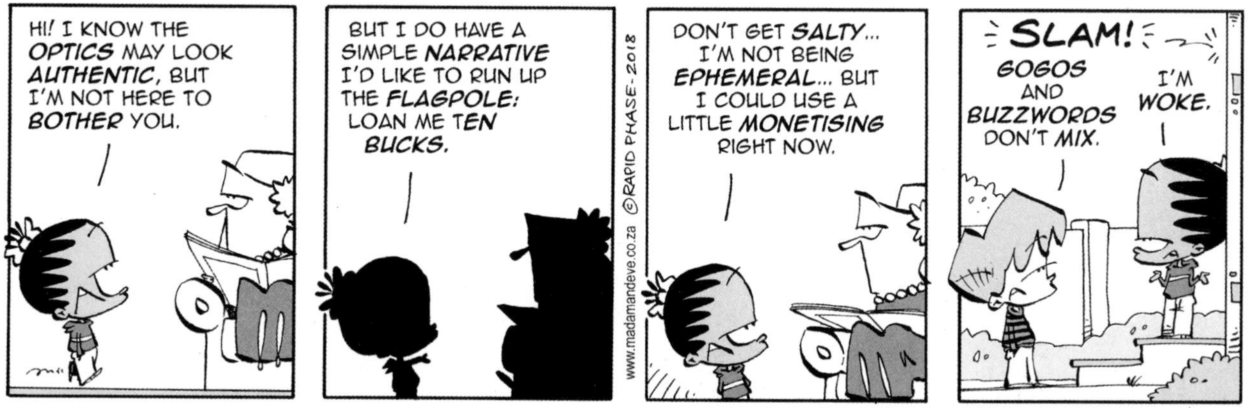
HI! I KNOW THE OPTICS MAY LOOK AUTHENTIC, BUT I'M NOT HERE TO BOTHER YOU.
BUT I DO HAVE A SIMPLE NARRATIVE I'D LIKE TO RUN UP THE FLAGPOLE: LOAN ME TEN BUCKS.
www.madamandeve.co.za ©RAPID PHASE·2018
DON'T GET SALTY... I'M NOT BEING EPHEMERAL... BUT I COULD USE A LITTLE MONETISING RIGHT NOW.
SLAM!
GOGOS AND BUZZWORDS DON'T MIX.
I'M WOKE.

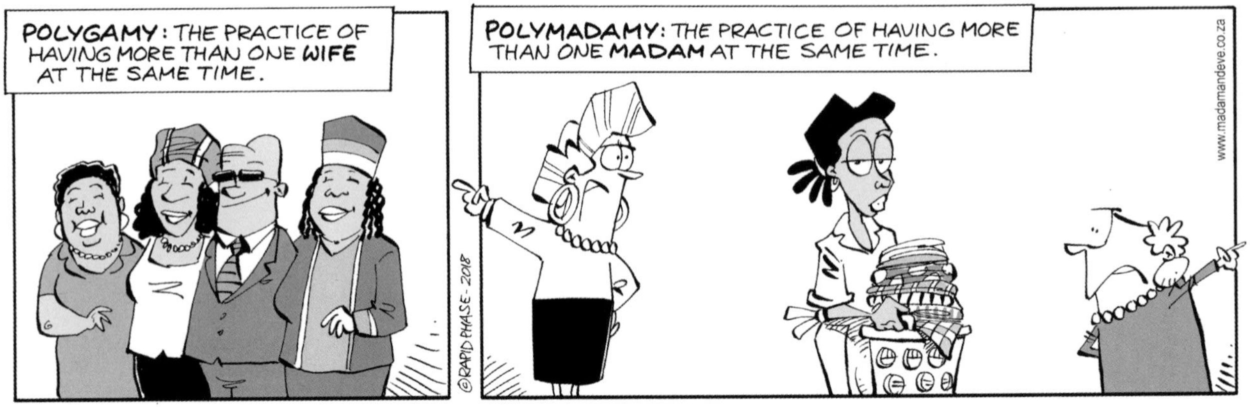
POLYGAMY: THE PRACTICE OF HAVING MORE THAN ONE WIFE AT THE SAME TIME.
©RAPID PHASE · 2018
POLYMADAMY: THE PRACTICE OF HAVING MORE THAN ONE MADAM AT THE SAME TIME.
www.madamandeve.co.za

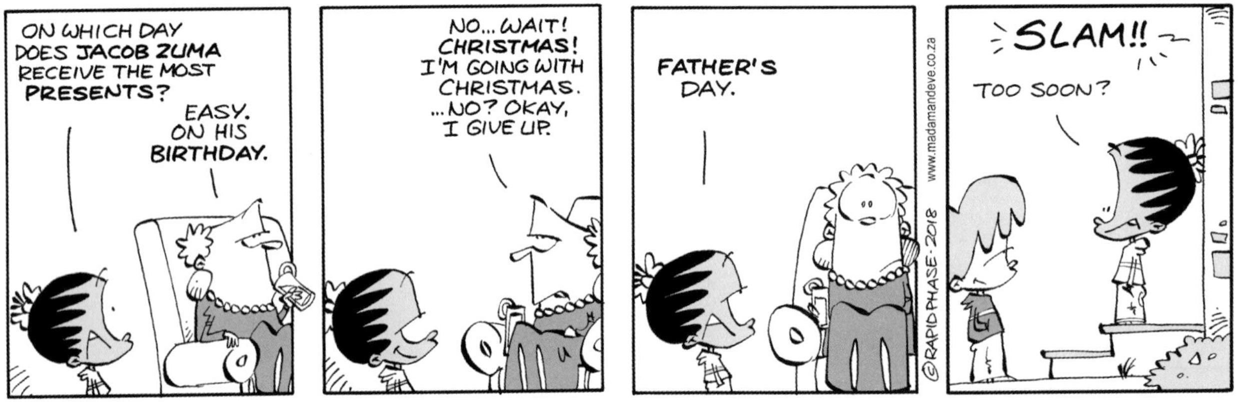
ON WHICH DAY DOES JACOB ZUMA RECEIVE THE MOST PRESENTS?
EASY. ON HIS BIRTHDAY.
NO... WAIT! CHRISTMAS! I'M GOING WITH CHRISTMAS. ...NO? OKAY, I GIVE UP.
FATHER'S DAY.
©RAPID PHASE · 2018
www.madamandeve.co.za
SLAM!!
TOO SOON?

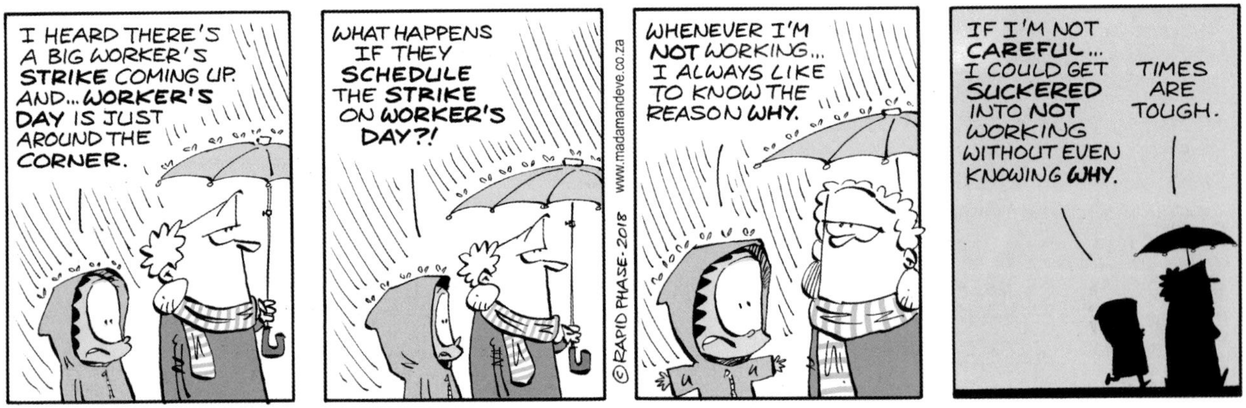
I HEARD THERE'S A BIG WORKER'S STRIKE COMING UP. AND... WORKER'S DAY IS JUST AROUND THE CORNER.
WHAT HAPPENS IF THEY SCHEDULE THE STRIKE ON WORKER'S DAY?!
©RAPID PHASE · 2018
www.madamandeve.co.za
WHENEVER I'M NOT WORKING... I ALWAYS LIKE TO KNOW THE REASON WHY.
IF I'M NOT CAREFUL... I COULD GET SUCKERED INTO NOT WORKING WITHOUT EVEN KNOWING WHY.
TIMES ARE TOUGH.

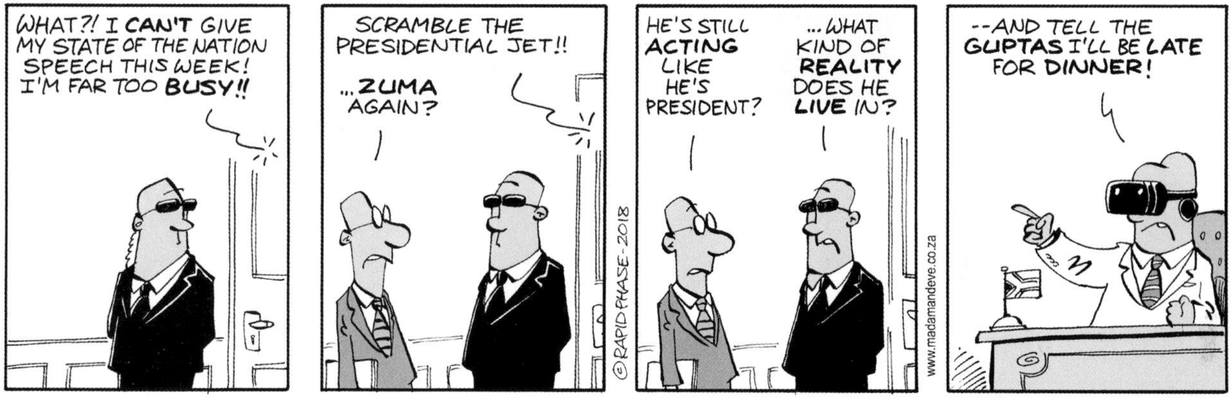
WHAT?! I **CAN'T** GIVE MY STATE OF THE NATION SPEECH THIS WEEK! I'M FAR TOO **BUSY**!!
SCRAMBLE THE PRESIDENTIAL JET!!
...**ZUMA** AGAIN?
©RAPID PHASE-2018
HE'S STILL **ACTING** LIKE HE'S PRESIDENT?
...WHAT KIND OF **REALITY** DOES HE **LIVE** IN?
www.madamandeve.co.za
--AND TELL THE **GUPTAS** I'LL BE **LATE** FOR **DINNER**!

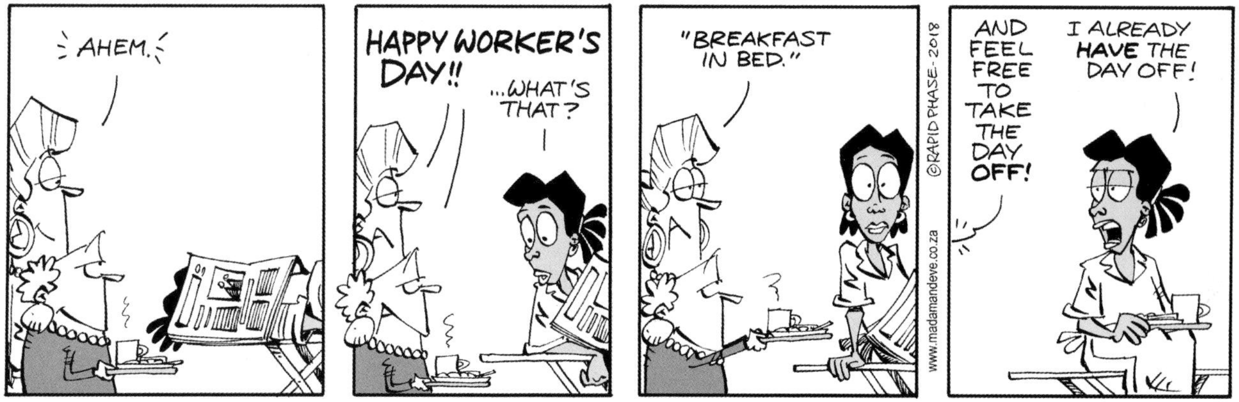
AHEM.
HAPPY WORKER'S DAY!!
...WHAT'S THAT?
"BREAKFAST IN BED."
©RAPID PHASE-2018
www.madamandeve.co.za
AND FEEL FREE TO TAKE THE DAY **OFF!**
I ALREADY **HAVE** THE DAY OFF!

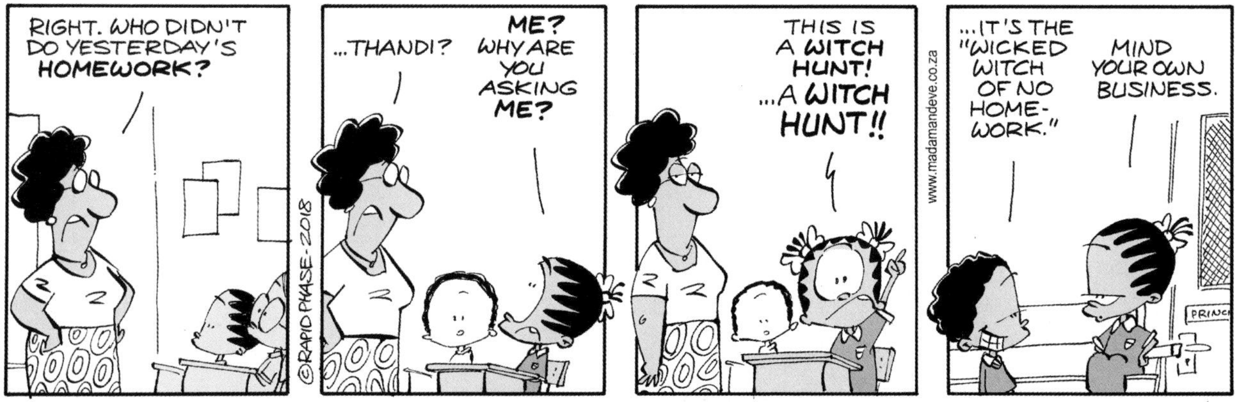
RIGHT. WHO DIDN'T DO YESTERDAY'S **HOMEWORK?**
...THANDI?
ME? WHY ARE YOU ASKING **ME?**
©RAPID PHASE-2018
THIS IS A **WITCH HUNT!** ...A **WITCH HUNT!!**
www.madamandeve.co.za
...IT'S THE "WICKED WITCH OF NO HOME-WORK."
MIND YOUR OWN BUSINESS.

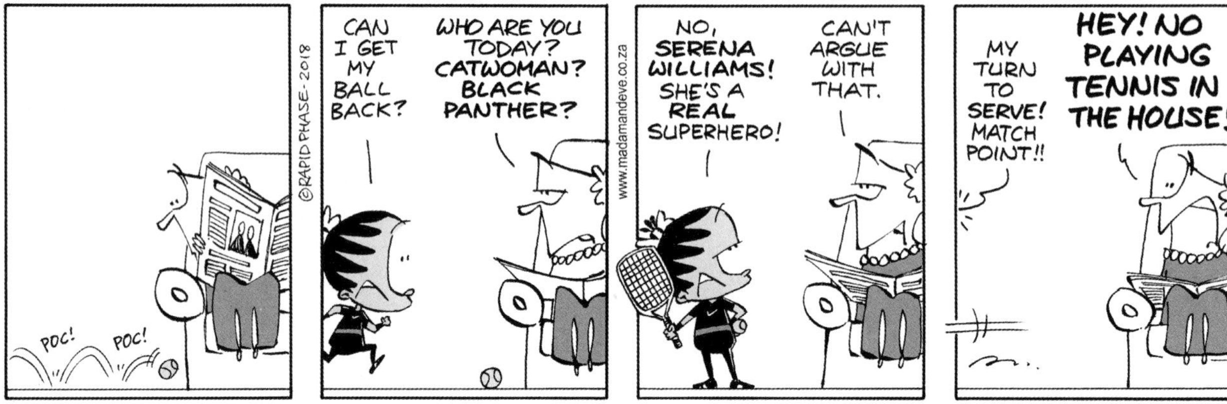
POC!
POC!
©RAPID PHASE - 2018
CAN I GET MY BALL BACK?
WHO ARE YOU TODAY? CATWOMAN? BLACK PANTHER?
www.madamandeve.co.za
NO, SERENA WILLIAMS! SHE'S A REAL SUPERHERO!
CAN'T ARGUE WITH THAT.
MY TURN TO SERVE! MATCH POINT!!
HEY! NO PLAYING TENNIS IN THE HOUSE!

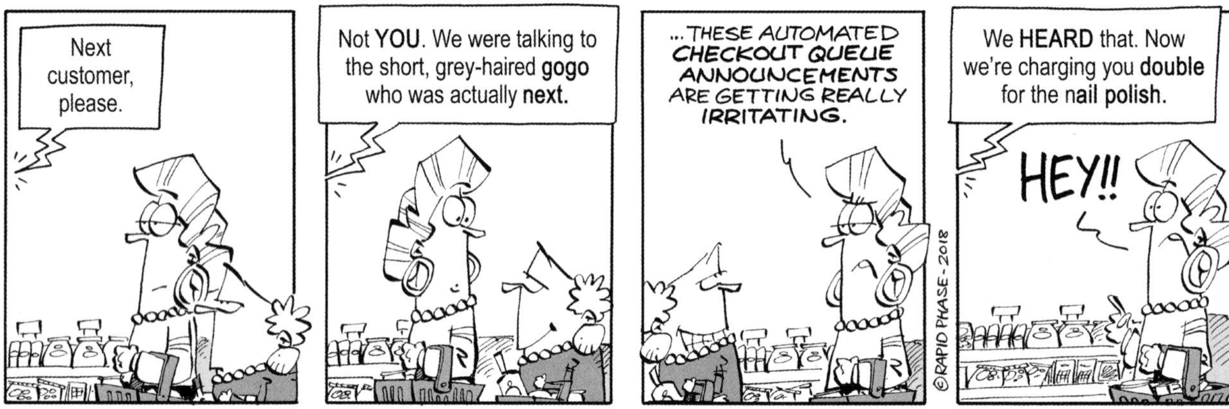
Next customer, please.
Not YOU. We were talking to the short, grey-haired gogo who was actually next.
...THESE AUTOMATED CHECKOUT QUEUE ANNOUNCEMENTS ARE GETTING REALLY IRRITATING.
©RAPID PHASE - 2018
We HEARD that. Now we're charging you double for the nail polish.
HEY!!

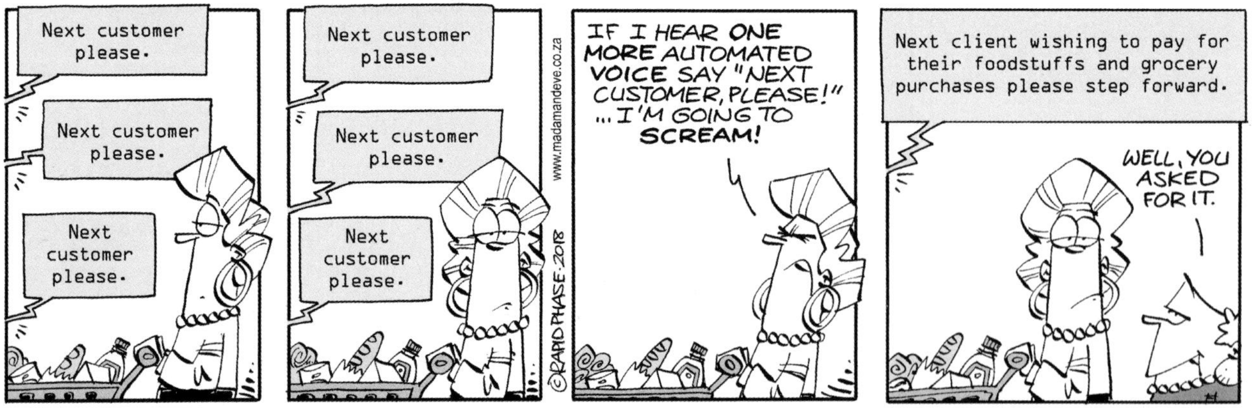
Next customer please.
Next customer please.
Next customer please.
Next customer please.
Next customer please.
Next customer please.
www.madamandeve.co.za
©RAPID PHASE - 2018
IF I HEAR ONE MORE AUTOMATED VOICE SAY "NEXT CUSTOMER, PLEASE!" ... I'M GOING TO SCREAM!
Next client wishing to pay for their foodstuffs and grocery purchases please step forward.
WELL, YOU ASKED FOR IT.

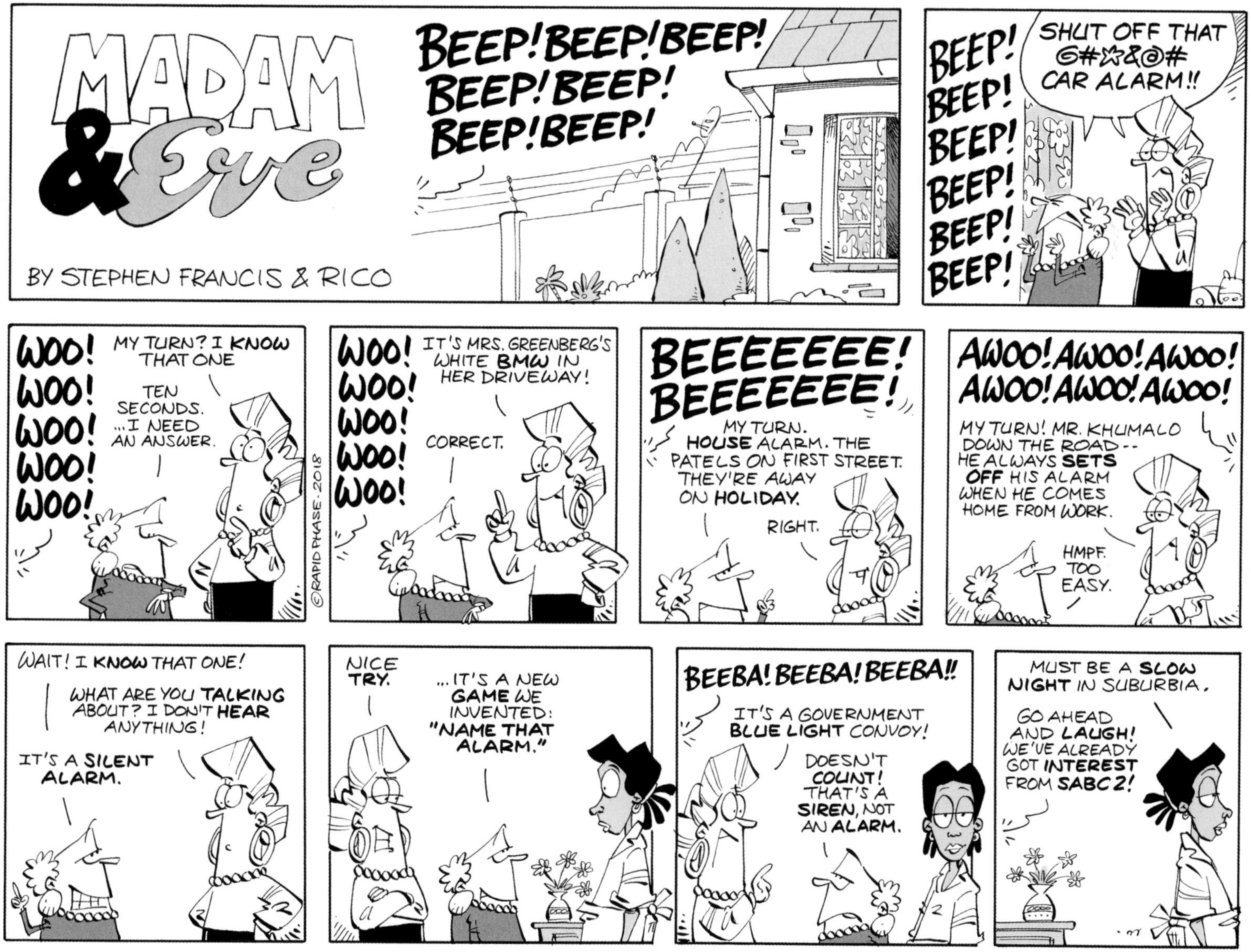

MADAM & Eve
BY STEPHEN FRANCIS & RICO
BEEP! BEEP! BEEP! BEEP! BEEP! BEEP! BEEP! BEEP!
BEEP! BEEP! BEEP! BEEP! BEEP! BEEP!
SHUT OFF THAT @#☆&@# CAR ALARM!!
WOO! WOO! WOO! WOO! WOO! WOO!
MY TURN? I KNOW THAT ONE
TEN SECONDS. ...I NEED AN ANSWER.
WOO! WOO! WOO! WOO! WOO!
IT'S MRS. GREENBERG'S WHITE BMW IN HER DRIVEWAY!
CORRECT.
©RAPID PHASE . 2018
BEEEEEEE! BEEEEEEE!
MY TURN. HOUSE ALARM. THE PATELS ON FIRST STREET. THEY'RE AWAY ON HOLIDAY.
RIGHT.
AWOO! AWOO! AWOO! AWOO! AWOO! AWOO!
MY TURN! MR. KHUMALO DOWN THE ROAD -- HE ALWAYS SETS OFF HIS ALARM WHEN HE COMES HOME FROM WORK.
HMPF. TOO EASY.
WAIT! I KNOW THAT ONE!
WHAT ARE YOU TALKING ABOUT? I DON'T HEAR ANYTHING!
IT'S A SILENT ALARM.
NICE TRY.
...IT'S A NEW GAME WE INVENTED: "NAME THAT ALARM."
BEEBA! BEEBA! BEEBA!!
IT'S A GOVERNMENT BLUE LIGHT CONVOY!
DOESN'T COUNT! THAT'S A SIREN, NOT AN ALARM.
MUST BE A SLOW NIGHT IN SUBURBIA.
GO AHEAD AND LAUGH! WE'VE ALREADY GOT INTEREST FROM SABC 2!

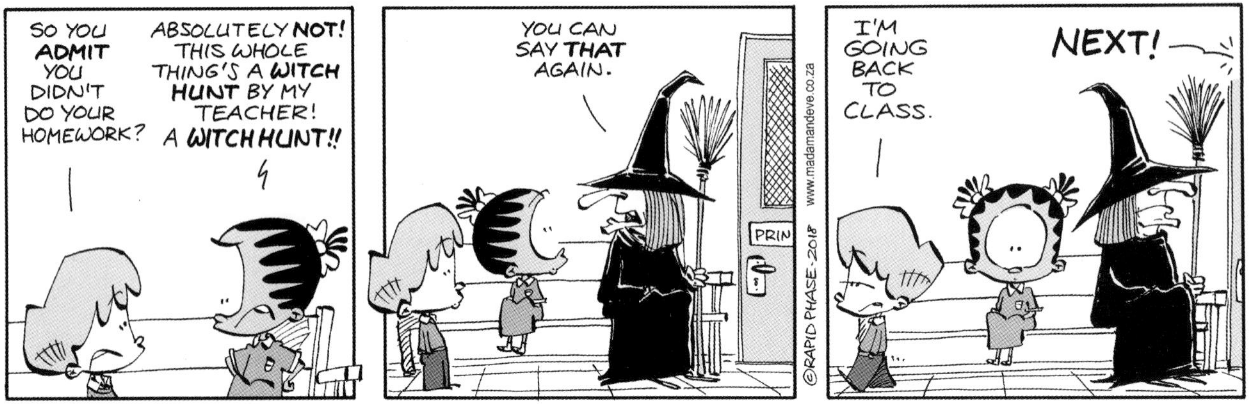
SO YOU ADMIT YOU DIDN'T DO YOUR HOMEWORK?
ABSOLUTELY NOT! THIS WHOLE THING'S A WITCH HUNT BY MY TEACHER! A WITCH HUNT!!
YOU CAN SAY THAT AGAIN.
PRIN
www.madamandeve.co.za
©RAPID PHASE-2018
I'M GOING BACK TO CLASS.
NEXT!

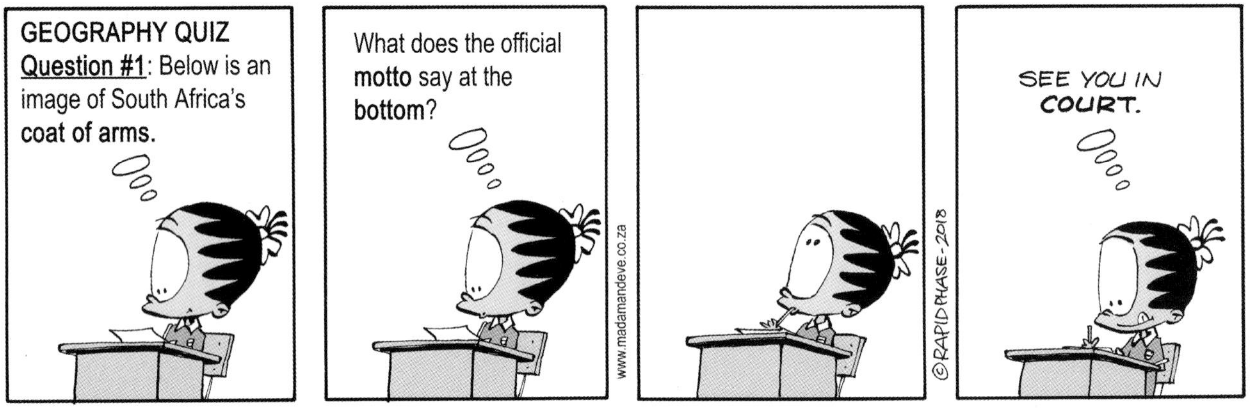
GEOGRAPHY QUIZ
Question #1: Below is an image of South Africa's coat of arms.
What does the official motto say at the bottom?
www.madamandeve.co.za
©RAPID PHASE-2018
SEE YOU IN COURT.

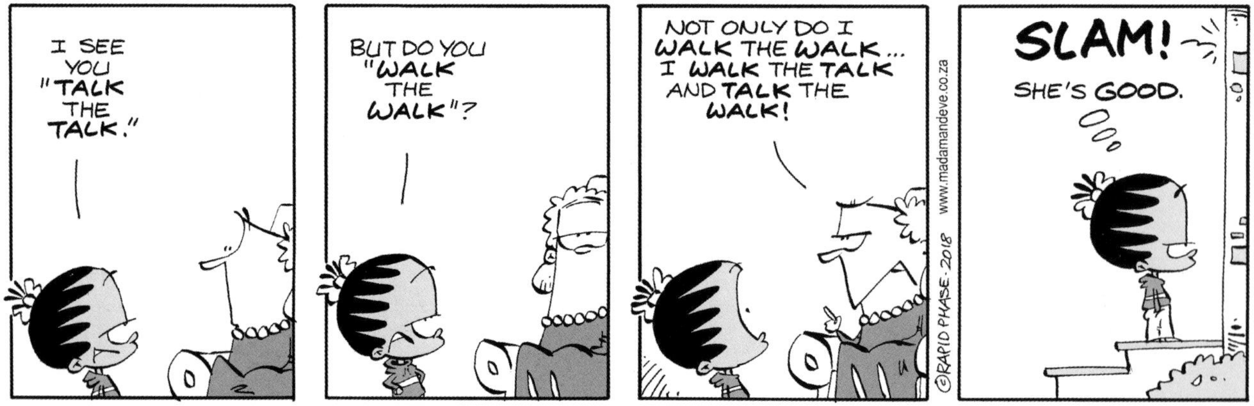
I SEE YOU "TALK THE TALK."
BUT DO YOU "WALK THE WALK"?
NOT ONLY DO I WALK THE WALK... I WALK THE TALK AND TALK THE WALK!
www.madamandeve.co.za
©RAPID PHASE-2018
SLAM!
SHE'S GOOD.

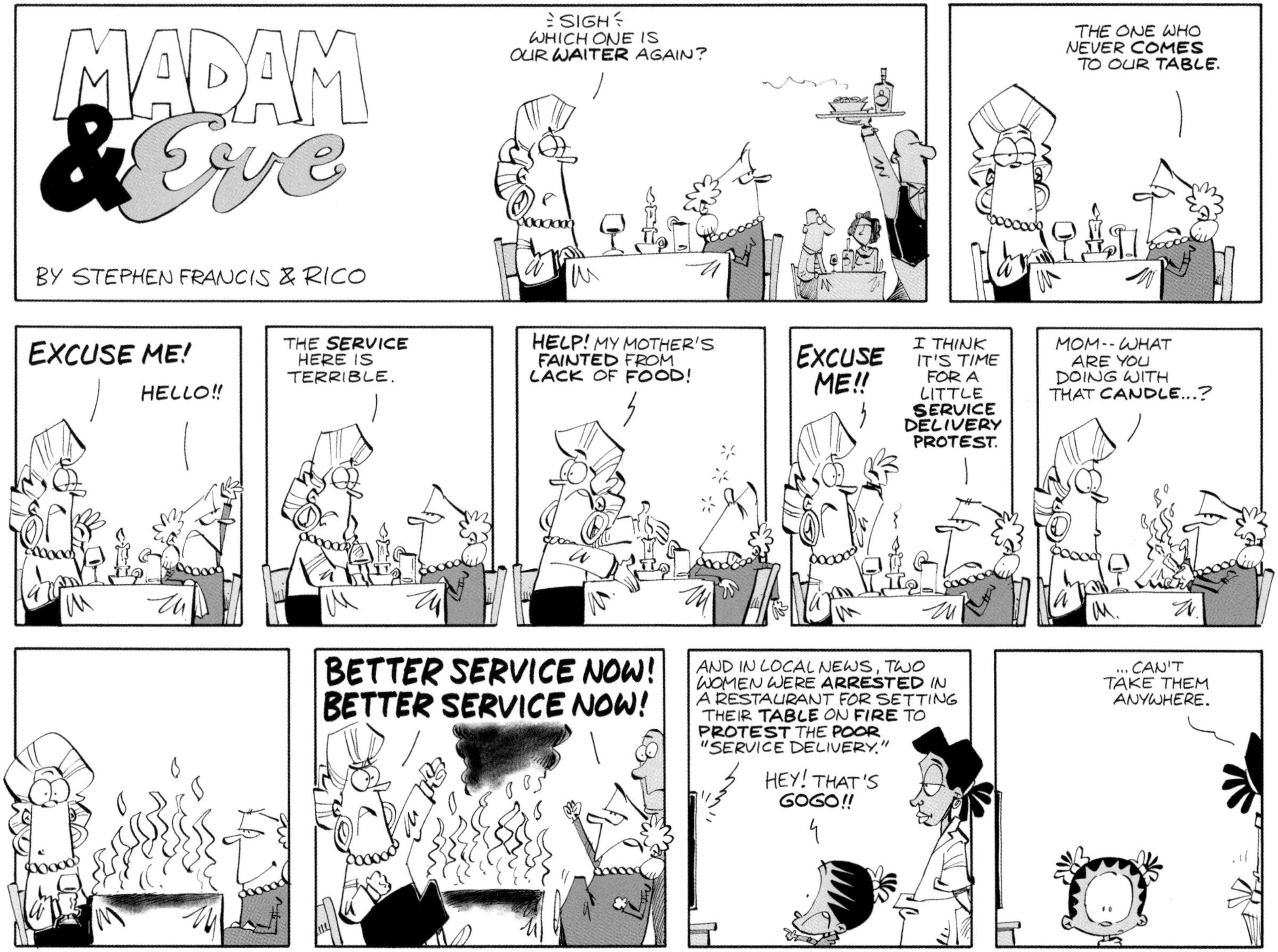
MADAM & Eve
BY STEPHEN FRANCIS & RICO
SIGH
WHICH ONE IS OUR WAITER AGAIN?
THE ONE WHO NEVER COMES TO OUR TABLE.
EXCUSE ME!
HELLO!!
THE SERVICE HERE IS TERRIBLE.
HELP! MY MOTHER'S FAINTED FROM LACK OF FOOD!
EXCUSE ME!!
I THINK IT'S TIME FOR A LITTLE SERVICE DELIVERY PROTEST.
MOM-- WHAT ARE YOU DOING WITH THAT CANDLE...?
BETTER SERVICE NOW! BETTER SERVICE NOW!
AND IN LOCAL NEWS, TWO WOMEN WERE ARRESTED IN A RESTAURANT FOR SETTING THEIR TABLE ON FIRE TO PROTEST THE POOR "SERVICE DELIVERY."
HEY! THAT'S GOGO!!
...CAN'T TAKE THEM ANYWHERE.

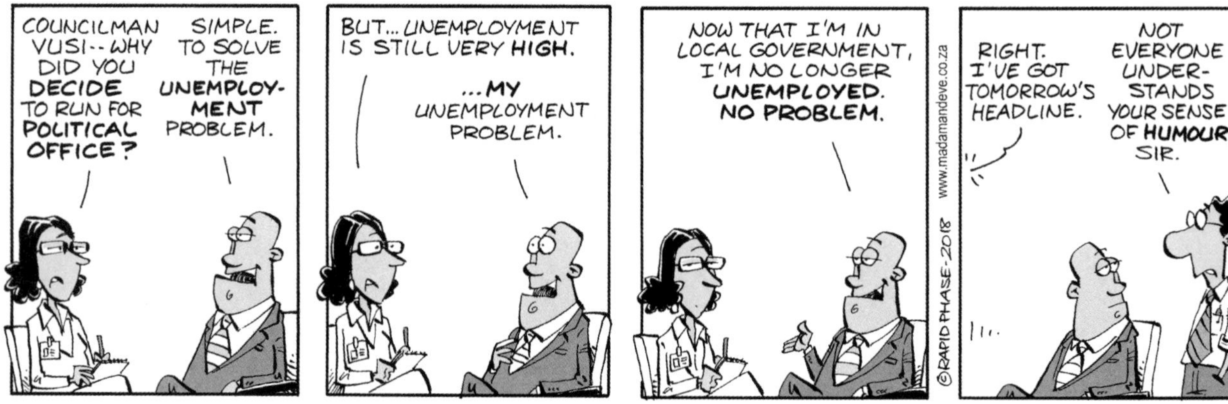

COUNCILMAN VUSI -- WHY DID YOU **DECIDE** TO RUN FOR **POLITICAL OFFICE?**
SIMPLE. TO SOLVE THE **UNEMPLOYMENT** PROBLEM.
BUT... UNEMPLOYMENT IS STILL VERY **HIGH.**
... **MY** UNEMPLOYMENT PROBLEM.
NOW THAT I'M IN LOCAL GOVERNMENT, I'M NO LONGER **UNEMPLOYED. NO PROBLEM.**
©RAPID PHASE-2018 www.madamandeve.co.za
RIGHT. I'VE GOT TOMORROW'S HEADLINE.
NOT EVERYONE UNDERSTANDS YOUR SENSE OF **HUMOUR**, SIR.

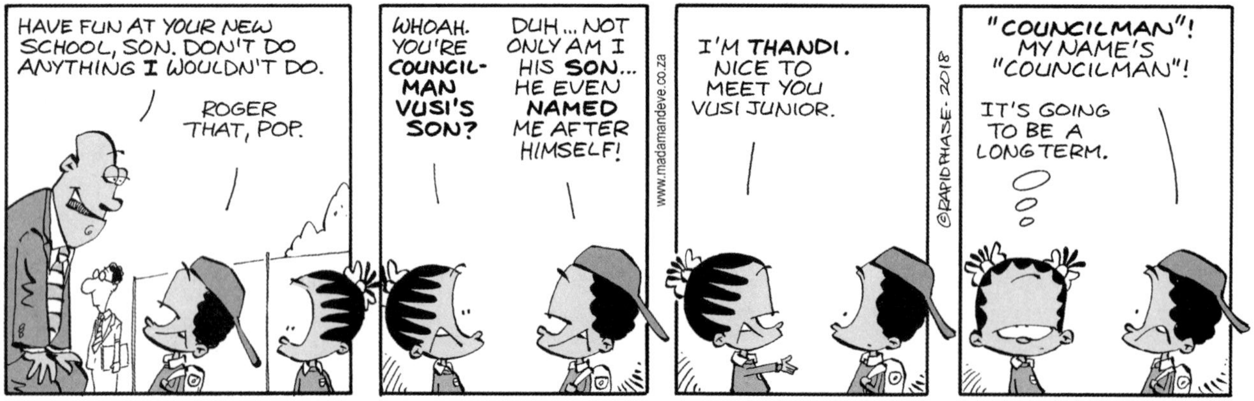

HAVE FUN AT YOUR NEW SCHOOL, SON. DON'T DO ANYTHING **I** WOULDN'T DO.
ROGER THAT, POP.
WHOAH. YOU'RE **COUNCILMAN VUSI'S SON?**
DUH ... NOT ONLY AM I HIS **SON**... HE EVEN **NAMED** ME AFTER HIMSELF!
www.madamandeve.co.za
I'M **THANDI.** NICE TO MEET YOU VUSI JUNIOR.
©RAPID PHASE-2018
"COUNCILMAN"! MY NAME'S "COUNCILMAN"!
IT'S GOING TO BE A LONG TERM.

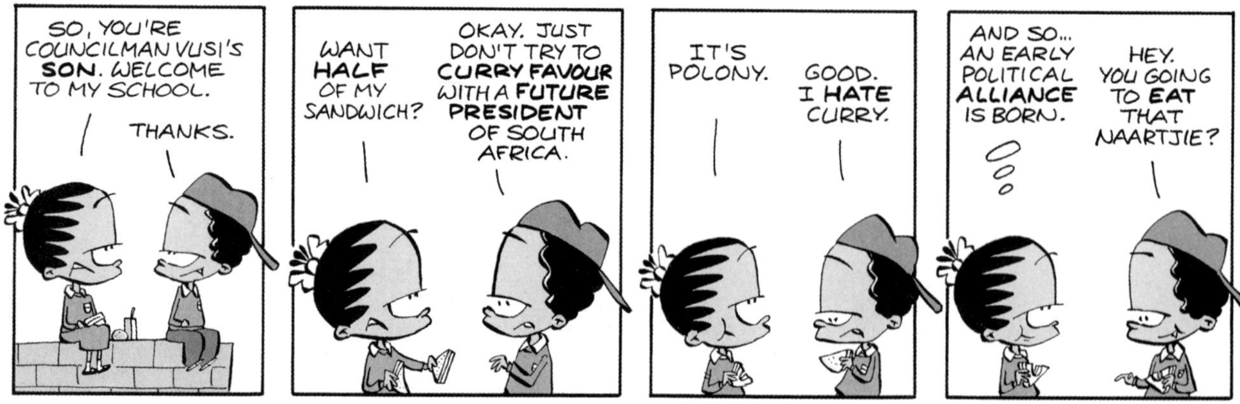

SO, YOU'RE COUNCILMAN VUSI'S **SON**. WELCOME TO MY SCHOOL.
THANKS.
WANT **HALF** OF MY SANDWICH?
OKAY. JUST DON'T TRY TO **CURRY FAVOUR** WITH A **FUTURE PRESIDENT** OF SOUTH AFRICA.
IT'S POLONY.
GOOD. I **HATE** CURRY.
AND SO... AN EARLY POLITICAL **ALLIANCE** IS BORN.
HEY. YOU GOING TO **EAT** THAT NAARTJIE?

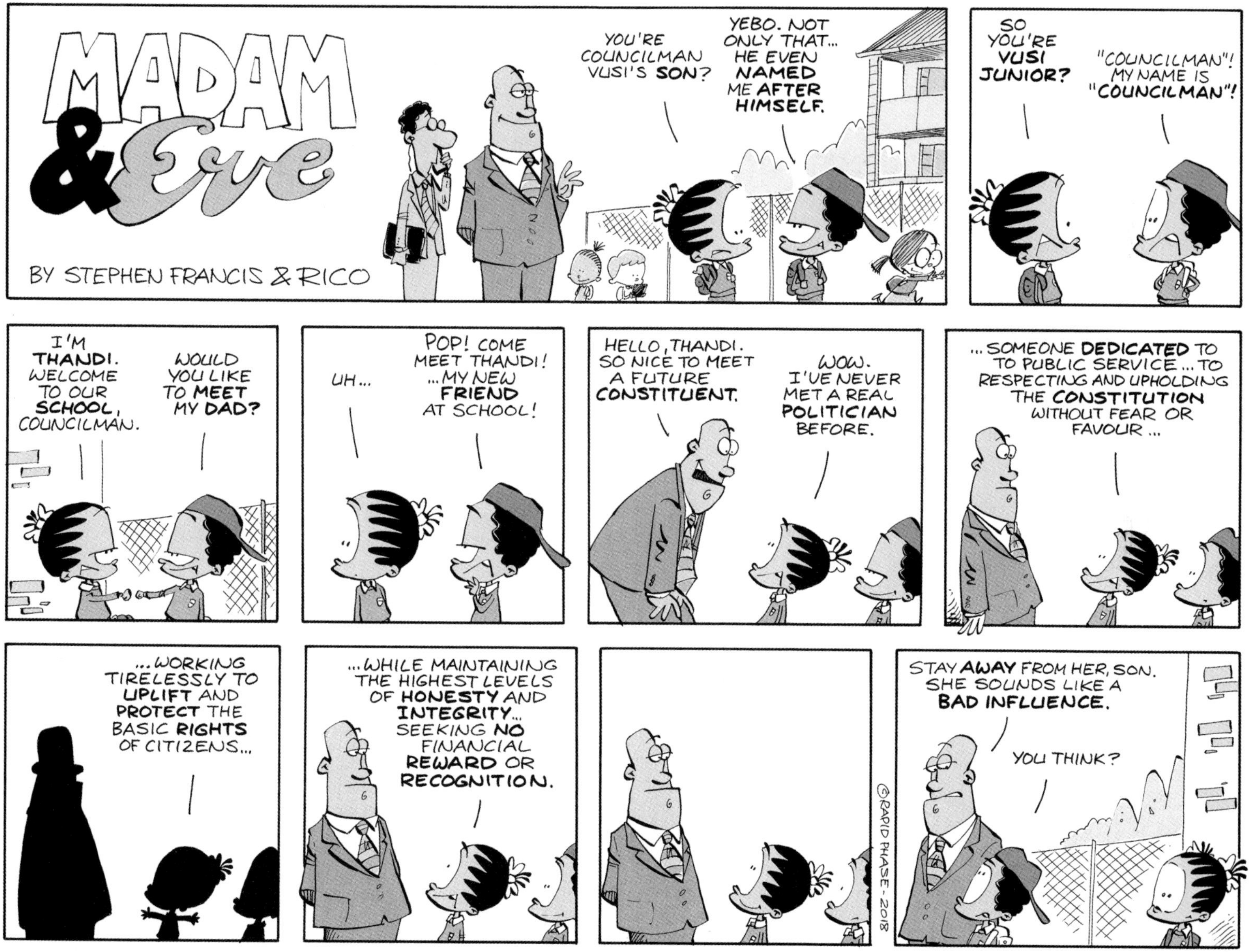
MADAM & Eve
BY STEPHEN FRANCIS & RICO
YOU'RE COUNCILMAN VUSI'S SON?
YEBO. NOT ONLY THAT... HE EVEN NAMED ME AFTER HIMSELF.
SO YOU'RE VUSI JUNIOR?
"COUNCILMAN"! MY NAME IS "COUNCILMAN"!
I'M THANDI. WELCOME TO OUR SCHOOL, COUNCILMAN.
WOULD YOU LIKE TO MEET MY DAD?
UH...
POP! COME MEET THANDI! ...MY NEW FRIEND AT SCHOOL!
HELLO, THANDI. SO NICE TO MEET A FUTURE CONSTITUENT.
WOW. I'VE NEVER MET A REAL POLITICIAN BEFORE.
...SOMEONE DEDICATED TO TO PUBLIC SERVICE ... TO RESPECTING AND UPHOLDING THE CONSTITUTION WITHOUT FEAR OR FAVOUR ...
...WORKING TIRELESSLY TO UPLIFT AND PROTECT THE BASIC RIGHTS OF CITIZENS...
...WHILE MAINTAINING THE HIGHEST LEVELS OF HONESTY AND INTEGRITY... SEEKING NO FINANCIAL REWARD OR RECOGNITION.
©RAPID PHASE - 2018
STAY AWAY FROM HER, SON. SHE SOUNDS LIKE A BAD INFLUENCE.
YOU THINK?

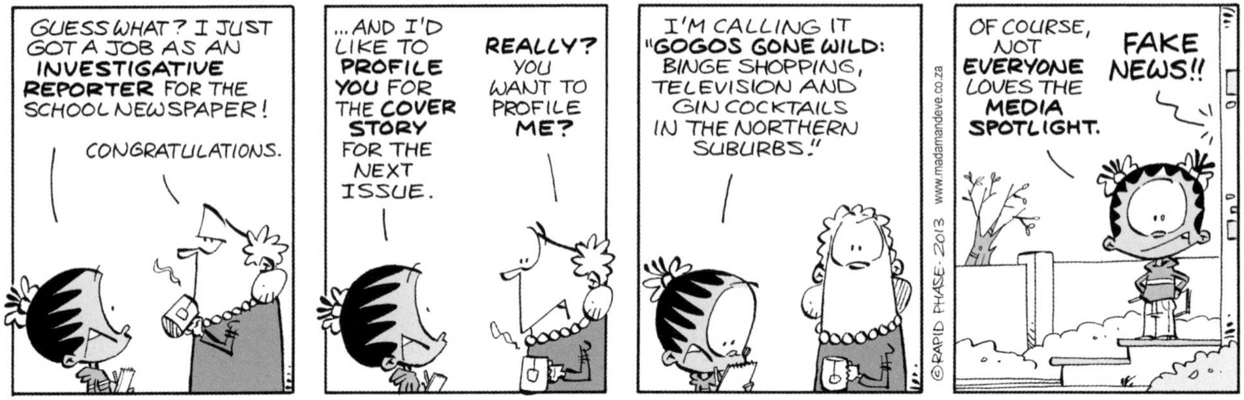
GUESS WHAT? I JUST GOT A JOB AS AN **INVESTIGATIVE REPORTER** FOR THE SCHOOL NEWSPAPER!
CONGRATULATIONS.
...AND I'D LIKE TO **PROFILE YOU** FOR THE **COVER STORY** FOR THE NEXT ISSUE.
REALLY? YOU WANT TO PROFILE **ME?**
I'M CALLING IT **"GOGOS GONE WILD:** BINGE SHOPPING, TELEVISION AND GIN COCKTAILS IN THE NORTHERN SUBURBS."
©RAPID PHASE - 2013 www.madamandeve.co.za
OF COURSE, NOT **EVERYONE** LOVES THE **MEDIA SPOTLIGHT.**
FAKE NEWS!!

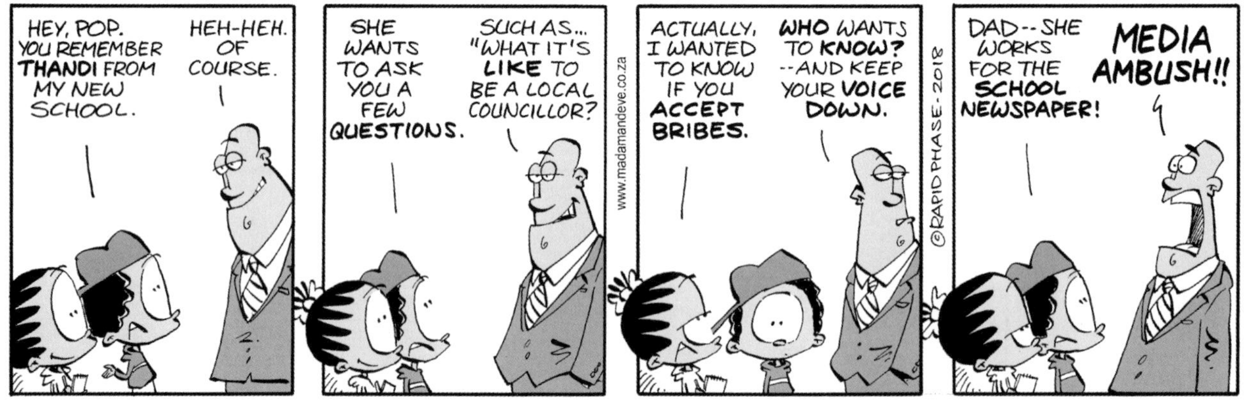
HEY, POP. YOU REMEMBER **THANDI** FROM MY NEW SCHOOL.
HEH-HEH. OF COURSE.
SHE WANTS TO ASK YOU A FEW **QUESTIONS.**
SUCH AS... "WHAT IT'S **LIKE** TO BE A LOCAL COUNCILLOR?
www.madamandeve.co.za
ACTUALLY, I WANTED TO KNOW IF YOU **ACCEPT BRIBES.**
WHO WANTS TO **KNOW?** --AND KEEP YOUR **VOICE DOWN.**
©RAPID PHASE - 2018
DAD-- SHE WORKS FOR THE **SCHOOL NEWSPAPER!**
MEDIA AMBUSH!!

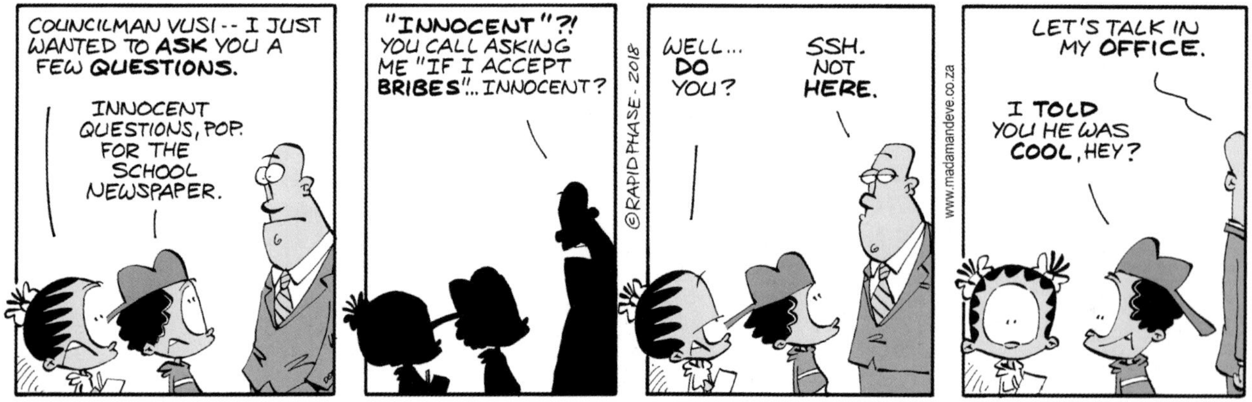
COUNCILMAN VUSI -- I JUST WANTED TO **ASK** YOU A FEW **QUESTIONS.**
INNOCENT QUESTIONS, POP. FOR THE SCHOOL NEWSPAPER.
"INNOCENT"?! YOU CALL ASKING ME "IF I ACCEPT **BRIBES**"... INNOCENT?
©RAPID PHASE - 2018
WELL... **DO** YOU?
SSH. NOT **HERE.**
www.madamandeve.co.za
LET'S TALK IN MY **OFFICE.**
I **TOLD** YOU HE WAS **COOL**, HEY?

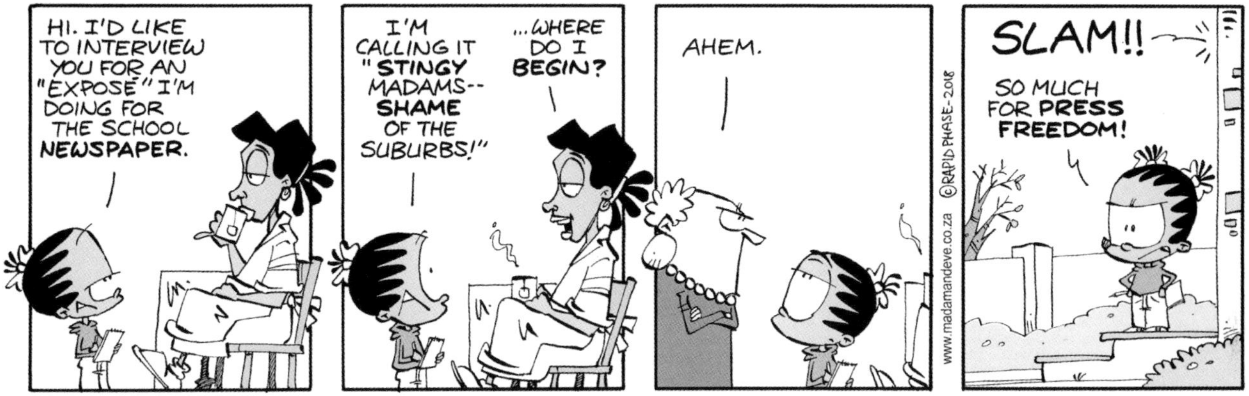
HI. I'D LIKE TO INTERVIEW YOU FOR AN "EXPOSÉ" I'M DOING FOR THE SCHOOL **NEWSPAPER**.
I'M CALLING IT "**STINGY** MADAMS-- **SHAME** OF THE SUBURBS!"
...WHERE DO I **BEGIN**?
AHEM.
SLAM!!
SO MUCH FOR **PRESS FREEDOM**!
www.madamandeve.co.za ©RAPID PHASE-2018

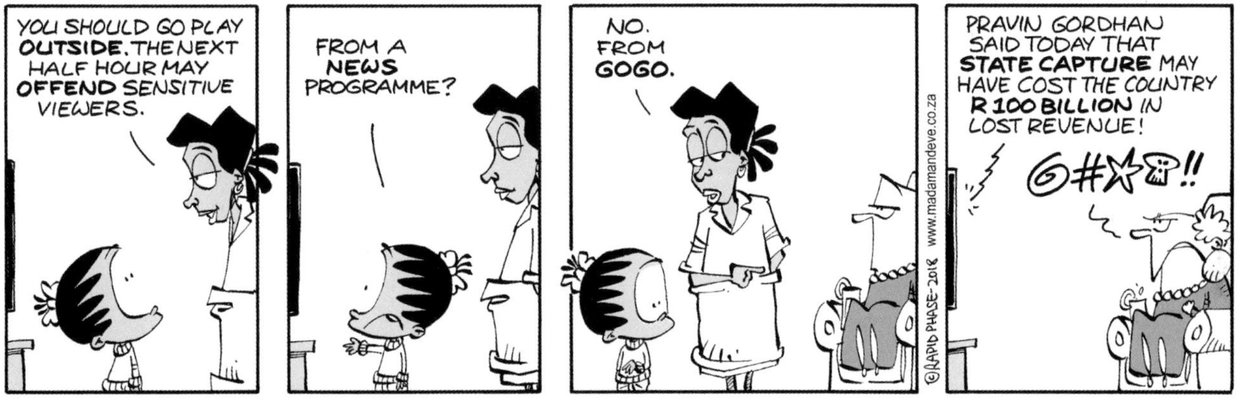
YOU SHOULD GO PLAY **OUTSIDE**. THE NEXT HALF HOUR MAY **OFFEND** SENSITIVE VIEWERS.
FROM A **NEWS** PROGRAMME?
NO. FROM **GOGO**.
PRAVIN GORDHAN SAID TODAY THAT **STATE CAPTURE** MAY HAVE COST THE COUNTRY **R 100 BILLION** IN LOST REVENUE!
©RAPID PHASE-2018 www.madamandeve.co.za

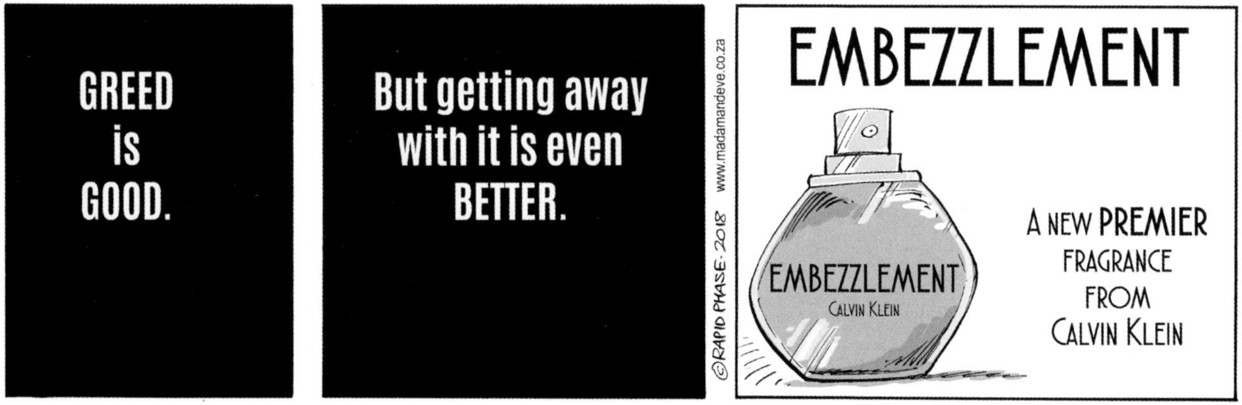
GREED is GOOD.
But getting away with it is even BETTER.
©RAPID PHASE-2018 www.madamandeve.co.za
EMBEZZLEMENT
EMBEZZLEMENT
CALVIN KLEIN
A NEW PREMIER FRAGRANCE FROM CALVIN KLEIN

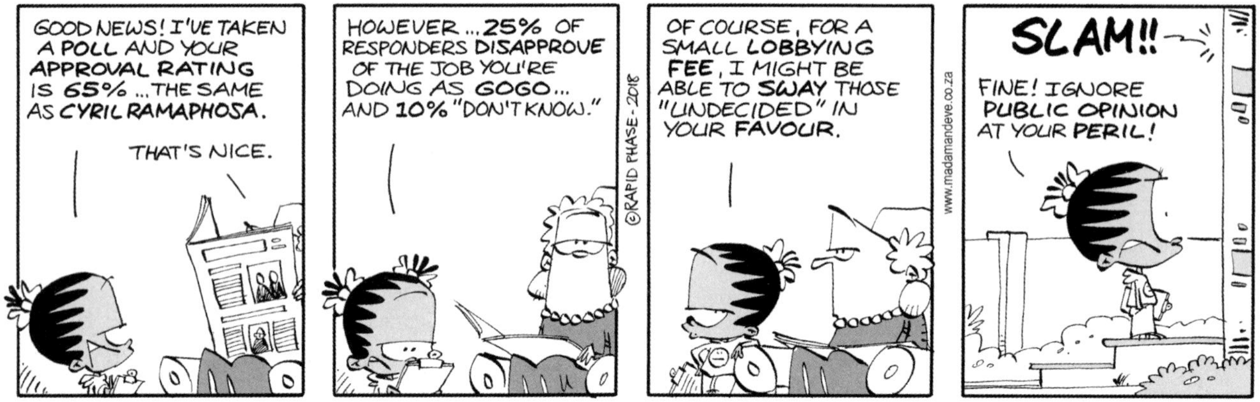
GOOD NEWS! I'VE TAKEN A POLL AND YOUR APPROVAL RATING IS 65% ...THE SAME AS CYRIL RAMAPHOSA.
THAT'S NICE.
HOWEVER ... 25% OF RESPONDERS DISAPPROVE OF THE JOB YOU'RE DOING AS GOGO... AND 10% "DON'T KNOW."
©RAPID PHASE - 2018
OF COURSE, FOR A SMALL LOBBYING FEE, I MIGHT BE ABLE TO SWAY THOSE "UNDECIDED" IN YOUR FAVOUR.
www.madamandeve.co.za
SLAM!!
FINE! IGNORE PUBLIC OPINION AT YOUR PERIL!

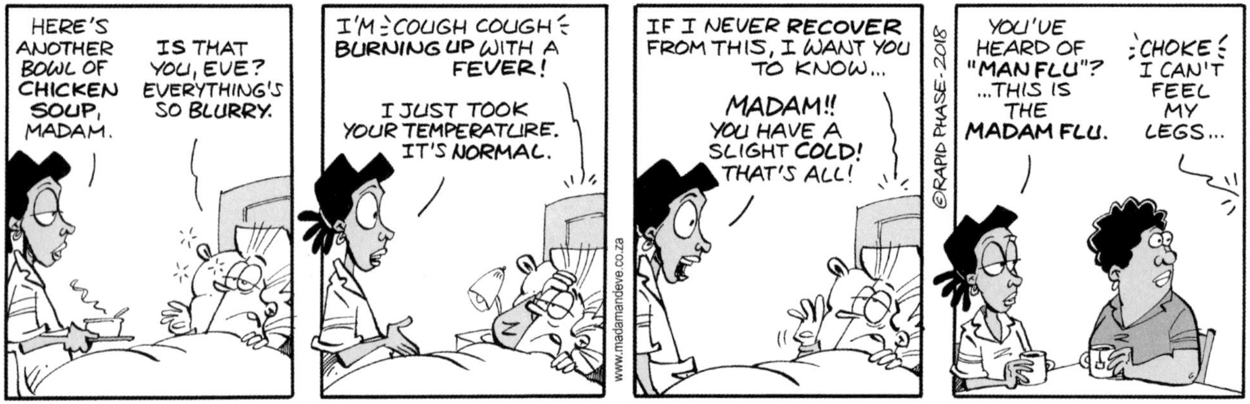
HERE'S ANOTHER BOWL OF CHICKEN SOUP, MADAM.
IS THAT YOU, EVE? EVERYTHING'S SO BLURRY.
I'M ⸗COUGH COUGH⸗ BURNING UP WITH A FEVER!
I JUST TOOK YOUR TEMPERATURE. IT'S NORMAL.
www.madamandeve.co.za
IF I NEVER RECOVER FROM THIS, I WANT YOU TO KNOW...
MADAM!! YOU HAVE A SLIGHT COLD! THAT'S ALL!
©RAPID PHASE - 2018
YOU'VE HEARD OF "MAN FLU"? ...THIS IS THE MADAM FLU.
⸗CHOKE⸗ I CAN'T FEEL MY LEGS...

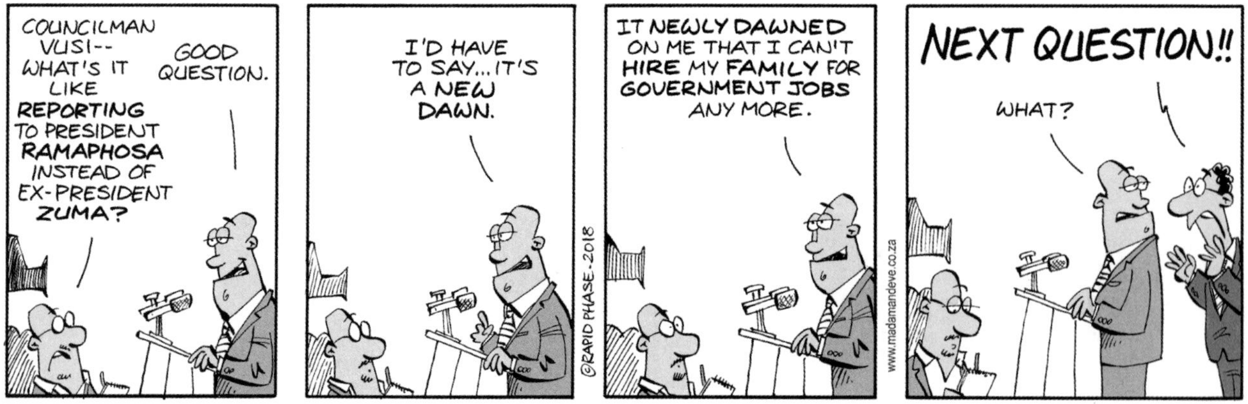
COUNCILMAN VUSI-- WHAT'S IT LIKE REPORTING TO PRESIDENT RAMAPHOSA INSTEAD OF EX-PRESIDENT ZUMA?
GOOD QUESTION.
I'D HAVE TO SAY... IT'S A NEW DAWN.
©RAPID PHASE - 2018
IT NEWLY DAWNED ON ME THAT I CAN'T HIRE MY FAMILY FOR GOVERNMENT JOBS ANY MORE.
www.madamandeve.co.za
NEXT QUESTION!!
WHAT?

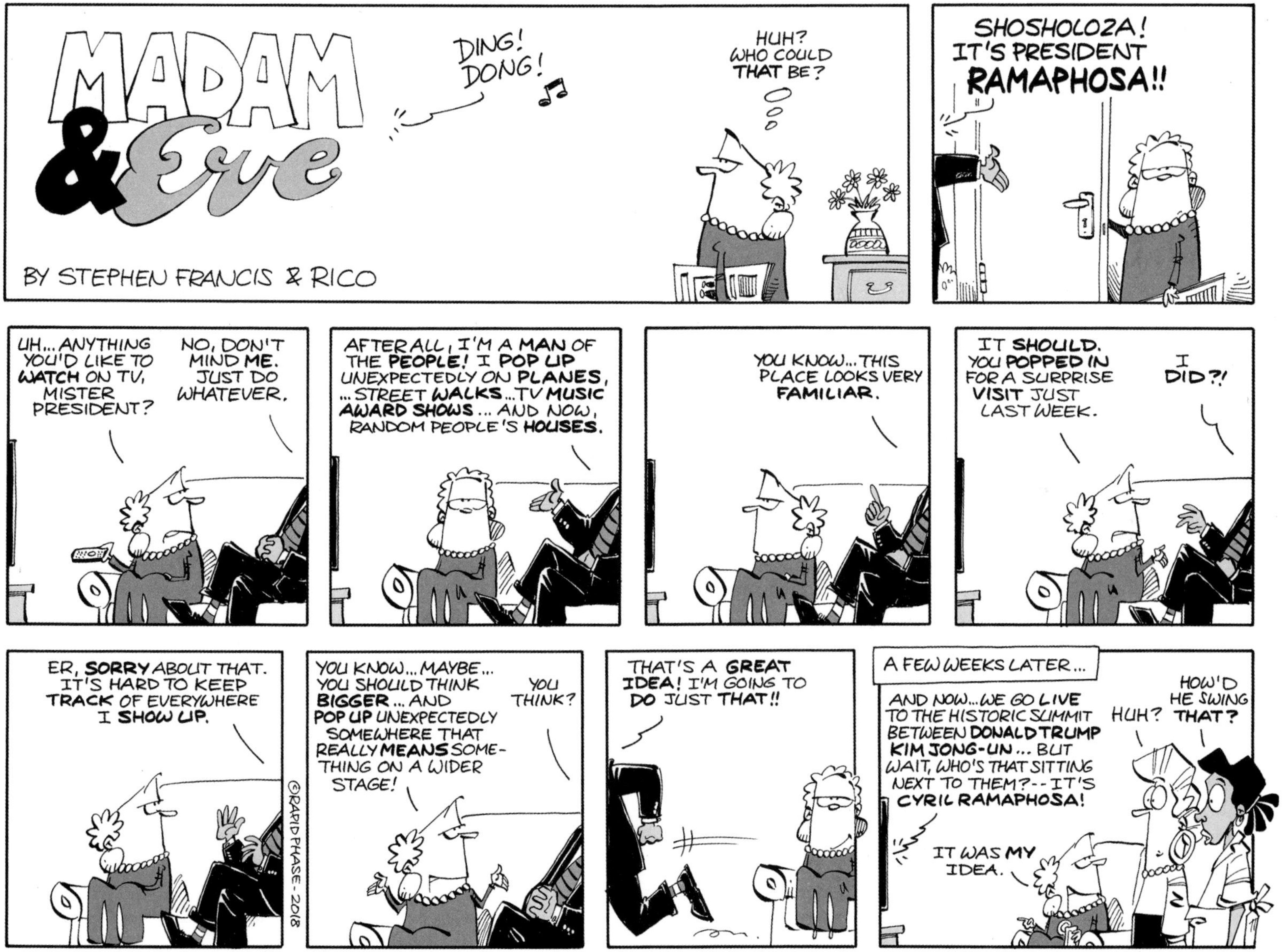
MADAM & Eve
BY STEPHEN FRANCIS & RICO
DING! DONG!
HUH? WHO COULD **THAT** BE?
SHOSHOLOZA! IT'S PRESIDENT **RAMAPHOSA!!**
UH... ANYTHING YOU'D LIKE TO **WATCH** ON TV, MISTER PRESIDENT?
NO, DON'T MIND **ME**. JUST DO WHATEVER.
AFTER ALL, I'M A **MAN** OF THE **PEOPLE!** I **POP UP** UNEXPECTEDLY ON **PLANES**, ... STREET **WALKS**... TV **MUSIC AWARD SHOWS**... AND NOW, RANDOM PEOPLE'S **HOUSES**.
YOU KNOW... THIS PLACE LOOKS VERY **FAMILIAR**.
IT **SHOULD**. YOU **POPPED IN** FOR A SURPRISE **VISIT** JUST LAST WEEK.
I **DID?!**
ER, **SORRY** ABOUT THAT. IT'S HARD TO KEEP **TRACK** OF EVERYWHERE I **SHOW UP**.
©RAPIDPHASE-2018
YOU KNOW... MAYBE... YOU SHOULD THINK **BIGGER**... AND **POP UP** UNEXPECTEDLY SOMEWHERE THAT REALLY **MEANS** SOMETHING ON A WIDER STAGE!
YOU THINK?
THAT'S A **GREAT IDEA!** I'M GOING TO **DO** JUST **THAT!!**
A FEW WEEKS LATER...
AND NOW... WE GO **LIVE** TO THE HISTORIC SUMMIT BETWEEN **DONALD TRUMP KIM JONG-UN**... BUT WAIT, WHO'S THAT SITTING NEXT TO THEM?-- IT'S **CYRIL RAMAPHOSA!**
HUH?
HOW'D HE SWING **THAT?**
IT WAS **MY** IDEA.

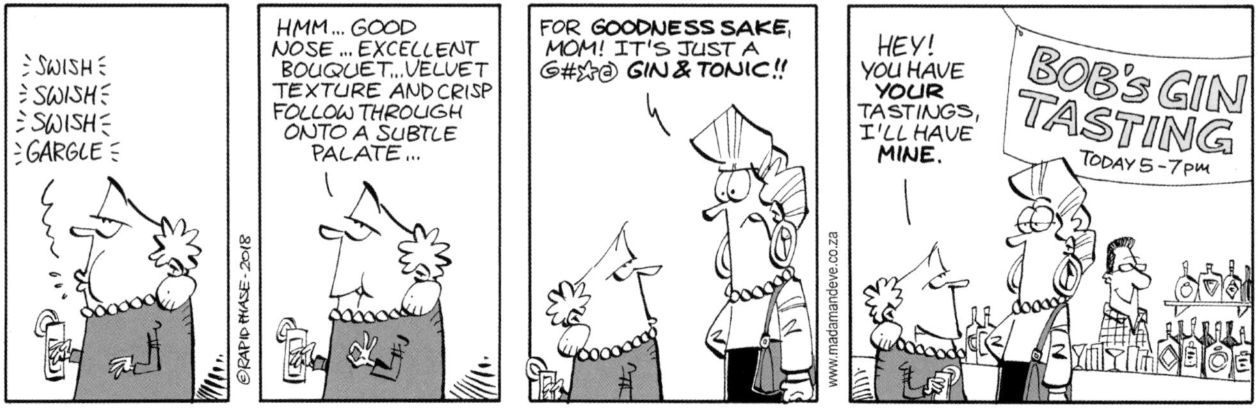
SWISH SWISH SWISH GARGLE
HMM... GOOD NOSE... EXCELLENT BOUQUET... VELVET TEXTURE AND CRISP FOLLOW THROUGH ONTO A SUBTLE PALATE...
©RAPID PHASE - 2018
FOR GOODNESS SAKE, MOM! IT'S JUST A G#☆@ GIN & TONIC!!
www.madamandeve.co.za
HEY! YOU HAVE YOUR TASTINGS, I'LL HAVE MINE.
BOB's GIN TASTING
TODAY 5 - 7pm

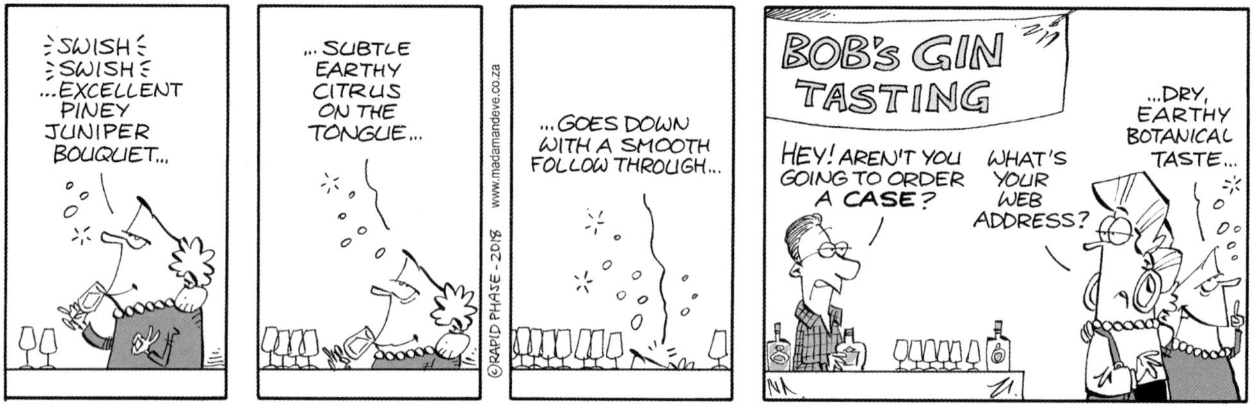
SWISH SWISH ...EXCELLENT PINEY JUNIPER BOUQUET...
...SUBTLE EARTHY CITRUS ON THE TONGUE...
©RAPID PHASE - 2018 www.madamandeve.co.za
...GOES DOWN WITH A SMOOTH FOLLOW THROUGH...
BOB's GIN TASTING
HEY! AREN'T YOU GOING TO ORDER A CASE?
WHAT'S YOUR WEB ADDRESS?
...DRY, EARTHY BOTANICAL TASTE...

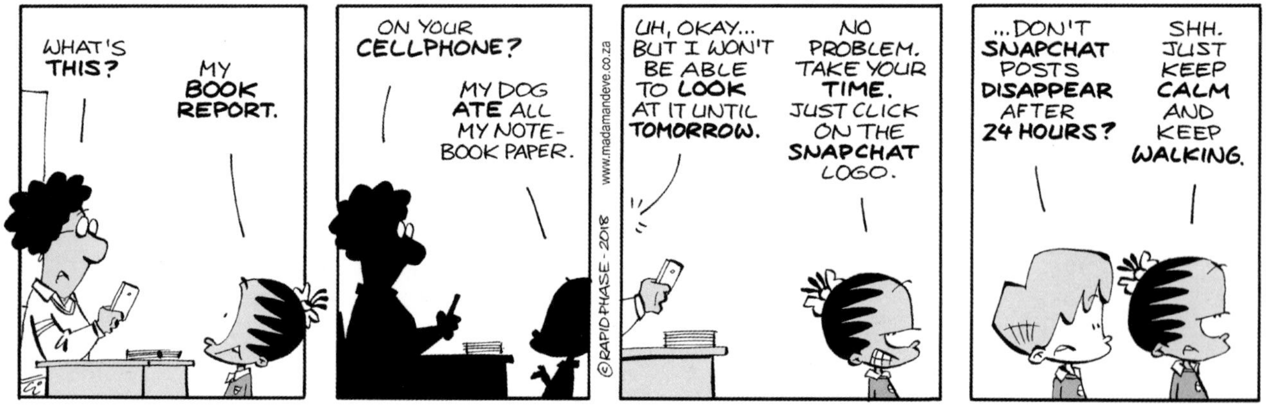
WHAT'S THIS?
MY BOOK REPORT.
ON YOUR CELLPHONE?
MY DOG ATE ALL MY NOTE-BOOK PAPER.
©RAPID PHASE - 2018 www.madamandeve.co.za
UH, OKAY... BUT I WON'T BE ABLE TO LOOK AT IT UNTIL TOMORROW.
NO PROBLEM. TAKE YOUR TIME. JUST CLICK ON THE SNAPCHAT LOGO.
...DON'T SNAPCHAT POSTS DISAPPEAR AFTER 24 HOURS?
SHH. JUST KEEP CALM AND KEEP WALKING.

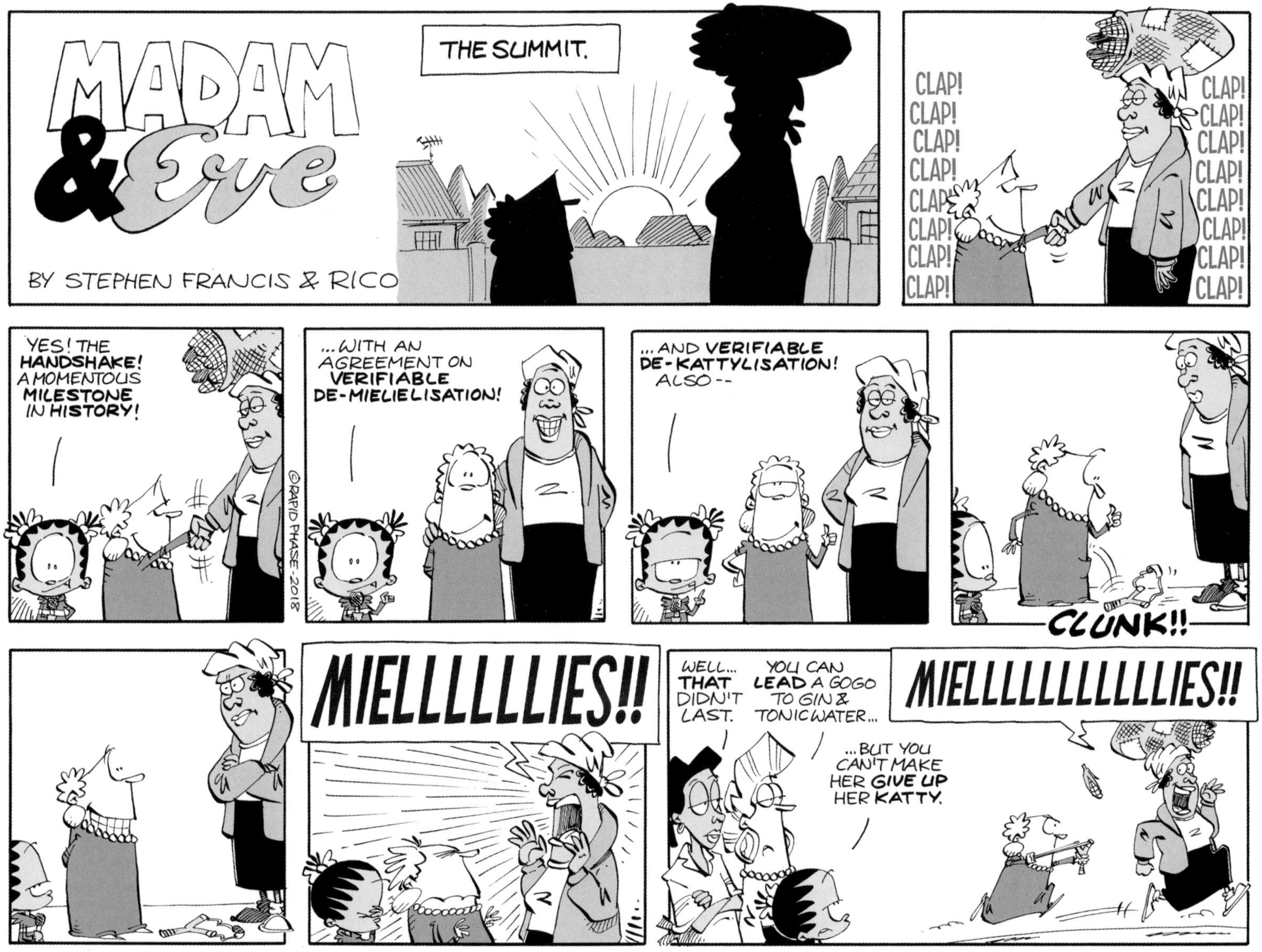
MADAM & Eve
THE SUMMIT.
BY STEPHEN FRANCIS & RICO
CLAP! CLAP! CLAP! CLAP! CLAP! CLAP! CLAP! CLAP!
CLAP! CLAP! CLAP! CLAP! CLAP! CLAP! CLAP! CLAP!
YES! THE HANDSHAKE! A MOMENTOUS MILESTONE IN HISTORY!
©RAPID PHASE · 2018
...WITH AN AGREEMENT ON VERIFIABLE DE-MIELIELISATION!
...AND VERIFIABLE DE-KATTYLISATION! ALSO --
CLUNK!!
MIELLLLLLIES!!
WELL... THAT DIDN'T LAST.
YOU CAN LEAD A GOGO TO GIN & TONIC WATER...
...BUT YOU CAN'T MAKE HER GIVE UP HER KATTY.
MIELLLLLLLLLLLLIES!!

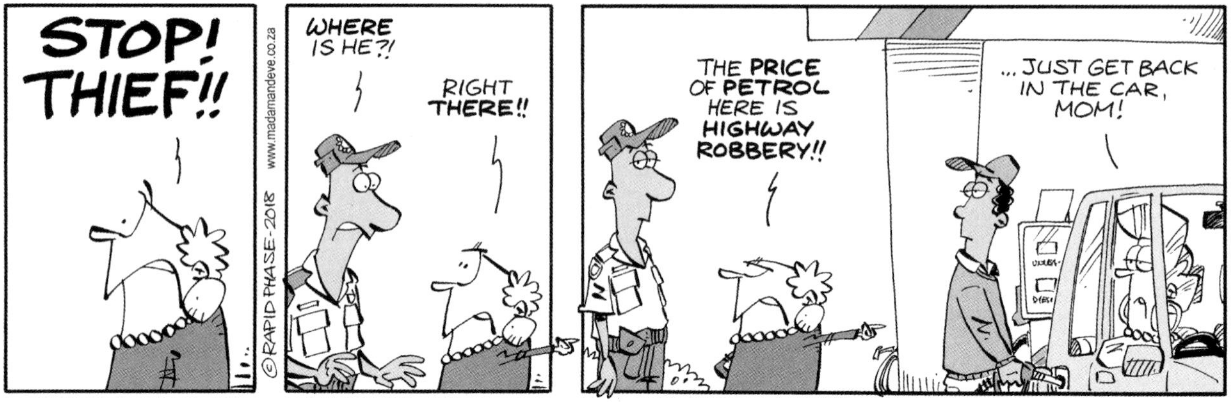
STOP! THIEF!!
WHERE IS HE?!
RIGHT THERE!!
©RAPID PHASE-2018 www.madamandeve.co.za
THE PRICE OF PETROL HERE IS HIGHWAY ROBBERY!!
... JUST GET BACK IN THE CAR, MOM!

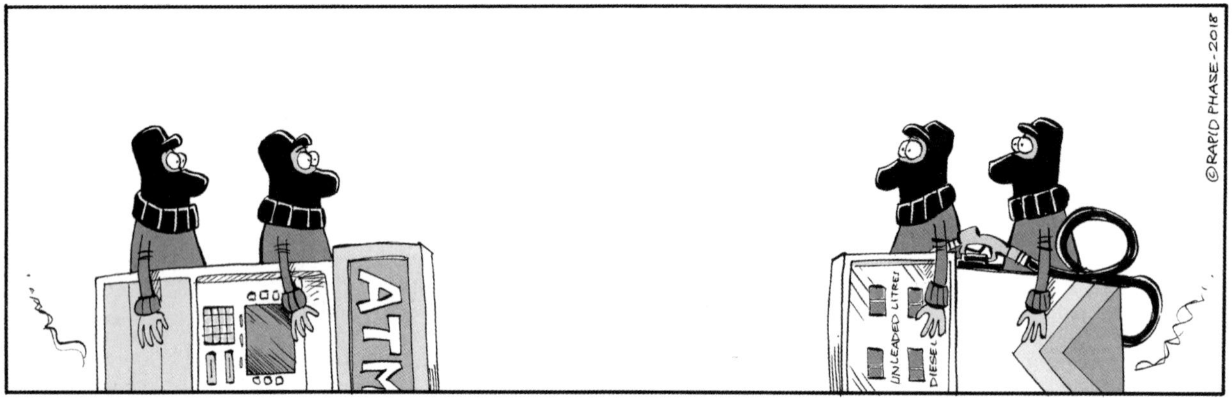
ATM
UNLEADED LITRES
DIESEL
©RAPID PHASE-2018

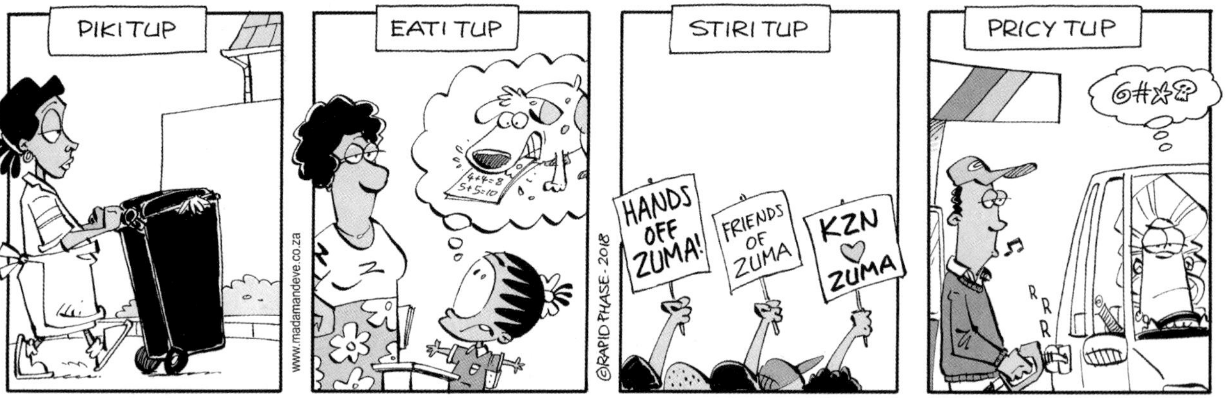
PIKITUP
EATI TUP
4+4=8
5+5=10
www.madamandeve.co.za
STIRI TUP
HANDS OFF ZUMA!
FRIENDS OF ZUMA
KZN ♥ ZUMA
©RAPID PHASE-2018
PRICY TUP
RRR

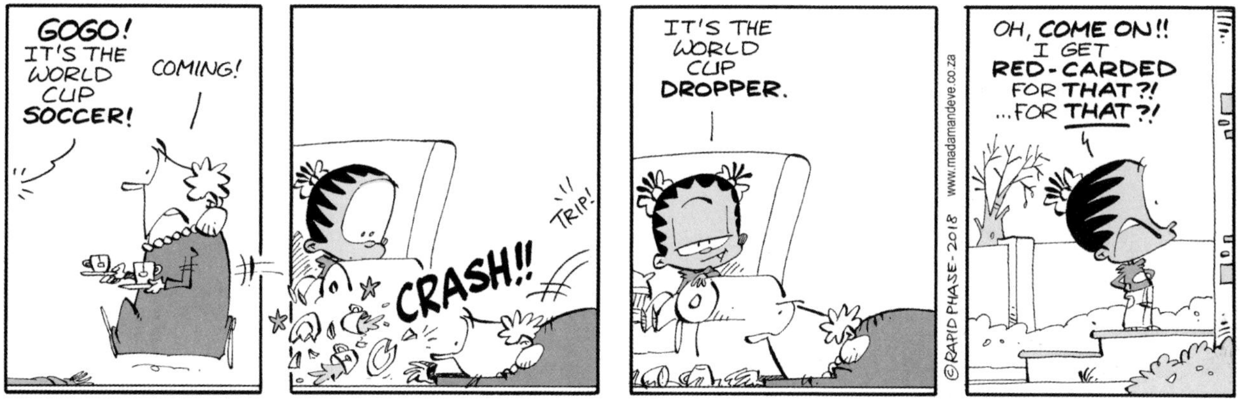
GOGO! IT'S THE WORLD CUP SOCCER!
COMING!
CRASH!!
TRIP!
IT'S THE WORLD CUP DROPPER.
www.madamandeve.co.za
©RAPID PHASE-2018
OH, COME ON!! I GET RED-CARDED FOR THAT?! ...FOR THAT?!

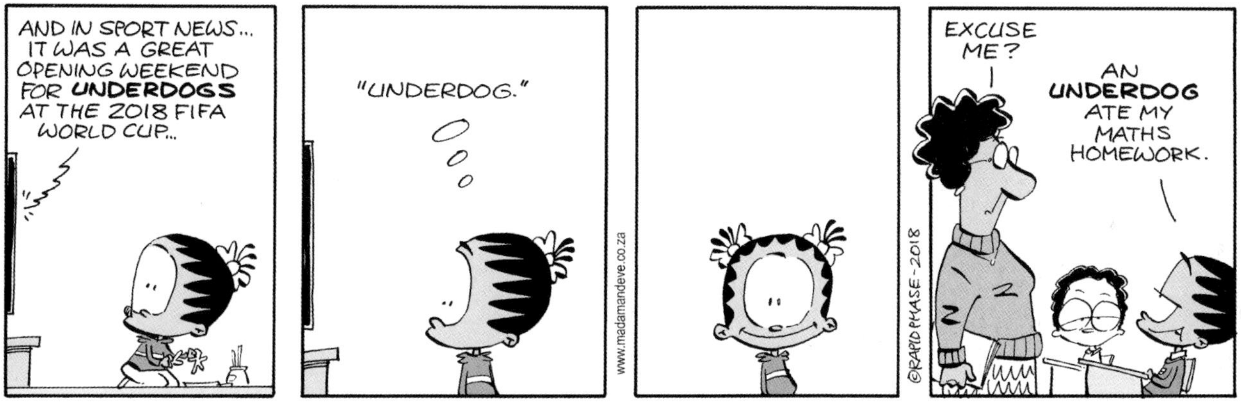
AND IN SPORT NEWS... IT WAS A GREAT OPENING WEEKEND FOR UNDERDOGS AT THE 2018 FIFA WORLD CUP...
"UNDERDOG."
www.madamandeve.co.za
©RAPID PHASE-2018
EXCUSE ME?
AN UNDERDOG ATE MY MATHS HOMEWORK.

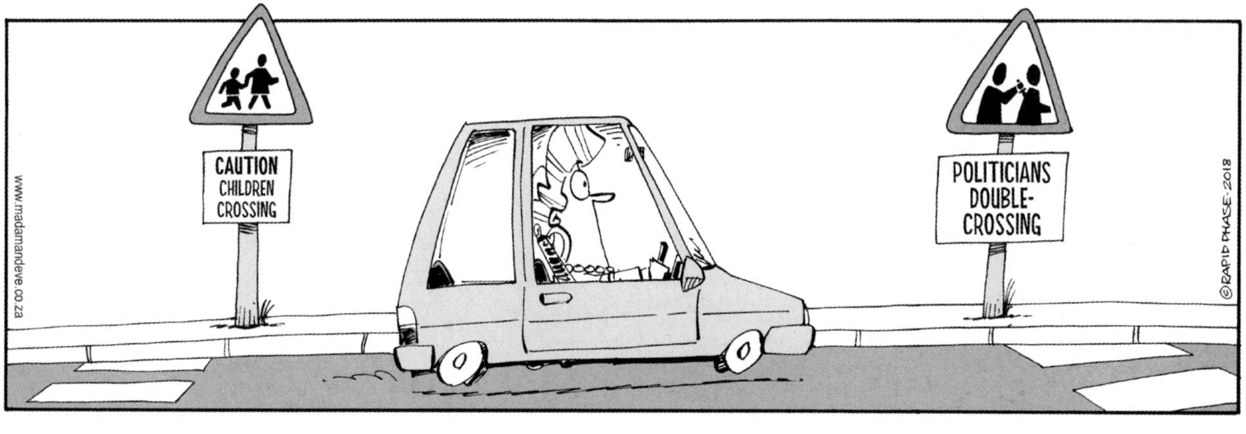
www.madamandeve.co.za
CAUTION
CHILDREN
CROSSING
POLITICIANS
DOUBLE-
CROSSING
©RAPID PHASE-2018

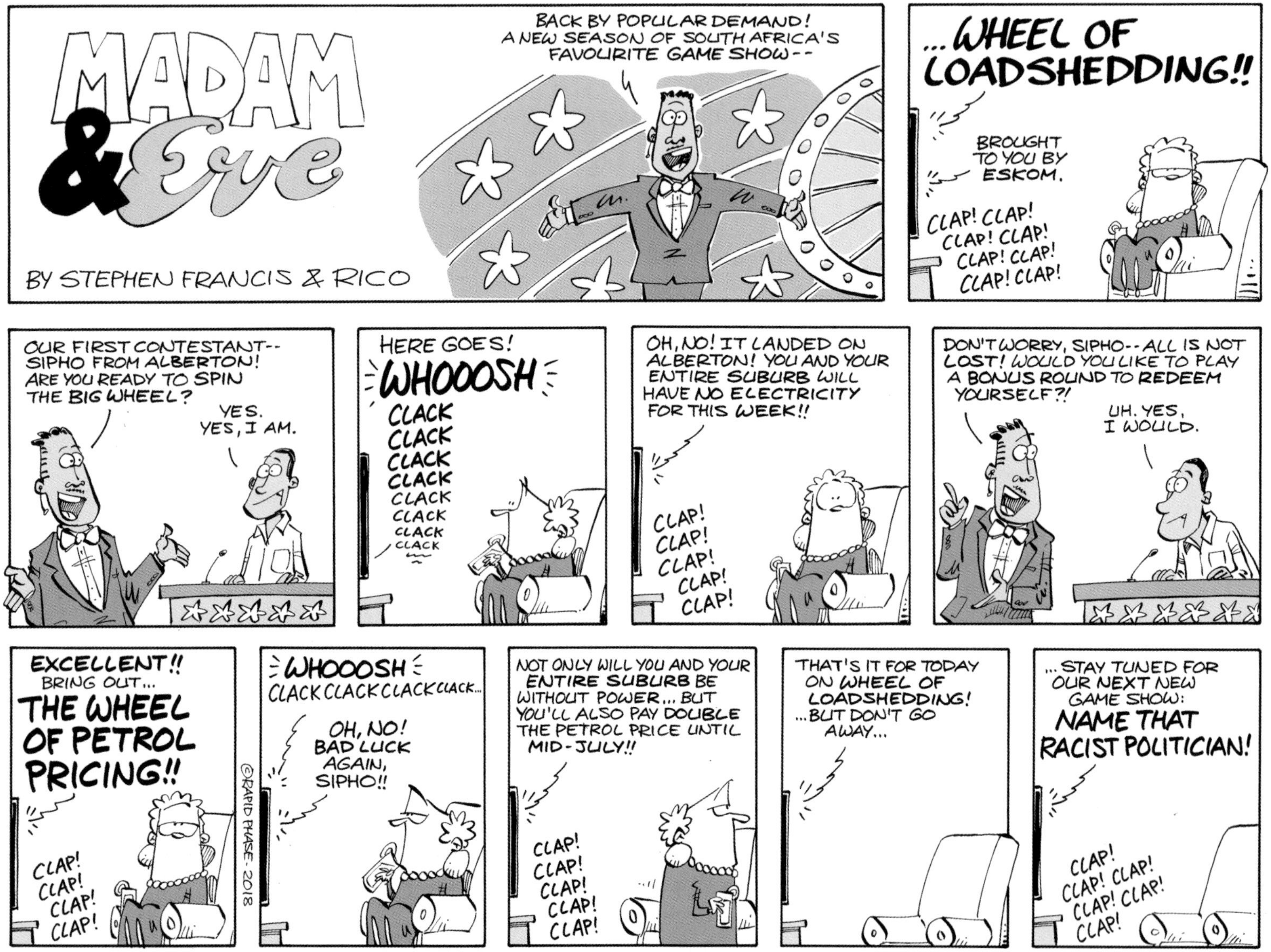
MADAM & Eve
BY STEPHEN FRANCIS & RICO
BACK BY POPULAR DEMAND! A NEW SEASON OF SOUTH AFRICA'S FAVOURITE GAME SHOW--
...WHEEL OF LOADSHEDDING!!
BROUGHT TO YOU BY ESKOM.
CLAP! CLAP! CLAP! CLAP! CLAP! CLAP! CLAP! CLAP!
OUR FIRST CONTESTANT-- SIPHO FROM ALBERTON! ARE YOU READY TO SPIN THE BIG WHEEL?
YES. YES, I AM.
HERE GOES!
WHOOOSH
CLACK CLACK CLACK CLACK CLACK CLACK CLACK CLACK
OH, NO! IT LANDED ON ALBERTON! YOU AND YOUR ENTIRE SUBURB WILL HAVE NO ELECTRICITY FOR THIS WEEK!!
CLAP! CLAP! CLAP! CLAP! CLAP!
DON'T WORRY, SIPHO--ALL IS NOT LOST! WOULD YOU LIKE TO PLAY A BONUS ROUND TO REDEEM YOURSELF?!
UH. YES, I WOULD.
EXCELLENT!! BRING OUT... THE WHEEL OF PETROL PRICING!!
CLAP! CLAP! CLAP! CLAP!
©RAPID PHASE · 2018
WHOOOSH
CLACK CLACK CLACK CLACK...
OH, NO! BAD LUCK AGAIN, SIPHO!!
NOT ONLY WILL YOU AND YOUR ENTIRE SUBURB BE WITHOUT POWER... BUT YOU'LL ALSO PAY DOUBLE THE PETROL PRICE UNTIL MID-JULY!!
CLAP! CLAP! CLAP! CLAP! CLAP!
THAT'S IT FOR TODAY ON WHEEL OF LOADSHEDDING! ...BUT DON'T GO AWAY...
...STAY TUNED FOR OUR NEXT NEW GAME SHOW: NAME THAT RACIST POLITICIAN!
CLAP! CLAP! CLAP! CLAP! CLAP! CLAP!

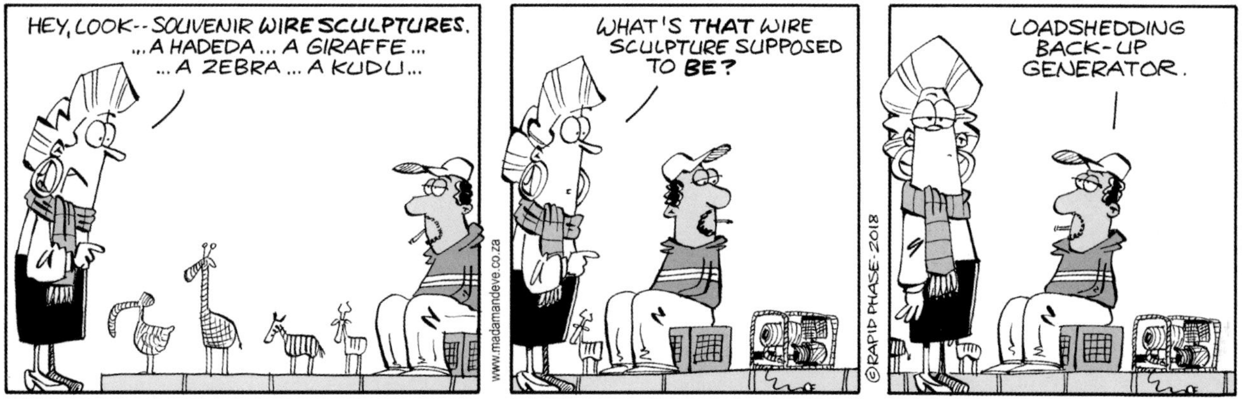
HEY, LOOK-- SOUVENIR **WIRE SCULPTURES**. ... A HADEDA ... A GIRAFFE ... ... A ZEBRA ... A KUDU ...
www.madamandeve.co.za
WHAT'S **THAT** WIRE SCULPTURE SUPPOSED TO **BE?**
©RAPID PHASE: 2018
LOADSHEDDING BACK-UP GENERATOR.

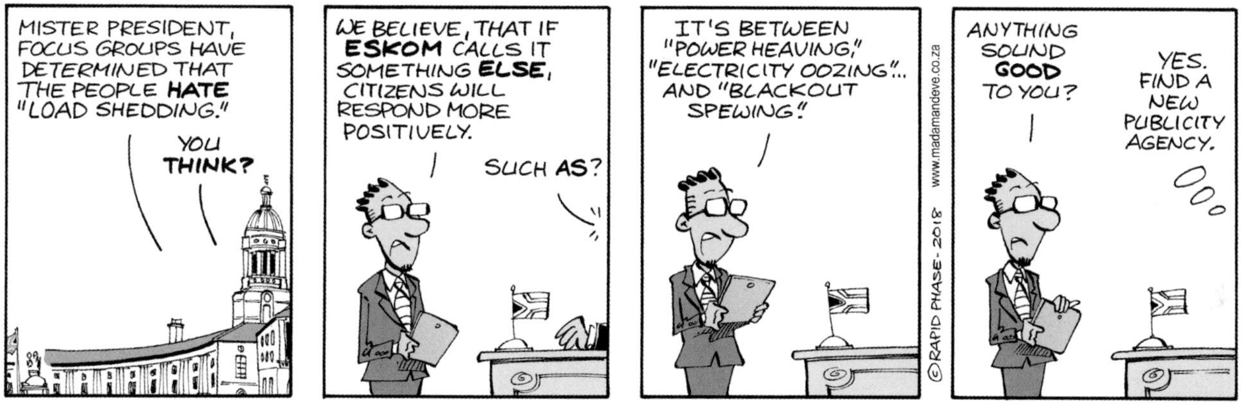
MISTER PRESIDENT, FOCUS GROUPS HAVE DETERMINED THAT THE PEOPLE **HATE** "LOAD SHEDDING."
YOU **THINK?**
WE BELIEVE, THAT IF **ESKOM** CALLS IT SOMETHING **ELSE**, CITIZENS WILL RESPOND MORE POSITIVELY.
SUCH **AS**?
IT'S BETWEEN "POWER HEAVING," "ELECTRICITY OOZING"... AND "BLACKOUT SPEWING!"
www.madamandeve.co.za
©RAPID PHASE - 2018
ANYTHING SOUND **GOOD** TO YOU?
YES. FIND A NEW PUBLICITY AGENCY.

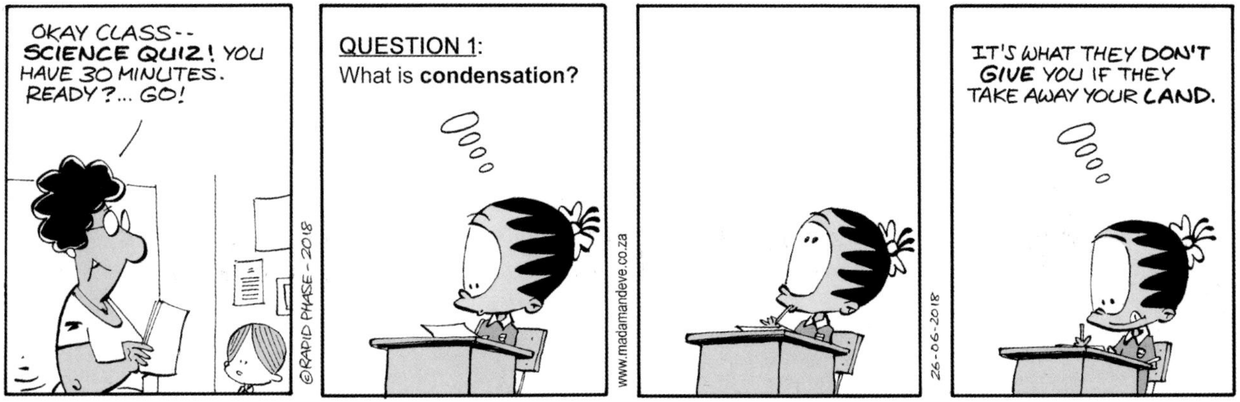
OKAY CLASS-- **SCIENCE QUIZ!** YOU HAVE 30 MINUTES. READY?... GO!
©RAPID PHASE - 2018
QUESTION 1:
What is **condensation?**
www.madamandeve.co.za
26-06-2018
IT'S WHAT THEY **DON'T GIVE** YOU IF THEY TAKE AWAY YOUR **LAND**.

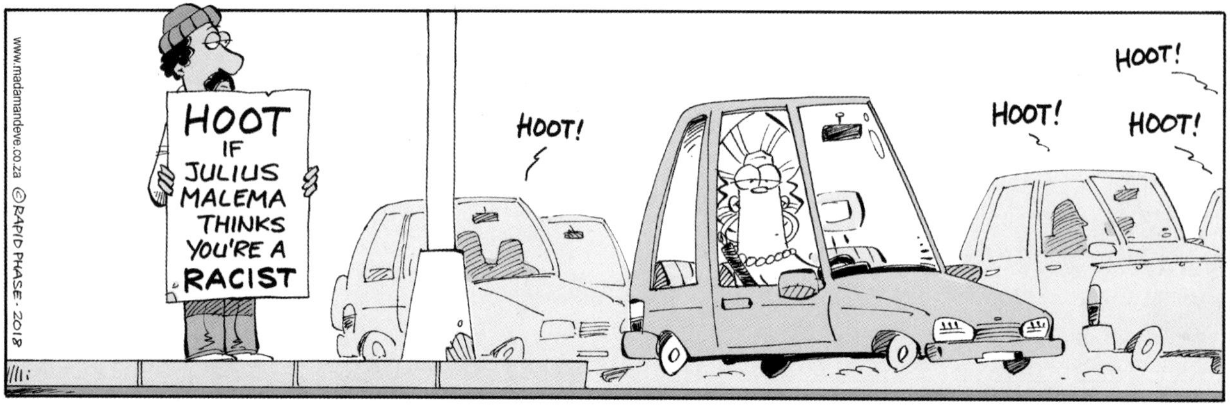
www.madamandeve.co.za ©RAPID PHASE · 2018
HOOT IF JULIUS MALEMA THINKS YOU'RE A RACIST
HOOT!
HOOT!
HOOT!
HOOT!

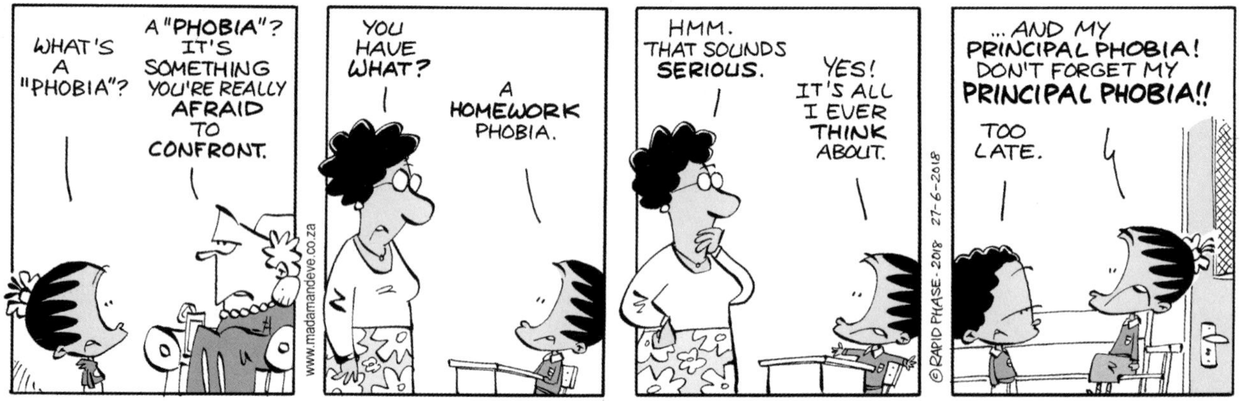
WHAT'S A "PHOBIA"?
A "PHOBIA"? IT'S SOMETHING YOU'RE REALLY AFRAID TO CONFRONT.
www.madamandeve.co.za
YOU HAVE WHAT?
A HOMEWORK PHOBIA.
HMM. THAT SOUNDS SERIOUS.
YES! IT'S ALL I EVER THINK ABOUT.
©RAPID PHASE · 2018 27-6-2018
...AND MY PRINCIPAL PHOBIA! DON'T FORGET MY PRINCIPAL PHOBIA!!
TOO LATE.

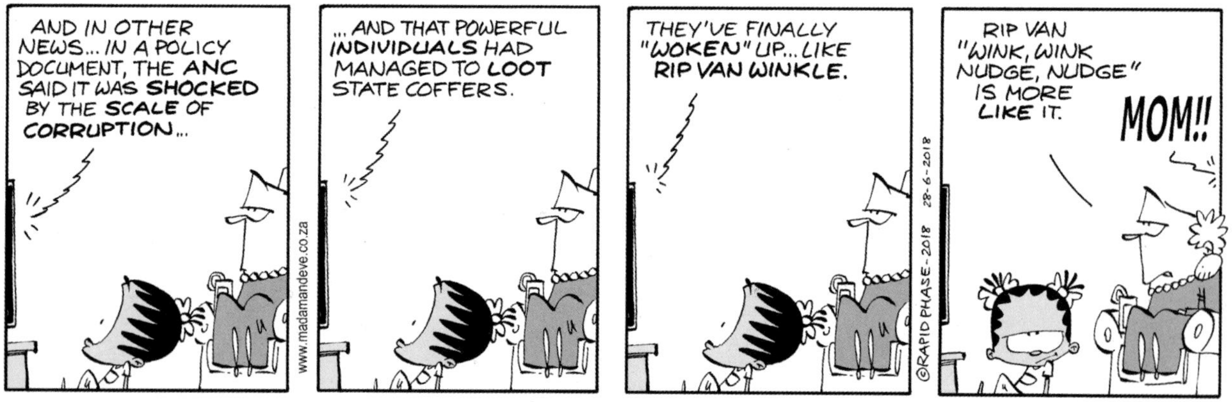
AND IN OTHER NEWS... IN A POLICY DOCUMENT, THE ANC SAID IT WAS SHOCKED BY THE SCALE OF CORRUPTION...
www.madamandeve.co.za
...AND THAT POWERFUL INDIVIDUALS HAD MANAGED TO LOOT STATE COFFERS.
THEY'VE FINALLY "WOKEN" UP... LIKE RIP VAN WINKLE.
©RAPID PHASE · 2018 28-6-2018
RIP VAN "WINK, WINK NUDGE, NUDGE" IS MORE LIKE IT.
MOM!!

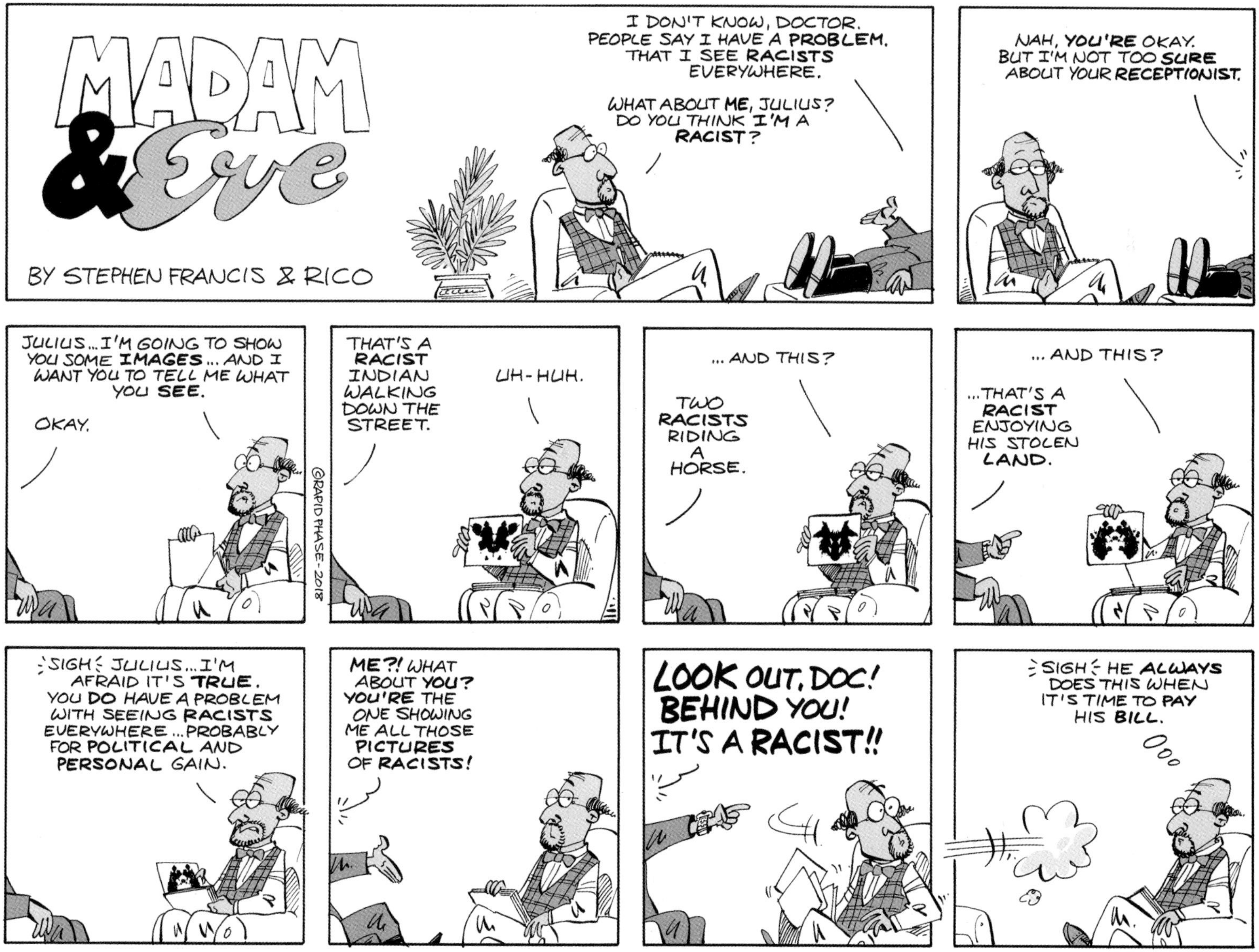
MADAM & Eve
BY STEPHEN FRANCIS & RICO
I DON'T KNOW, DOCTOR. PEOPLE SAY I HAVE A PROBLEM. THAT I SEE RACISTS EVERYWHERE.
WHAT ABOUT ME, JULIUS? DO YOU THINK I'M A RACIST?
NAH, YOU'RE OKAY. BUT I'M NOT TOO SURE ABOUT YOUR RECEPTIONIST.
JULIUS... I'M GOING TO SHOW YOU SOME IMAGES... AND I WANT YOU TO TELL ME WHAT YOU SEE.
OKAY.
©RAPID PHASE-2018
THAT'S A RACIST INDIAN WALKING DOWN THE STREET.
UH-HUH.
... AND THIS?
TWO RACISTS RIDING A HORSE.
... AND THIS?
...THAT'S A RACIST ENJOYING HIS STOLEN LAND.
SIGH JULIUS... I'M AFRAID IT'S TRUE. YOU DO HAVE A PROBLEM WITH SEEING RACISTS EVERYWHERE... PROBABLY FOR POLITICAL AND PERSONAL GAIN.
ME?! WHAT ABOUT YOU? YOU'RE THE ONE SHOWING ME ALL THOSE PICTURES OF RACISTS!
LOOK OUT, DOC! BEHIND YOU! IT'S A RACIST!!
SIGH HE ALWAYS DOES THIS WHEN IT'S TIME TO PAY HIS BILL.

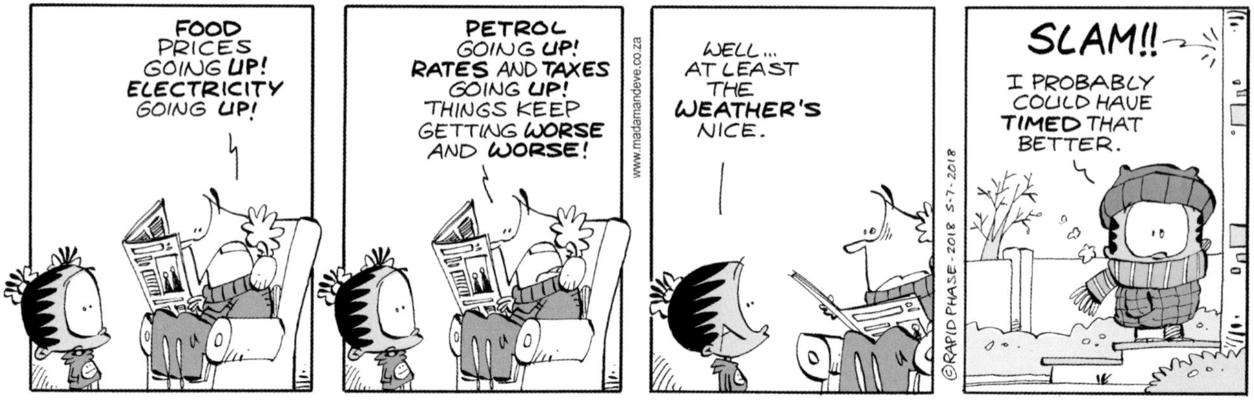
FOOD PRICES GOING UP! ELECTRICITY GOING UP!
PETROL GOING UP! RATES AND TAXES GOING UP! THINGS KEEP GETTING WORSE AND WORSE!
www.madamandeve.co.za
WELL... AT LEAST THE WEATHER'S NICE.
©RAPID PHASE - 2018 5-7-2018
SLAM!!
I PROBABLY COULD HAVE TIMED THAT BETTER.

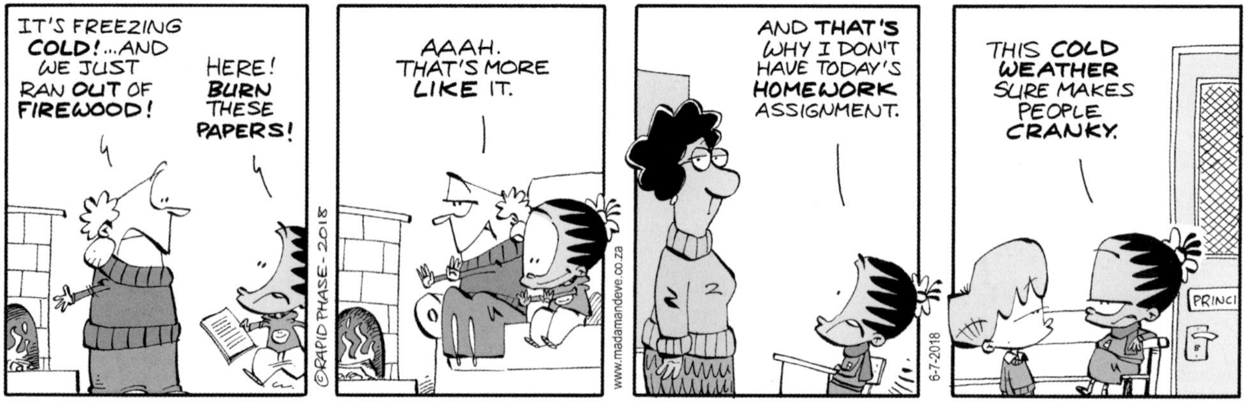
IT'S FREEZING COLD!...AND WE JUST RAN OUT OF FIREWOOD!
HERE! BURN THESE PAPERS!
©RAPID PHASE - 2018
AAAH. THAT'S MORE LIKE IT.
www.madamandeve.co.za
AND THAT'S WHY I DON'T HAVE TODAY'S HOMEWORK ASSIGNMENT.
6-7-2018
THIS COLD WEATHER SURE MAKES PEOPLE CRANKY.
PRINCI

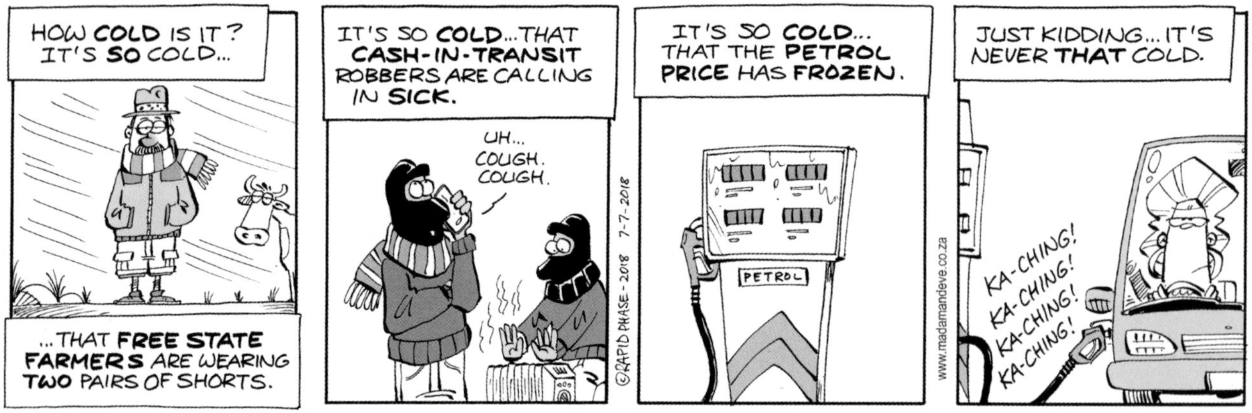
HOW COLD IS IT? IT'S SO COLD...
...THAT FREE STATE FARMERS ARE WEARING TWO PAIRS OF SHORTS.
IT'S SO COLD...THAT CASH-IN-TRANSIT ROBBERS ARE CALLING IN SICK.
UH... COUGH. COUGH.
©RAPID PHASE - 2018 7-7-2018
IT'S SO COLD... THAT THE PETROL PRICE HAS FROZEN.
PETROL
JUST KIDDING... IT'S NEVER THAT COLD.
www.madamandeve.co.za
KA-CHING! KA-CHING! KA-CHING! KA-CHING!

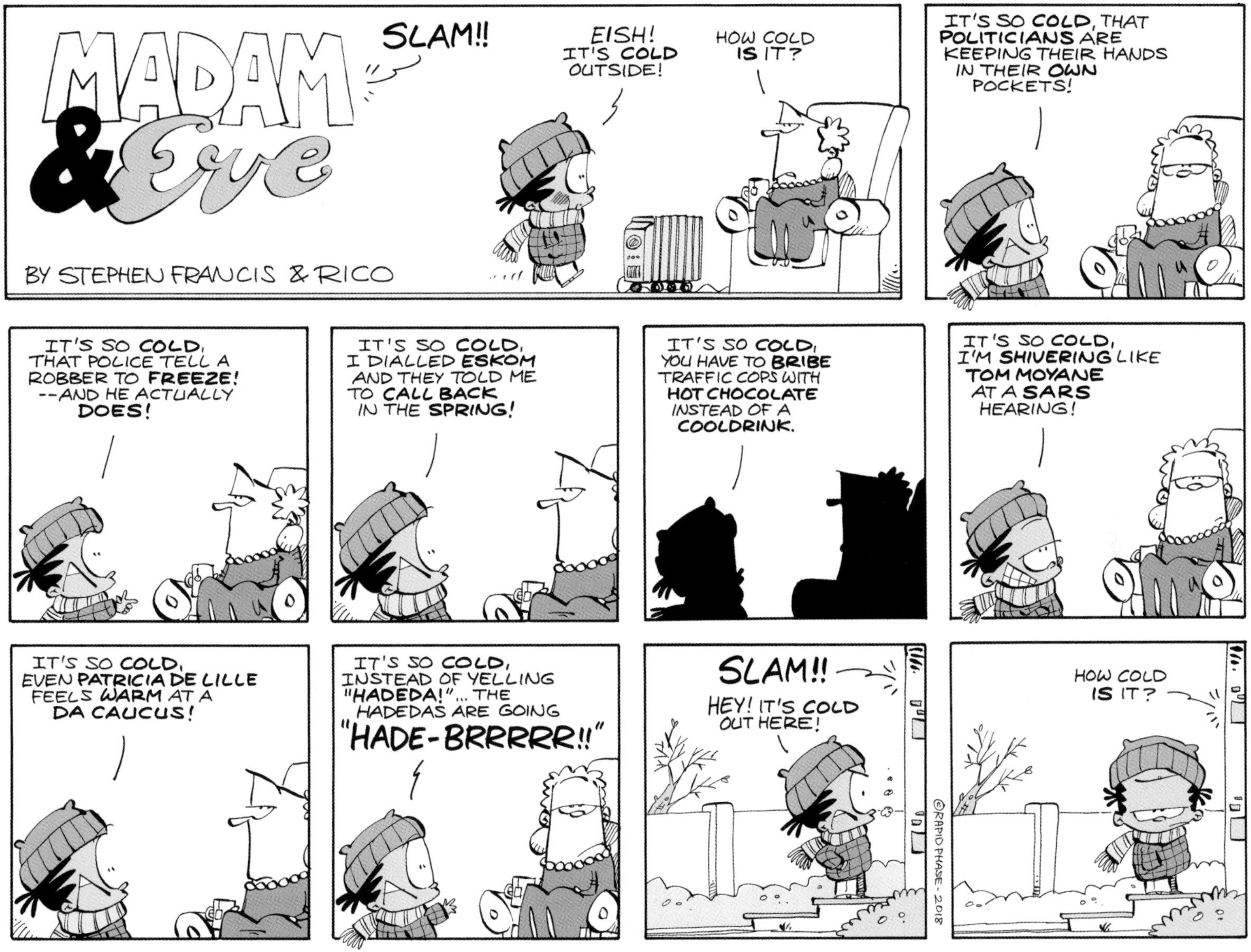
MADAM & Eve
BY STEPHEN FRANCIS & RICO
SLAM!!
EISH! IT'S COLD OUTSIDE!
HOW COLD IS IT?
IT'S SO COLD, THAT POLITICIANS ARE KEEPING THEIR HANDS IN THEIR OWN POCKETS!
IT'S SO COLD, THAT POLICE TELL A ROBBER TO FREEZE! --AND HE ACTUALLY DOES!
IT'S SO COLD, I DIALLED ESKOM AND THEY TOLD ME TO CALL BACK IN THE SPRING!
IT'S SO COLD, YOU HAVE TO BRIBE TRAFFIC COPS WITH HOT CHOCOLATE INSTEAD OF A COOLDRINK.
IT'S SO COLD, I'M SHIVERING LIKE TOM MOYANE AT A SARS HEARING!
IT'S SO COLD, EVEN PATRICIA DE LILLE FEELS WARM AT A DA CAUCUS!
IT'S SO COLD, INSTEAD OF YELLING "HADEDA!"... THE HADEDAS ARE GOING "HADE-BRRRRR!!"
SLAM!!
HEY! IT'S COLD OUT HERE!
©RAPID PHASE - 2018
HOW COLD IS IT?

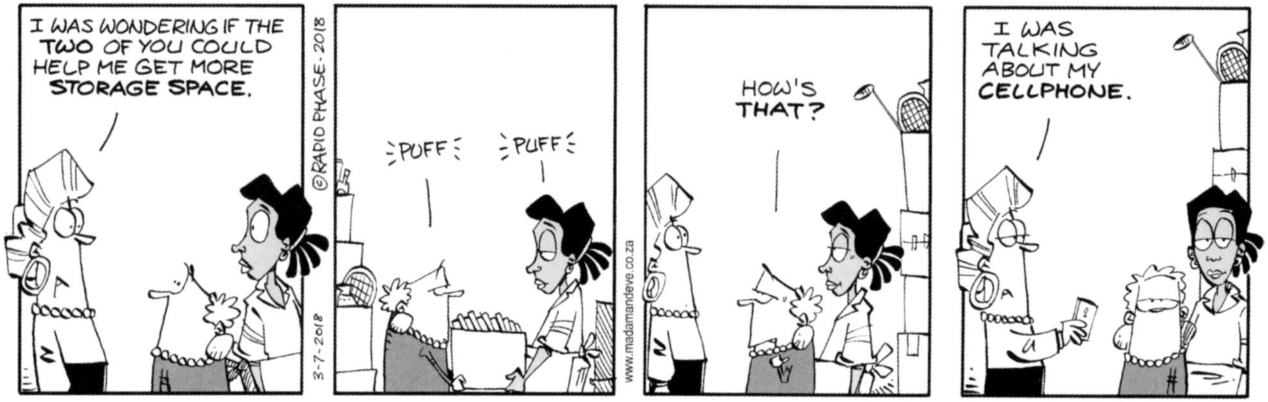
I WAS WONDERING IF THE TWO OF YOU COULD HELP ME GET MORE STORAGE SPACE.
©RAPID PHASE · 2018
3-7-2018
PUFF
PUFF
www.madamandeve.co.za
HOW'S THAT?
I WAS TALKING ABOUT MY CELLPHONE.

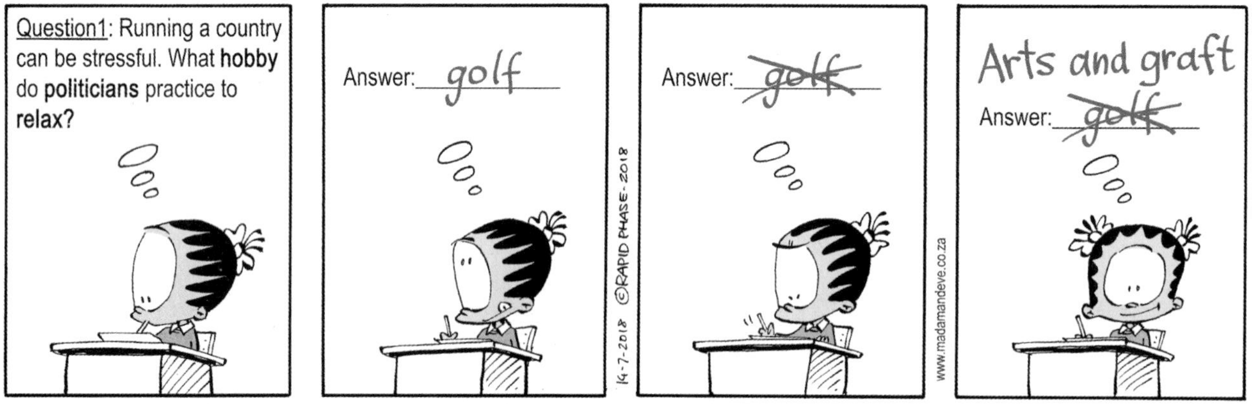
Question1: Running a country can be stressful. What hobby do politicians practice to relax?
Answer: golf
14-7-2018
©RAPID PHASE · 2018
Answer: ~~golf~~
www.madamandeve.co.za
Arts and graft
Answer: ~~golf~~

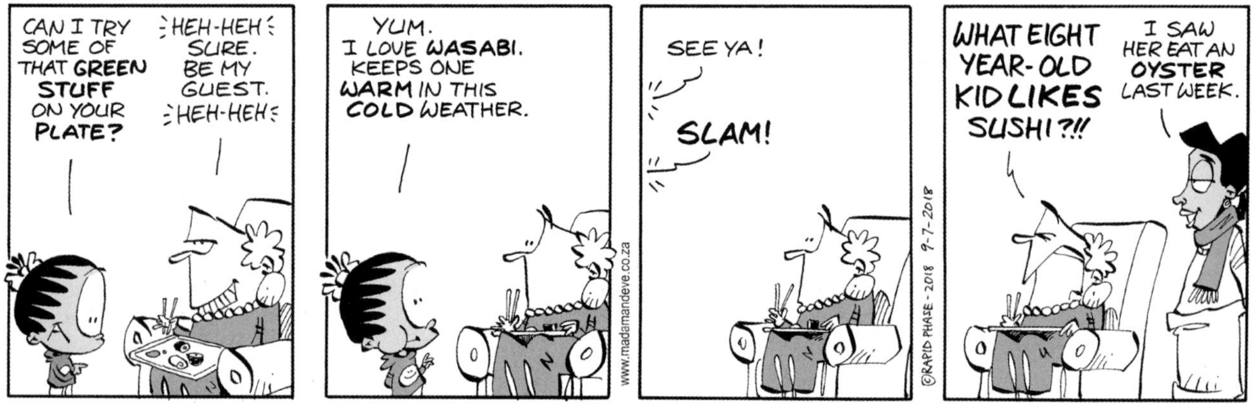
CAN I TRY SOME OF THAT GREEN STUFF ON YOUR PLATE?
HEH-HEH SURE. BE MY GUEST. HEH-HEH
YUM. I LOVE WASABI. KEEPS ONE WARM IN THIS COLD WEATHER.
www.madamandeve.co.za
SEE YA!
SLAM!
9-7-2018
©RAPID PHASE · 2018
WHAT EIGHT YEAR-OLD KID LIKES SUSHI?!!
I SAW HER EAT AN OYSTER LAST WEEK.

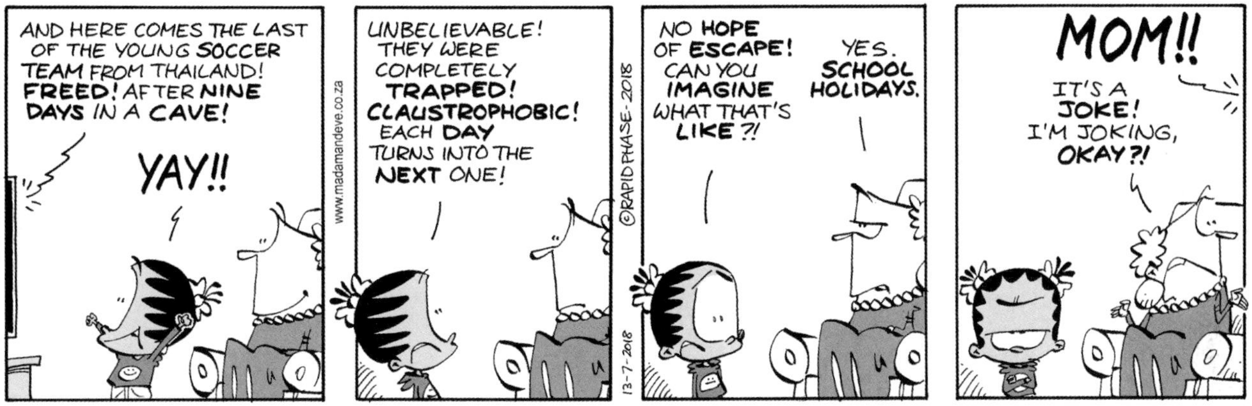
AND HERE COMES THE LAST OF THE YOUNG SOCCER TEAM FROM THAILAND! FREED! AFTER NINE DAYS IN A CAVE!
YAY!!
www.madamandeve.co.za
UNBELIEVABLE! THEY WERE COMPLETELY TRAPPED! CLAUSTROPHOBIC! EACH DAY TURNS INTO THE NEXT ONE!
©RAPID PHASE-2018
13-7-2018
NO HOPE OF ESCAPE! CAN YOU IMAGINE WHAT THAT'S LIKE?!
YES. SCHOOL HOLIDAYS.
MOM!!
IT'S A JOKE! I'M JOKING, OKAY?!

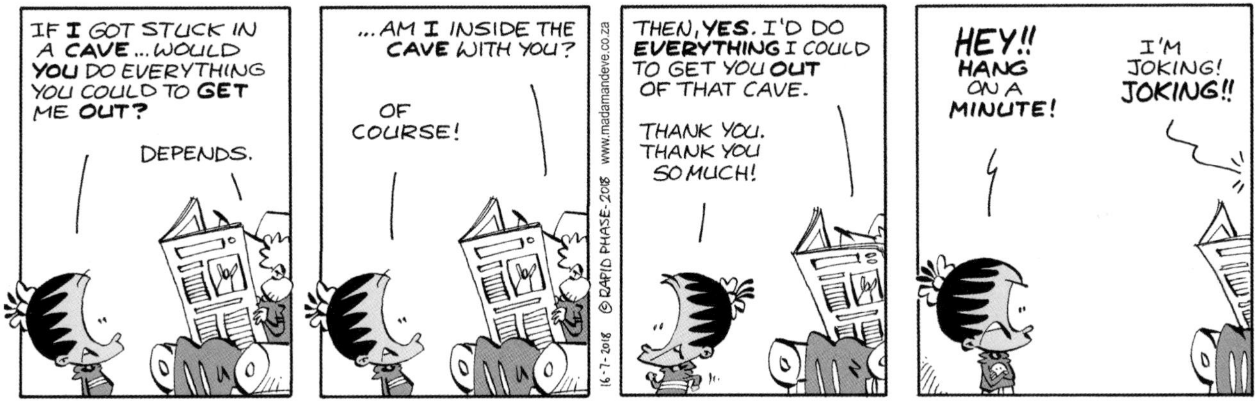
IF I GOT STUCK IN A CAVE... WOULD YOU DO EVERYTHING YOU COULD TO GET ME OUT?
DEPENDS.
...AM I INSIDE THE CAVE WITH YOU?
OF COURSE!
www.madamandeve.co.za
© RAPID PHASE-2018
16-7-2018
THEN, YES. I'D DO EVERYTHING I COULD TO GET YOU OUT OF THAT CAVE.
THANK YOU. THANK YOU SO MUCH!
HEY!! HANG ON A MINUTE!
I'M JOKING! JOKING!!

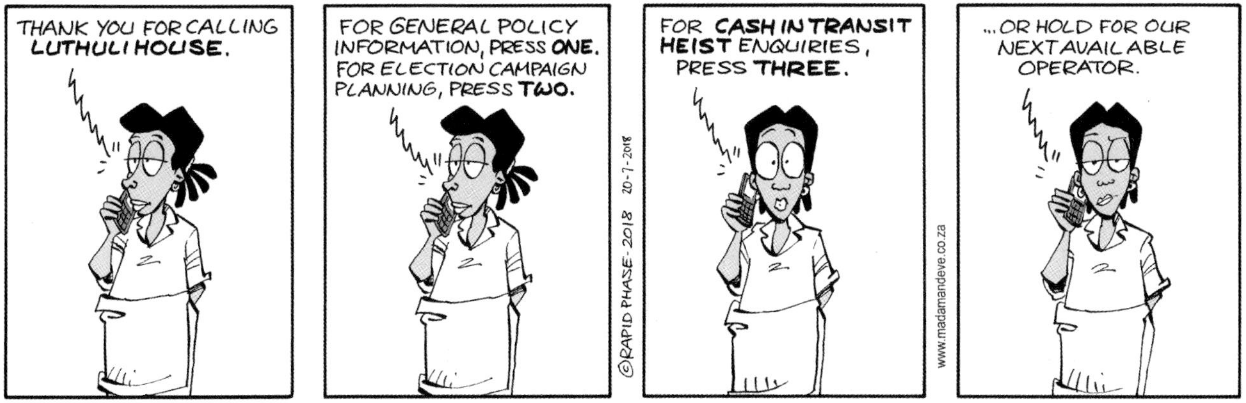
THANK YOU FOR CALLING LUTHULI HOUSE.
FOR GENERAL POLICY INFORMATION, PRESS ONE. FOR ELECTION CAMPAIGN PLANNING, PRESS TWO.
20-7-2018
©RAPID PHASE-2018
FOR CASH IN TRANSIT HEIST ENQUIRIES, PRESS THREE.
www.madamandeve.co.za
...OR HOLD FOR OUR NEXT AVAILABLE OPERATOR.

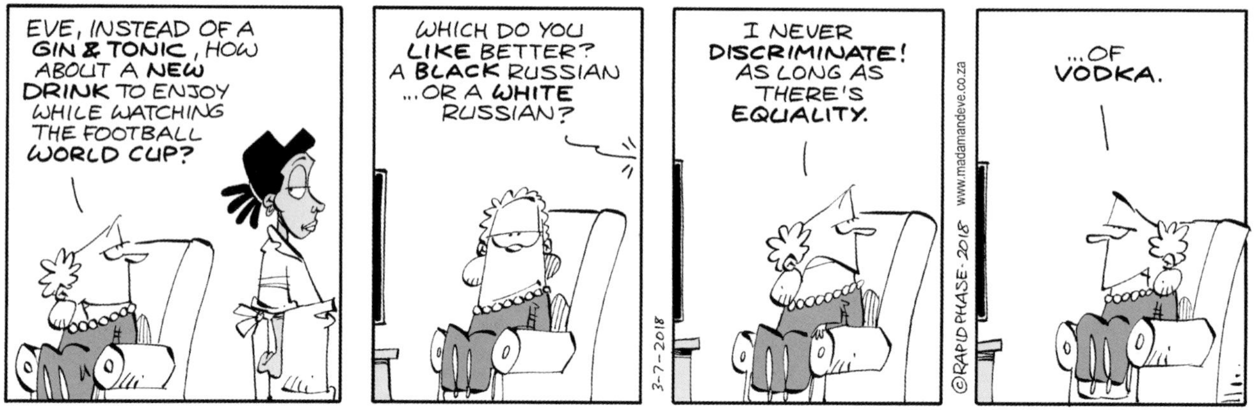
EVE, INSTEAD OF A GIN & TONIC, HOW ABOUT A NEW DRINK TO ENJOY WHILE WATCHING THE FOOTBALL WORLD CUP?
WHICH DO YOU LIKE BETTER? A BLACK RUSSIAN ...OR A WHITE RUSSIAN?
3-7-2018
I NEVER DISCRIMINATE! AS LONG AS THERE'S EQUALITY.
©RAPID PHASE - 2018 www.madamandeve.co.za
...OF VODKA.
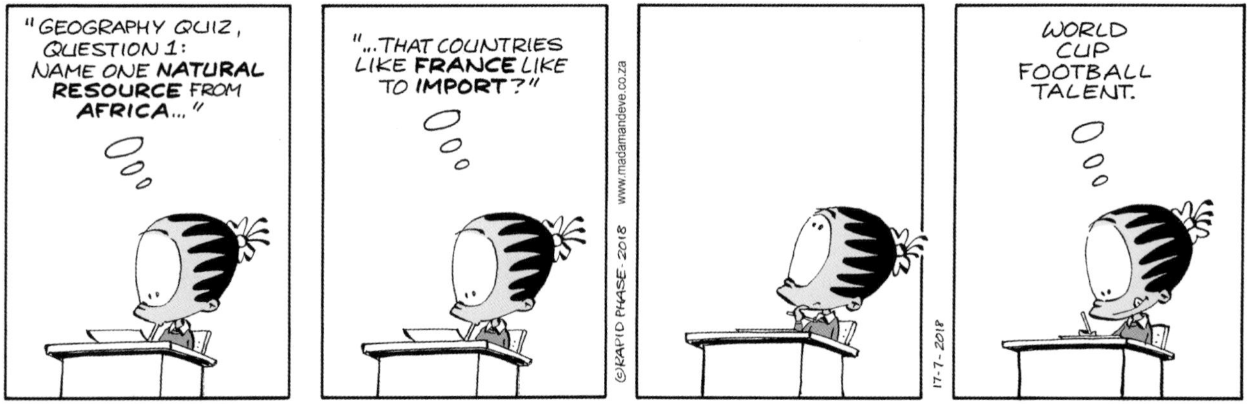
"GEOGRAPHY QUIZ, QUESTION 1: NAME ONE NATURAL RESOURCE FROM AFRICA..."
"...THAT COUNTRIES LIKE FRANCE LIKE TO IMPORT?"
©RAPID PHASE - 2018 www.madamandeve.co.za
17-7-2018
WORLD CUP FOOTBALL TALENT.
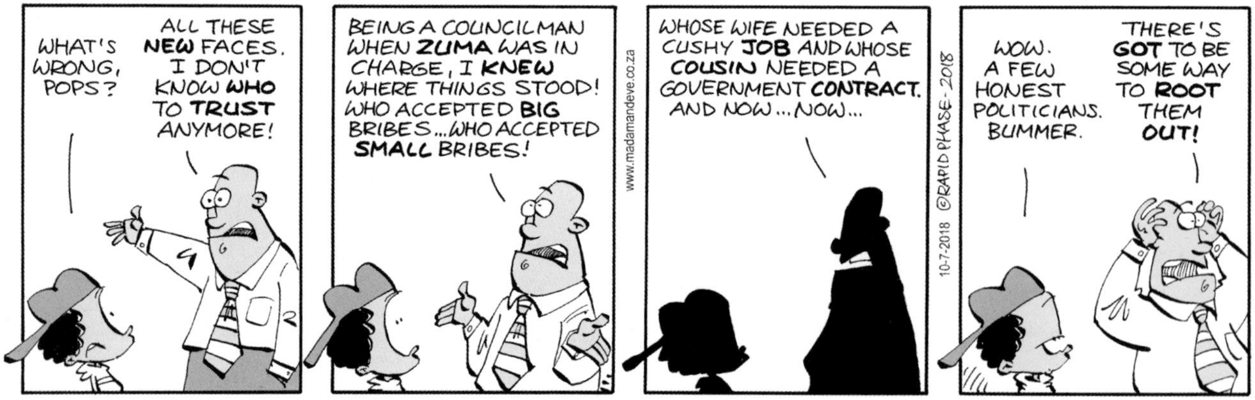
WHAT'S WRONG, POPS?
ALL THESE NEW FACES. I DON'T KNOW WHO TO TRUST ANYMORE!
BEING A COUNCILMAN WHEN ZUMA WAS IN CHARGE, I KNEW WHERE THINGS STOOD! WHO ACCEPTED BIG BRIBES...WHO ACCEPTED SMALL BRIBES!
www.madamandeve.co.za
WHOSE WIFE NEEDED A CUSHY JOB AND WHOSE COUSIN NEEDED A GOVERNMENT CONTRACT. AND NOW...NOW...
10-7-2018 ©RAPID PHASE - 2018
WOW. A FEW HONEST POLITICIANS. BUMMER.
THERE'S GOT TO BE SOME WAY TO ROOT THEM OUT!

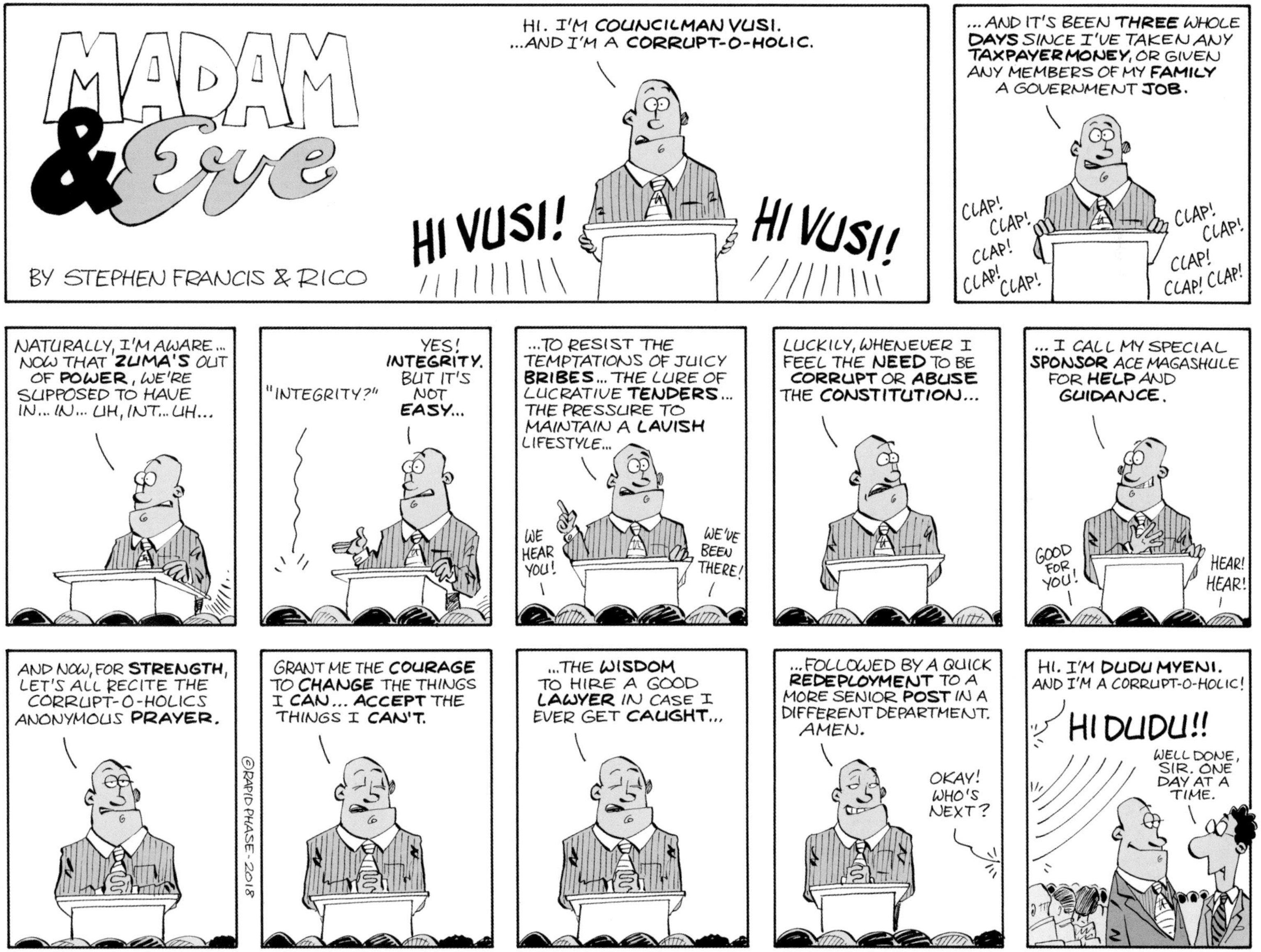
MADAM & Eve
BY STEPHEN FRANCIS & RICO
HI. I'M COUNCILMAN VUSI. ...AND I'M A CORRUPT-O-HOLIC.
HI VUSI!
HI VUSI!
...AND IT'S BEEN THREE WHOLE DAYS SINCE I'VE TAKEN ANY TAXPAYER MONEY, OR GIVEN ANY MEMBERS OF MY FAMILY A GOVERNMENT JOB.
CLAP! CLAP! CLAP! CLAP! CLAP!
CLAP! CLAP! CLAP! CLAP! CLAP!
NATURALLY, I'M AWARE... NOW THAT ZUMA'S OUT OF POWER, WE'RE SUPPOSED TO HAVE IN... IN... UH, INT... UH...
"INTEGRITY?"
YES! INTEGRITY. BUT IT'S NOT EASY...
...TO RESIST THE TEMPTATIONS OF JUICY BRIBES... THE LURE OF LUCRATIVE TENDERS... THE PRESSURE TO MAINTAIN A LAVISH LIFESTYLE...
WE HEAR YOU!
WE'VE BEEN THERE!
LUCKILY, WHENEVER I FEEL THE NEED TO BE CORRUPT OR ABUSE THE CONSTITUTION...
... I CALL MY SPECIAL SPONSOR ACE MAGASHULE FOR HELP AND GUIDANCE.
GOOD FOR YOU!
HEAR! HEAR!
AND NOW, FOR STRENGTH, LET'S ALL RECITE THE CORRUPT-O-HOLICS ANONYMOUS PRAYER.
©RAPID PHASE-2018
GRANT ME THE COURAGE TO CHANGE THE THINGS I CAN... ACCEPT THE THINGS I CAN'T.
...THE WISDOM TO HIRE A GOOD LAWYER IN CASE I EVER GET CAUGHT...
...FOLLOWED BY A QUICK REDEPLOYMENT TO A MORE SENIOR POST IN A DIFFERENT DEPARTMENT. AMEN.
OKAY! WHO'S NEXT?
HI. I'M DUDU MYENI. AND I'M A CORRUPT-O-HOLIC!
HI DUDU!!
WELL DONE, SIR. ONE DAY AT A TIME.

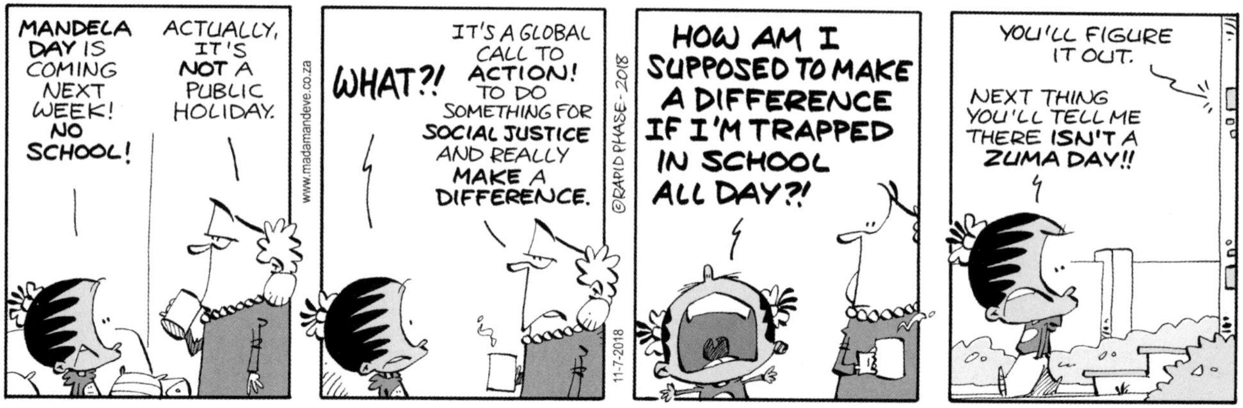
MANDELA DAY IS COMING NEXT WEEK! NO SCHOOL!
ACTUALLY, IT'S NOT A PUBLIC HOLIDAY.
www.madamandeve.co.za
WHAT?!
IT'S A GLOBAL CALL TO ACTION! TO DO SOMETHING FOR SOCIAL JUSTICE AND REALLY MAKE A DIFFERENCE.
©RAPID PHASE - 2018
11-7-2018
HOW AM I SUPPOSED TO MAKE A DIFFERENCE IF I'M TRAPPED IN SCHOOL ALL DAY?!
YOU'LL FIGURE IT OUT.
NEXT THING YOU'LL TELL ME THERE ISN'T A ZUMA DAY!!

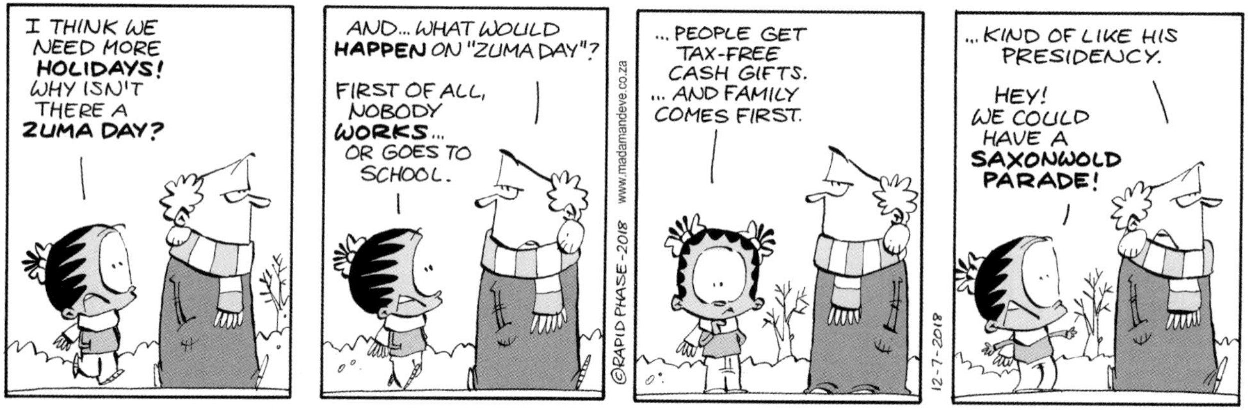
I THINK WE NEED MORE HOLIDAYS! WHY ISN'T THERE A ZUMA DAY?
AND... WHAT WOULD HAPPEN ON "ZUMA DAY"?
FIRST OF ALL, NOBODY WORKS... OR GOES TO SCHOOL.
www.madamandeve.co.za
©RAPID PHASE - 2018
... PEOPLE GET TAX-FREE CASH GIFTS. ... AND FAMILY COMES FIRST.
12-7-2018
... KIND OF LIKE HIS PRESIDENCY.
HEY! WE COULD HAVE A SAXONWOLD PARADE!

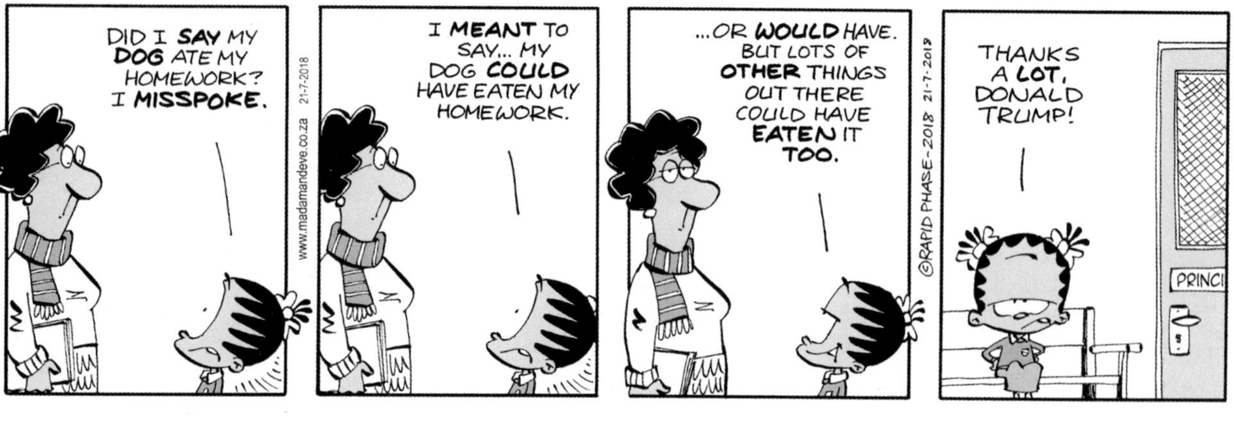
DID I SAY MY DOG ATE MY HOMEWORK? I MISSPOKE.
21-7-2018
www.madamandeve.co.za
I MEANT TO SAY... MY DOG COULD HAVE EATEN MY HOMEWORK.
...OR WOULD HAVE. BUT LOTS OF OTHER THINGS OUT THERE COULD HAVE EATEN IT TOO.
©RAPID PHASE - 2018 21-7-2018
THANKS A LOT, DONALD TRUMP!
PRINCI

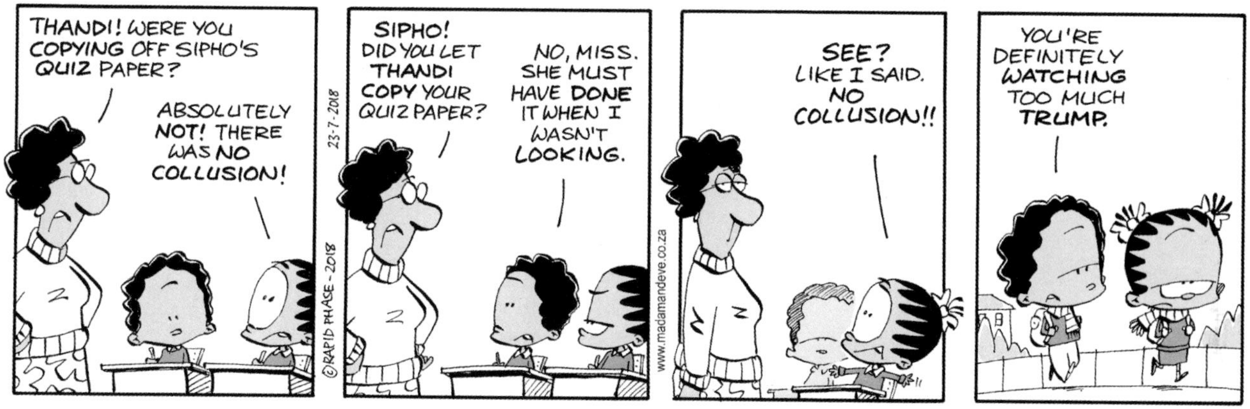
THANDI! WERE YOU COPYING OFF SIPHO'S QUIZ PAPER?
ABSOLUTELY NOT! THERE WAS NO COLLUSION!
23-7-2018
©RAPID PHASE - 2018
SIPHO! DID YOU LET THANDI COPY YOUR QUIZ PAPER?
NO, MISS. SHE MUST HAVE DONE IT WHEN I WASN'T LOOKING.
www.madamandeve.co.za
SEE? LIKE I SAID. NO COLLUSION!!
YOU'RE DEFINITELY WATCHING TOO MUCH TRUMP.

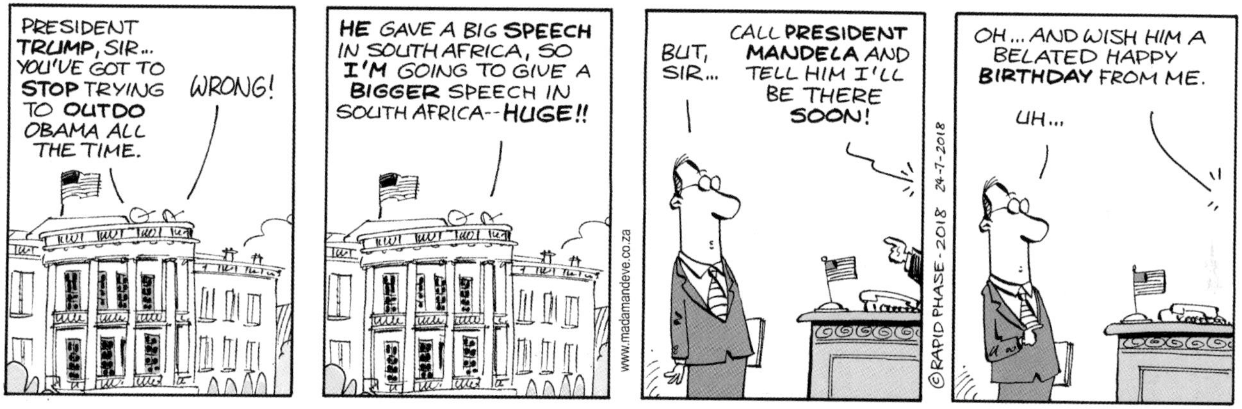
PRESIDENT TRUMP, SIR... YOU'VE GOT TO STOP TRYING TO OUTDO OBAMA ALL THE TIME.
WRONG!
HE GAVE A BIG SPEECH IN SOUTH AFRICA, SO I'M GOING TO GIVE A BIGGER SPEECH IN SOUTH AFRICA--HUGE!!
www.madamandeve.co.za
BUT, SIR...
CALL PRESIDENT MANDELA AND TELL HIM I'LL BE THERE SOON!
©RAPID PHASE - 2018 24-7-2018
OH... AND WISH HIM A BELATED HAPPY BIRTHDAY FROM ME.
UH...

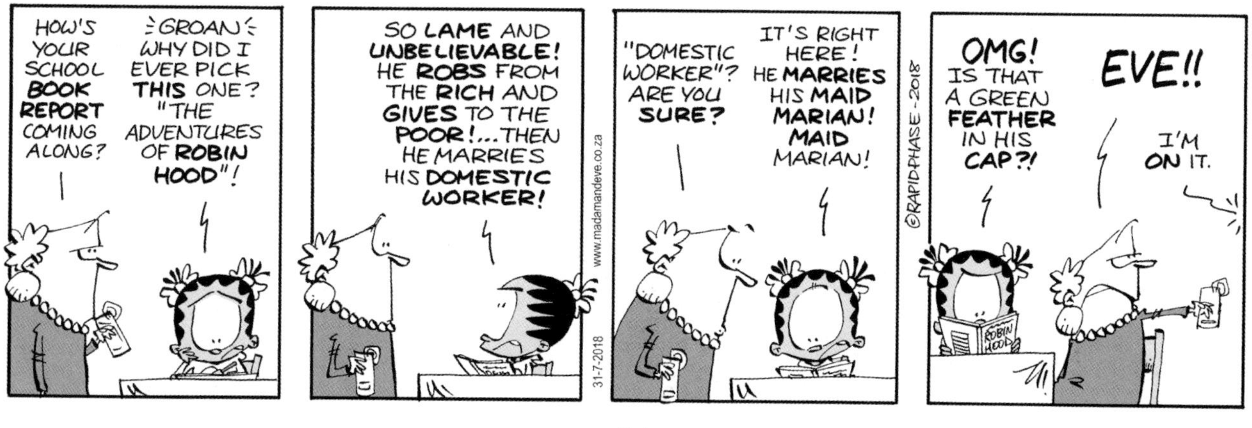
HOW'S YOUR SCHOOL BOOK REPORT COMING ALONG?
GROAN
WHY DID I EVER PICK THIS ONE? "THE ADVENTURES OF ROBIN HOOD"!
SO LAME AND UNBELIEVABLE! HE ROBS FROM THE RICH AND GIVES TO THE POOR!...THEN HE MARRIES HIS DOMESTIC WORKER!
31-7-2018
www.madamandeve.co.za
"DOMESTIC WORKER"? ARE YOU SURE?
IT'S RIGHT HERE! HE MARRIES HIS MAID MARIAN! MAID MARIAN!
©RAPIDPHASE - 2018
OMG! IS THAT A GREEN FEATHER IN HIS CAP?!
EVE!!
I'M ON IT.
ROBIN HOOD

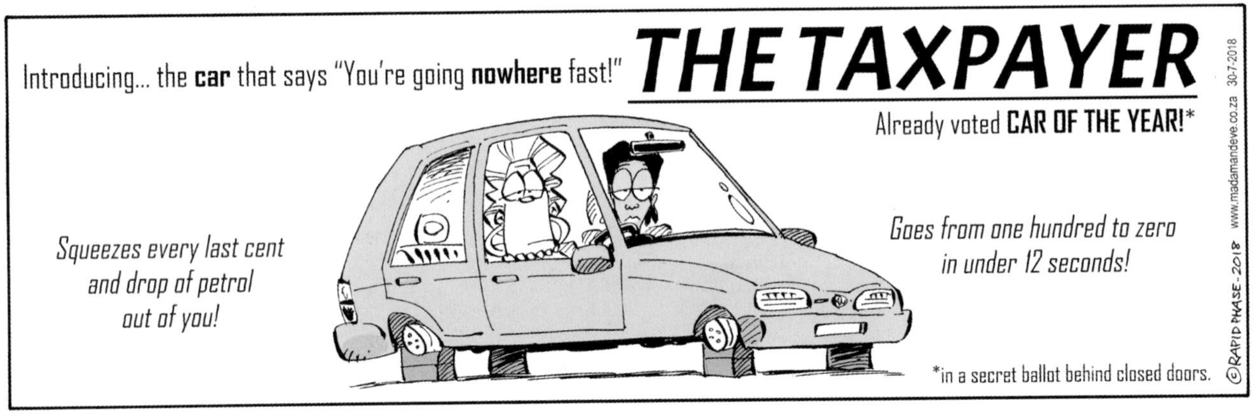
Introducing... the **car** that says "You're going **nowhere** fast!"
THE TAXPAYER
Already voted **CAR OF THE YEAR!***
Squeezes every last cent and drop of petrol out of you!
Goes from one hundred to zero in under 12 seconds!
*in a secret ballot behind closed doors.
www.madamandeve.co.za 30-7-2018
©RAPID PHASE-2018

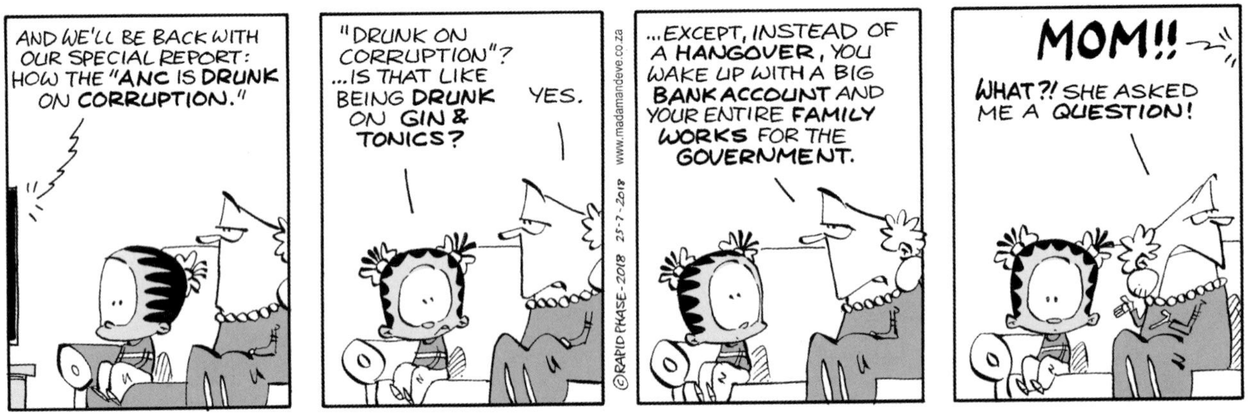
AND WE'LL BE BACK WITH OUR SPECIAL REPORT: HOW THE "**ANC** IS **DRUNK** ON **CORRUPTION**."
"DRUNK ON CORRUPTION"? ...IS THAT LIKE BEING **DRUNK** ON **GIN & TONICS**?
YES.
www.madamandeve.co.za ©RAPID PHASE-2018 25-7-2018
...EXCEPT, INSTEAD OF A **HANGOVER**, YOU WAKE UP WITH A BIG **BANK ACCOUNT** AND YOUR ENTIRE **FAMILY WORKS** FOR THE **GOVERNMENT**.
MOM!!
WHAT?! SHE ASKED ME A **QUESTION**!

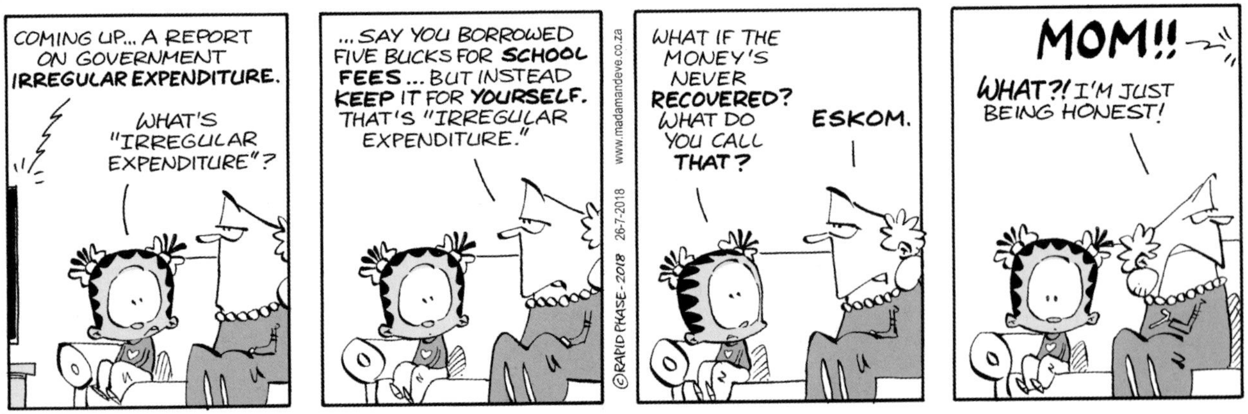
COMING UP... A REPORT ON GOVERNMENT **IRREGULAR EXPENDITURE**.
WHAT'S "IRREGULAR EXPENDITURE"?
...SAY YOU BORROWED FIVE BUCKS FOR **SCHOOL FEES**... BUT INSTEAD **KEEP IT** FOR **YOURSELF**. THAT'S "IRREGULAR EXPENDITURE."
www.madamandeve.co.za ©RAPID PHASE-2018 26-7-2018
WHAT IF THE MONEY'S NEVER **RECOVERED**? WHAT DO YOU CALL **THAT**?
ESKOM.
MOM!!
WHAT?! I'M JUST BEING HONEST!

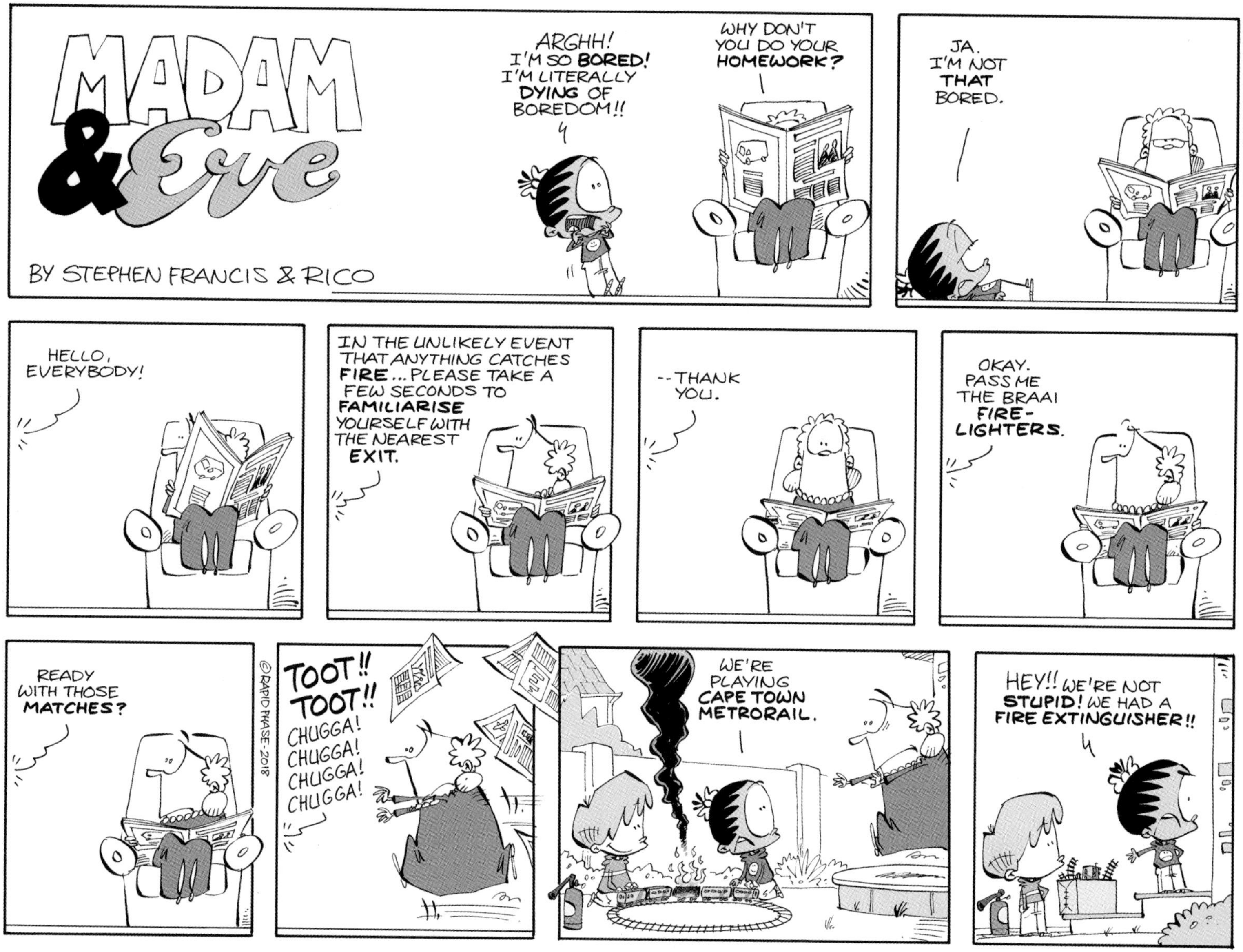
MADAM & Eve
BY STEPHEN FRANCIS & RICO
ARGHH! I'M SO BORED! I'M LITERALLY DYING OF BOREDOM!!
WHY DON'T YOU DO YOUR HOMEWORK?
JA. I'M NOT THAT BORED.
HELLO, EVERYBODY!
IN THE UNLIKELY EVENT THAT ANYTHING CATCHES FIRE... PLEASE TAKE A FEW SECONDS TO FAMILIARISE YOURSELF WITH THE NEAREST EXIT.
--THANK YOU.
OKAY. PASS ME THE BRAAI FIRE-LIGHTERS.
READY WITH THOSE MATCHES?
© RAPID PHASE 2018
TOOT!! TOOT!!
CHUGGA! CHUGGA! CHUGGA! CHUGGA!
WE'RE PLAYING CAPE TOWN METRORAIL.
HEY!! WE'RE NOT STUPID! WE HAD A FIRE EXTINGUISHER!!

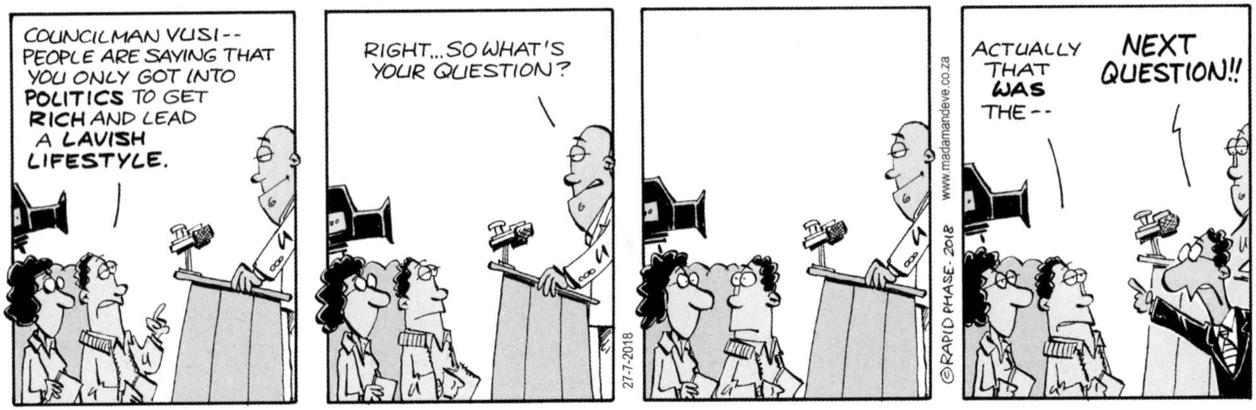
COUNCILMAN VUSI-- PEOPLE ARE SAYING THAT YOU ONLY GOT INTO **POLITICS** TO GET **RICH** AND LEAD A **LAVISH LIFESTYLE.**
RIGHT... SO WHAT'S YOUR QUESTION?
27-7-2018
www.madamandeve.co.za
©RAPID PHASE-2018
ACTUALLY THAT **WAS** THE--
NEXT QUESTION!!

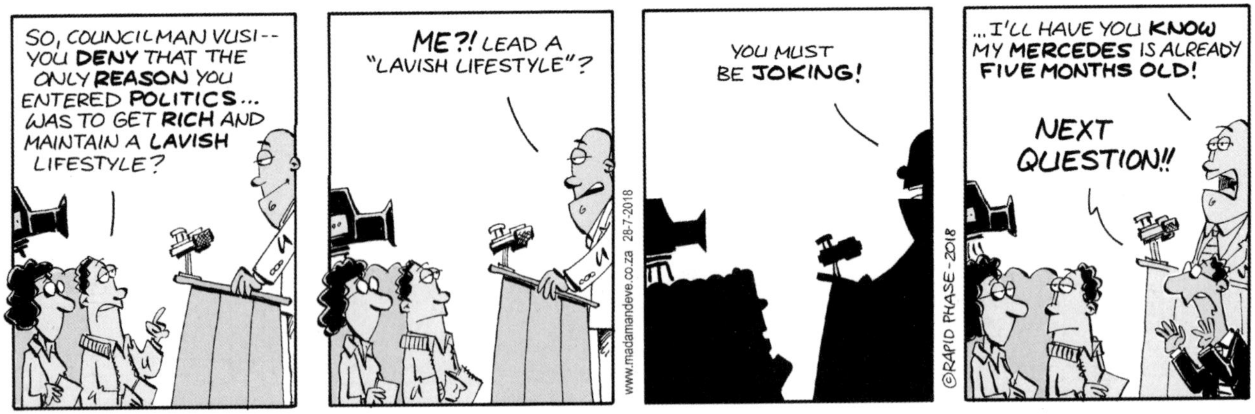
SO, COUNCILMAN VUSI-- YOU **DENY** THAT THE ONLY **REASON** YOU ENTERED **POLITICS**... WAS TO GET **RICH** AND MAINTAIN A **LAVISH** LIFESTYLE?
ME?! LEAD A "LAVISH LIFESTYLE"?
www.madamandeve.co.za 28-7-2018
YOU MUST BE **JOKING!**
©RAPID PHASE-2018
...I'LL HAVE YOU **KNOW** MY **MERCEDES** IS ALREADY **FIVE MONTHS OLD!**
NEXT QUESTION!!

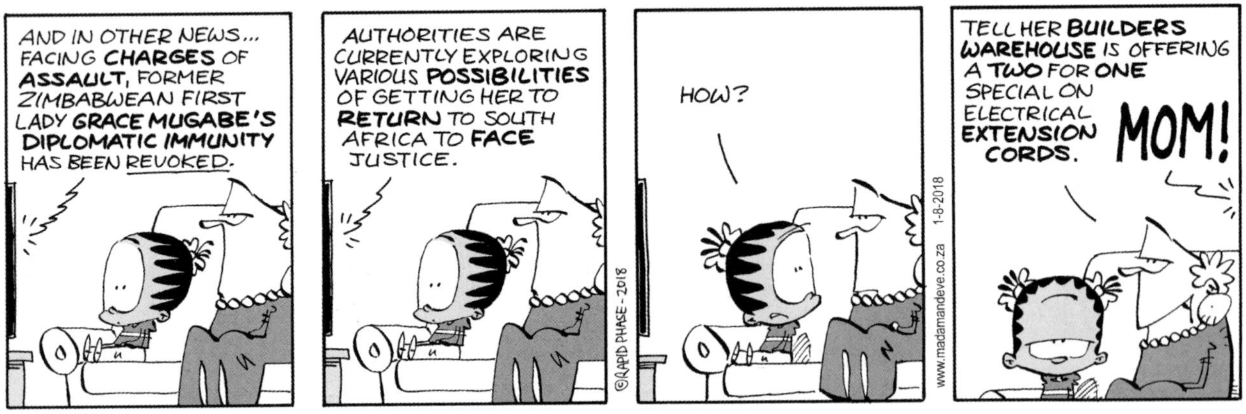
AND IN OTHER NEWS... FACING **CHARGES** OF **ASSAULT**, FORMER ZIMBABWEAN FIRST LADY **GRACE MUGABE'S DIPLOMATIC IMMUNITY** HAS BEEN REVOKED.
AUTHORITIES ARE CURRENTLY EXPLORING VARIOUS **POSSIBILITIES** OF GETTING HER TO **RETURN** TO SOUTH AFRICA TO **FACE** JUSTICE.
©RAPID PHASE-2018
HOW?
www.madamandeve.co.za 1-8-2018
TELL HER **BUILDERS WAREHOUSE** IS OFFERING A **TWO** FOR **ONE** SPECIAL ON ELECTRICAL **EXTENSION CORDS.**
MOM!

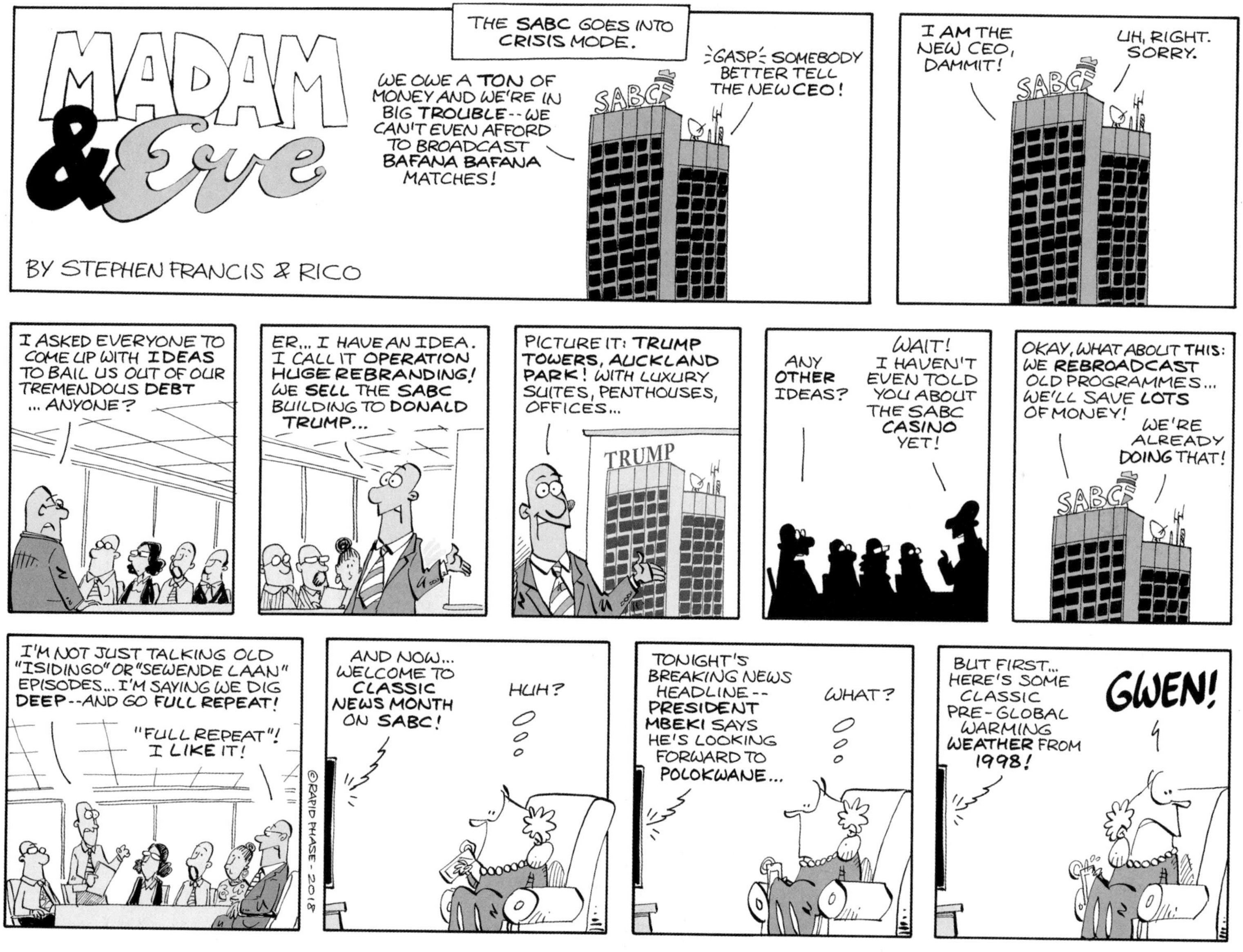

MADAM & Eve
BY STEPHEN FRANCIS & RICO
THE SABC GOES INTO CRISIS MODE.
WE OWE A TON OF MONEY AND WE'RE IN BIG TROUBLE--WE CAN'T EVEN AFFORD TO BROADCAST BAFANA BAFANA MATCHES!
SABC
-GASP- SOMEBODY BETTER TELL THE NEW CEO!
I AM THE NEW CEO, DAMMIT!
UH, RIGHT. SORRY.
I ASKED EVERYONE TO COME UP WITH IDEAS TO BAIL US OUT OF OUR TREMENDOUS DEBT ... ANYONE?
ER... I HAVE AN IDEA. I CALL IT OPERATION HUGE REBRANDING! WE SELL THE SABC BUILDING TO DONALD TRUMP...
PICTURE IT: TRUMP TOWERS, AUCKLAND PARK! WITH LUXURY SUITES, PENTHOUSES, OFFICES...
TRUMP
ANY OTHER IDEAS?
WAIT! I HAVEN'T EVEN TOLD YOU ABOUT THE SABC CASINO YET!
OKAY, WHAT ABOUT THIS: WE REBROADCAST OLD PROGRAMMES... WE'LL SAVE LOTS OF MONEY!
WE'RE ALREADY DOING THAT!
I'M NOT JUST TALKING OLD "ISIDINGO" OR "SEWENDE LAAN" EPISODES... I'M SAYING WE DIG DEEP--AND GO FULL REPEAT!
"FULL REPEAT"! I LIKE IT!
©RAPID PHASE - 2018
AND NOW... WELCOME TO CLASSIC NEWS MONTH ON SABC!
HUH?
TONIGHT'S BREAKING NEWS HEADLINE-- PRESIDENT MBEKI SAYS HE'S LOOKING FORWARD TO POLOKWANE...
WHAT?
BUT FIRST... HERE'S SOME CLASSIC PRE-GLOBAL WARMING WEATHER FROM 1998!
GWEN!

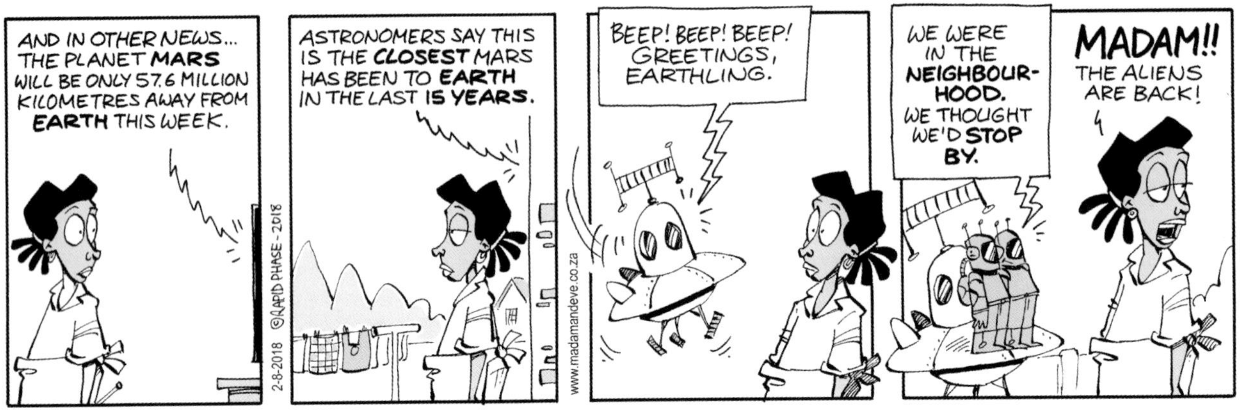
AND IN OTHER NEWS... THE PLANET **MARS** WILL BE ONLY 57.6 MILLION KILOMETRES AWAY FROM **EARTH** THIS WEEK.
2-8-2018 ©RAPID PHASE-2018
ASTRONOMERS SAY THIS IS THE **CLOSEST** MARS HAS BEEN TO **EARTH** IN THE LAST **15 YEARS.**
www.madamandeve.co.za
BEEP! BEEP! BEEP! GREETINGS, EARTHLING.
WE WERE IN THE **NEIGHBOUR-HOOD.** WE THOUGHT WE'D **STOP BY.**
MADAM!! THE ALIENS ARE BACK!

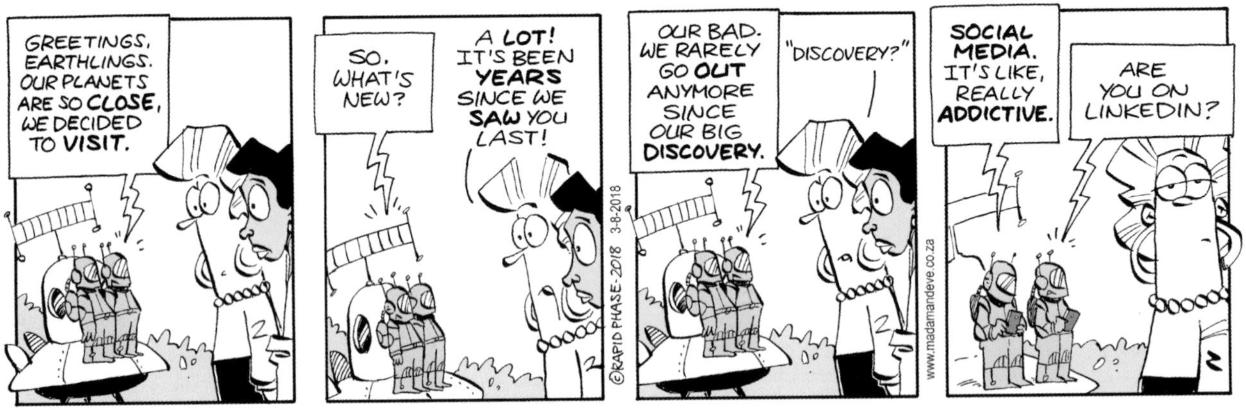
GREETINGS, EARTHLINGS. OUR PLANETS ARE SO **CLOSE,** WE DECIDED TO **VISIT.**
SO. WHAT'S NEW?
A **LOT!** IT'S BEEN **YEARS** SINCE WE **SAW** YOU LAST!
©RAPID PHASE-2018 3-8-2018
OUR BAD. WE RARELY GO **OUT** ANYMORE SINCE OUR BIG **DISCOVERY.**
"DISCOVERY?"
www.madamandeve.co.za
SOCIAL MEDIA. IT'S LIKE, REALLY **ADDICTIVE.**
ARE YOU ON LINKEDIN?

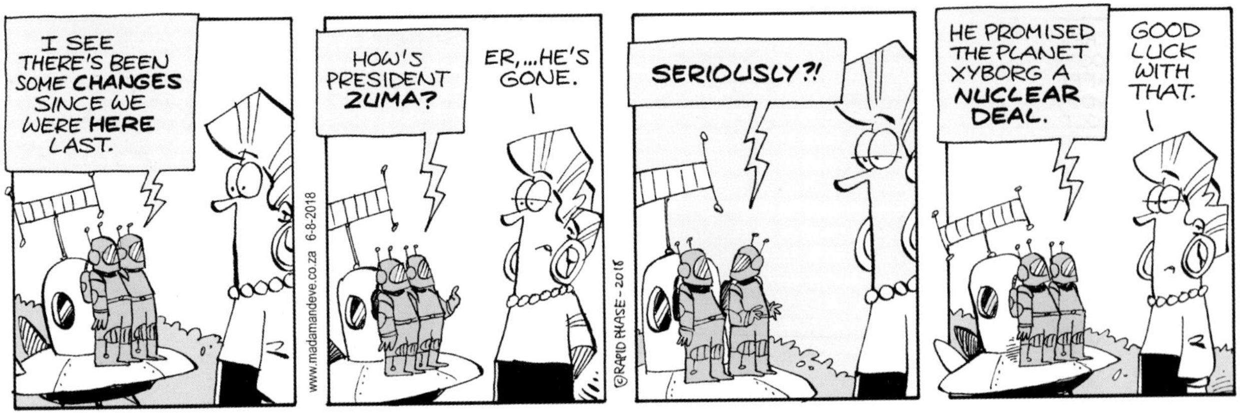
I SEE THERE'S BEEN SOME **CHANGES** SINCE WE WERE **HERE** LAST.
www.madamandeve.co.za 6-8-2018
HOW'S PRESIDENT **ZUMA?**
ER, ...HE'S GONE.
©RAPID PHASE-2018
SERIOUSLY?!
HE PROMISED THE PLANET XYBORG A **NUCLEAR DEAL.**
GOOD LUCK WITH THAT.

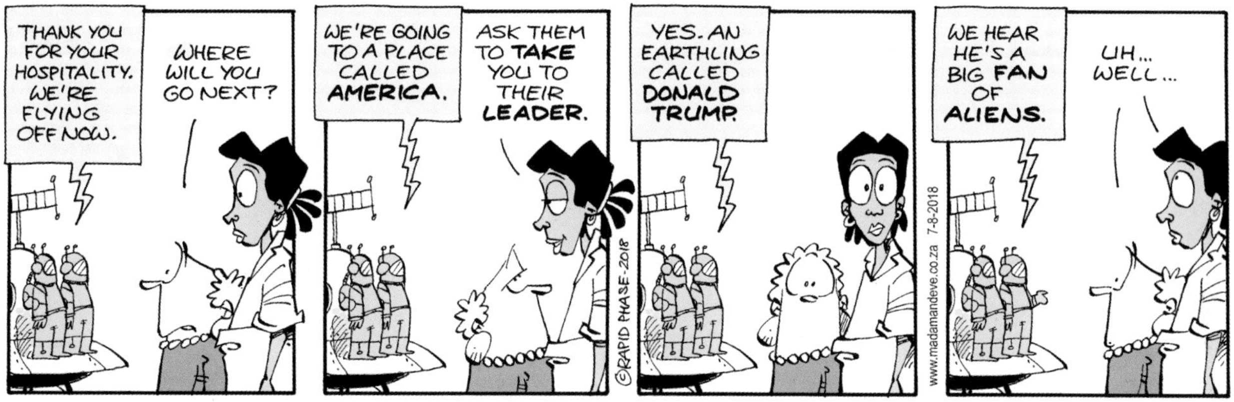
THANK YOU FOR YOUR HOSPITALITY. WE'RE FLYING OFF NOW.
WHERE WILL YOU GO NEXT?
WE'RE GOING TO A PLACE CALLED **AMERICA**.
ASK THEM TO **TAKE** YOU TO THEIR **LEADER**.
©RAPID PHASE-2018
YES. AN EARTHLING CALLED **DONALD TRUMP**.
www.madamandeve.co.za 7-8-2018
WE HEAR HE'S A BIG **FAN** OF **ALIENS**.
UH... WELL...

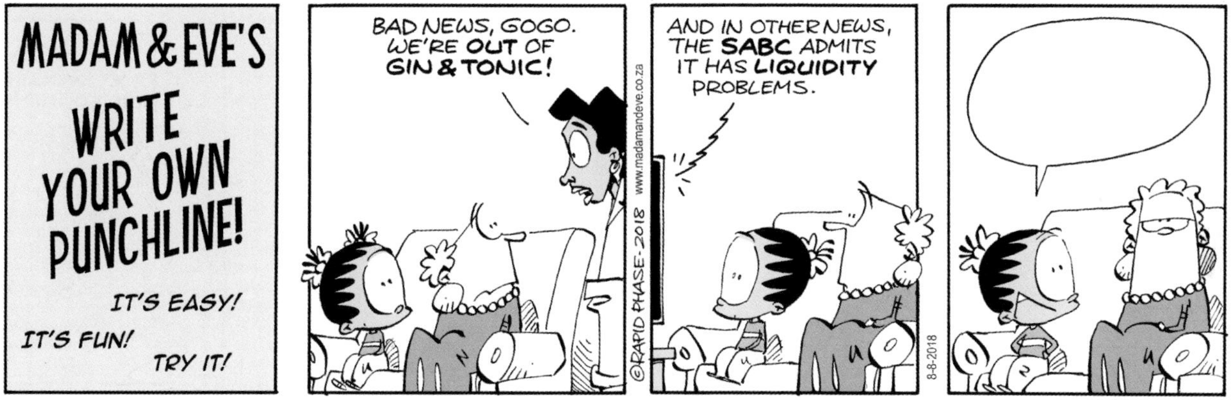
MADAM & EVE'S
WRITE YOUR OWN PUNCHLINE!
IT'S EASY!
IT'S FUN!
TRY IT!
BAD NEWS, GOGO. WE'RE **OUT** OF **GIN & TONIC**!
©RAPID PHASE-2018 www.madamandeve.co.za
AND IN OTHER NEWS, THE **SABC** ADMITS IT HAS **LIQUIDITY** PROBLEMS.
8-8-2018

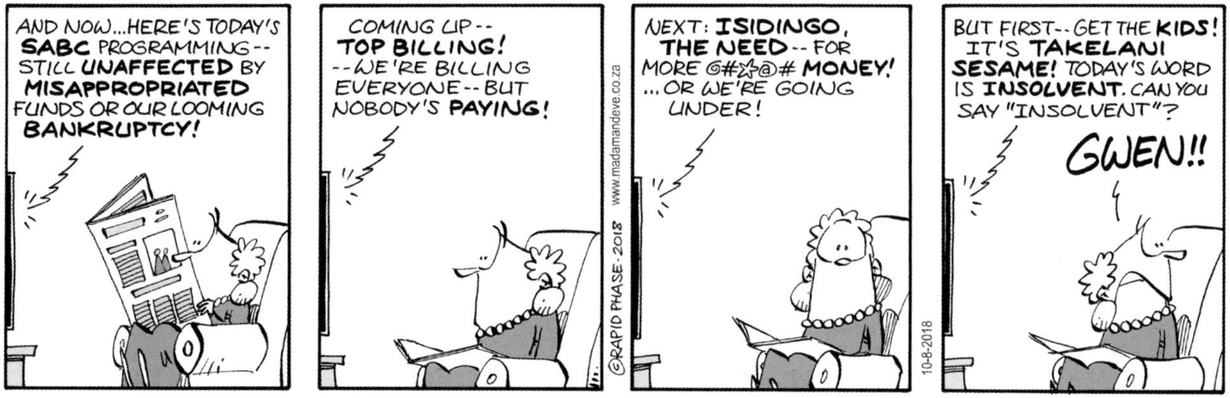
AND NOW...HERE'S TODAY'S **SABC** PROGRAMMING-- STILL **UNAFFECTED** BY **MISAPPROPRIATED** FUNDS OR OUR LOOMING **BANKRUPTCY**!
COMING UP-- **TOP BILLING**! --WE'RE BILLING EVERYONE--BUT NOBODY'S **PAYING**!
©RAPID PHASE-2018 www.madamandeve.co.za
NEXT: **ISIDINGO, THE NEED**--FOR MORE @#☆@# **MONEY**! ...OR WE'RE GOING UNDER!
10-8-2018
BUT FIRST--GET THE **KIDS**! IT'S **TAKELANI SESAME**! TODAY'S WORD IS **INSOLVENT**. CAN YOU SAY "INSOLVENT"?
GWEN!!

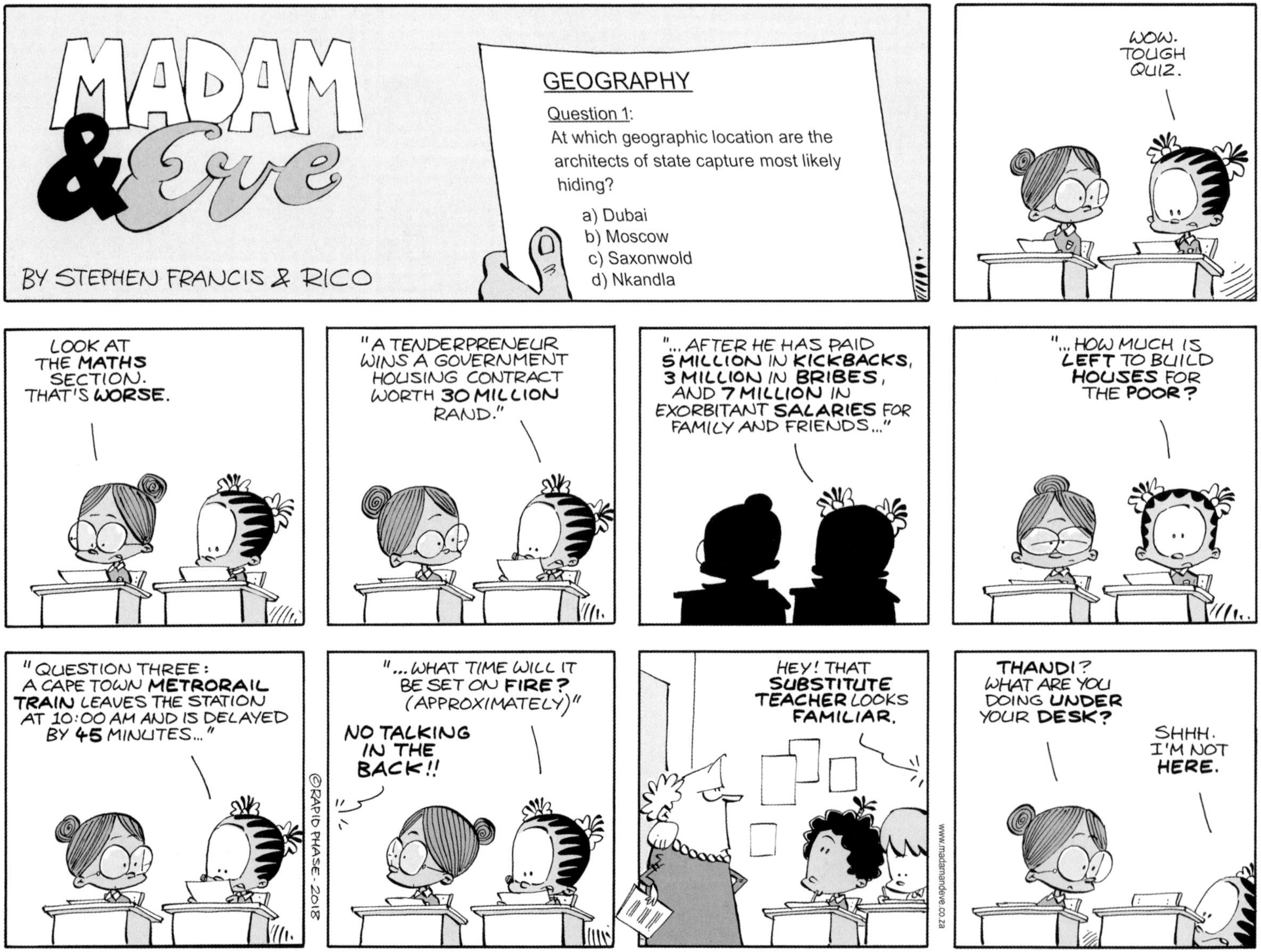
MADAM & Eve
BY STEPHEN FRANCIS & RICO
GEOGRAPHY
Question 1:
At which geographic location are the architects of state capture most likely hiding?
a) Dubai
b) Moscow
c) Saxonwold
d) Nkandla
WOW. TOUGH QUIZ.
LOOK AT THE MATHS SECTION. THAT'S WORSE.
"A TENDERPRENEUR WINS A GOVERNMENT HOUSING CONTRACT WORTH 30 MILLION RAND."
"... AFTER HE HAS PAID 5 MILLION IN KICKBACKS, 3 MILLION IN BRIBES, AND 7 MILLION IN EXORBITANT SALARIES FOR FAMILY AND FRIENDS..."
"... HOW MUCH IS LEFT TO BUILD HOUSES FOR THE POOR?
"QUESTION THREE: A CAPE TOWN METRORAIL TRAIN LEAVES THE STATION AT 10:00 AM AND IS DELAYED BY 45 MINUTES..."
©RAPID PHASE. 2018
"... WHAT TIME WILL IT BE SET ON FIRE? (APPROXIMATELY)"
NO TALKING IN THE BACK!!
HEY! THAT SUBSTITUTE TEACHER LOOKS FAMILIAR.
www.madamandeve.co.za
THANDI? WHAT ARE YOU DOING UNDER YOUR DESK?
SHHH. I'M NOT HERE.

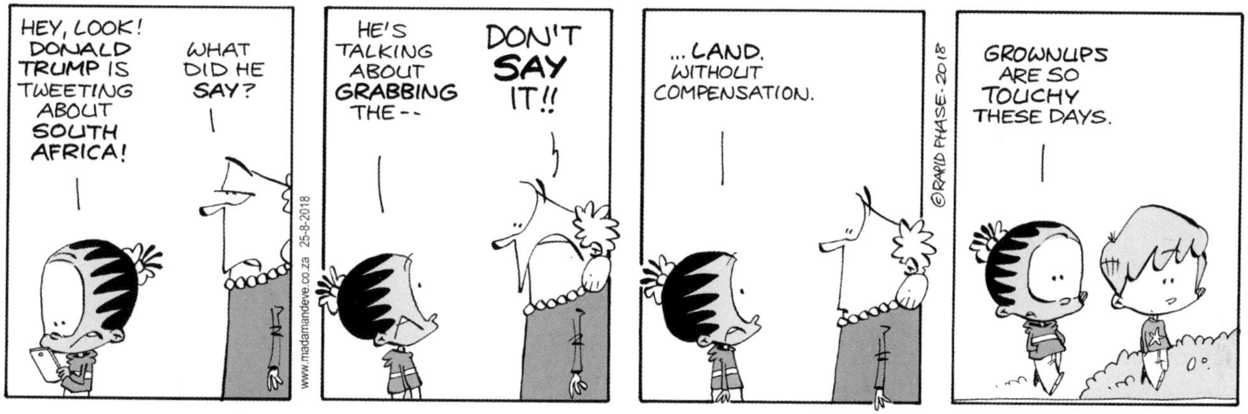

HEY, LOOK! DONALD TRUMP IS TWEETING ABOUT SOUTH AFRICA!
WHAT DID HE SAY?
www.madamandeve.co.za 25-8-2018
HE'S TALKING ABOUT GRABBING THE--
DON'T SAY IT!!
...LAND. WITHOUT COMPENSATION.
©RAPID PHASE-2018
GROWNUPS ARE SO TOUCHY THESE DAYS.

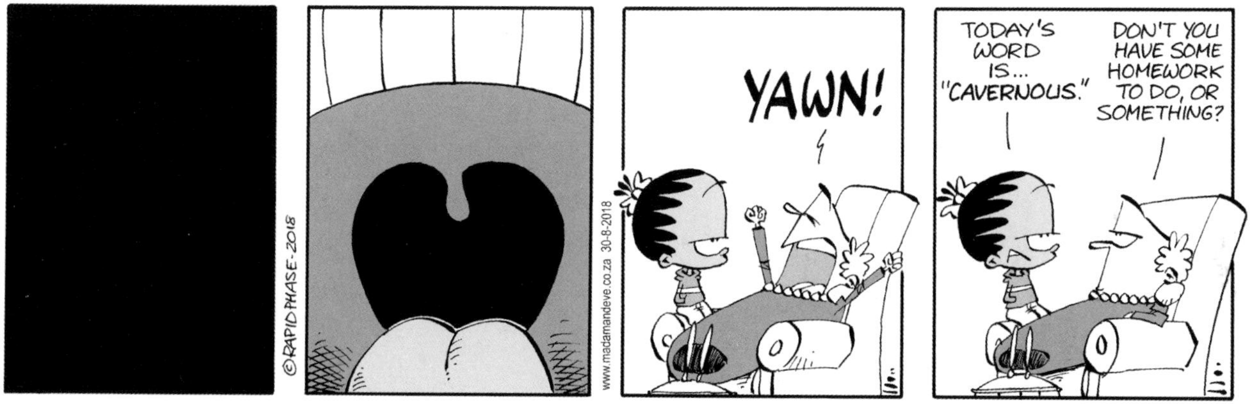

©RAPID PHASE-2018
www.madamandeve.co.za 30-8-2018
YAWN!
TODAY'S WORD IS... "CAVERNOUS."
DON'T YOU HAVE SOME HOMEWORK TO DO, OR SOMETHING?

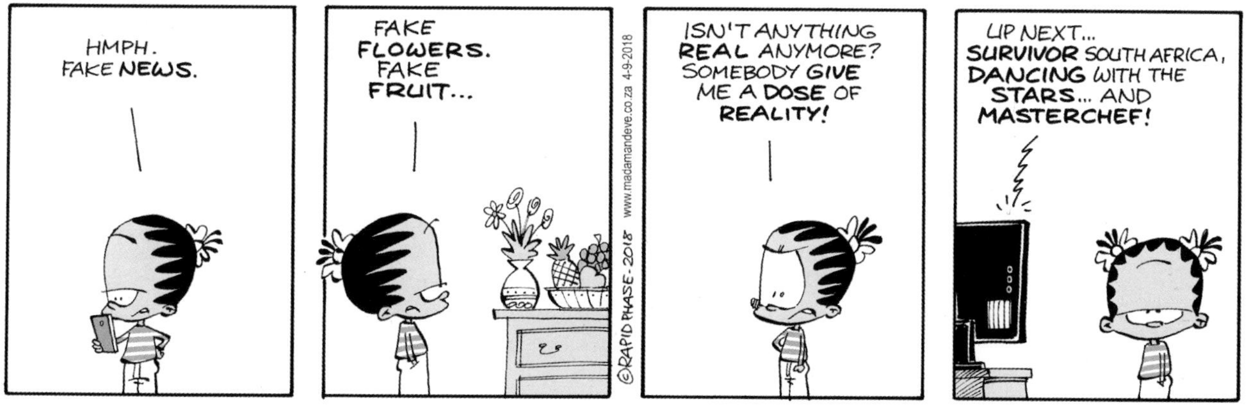

HMPH. FAKE NEWS.
FAKE FLOWERS. FAKE FRUIT...
©RAPID PHASE-2018 www.madamandeve.co.za 4-9-2018
ISN'T ANYTHING REAL ANYMORE? SOMEBODY GIVE ME A DOSE OF REALITY!
UP NEXT... SURVIVOR SOUTH AFRICA, DANCING WITH THE STARS... AND MASTERCHEF!

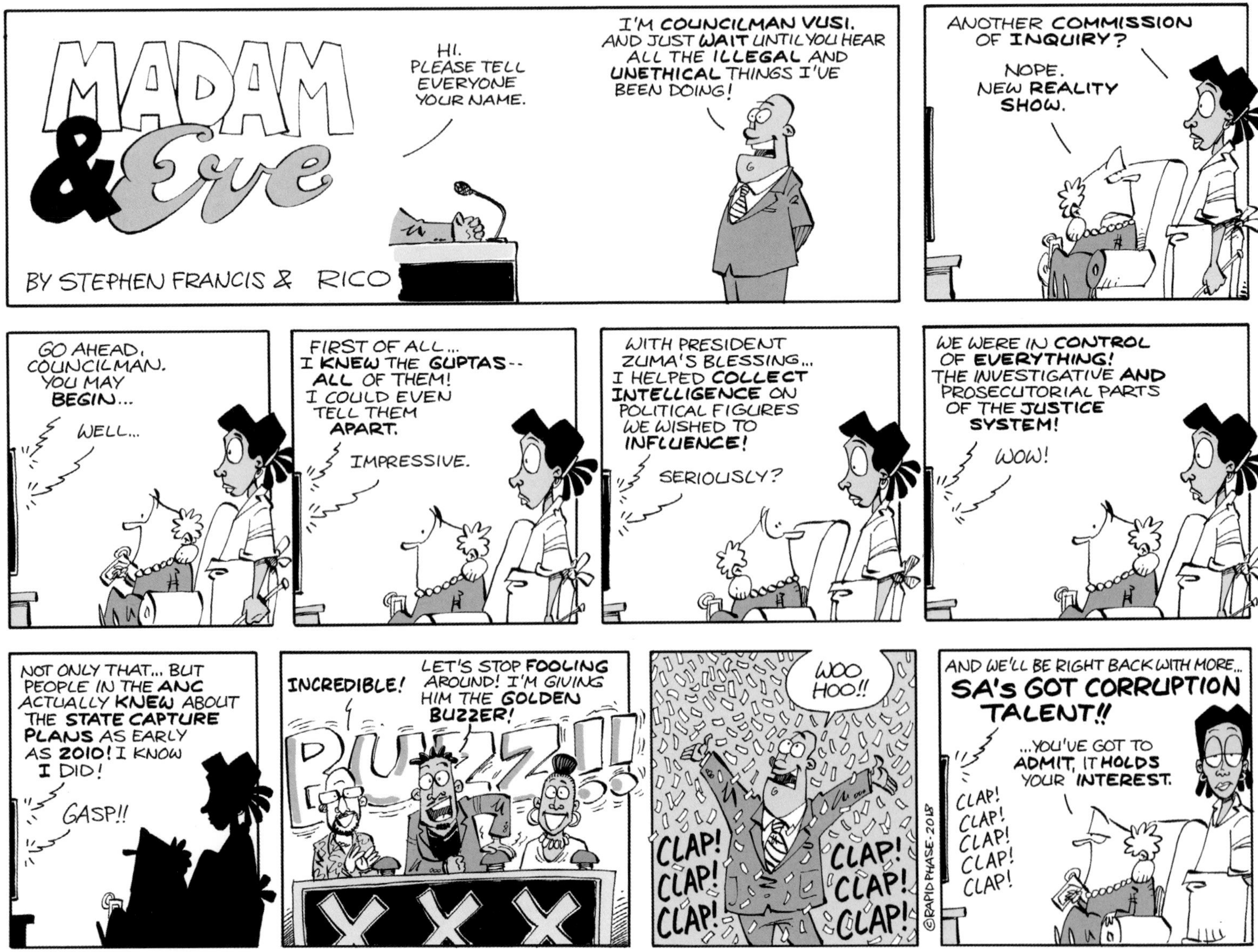
MADAM & Eve
BY STEPHEN FRANCIS & RICO
HI. PLEASE TELL EVERYONE YOUR NAME.
I'M COUNCILMAN VUSI. AND JUST WAIT UNTIL YOU HEAR ALL THE ILLEGAL AND UNETHICAL THINGS I'VE BEEN DOING!
ANOTHER COMMISSION OF INQUIRY?
NOPE. NEW REALITY SHOW.
GO AHEAD, COUNCILMAN. YOU MAY BEGIN...
WELL...
FIRST OF ALL... I KNEW THE GUPTAS-- ALL OF THEM! I COULD EVEN TELL THEM APART.
IMPRESSIVE.
WITH PRESIDENT ZUMA'S BLESSING... I HELPED COLLECT INTELLIGENCE ON POLITICAL FIGURES WE WISHED TO INFLUENCE!
SERIOUSLY?
WE WERE IN CONTROL OF EVERYTHING! THE INVESTIGATIVE AND PROSECUTORIAL PARTS OF THE JUSTICE SYSTEM!
WOW!
NOT ONLY THAT... BUT PEOPLE IN THE ANC ACTUALLY KNEW ABOUT THE STATE CAPTURE PLANS AS EARLY AS 2010! I KNOW I DID!
GASP!!
INCREDIBLE!
LET'S STOP FOOLING AROUND! I'M GIVING HIM THE GOLDEN BUZZER!
BUZZ!!
WOO HOO!!
CLAP! CLAP! CLAP!
CLAP! CLAP! CLAP!
©RAPID PHASE·2018
AND WE'LL BE RIGHT BACK WITH MORE... SA's GOT CORRUPTION TALENT!!
...YOU'VE GOT TO ADMIT, IT HOLDS YOUR INTEREST.
CLAP! CLAP! CLAP! CLAP! CLAP!

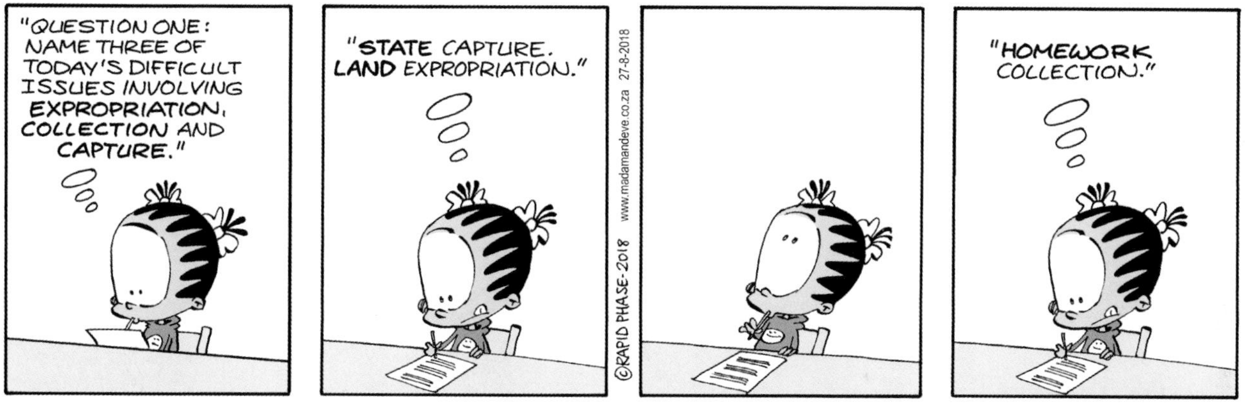
"QUESTION ONE: NAME THREE OF TODAY'S DIFFICULT ISSUES INVOLVING **EXPROPRIATION**, **COLLECTION** AND **CAPTURE**."
"**STATE** CAPTURE. **LAND** EXPROPRIATION."
©RAPID PHASE-2018 www.madamandeve.co.za 27-8-2018
"**HOMEWORK** COLLECTION."

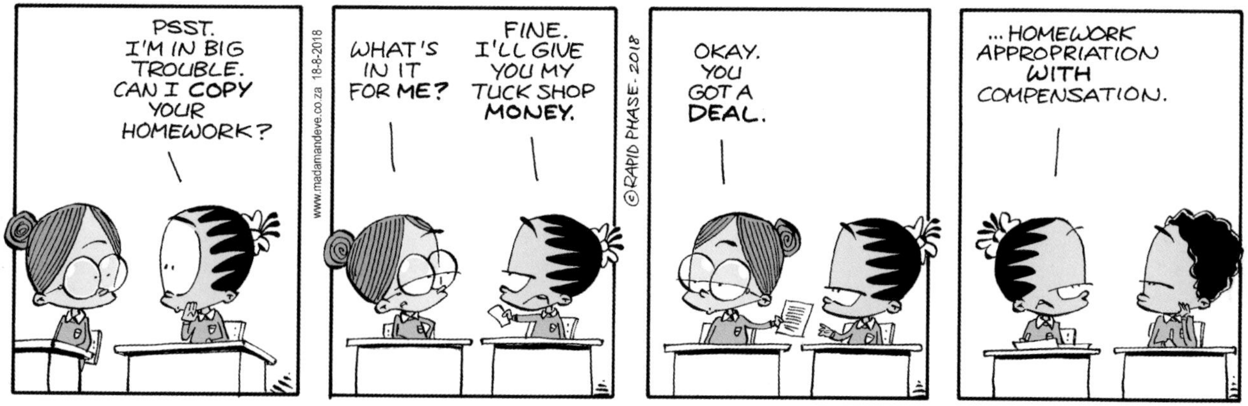
PSST. I'M IN BIG TROUBLE. CAN I **COPY** YOUR HOMEWORK?
www.madamandeve.co.za 18-8-2018
WHAT'S IN IT FOR **ME?**
FINE. I'LL GIVE YOU MY TUCK SHOP **MONEY.**
©RAPID PHASE-2018
OKAY. YOU GOT A **DEAL**.
...HOMEWORK APPROPRIATION **WITH** COMPENSATION.

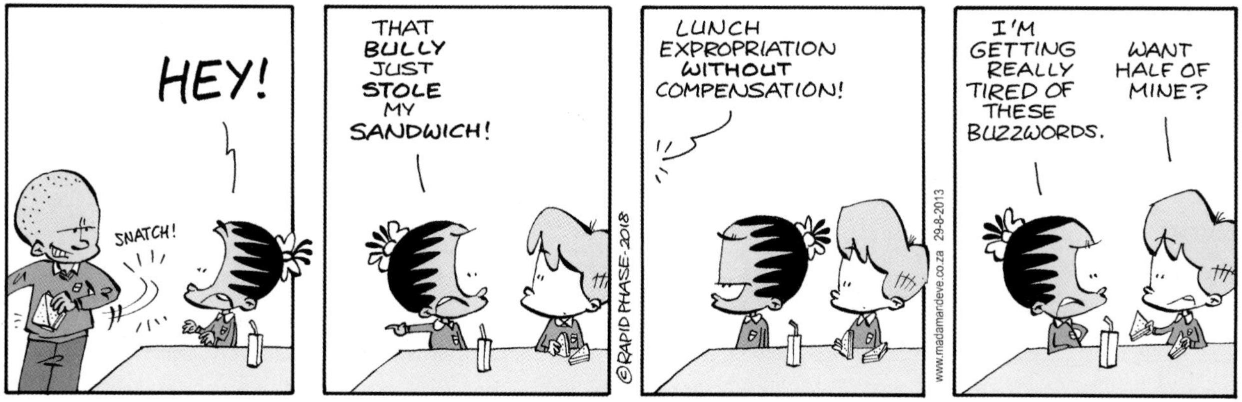
HEY!
SNATCH!
THAT **BULLY** JUST **STOLE** MY **SANDWICH!**
©RAPID PHASE-2018
LUNCH EXPROPRIATION **WITHOUT** COMPENSATION!
www.madamandeve.co.za 29-8-2013
I'M GETTING REALLY TIRED OF THESE BUZZWORDS.
WANT HALF OF MINE?

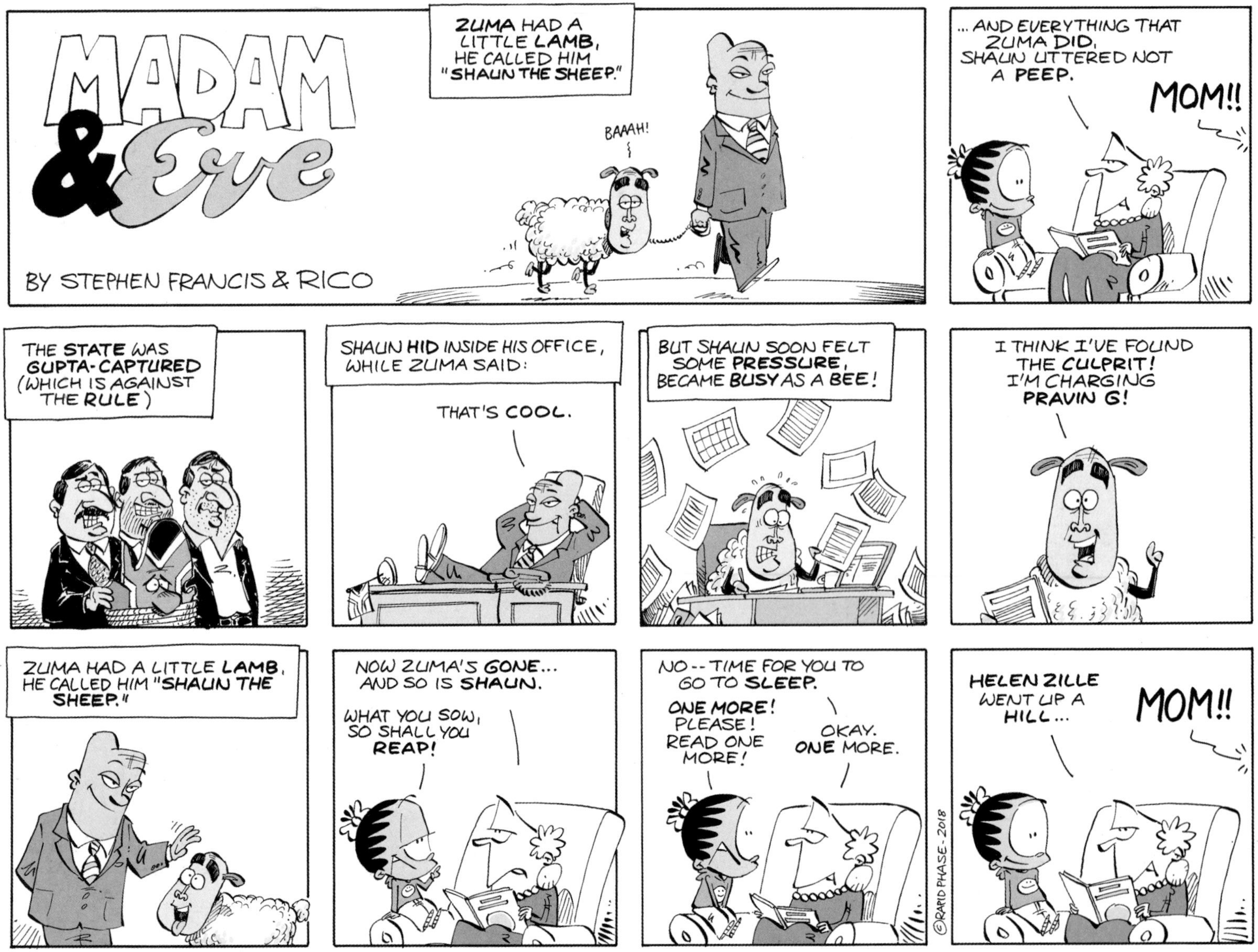
MADAM & Eve
BY STEPHEN FRANCIS & RICO
ZUMA HAD A LITTLE LAMB, HE CALLED HIM "SHAUN THE SHEEP."
BAAAH!
... AND EVERYTHING THAT ZUMA DID, SHAUN UTTERED NOT A PEEP.
MOM!!
THE STATE WAS GUPTA-CAPTURED (WHICH IS AGAINST THE RULE)
SHAUN HID INSIDE HIS OFFICE, WHILE ZUMA SAID:
THAT'S COOL.
BUT SHAUN SOON FELT SOME PRESSURE, BECAME BUSY AS A BEE!
I THINK I'VE FOUND THE CULPRIT! I'M CHARGING PRAVIN G!
ZUMA HAD A LITTLE LAMB, HE CALLED HIM "SHAUN THE SHEEP."
NOW ZUMA'S GONE... AND SO IS SHAUN.
WHAT YOU SOW, SO SHALL YOU REAP!
NO -- TIME FOR YOU TO GO TO SLEEP.
ONE MORE! PLEASE! READ ONE MORE!
OKAY. ONE MORE.
©RAPID PHASE - 2018
HELEN ZILLE WENT UP A HILL...
MOM!!